Rethinking Architectural Historiography

Rather than subscribing to a single position, this collection informs the reader about the current state of the discipline looking at changes across the broad field of methodological, theoretical and geographical plurality. Divided into three sections, *Rethinking Architectural Historiography* begins by renegotiating foundational and contemporary boundaries of architectural history in relation to other cognate fields. It then goes on to engage critically with past and present histories, disclosing assumptions, biases and absences in architectural historiography. It concludes by exploring the possibilities provided by new perspectives, and reframing the discipline in the light of new parameters and problematics.

Featuring distinctive contributions from authors with a range of expertise on the writing, teaching and practice of architectural history, this timely and internationally relevant title reflects upon the current changes in historiographical practice. This book explores potential openings that may contribute to further transformation of the discipline and theories of architectural historiography, and addresses the current question of the disciplinary particularity of architectural history.

Dana Arnold is Professor of Architectural History and Director at the Centre for Studies in Architecture and Urbanism, University of Southampton, UK.

Elvan Altan Ergut is Assistant Professor and Vice Chair in the Department of Architecture at Middle East Technical University, Ankara, Turkey.

Belgin Turan Özkaya is Associate Professor of Architectural History in the Department of Architecture at Middle East Technical University, Ankara, Turkey.

Rethinking Architectural Historiography

Edited by
Dana Arnold,
Elvan Altan Ergut
and
Belgin Turan Özkaya

LONDON AND NEW YORK

First published 2006
by Routledge
2 Park Square, Milton Park, Abingdon, Oxon OX14 4RN

Simultaneously published in the USA and Canada
by Routledge
270 Madison Ave, New York, NY10016

Routledge is an imprint of the Taylor & Francis Group, an informa business

© 2006 selection and editorial matter: Dana Arnold, Elvan Altan Ergut and Belgin Turan Özkaya; individual chapters: the contributors

Typeset in Galliard by
Florence Production Ltd, Stoodleigh, Devon
Printed and bound in Great Britain by
TJ International Ltd, Padstow, Cornwall

All rights reserved. No part of this book may be reprinted or reproduced or utilized in any form or by any electronic, mechanical, or other means, now known or hereafter invented, including photocopying and recording, or in any information storage or retrieval system, without permission in writing from the publishers.

British Library Cataloguing in Publication Data
A catalogue record for this book is available from the British Library

Library of Congress Cataloging in Publication Data
Rethinking architectural historiography/edited by Dana Arnold, Elvan Altan Ergut & Belgin Turan Özkaya.– 1st ed.
   p. cm.
   1. Architecture – Historiography. I. Arnold, Dana. II. Altan Ergut, Elvan. III. Turan Özkaya, Belgin.
NA190.R48 2006
720.9–dc22   2006001550

ISBN10: 0–415–36082–X (hbk)
ISBN10: 0–415–36085–4 (pbk)

ISBN13: 978–0–415–36082–1 (hbk)
ISBN13: 978–0–415–36085–2 (pbk)

Contents

List of figures vii
Notes on contributors ix

Preface xv
DANA ARNOLD

Introduction: mapping architectural historiography 1
ELVAN ALTAN ERGUT AND BELGİN TURAN ÖZKAYA

PART I
Boundaries **15**

1 **Art history and architectural history** 17
   ERIC C. FERNIE

2 **Buildings archaeology: context and points of convergence** 24
   ROGER H. LEECH

3 **Architecture as evidence** 36
   ANDREW BALLANTYNE

4 **Program and programs** 50
   CHRISTIAN F. OTTO

5 **Hercules at the roundabout: multidisciplinary choice in the history of architecture** 60
   FİKRET YEGÜL

6 **Frontiers of fear: architectural history, the anchor and the sail** 74
   SUNA GÜVEN

PART II
Critical engagements 83

7 Questions of Ottoman identity and architectural history 85
TÜLAY ARTAN

8 *In Ordinary Time*: considerations on a video installation by Iñigo Manglano Ovalle and the New National Gallery in Berlin by Mies van der Rohe 110
EDWARD DIMENDBERG

9 Reopening the question of document in architectural historiography: reading (writing) Filarete's treatise on architecture for (in) Piero de' Medici's study 121
SEVİL ENGİNSOY EKİNCİ

10 From architectural history to spatial writing 135
JANE RENDELL

11 Presenting Ankara: popular conceptions of architecture and history 151
ELVAN ALTAN ERGUT

PART III
Reframings 169

12 Space, time, and architectural history 171
NANCY STIEBER

13 Visuality and architectural history 183
BELGİN TURAN ÖZKAYA

14 The digital disciplinary divide: reactions to historical virtual reality models 200
DIANE FAVRO

15 The afterlife of buildings: architecture and Walter Benjamin's theory of history 215
PATRICIA A. MORTON

16 Beyond a boundary: towards an architectural history of the non-east 229
DANA ARNOLD

Index 246

Figures

1.1	Speyer Cathedral from the south-east	18
2.1	Trinity Area of Frome; plans of houses in Castle Street	27
2.2	The redevelopment of St Bartholomew's Fair, London, c.1598–c.1616	29
2.3	The St Michael's Hill precinct of Bristol University	30
2.4	Alleynedale House, Barbados	32
5.1	Luis Barragan: San Cristobal Stables and Egerstom House, Mexico City, 1968	68
5.2	Carlo Scarpa: main door of the Banca Popolare di Verona, Verona, 1973	68
5.3	Sedad Hakkı Eldem: Şark Kahvesi (Oriental Café), İstanbul, 1948	69
5.4	Fikret Yegül: Country House, Gölcük-Ödemiş, Turkey, 1999	69
6.1	Figure from Book 5, *Vitruvius*, Rusconi edition, Venice, 1590	80
8.1	Iñigo Manglano Ovalle: *In Ordinary Time*, 2001	115
8.2	Iñigo Manglano Ovalle: *In Ordinary Time*, 2001	115
11.1a	*Anıtkabir*, Mausoleum of Atatürk in Ankara; Emin Onat and Orhan Arda, 1942	152
11.1b	Model of *Anıtkabir* in Miniaturk, İstanbul	153
11.2	Photographs of Ankara in 1923 and 1933	156
11.3	Postcard showing *Hisar*, the citadel of Ankara	158
11.4	Postcard showing *Atakule*, the tower and shopping mall in Ankara; Ragıp Buluç, 1986	162
13.1	Aldo Rossi: detail from the *Teatro Domestico* for the exhibition *Il Progetto Domestico* at the Milan Triennial, 1986	191
13.2	Mario Sironi: *Paesaggio urbano*	193
13.3	Aldo Rossi: *Città con Architetture e Monumenti*, 1972	195
13.4	Aldo Rossi: *Senza titolo su un'antica carta francese*, printed in 1989	196

14.1	Recreated Arch of Septimius Severus	203
14.2	Colosseum with coded circulation paths	204
14.3	Sequential views flying down into Roman Forum Model	205
14.4	Lightscape analysis of Curia (Senate House) model, Rome	209
15.1	Galerie Vivienne, Paris, 1823, interior view	219
15.2	Passage de Choiseul, Paris, 1824, exterior view	221

Contributors

Dana Arnold is Professor of Architectural History and Director of the Centre for Studies in Architecture and Urbanism at the University of Southampton, UK. Her recent books include: *Rural Urbanism: London Landscapes in the Early Nineteenth Century* (2006); *Art History: A Very Short Introduction* (2004); *Reading Architectural History* (2002); and *Representing the Metropolis* (2000). She has edited several volumes, the latest of which include *Cultural Identities and the Aesthetics of Britishness* (2004); (with Andrew Ballantyne) *Architecture as Experience* (2004); (with Margaret Iversen) *Art and Thought* (2003). She has held fellowships at the University of Cambridge, Yale University and the Getty Research Institute, Los Angeles and has been a visiting professor at various instutions in the UK, US and Canada. Her forthcoming book on the hospital in London will be published by Routledge.

Tülay Artan teaches Ottoman history at Sabancı University in İstanbul. Her interests include a variety of topics in seventeenth- and eighteenth-century Ottoman political and cultural history. Her numerous articles focus on the marriages and households of Ottoman princesses, on İstanbul's urban and architectural history, and on eighteenth-century material culture and elite consumption. She has been the co-organizer and catalogue editor for several exhibitions, including 'The Splendour of the Ottoman Sultans' (Memphis, 1993), 'Palace of Gold and Light' (Washington DC, 2000) and 'Mothers, Goddesses and Sultanas' (Brussels, 2004). She is currently working on a book on the eighteenth-century grandvizieral household.

Andrew Ballantyne is Professor of Architecture at the University of Newcastle upon Tyne, UK, where he directs architecture research in the Tectonic Cultures Research Group. He studied and practised architecture before taking up academic positions in research and teaching. He has worked with archaeologists in the UK and Greece, and has written extensively in the fields of architectural history and theory. His books include *Architecture, Landscape and Liberty* (1997), *What is Architecture?* (2002),

Architecture: A Very Short Introduction (2002), *Architectures* (2004), *Architecture Theory: A Reader in Philosophy and Culture* (2005) and (with Dana Arnold) *Architecture as Experience* (2004). He is currently leading a project investigating Mock-Tudor architecture and its spread around the globe.

Edward Dimendberg is Associate Professor of Film and Media Studies and Visual Studies at the University of California, Irvine. The recipient of fellowships from the J. Paul Getty Trust, the Graham Foundation, the Canadian Centre for Architecture and the German Fulbright Commission, he is also a member of the editorial board of the journal *October*, multimedia editor of the *Journal of the Society of Architectural Historians* and a general editor of the *Weimar and Now: German Cultural Criticism* book series. He is the author of *Excluded Middle: Toward a Reflective Architecture and Urbanism* (2001) and *Film Noir and the Spaces of Modernity* (2004) and co-editor (with Anton Kaes and Martin Jay) of *The Weimar Republic Sourcebook* (1994). At present he is completing books on the architecture of Diller Scofidio + Renfro, and Los Angeles documentary media.

Sevil Enginsoy Ekinci trained as an architect and architectural historian at Middle East Technical University (BArch, MA) and Cornell University (PhD) by receiving several research and travel grants. She presently teaches courses on architectural history at the Department of Architecture, METU, where she also previously taught in the design studios. She has presented papers at many international conferences, and is currently preparing them for publication. Among these articles are 'Building Commodity: Consumption/Production of a 19th Century Ottoman/British "Iron House for a Corn-Mill"', 'Building/Writing *Fantasia*: The Eroticism of Filarete's Architectural Theory' and 'Remapping Architectural Encounters between "East" and "West" in the Fifteenth Century: Filarete's Travel to İstanbul'.

Elvan Altan Ergut is Assistant Professor and Vice Chair at the Department of Architecture, Middle East Technical University, Ankara, Turkey. She received her BArch and MA in History of Architecture from Middle East Technical University, and her PhD in Art History from the State University of New York at Binghamton with a dissertation on the relationship between architecture and nationalism in early Republican Turkey. Her research areas include architecture in the nineteenth and twentieth centuries and architectural historiography. She is currently editing two volumes on twentieth-century architecture in Turkey, and local modernisms in Turkish provinces.

Diane Favro is a Professor of Architecture and Urban Design at UCLA. Her research focuses on Roman urbanism, women in architecture and the pedagogy of architectural history. Among her publications are (with Zeynep Çelik and Richard Ingersoll) *Streets: Critical Perspectives on Public Space*

(1994), *The Urban Image of Augustan Rome* (1996) and the forthcoming chapter, 'Making Rome a World City', in the *Cambridge Companion to the Age of Augustus*, edited by Karl Galinsky. She is Director of the UCLA Experiential Technology Center and recently ended a term as President of the International Society of Architectural Historians.

Eric C. Fernie retired as Director of the Courtauld Institute of Art of the University of London in 2003 and is currently President of the Society of Antiquaries of London. He is a fellow of the British Academy and the Royal Society of Edinburgh. His books include *The Architecture of the Anglo-Saxons* (1983), *An Architectural History of Norwich Cathedral* (1993), *Art History and its Methods* (1995) and *The Architecture of Norman England* (2000). He has also published over fifty papers in refereed journals.

Suna Güven has been teaching Architectural History at Middle East Technical University in Ankara since 1985. She is one of the founders and current Head of the graduate programme in Architectural History, which began graduating students in 1990. Her area of specialization is Roman architecture and she also has an interest in the Latin medieval architecture of Cyprus. She has authored the first translation in Turkish of Vitruvius' *Ten Books on Architecture*. Her recent research and publications concern investigations on identity and the multifaceted aspects of centre and periphery in Roman architecture.

Roger H. Leech is a Visiting Professor at the University of Southampton, UK. He was formerly Head of Archaeology at the Royal Commission on the Historical Monuments of England (now part of English Heritage), is a former President of the Society for Post Medieval Archaeology and was earlier Director of the Cumbria and Lancashire Archaeological Unit at the University of Lancaster. His main research interests are in the historical archaeology of the early modern city and of the Atlantic world in the seventeenth and subsequent centuries, on which he has published widely. He is currently completing a study of town houses in Bristol and is undertaking, with colleagues from National Museums Liverpool and Bristol City Museum in England, and Mercer University, Mary Washington College and the University of Virginia in the United States, a project on the colonial landscape of the eastern Caribbean, funded to date by the British Academy and the Society of Antiquaries.

Patricia A. Morton is Chair of the History of Art Department, Associate Professor of Architectural History and Director of the Culver Center of the Arts at the University of California, Riverside. The Getty Research Institute, the University of California Humanities Research Institute and the National Endowment for the Arts, among other institutions, have awarded her grants and fellowships. Her book on the 1931 Colonial Exposition in Paris, *Hybrid Modernities*, was published in 2000 by MIT Press and in Japan by Brücke in 2002. Her current research focuses on 'bad taste' in 1960s' architecture and its relation to postmodern architecture. She is editing a volume of essays on taste and popular culture in the 1960s and has published widely on architectural history and issues of race, gender and marginality. In spring 1999, she was a Fulbright Senior Scholar at the Department of the History of Ideas in Umeå, Sweden. She has been a Director of the Los Angeles Forum for Architecture and a member of the *Journal of Architectural Education* Editorial Board.

Christian F. Otto Professor of the History of Architecture and Urbanism at Cornell University, works primarily on eighteenth-century and Modern architecture history and urbanism. He has special interests in questions of method, historiography and pedagogy. His publications include *Space Into Light. The Churches of Balthasar Neumann* (1979), (with Richard Pommer) *Weissenhof 1927 and the Modern Movement in Architecture* (1991), scholarly articles, reviews and encyclopedia entries. He edited (with Mark Ashton) *The Utility of Splendor, Ceremony, Social Life, and Architecture at the Court of Bavaria, 1600–1800* (1993) by Samuel John Klingensmith, and from 1974–81 he served as editor of the *Journal of the Society of Architectural Historians*. His professional honours include support from both the Graham and Kaufmann foundations, the National Endowment for the Humanities, the Institute for Advanced Study, and the Fulbright Commission. He was named Outstanding Educator (1997) and Paramount Professor (1992) at Cornell University.

Jane Rendell is Reader in Architecture and Art and Director of Architectural Research at the Bartlett, University College London. An architectural designer and historian, art critic and writer, she is author of *The Pursuit of Pleasure* (2002), editor of 'A Place Between', *Public Art Journal* (1999) and co-editor of *Strangely Familiar* (1995), *Gender Space Architecture* (1999), *Intersections* (2000) and *The Unknown City* (2000). She is currently completing a new book, *From Art to Architecture*, and working on a project of site-specific writings. Her interest is in the relationship between disciplines: feminist theory and architectural history, fine art practice and architectural design, and critical theory and creative writing practice.

Nancy Stieber is Associate Professor in the Art Department at the University of Massachusetts Boston. She has written extensively on Dutch housing, architecture and urbanism of the nineteenth and twentieth centuries. Her 1998 book, *Housing Design and Society in Amsterdam: Reconfiguring Urban Order and Identity, 1900–1920*, won the 1999 Spiro Kostof Award. She is currently writing a book on the visual imagining of Amsterdam around 1900 entitled *The Metaphorical City: Representations of Fin-de-Siècle Amsterdam*. Professor Stieber has been the recipient of numerous grants, including support from the J. Paul Getty Foundation and the Radcliffe Institute for Advanced Study. From 2003 to 2006, she has been the editor of the *Journal of the Society of Architectural Historians*.

Belgin Turan Özkaya is Associate Professor of Architectural History at Middle East Technical University in Ankara. She received her PhD in the History of Architecture and Urbanism from Cornell University, and was a fellow at the 1999 Getty Summer Institute in Visual Studies and Art History and a Visiting Scholar at the Canadian Centre for Architecture in 2000–1. She has published on the Italian *Tendenza*, Ottoman–Venetian relations and historiography in journals such as the *Journal of Architectural Education* and the *Harvard Design Magazine* and in collections such as *After Orientalism*. Her work is located at the interstices of architectural history and contemporary interdisciplinary theory. Currently, she is working on an edited volume on visuality and architecture.

Fikret Yegül is a Professor in the Department of the History of Art and Architecture, University of California, Santa Barbara. His book *Baths and Bathing in Classical Antiquity* is the recipient of the 1994 Alice Davis Hitchcock Award of the Society of Architectural Historians. Other books include *The Bath-Gymnasium Complex at Sardis* (1986), *Gentlemen of Instinct and Breeding: Architecture at the American Academy in Rome, 1894–1940* (1991) and *The City of Sardis: Approaches in Graphic Recording*, co-authored (2003). His recent publications include 'Memory, Metaphor and Meaning in the Cities of Asia Minor', in *Romanization and the City: Creation, Transformations and Failures*, a supplement of the *Journal of Roman Archaeology*, edited by Elizabeth Fentress (2000) and 'Building a Roman Bath for the Cameras', *Journal of Roman Archaeology* (2003). Among Yegül's fellowships are the Fulbright, the Ailsa Mellon Bruce Senior Fellowship (CASVA) and the American Research Center in Turkey (ARIT). He was the Resident in Classical Studies at the American Academy in Rome (RAAR) in 1998.

Preface

Can architecture have a history? We think about architecture as being timeless, the 'beauty' of its aesthetic having meaning, significance and appeal to humankind across the ages. At least this usually applies to our ideas about polite architecture, in other words architecture with a 'known' architect and designed in a recognizable 'style'. This kind of visual material can have an autonomous existence – we can enjoy looking at it for its own sake and enjoy it, independent of any knowledge of its context, although of course viewers from different periods or cultures may see the same object in contrasting ways. For architecture to have a history we expect not only a timeless quality but also some kind of sequence or progression, as this is what history leads us to expect. Our history books are full of events in the past that are presented as part of either the continual movement towards improvement, or as stories about great men or as epochs of time that stand out from others. As the coming together of the two separate strands – architecture and the forces of history – we see how history reorders visual experience to give us a history of architecture.

When we look at a building, we often ask the following questions: who made it?; what is it for?; when was it completed? These are quite valid questions that are often anticipated and answered in, for example, the captions to illustrations in books and guides to historic buildings. For those of us also interested in the question how?, information on the building techniques used might help us to appreciate further the skill of the architect. The important thing to note about this kind of architectural appreciation is that it requires no knowledge of architectural history. The history of an individual building is contained within itself and can be found in the answers to the questions who, what, when, and how. This acts as a kind of pedigree for the work and might be used to help prove that it is an authentic work by a given architect.

Is there then a distinction to be made between the interaction of architecture and history, and architectural history? That is to say that histories of architecture can have a single focus on style or the work in relation to the biography of the artist, where our expectations of a progressive history are inflected on the visual. What I am suggesting here is that we turn the question on its head and put architecture in the driving seat, so to speak. By using architecture as our starting point we can see the complex and intertwined strands that make up architectural history. This implies that architectural history is a subject or academic field of enquiry in its own right, rather than the result of the rules of one discipline – history – being applied to another – architecture.

This volume investigates how architectural histories have been formulated and the impact these processes continue to have on our understanding of the built environment. To understand and to re-think architectural historiography it is important to discuss what kind of archive architectural history can draw upon, as the range of material used to construct these histories extends well beyond the works themselves. For instance, history has its documents, written records of the past; archaeology focuses on the material record, physical remains of the past; whilst anthropology looks to social rituals and cultural practices as a way of understanding past and present peoples. Architectural history can draw upon all these archives in addition to the primary archive of the building. In this way, architectural history is the stepping-stone into various ways of interpreting and understanding the past.

In contradiction to this, what is known as the 'canon' of architecture regiments our understanding and interpretation of the evidence. Architects and buildings that comprise the canon are usually seen as being of the highest quality. Consequently the canon plays an important role in the institutionalization of architecture, as new works can be judged against it. As such it is a means of imposing hierarchical relationships on groups of objects which usually favours the individual genius and the idea of the 'masterpiece'. Moreover, the canon promotes the idea that certain cultural objects or styles of architecture have more value (both historical and monetary) than others.

Architectural history is also the art of story telling, which is often seen as one of the most important functions of writing histories and fundamental to the nature of the discipline. A story requires a beginning, middle and end, based on a series of events that take place over a period of time. Two orders of narrative used frequently in architectural history are the narrative of style and the narrative of the author (architect). Style allows the ordering of architectural production whether anonymous or not through aesthetic categories. The heterogeneity, discordance and lack of synchronization between different strands of architectural production can then be sorted into movements coming into ascendancy and then declining. This is evident in stylistic histories where teleological patterns of stylistic dominance and recession are imposed. The choice of narrative creates a dialogue between both past and present; and author and archive. The former remains fluid being as much part of its moment of creation and subject, therefore, to contemporary and subsequent intellectual fashions. The latter can have the aura of objective truth, seeming to give the reader direct contact with the past. But this is an intellectual sleight of hand as the absence of the first person in much academic writing only masks the subjective authorial choices that have been made. At this point I would add a third party to this perceived dialogue between the architectural historian and their narrative – the reader. What do we bring to and what do we want from these discourses? And what is our 'experience' of the past?

This book attempts to address these issues within an international and transdisciplinary frame. Indeed the volume benefits from the interaction of a range of scholars at four recent colloquia and offers a synthesis of thinking on and rethinking of architectural historiography. The enquiry into the parameters and boundaries of architectural history began at a conference *Architectural History: Between History and Archaeology?*.[1] Here the somewhat ambiguous existence of architectural history as an academic discipline came under scrutiny from archaeologists, classical scholars, and both art and architectural historians. A central theme was that although buildings constitute one of the central objects of enquiry for archaeologists, and although, of all cultural artefacts, buildings are the most directly linked not only to social history but also to political history, the study of the history of architecture[2] is rarely taught or researched in university departments of archaeology or history. Rather, the history of architecture is the institutional preserve of departments of architecture or of the history of art. This has serious consequences for the way in which the history of architecture is studied. Putting the history of architecture within the context of disciplines whose primary concern is properly with aesthetics encourages the architectural historian to ignore the wider context by focusing solely on authorial authenticity, the link between the individual maker and the individual work, and the aesthetics of style. If freed from the expectations that it should be studied only within the confines of art history, the architectural history is well placed to have a radical impact upon the terms in which the past is studied. Are the differences between the skills needed for reading documents, on the one hand, and those needed for analysing the material evidence, on the other, a sufficient justification for dividing the proper subject, the past, into two disciplines called history and archaeology? With the archaeologist, the architectural historian must place buildings in their physical and topographical contexts and within their own craft and design tradition. But with the historian, the architectural historian must place buildings both in their wider political and social context, and in the more particular social and economic context, which can be reconstructed only from the detailed records of the commercial and other transactions that surrounded the building decisions.

The conference aimed to explore the tensions between the methods and approaches of history, archaeology and architectural history, looking for the distinctive character of each field of enquiry as well as points of convergence. Just as both the history of academic professionalization and the history of the practice of architecture are relevant to the current divisions within the subject, so too the reassessment of the extent to which the standard accepted usage of the subject labels (and the term 'subject', itself) clarifies or obfuscates their relationship has wide implications for the future shape of the academy. These concerns were discussed further in a conference organized by the Middle East Technical University, Ankara, *Rethinking Architectural Historiography* that provided a forum for an international group of scholars.[3] The exchange between these different intellectual and geographical/cultural contexts, mainly from British, American and Turkish Academia revealed the need for further discussions on architectural historiography across that broad territory. This was the catalyst for the very fruitful and enjoyable collaboration between Elvan Altan Ergut, Belgin Turan Özkaya and myself. It became evident that these issues could be expanded to look at the imperialist Eurocentric ways in which architectural histories have been constructed. And in response to this opportunity the ongoing interaction between an international body of scholars, of which this volume is a part, was initiated by the colloquium, *The Black Sea: Architectural History Between East and West*.[4] The principal concern here was the extraordinary reach of western imperialism in the nineteenth and early twentieth centuries as a predominant aspect of geopolitical history. Neither Rome, nor Byzantium, nor Spain at the height of its glory came close to the imperial scope of France, the United States, and particularly Great Britain in these years. Culture and politics co-operated, knowingly and unknowingly, to produce a system of domination that involved more than military might – to produce a western sovereignty that extended over forms, images and the very imaginations of both the dominators and the dominated. The result was a 'consolidated vision' that affirmed not only the Europeans' right to rule but also their obligation to do so. Architecture remains one of the most potent symbols of the civilization and culture of both colonizer and colonized, and is thus germane to this 'vision'. In terms of architectural history this has led to the establishing of canonical histories and narratives that privilege western traditions of thinking, modes of production and aesthetics.

In the last twenty years post-colonial theorists have argued that 'the Orient' was constructed by westerners as an explanation of the nature of the west so making 'the Orient' a reflective tool to articulate the existence and justify the behaviour of the 'Occidental' colonial powers. But by contrast, this colloquium looked at the mechanisms involved in the creation of a 'consolidated vision' and in exploring alternative narratives. Whereas post-colonial studies establish the western hegemony that is a necessary part of its discourse, this colloquium attempted to fracture that colonial monolith to examine the strategies used in the telling of the various narratives of architectural history. The papers and discussion began the process of unpacking this vision across a broad time span and cross-disciplinary subjects from both a 'western' and an 'eastern' perspective. The geopolitical landscape and history of the Black Sea Region provided an appropriate starting point to consider how a specific areas of study have been formulated either within or without western paradigms. The broader intention was to challenge established post-colonial discourses, which despite claims to liberate non western material from the colonising frame, continue to see it within western/non-western formula, i.e. it is defined by what it is not – it remains 'other'. Indeed, this raises the interesting possibility of looking at architectural history within the paradigm of the 'non-east'. But the collective interest of this colloquium pointed the way to a kind of 'unlearning' of the discourses of architectural history by revisiting the cultural formulations behind their making in both the east and the west as a means of learning about ourselves.

These interests were the focus of the conference session *Ambivalent Geographies: Situating Difference in Architectural History*[5] that enabled exchange between different intellectual and geographical/cultural contexts for architectural history across a broad territory. It became clear that architectural history has been transformed in recent decades as a field of academic inquiry with the expansion of frameworks, subject matters, themes and methods of the discipline in line with critical scholarship in the humanities and social sciences. Most often productive interaction with different disciplines and theories has provided new perspectives and conceptual grounding, and examples of architectural history along these new lines have proliferated, including the study of architecture produced in 'distant' and 'different' geographies that have been put under the totalizing rubric of the 'non-west'. By taking issue with such simplistic positions, speakers aimed to open up further the spatial boundaries of architecture, in order to contribute to the ongoing transformation of architectural history.

Such is the narrative, so far, of the evolution of this ongoing dialogue. The chapters in this book represent the various stages as well as points of convergence and divergence in our project. The next colloquium is already in place where the aim is to problematize geographical difference – a complex category which may work in unexpected and ambivalent ways. A group of international scholars met in Ankara earlier this year to discuss the theme *Towards an Architectural History of the Non-East* and it is hoped that this colloquium will be the prompt for the formation of a global network to enable the exchange of ideas.[6] While acknowledging the changes in the geographical frames of reference for the discipline, which have defined new objects of study and scopes of inquiry, speakers will seek to go beyond the trope of east versus west that had not only dominated the earlier colonizing projects, but also casts its shadow on some recent discourses that aim to dismantle the legacies of colonialism. The interest here is in fracturing the 'consolidated vision' that privileges the 'West' through essentializing and dualistic perspectives, and perpetuates the misrecognition regarding the totality and unity of cultures. The project is part of an attempt to actively open up the boundaries between putative totalities of culture in order to write different histories, particularly the intertwined histories of seemingly distant geographies. Instead of colonising the 'non-west' by mapping it using western narrative structures, we must appreciate its complexity and diversity, as well as the different sets of values that operate within its various cultural frames.

This project continues to benefit from the generous support of funding bodies whose wide-ranging interests are brought together in this truly collaborative project that crosses geographical, disciplinary and methodological boundaries. I would like to acknowledge them on behalf of all who have benefited at the various meetings from the generosity of The British Academy Black Sea Initiative, The British Institute of Archaeology, Ankara, the Centre for Research in Arts, Social Sciences and the Humanities (CRASSH), University of Cambridge, King's College, Cambridge, Institut national d'histoire de l'art, Paris; Society of Architectural Historians, USA, The University of Southampton, Turkish Academy of Sciences (TÜBA) and Turkish Scientific and Technological Research Council (TÜBITAK), and the Graduate Program in Architectural History and the Faculty of Architecture at Middle East Technical University. Finally, thanks must go to Caroline Mallinder at Routledge who has supported this volume that enables us to state where we are now in an continuing, and we hope expanding, discourse.

Notes

1 *Architectural History: Between History and Archaeology?* convened by Eric Fernie, Robin Osborne and me hosted by CRASSH (Centre for Research in Arts, Social Science and Humanities) and King's College Cambridge in November 2003.
2 The term 'History of Architecture' is used here to connote architecture when studied through the lens of another discipline.
3 *Rethinking Architectural Historiography* organized by Elvan Altan Ergut, Sevil Enginsoy Ekinci, Suna Güven and Belgin Turan Özkaya, with the support of Turkish Academy of Sciences (TÜBA) and Turkish Scientific and Technological Research Council (TÜBITAK), and Middle East Technical University 18–19 March 2004.
4 *The Black Sea: Architectural History between East and West* organized by Dana Arnold with the support of the British Institute of Archaeology at Ankara through the British Academy Black Sea Initiative, at the University of Southampton in UK in November 2004.
5 *Ambivalent Geographies: Situating Difference in Architectural History* organized by Elvan Altan Ergut and Belgin Turan Özkaya at 'Changing Boundaries: Architectural History in Transition' conference of the Society of Architectural Historians and Institut national d'histoire de l'art in Paris between August 31–September 4, 2005.
6 *Towards an Architectural History of the Non-East*, organized by Dana Arnold, funded by the British Institute of Archaeology Ankara, hosted by Middle East Technical University 27–29 April 2006.

Dana Arnold
London 2006

Introduction
Mapping architectural historiography

*Elvan Altan Ergut and
Belgin Turan Özkaya*

> This is a beautiful and ingenious machine, very useful and convenient for anyone who takes pleasure in study.... For with this machine a man can see and turn through a large number of books without moving from one spot...
> This wheel is ... constructed so that when the books are laid on their lecterns they never fall or move from the place where they are laid even when the wheel is turned and revolved all the way around. Indeed, they will always remain in the same position and will be displayed to the reader in the same way ... without any need to tie or hold them with anything. This wheel may be made as large or small as desired, provided the master craftsman who constructs it observes the proportions of each part of its components.[1]

This is the way Agostino Ramelli, a sixteenth-century royal engineer in the service of King Henry III of France, described an engraved design for a book lectern that he published alongside other designs for 'ingenious' machines of his, such as fountains and bird calls, machines for dragging heavy objects, and cranes. Ramelli's book wheel, conceived as a helping device for bringing diverse sources within the reach of those who delight in study, has a logic similar to that of this volume: *Rethinking Architectural Historiography* aims to assemble the current positions on architectural historiography without privileging any of them. In other words, it is an attempt at a cartography of a field that has been going through a major transformation over the last two decades. In *Rethinking Architectural Historiography*, as in the case of the open books on Ramelli's machine, illustrated on the cover of this volume, different positions, narratives and perspectives of architectural history are held at equal distance with the aim of making the present situation of the discipline available. Written by a group of international scholars who meditate on selected points of disciplinary change across a broad field of methodological, theoretical and geographical plurality not constrained to the West, the book does not subscribe to a single position. The 'machine' could have been made larger in order to incorporate more 'books'. *Rethinking Architectural Historiography*, however, does not aspire to be comprehensive; instead it highlights a series of salient points and examples that are efficiently representative of the condition of the field at large.

Elicited by the need to reflect upon the changing historiographical practice at this juncture, the book explores the potential openings that may contribute to the further transformation of the discipline, while concurrently problematizing the impact of such encounters with other disciplines and theories on architectural historiography. While doing this, first, the historical and contemporary boundaries of the discipline are discussed. Then, critical engagements with past and present histories that unearth the assumptions, biases and absences in conventional architectural history are brought in. Finally, the discipline is reframed in the light of new perspectives, parameters and problematics. As a result, the book raises a series of questions about interdisciplinarity and multidisciplinarity, and the potentials that they may provide for the discipline; about theories, methods, techniques, genres and tools, as well as assumptions and biases of the discipline; and about the disciplinary particularity of architectural history. Among the sundry questions and issues the volume raises is its intention to induce the reader to ponder on the question, 'What constitutes architectural history?'

Why mapping? Why now?

In line with critical scholarship in the humanities and social sciences in recent decades, architectural history has been transformed as a field of academic inquiry with the expansion of frameworks, subject matters, themes and methods of the discipline. Most often productive interaction with different disciplines and theories provided new perspectives and conceptual grounding, and examples of architectural historiography along these new lines have proliferated. Surprisingly, the transformation in the practice of the discipline has not been sufficiently reflected upon. This book aims to undertake the task.

Up until the late 1990s, the quite rare publications on architectural historiography opted to survey the ways and materials of studying past architectures. As prominent representatives of different genres, the British architectural historian David Watkin's *The Rise of Architectural History*, the *Architectural Design* profile, 'On the Methodology of Architectural History', and the American art and architectural historian Marvin Trachtenberg's *Art Bulletin* article, 'Some Observations on Recent Architectural History', should be mentioned. David Watkin's 1980 book, *The Rise of Architectural History*, is the first historical survey of (mainly British) scholarship in architectural historiography from the seventeenth century to the 1980s.[2] In 1981, Watkin's book was followed by the *Architectural Design* profile, 'On the Methodology of Architectural History', edited by the Greek architect and author Demetri Porphyrios, which delves into what he calls 'the epistemological foundations of the various architectural histories'[3] by juxtaposing excerpts from the works of 'canonical' art and architectural historians and thinkers with critical introductions written by a group of contemporary scholars. Marvin Trachtenberg's 1988 article, 'Some Observations on Recent Architectural History', on the other hand, was commissioned for *Art Bulletin* and gives an outlook on the architectural history literature published between the mid 1970s and the end of the 1980s.[4]

Since the end of the 1990s, on the other hand, a more pervasive, self-reflexive attitude has emerged as revealed in the leading journals of architectural history as well. Recent editors of the *Journal of the Society of Architectural Historians,* as one significant North American publication on architectural history, Nicholas Adams, Eve Blau, Zeynep Çelik and Nancy Stieber, have all focused on the changing nature of architectural history with a more favourable stance towards the new developments than the earlier writings.[5] Accordingly, the *JSAH* made a special issue on 'Architectural History' in September 1999 and in 2002 a three-issue query on 'Teaching Architectural History'. While the latter, edited by Zeynep Çelik, surveyed the situation of architectural history in different educational and geographical contexts from South Asia to Europe and from North Africa to Latin America, the former, under the editorship of Eve Blau, tackled different aspects of the discipline from institutional frameworks to study areas together with emerging perspectives and parameters in North American scholarship. In addition, the all-important history–theory interface was highlighted by, among others, the *Journal of Architectural Education* in a 1999 special issue on 'Critical Historiography', edited by Kazys Varnelis,[6] and in *InterSections: Architectural Histories and Critical Theories,* the volume edited by Iain Borden and Jane Rendell in 2000, which argues for theoretical and interdisciplinary openings for architectural history.

Despite the increasing interest in the methodologies, techniques, and internal mechanisms and institutional contexts of the discipline since the publication of *The Rise of Architectural History,* books that are exclusively on architectural historiography are virtually non-existent. Recent publications that focus on the discipline of architectural history, architectural epistemology and education or on the interface of architectural history with other disciplines and theories touch upon architectural historiography at different levels without concentrating on the subject. To name a few significant examples since the beginning of the 1990s, Eric Fernie's *Art History and Its Methods, The Architectural Historian in America,* edited by Elisabeth Blair MacDougall, *The Education of the Architect: Historiography, Urbanism, and the Growth of Architectural Knowledge,* edited by Martha Pollak, and *The History of History in American Schools of Architecture,* edited by Gwendolyn Wright and Janet Parks, all in one way or another bring up historiography as part of their different agendas.[7] Dana Arnold's *Reading Architectural History* of 2002, which focuses on architectural history texts themselves and rereads them through the lens of social and cultural theory to reveal the productive potential of these texts, which might have been hitherto overlooked, is a major exception in that regard.[8] *Rethinking Architectural Historiography* complements the terrain covered by *Reading Architectural History* in terms of engagement with existing architectural histories. On the other hand, the self-reflexive attitude in recent publications that write history through encounters with different theories, disciplines and perspectives is relevant for *Rethinking Architectural Historiography* as well. As mentioned before, these constitute its major concerns in its mapping of the discipline in order to investigate the current state of architectural historiography.

Boundaries

Today architectural history is written mostly by people who define themselves as architectural historians, but contribution to the field is not the exclusive right of the architectural historian. Many art historians, archaeologists and other academicians and scholars are in one way or another adding to the expanding architectural history scholarship. The backgrounds of architectural historians may vary as well; they have PhD degrees less in architectural history than art history, archaeology and architecture or in programmes that focus on history and theory. In North America, for instance, although architectural history has been taught as part of liberal arts and humanities programmes and on and off at schools of architecture since the end of the nineteenth century, the first advanced programmes on the subject were instituted only in the 1960s. Also, the Society of Architectural Historians, arguably the first society of architectural historians in the world, was founded only in 1940 and continued to hold its meetings for some time together with the College Art Association – the organization of art historians.

The varying degrees and backgrounds of people who are contributing to architectural history scholarship makes futile, in Eric Fernie's words, 'the academic turf wars' based on historians' backgrounds and degrees. Rather than that, our interest in the first section of the book is in the changing boundaries of architectural history in relation to its disciplinary 'constituent facts'. We employ the term 'constituent fact' differently from Sigfried Giedion's use of it,[9] to point at those processes, materials and properties that make architectural history. If we proceed with the renowned concept of Giedion, those 'constituent facts' are also indices of the disciplines that architectural history is historically and currently entwined with, i.e. art history, archaeology, history and architecture.

Architectural history can be defined as having a multidisciplinary base located at the interstices of architecture as, in Fikret Yegül's words, 'the parent discipline', with those other disciplines that historically preceded architectural history as academically sanctioned autonomous disciplines. Yet, the art historian Alina Payne, in a 1999 article, has reminded us that in the past art historians, by studying architecture, made important contributions not only to architectural but to art history as well.[10] In the North American context, she observes that all very useful dialogue between architectural history and history of art has been suspended due to the deepening focus of each. In addition, the American architectural historian, Katherine Fischer Taylor, within the context of a discussion of architecture's place in art history, argues for the distinctive nature of architecture as an object of historical study that can enrich art history by pointing at 'the aesthetic stakes in a sociocultural analysis of buildings that considers both their significance as spaces of social performance and their necessarily formal materiality'.[11] Taking issue with art history's emphasis on (two-dimensional) pictoriality, Fischer Taylor highlights art history and architectural history's common ground of visual analysis that other related humanistic and social disciplines, such as geography, do not possess. Expanding on the 'in-betweenness' of architectural history, Dana Arnold and Robin Osborne, on the other hand, query architectural history's position between archaeology and history as a practice based on analysing material evidence (i.e. buildings, as does archaeology) and utilizing textual evidence (as does history), and delineate the pitfalls of teleological and aesthetical formulations of architectural history.[12]

All these debates evince the essentially multifaceted nature of architectural history. Architectural history shares a material component with art history and archaeology in the sense of the existence of a tactile object of study, and a textual component with the discipline of history in the form of written and visual documents. As Andrew Ballantyne has noted in this volume, the material evidence (the building) may not be enough in itself; it has to be supplemented with the knowledge of the 'context' that can be acquired from textual evidence. And the built space, often shaped by 'aesthetic' concerns, constitutes a setting for 'social performance' that renders historical study of architecture an enterprise about aesthetical, utilitarian and social issues.

The essays in the first part illuminate these different facets of studying past architectures. They renegotiate historical and contemporary boundaries of architectural history vis-à-vis other related fields of art history, archaeology and architecture to different effect. The study of architectural history under art history constitutes the core of Eric Fernie's opening essay, 'Art history and architectural history'. While giving their due to the criticisms directed at stylistic analysis and connoisseurship when they operate as tools for endorsing absolute aesthetic values, he rethinks these conventional methods of art history by locating them in the social realm. Hence, he powerfully argues for the relevance of changing the questions rather than the methods and studying the changing social meanings of style for understanding societies.

Roger Leech, in 'Buildings archaeology: contexts and points of convergence', presents a very different view of architectural history as he discusses it in relation to the practice of archaeology. Through case studies in which Leech was personally involved, the contrasting approaches to recording buildings and constructing their histories within and without the discipline of archaeology are outlined. Unlike many other examples in this volume, Leech's buildings are vernacular and so some of the archival information that may be more readily available for polite architecture can be missing or never existed. Leech argues that archaeology and architectural history are complementary and together provide the fullest possible account of the building. Moreover, his essay indicates how the practice of recording buildings has been institutionalized within the heritage and preservation sector in the UK – but not without lively debate.

Christian F. Otto's essay, 'Program and programs', informs us about the other and more recent address of architectural history – the professional architecture school. He traces the emergence of architectural history as an advanced field of study different from art history and in integration with a design curriculum as exemplified in the specific case of Cornell University. While shedding light on this important and still evolving North American case, he draws the lines between the historian's task and the pragmatic use of history in design studios.

Fikret Yegül's essay, 'Hercules at the roundabout: multidisciplinary choice in the history of architecture', on the other hand, takes us on a tour of potential openings for architectural history. After gauging different models and paradigms, we go back to architecture itself, what he deems the fundamental discipline for the study of architectural history. Yegül argues that, more than any other extra-disciplinary outlook, architectural history should base itself on what is specific to architecture. Andrew Ballantyne's essay, 'Architecture as evidence', counterpoises this and Eric Fernie's positions from different angles. In contradistinction to Yegül's privileging of the phenomenological architectural object, and in a different tone than that of Fernie's reading of the social from the stylistic, the essay argues about the ambiguity of the material evidence (i.e. the building itself) for the historical study of architecture. Ballantyne argues that the architectural object can speak to us only with the aid of the knowledge of its context furnished by textual evidence, and usually what it conveys is more about its perception in a certain framework rather than a trans-historical truth.

The concluding essay of the first part, Suna Güven's 'Frontiers of fear: architectural history, the anchor and the sail', emphatically delineates the pliable nature of architectural history. After pointing out the essentially daunting work that awaits an architectural historian due to the sheer amount of objects of study, together with their folded histories and the sundry perspectives that can be adopted, it characterizes the working of architectural history as one of alternating exploration and absorption, and paves the way for the coming essays in the volume that one way or the other explore new territories in the form of either new problematics, theories or new perspectives.

Critical engagements

Architectural history, so we are told, and so we repeatedly tell ourselves, is in crisis; not necessarily in the life-threatening, medical sense of a turning point for better or worse in an acute disease or fever, but rather in the existential sense of being in a state of transition – at a critical point of decision in which change is imminent. As John Pinto pointed out two years ago in his 2000 plenary address, when he invoked the Chinese ideogram for crisis, such conditions combine danger with opportunity. I would like to take this idea a step further and to suggest that not only are there both positive and negative aspects to crisis, but that crisis itself is a good thing for a discipline; it is, moreover, inherent in historical thinking, and therefore intrinsic to our discipline.[13]

Thus, the former editor of the *Journal of the Society of Architectural Historians*, Eve Blau, in her plenary address at the 2002 SAH Meeting in Richmond, describes her position on the 'disciplinary crisis of architectural history'. Based on the Italian architectural historian Manfredo Tafuri's conflation of the 'project of history' with 'a project of crisis' in the sense of being never definitive but always provisional and querying its material, she contends that

> Crisis conceived in this way is not only a sign of vitality and resistance – it is a critical habit of mind and a fundamental condition of historical thinking. It would seem that a discipline whose project is to understand change must repeatedly throw itself into crisis.[14]

Such a conceptualization of the discipline of (architectural) history is both historically and heuristically accurate – it is a reminder of the immanent non-stagnant nature of studying history and situates the (architectural) historian as an agent who can utilize the 'crisis' to positive effect. Change in the way the discipline, which studies change, operates is not a recent phenomenon. Since its formal inception as an autonomous, academic discipline in the nineteenth century, history itself has gone through different phases and conceptualizations, from simple causal, linear explanatory models to teleological, totalistic Hegelian formulations, and from structuralist history of multiple historical times to more recent post-structuralist micro-history and discourse analysis, traces of all of which can be found in today's different 'schools' of history. On the other hand, this is not to say that the pace of change in ways of writing history has not accelerated in the second half of the twentieth century, with proliferating 'schools', from the aforementioned structuralist history and post-structuralist micro-history to discourse analysis, and from earlier formulations of social history to the ensuing various paradigms such as gender, sexuality, post-colonial theory and different critiques of globalization and locality. The consequent development of a pervasive self-reflexive attitude in architectural historiography since the 1990s, along the lines of the changes in the humanities and social sciences in general, resulted in not only new subject matters, but also new methodologies, paradigms and perspectives. Accordingly, the existing scholarship of architectural history began to be questioned.

The material evidence (the built space) and the textual evidence (written and visual documents) that have been pointed out in the above discussion on the disciplinary boundaries are two of the essential components, i.e. constituent facts, of writing architectural history. By analysing such evidences, the historian constructs a 'narrative', which is developed in relation to (or against) the existing scholarship. In the last decades, a growing literature started to query these different components of architectural historiography, and a series of questions was raised about the latent assumptions in the scholarship, about canonization of objects of study, and about not only the self-evidentiality of the document but also the objectivity of the historian, as well as the biases and absences in consequently formed narratives of history.

The essays in the second part thus critically engage with past and present histories and disclose dormant problematics in architectural historiography. They take issue with the conventional conceptualizations of those essential constituent facts of writing architectural history, from the existing scholarship to the architectural work, and from the document to the historian to the historical narrative. It opens with Tülay Artan's meticulous anatomizing of the scholarship on the Ottoman period. Artan, in her 'Questions of Ottoman identity and architectural history', by discussing a multitude of points from the reductive parameters to the nationalistic and anachronistic biases of Ottoman historiography, argues for the necessity of a new sociology (and historiography) of empire that will give its due to the complex Ottoman imperial cultural tradition, which was, in her words, more than 'a coherent blending of elements from the traditions out of which it had been forged'. The following essay, '*In Ordinary Time*: considerations on a video installation by Iñigo Manglano Ovalle and the New National Gallery in Berlin by Mies van der Rohe', critiques one of the most canonical works of modern architecture. Edward Dimendberg starts his essay by enunciating what is mostly overlooked in architectural history, i.e. the lived spatiality facilitated by built environment. Through a rereading of the New National Gallery as mediated by Iñigo Manglano Ovalle's video installation, *In Ordinary Time*, Dimendberg argues against its architect's claims and the modernist reception of the building, and highlights the potential that audio-visual media have for the comprehension of how built spaces are actually used.

Sevil Enginsoy Ekinci, on the other hand, in her essay 'Reopening the question of document in architectural historiography: reading (writing) Filarete's treatise on architecture for (in) Piero de' Medici's study', takes up the problem of the document in historiography in relation to the specific example of Filarete's *Trattato di Architettura*. By demonstrating how a document can operate in a multitude of ways not only as a textual but also as a material object and a socio-cultural commodity, and how 'reading of a document is not an instrumental but a stimulating practice that initiates the activity of writing history', Enginsoy Ekinci displaces the textual evidence from the realm of 'objective' knowledge to its historical and the historian's psychic sphere. The historian's subjectivity constitutes the crux of Jane Rendell's essay as well, which innovatively unveils the 'texts' that write the historian as much as the texts that she herself writes. Based on her own experience as an architectural historian and writer, Rendell, in 'From architectural history to spatial writing', traces the changing role of critical theory in the practice of architectural history and argues for an interdisciplinary architectural history located between history, theory and practice.

The chapter concludes with an engagement with that much maligned but just as resistant component of historiography – the narrative.[15] By stitching together information from a variety of sources, from official views of administrative authorities to tourist websites, Elvan Altan Ergut unearths three different imaginary Ankaras in her essay, 'Presenting Ankara: popular conceptions of architecture and history'. After showing the intermingled nature of these popular constructs both with each other and with scholarly narratives, she argues for the necessity of more inclusive historiographical approaches based on real and multiple identities rather than reductive ideological and popular views.

Reframings

The last five essays explore the potentialities provided by new perspectives and reframe the discipline in the light of new parameters and problematics. In order to contribute to the ongoing transformation of architectural historiography, they further open up the boundaries of the discipline. This is a task complementary to the 'practice' of critical engagement in that querying its conventions, genres, practices and methodologies, among others, constitutes one facet of the disciplinary transformation of architectural history, with appropriation and integration of new outlooks, paradigms and frameworks as the other. This section delineates that venturing into new territories is fraught not only with danger but also with opportunity, which keeps the discipline vigorous and ultimately is beneficial to it.

More importantly, the essays in this section do not conceive the opening up of the boundaries of the discipline as a one-way move on the part of architectural history that renders it a passive receptor of what is happening in other fields. Rather than that, they envisage the interaction with other fields as a two-way act, and highlight the hitherto curiously understated potential of architectural history in affecting other disciplines and fields. As evinced by the case of German thinker, Walter Benjamin, who was interested in architecture and urban space as part of his philosophical/historical project, and along the lines of Katherine Fischer Taylor's emphasis on the complex constitution of architecture as both visual and spatial, aesthetic and utilitarian, and social and material,[16] architectural history can guide other disciplines as well.

Hence, Nancy Stieber's reminder in this volume about the necessity of a dialogue between architectural historians – who, more than anyone else, can provide insights into the shaping of space and who, by doing so, can contribute 'in essential ways to the transdisciplinary discourse of space' – and cultural geographers, anthropologists and literary theorists who have been writing about space. Stieber's 'Space, time, and architectural history', which is the opening essay of the last part, is located on the imbrications of architectural history with a series of other fields, from geography to cultural studies to literary theory to postcolonial studies, particularly in terms of their mobilization of the category of space. In her essay, while acknowledging the benefits of being open to these fields and the interesting methods and problems defined outside architectural history, Nancy Stieber also argues that what the social and humanistic spatial studies lack – the empirically arrived, specific space – can be provided by architectural history, which, she argues, can then contribute a much-needed 'visual turn' to these disciplines.

The following two essays, too, investigate the intertwined zone of spatiality and visuality from different angles. The exploration of a common structural logic between the seemingly different media of pictorial, filmic and architectural spaces is at the centre of Belgin Turan Özkaya's essay, 'Visuality and architectural history'. After discussing the ramifications of the 'pictorial turn' in the humanities and social sciences for architectural history, Turan Özkaya argues that the object of architectural history, i.e. architecture, needs to be conceptualized as encompassing not only the built space but as a discursive and visual practice comprising diverse conceptual, representational, textual and spatial processes. Diane Favro, in her essay 'The digital disciplinary divide: reactions to historical virtual reality models', on the other hand, takes up a different aspect of recent developments – the all-important but hitherto under-theorized issue of the impact of new visual technologies on the study of historical architectures. On the basis of the reactions evoked by four-dimensional virtual reality models, Favro compellingly exposes the differing 'disciplinary eyes' of people coming from different fields, and argues for the necessity of studying past environments holistically by weaving together aesthetic, structural, theoretical, visual and experiential factors.

The architectural object as the material evidence of something beyond aesthetic realm and laden with the potential to demystify the phantasmagorias of modern life, those formulations of Walter Benjamin, are at the core of Patricia Morton's essay, 'The afterlife of buildings: architecture and Walter Benjamin's theory of history'. The 'afterlife' of architectural works and the non-progressive notion of history are the two axes around which Morton weaves her argument on the relevance of Benjamin's theory of history for a critical architectural historiography that will displace the emphasis from the heroic architect to the status of the work over time, and to the marginal and the neglected. The last essay, by Dana Arnold, engages with some threads pursued in several essays and argues for structural alterations in the discipline, namely for changing narrative and linguistic structures if a genuine understanding of the marginalized and the subjugated in architectural history is sought after. In that sense, 'Beyond a boundary: towards an architectural history of the non-east' concludes the volume with a critique of the current establishments as well as with a salutary opening to the future.

Notes

Many individuals and institutions contributed to the long process leading to the publication of this volume. Generous grants by Middle East Technical University, the Turkish Academy of Sciences (TÜBA) and the Turkish Scientific and Technological Research Council (TÜBITAK), and the support of Haluk Pamir, the Dean of the METU Faculty of Architecture, made it possible to organize the conference 'Rethinking Architectural Historiography' in Ankara, which has become one of the catalysts for this volume. We would like to thank the contributors of *Rethinking Architectural Historiography* for their collaboration and thought-provoking essays, and Caroline Mallinder, Georgina Johnson and the Routledge staff for their guidance and help. Our heartfelt gratitude goes to our co-editor, Dana Arnold, with whom scholarly pursuits turned into pleasurable journeys. We also are grateful to our families: working on this volume meant stealing from our time with them.

1 The full description is as follows:

> This is a beautiful and ingenious machine, very useful and convenient for anyone who takes pleasure in study, especially those who are indisposed and tormented by gout. For with this machine a man can see and turn through a large number of books without moving from one spot. Moreover, it has another fine convenience in that it occupies very little space in the place where it is set, as anyone of intelligence can clearly see from the drawing. This wheel is made in the manner shown, that is, it is constructed so that when the books are laid on their lecterns they never fall or move from the place where they are laid even when the wheel is turned and revolved all the way around. Indeed, they will always remain in the same position and will be displayed to the reader in the same way ... without any need to tie or hold them with anything. This wheel may be made as large or small as desired, provided the master craftsman who constructs it observes the proportions of each part of its components. He can do this very easily if he studies carefully all the parts of these small wheels of ours and the other devices in this machine. These parts are made in sizes proportionate to each other. To give a fuller understanding and comprehension to anyone who wishes to make and operate this machine, I have shown here separately and uncovered all the devices needed for it, so that anyone may understand them better and make use of them for his needs.

Agostino Ramelli, *The Various and Ingenious Machines of Agostino Ramelli* [*Le diverse et artificiose machine del Capitano Agostino Ramelli* (1588), Paris], translated from the Italian and French with a biographical sketch of the author by Martha Teach Gnudi; technical annotations and a pictorial glossary by Eugene S. Ferguson, Baltimore, MD, and London, 1976, 508.

We would like to thank Sevil Enginsoy Ekinci and Ela Kaçel for their help in tracking down Ramelli's text.

2 David Watkin, *The Rise of Architectural History*, London, 1980. Watkin himself mentions the more specifically focused works of Paul Frankl on the Gothic and Nikolaus Pevsner on the nineteenth century as important precedents of his book. See Paul Frankl, *The Gothic, Literary Sources and Interpretations through Eight Centuries*, Princeton, NJ, 1960; and Nikolaus Pevsner, *Some Architectural Writers of the Nineteenth Century*, Oxford, 1972.

3 Demetri Porphyrios, 'Introduction', in Demetri Prophyrios (ed.), 'On the Methodology of Architectural Historiography', *Architectural Design Profile*, 1981.
4 Marvin Trachtenberg, 'Some Observations on Recent Architectural History', *Art Bulletin*, LXX: 2, 1988, 208–41. Trachtenberg's essay surveys the architectural history literature under the headings of The Architect, The Single-Building Monograph, The Building Type, Styles and Periods, Urbanism, and Theory and Criticism.
5 Marvin Trachtenberg, for instance, does not have much sympathy for the developments that he analyses in the Theory and Criticism section of his essay on recent architectural history. See Nicholas Adams, 'Celebrating Tradition and Change', *Journal of the Society of Architectural Historians*, LII: 2, June 1993, 137–8; Eve Blau, 'Representing Architectural History', *Journal of the Society of Architectural Historians*, 56: 2, June 1997, 144–5; Zeynep Çelik, 'Expanding Frameworks', *Journal of the Society of Architectural Historians*, 59: 2, June 2000, 152–3; and Nancy Stieber, 'Architecture Between Disciplines', *Journal of the Society of Architectural Historians*, 62: 2, June 2003, 176–7.
6 Kazys Varnelis, 'Critical Historiography and the End of Theory', *Journal of Architectural Education*, 52: 4, May 1999, 95–6.
7 Eric Fernie (ed.), *Art History and Its Methods: A Critical Anthology*, London, 1995; Elisabeth Blair MacDougall (ed.), *The Architectural Historian in America*, Hanover, NH, and London, 1990; Martha Pollak (ed.), *The Education of the Architect: Historiography, Urbanism, and the Growth of Architectural Knowledge*, Cambridge, MA, and London, 1997; and Gwendolyn Wright and Janet Parks (eds), *The History of History in American Schools of Architecture 1865–1975*, New York, 1990. See also James S. Ackerman and Rhys Carpenter, *Art and Archaeology*, Englewood Cliffs, NJ, 1963; Iain Borden and David Dunster, *Architecture and the Sites of History*, New York, 1995; L. Groat and D. Wang, *Architectural Research Methods*, New York, 2002; Andrej Piotrowski and Julia Williams Robinson (eds), *The Discipline of Architecture*, Minneapolis, MN, and London, 2001; and Marcus Whiffen (ed.), *The History, Theory and Criticism of Architecture*, Cambridge, MA, 1965.
8 Dana Arnold, *Reading Architectural History*, London and New York, 2002.
9 Sigfried Giedion, *Space, Time and Architecture: The Growth of a New Tradition*, Cambridge, MA, 1941.
10 Alina Payne, 'Architectural History and the History of Art', *Journal of the Society of Architectural Historians*, 58: 3, September 1999, 292–300. Payne cites Donald Preziosi's *The Art of Art History: A Critical Anthology* of 1998 as an example that excludes architectural history.
11 Katherine Fischer Taylor, 'Architecture's Place in Art History: Art or Adjunct?', *Art Bulletin*, LXXXIII: 2, June 2001, 346.
12 Robin Osborne and Dana Arnold's unpublished statement for the conference *Architectural History: Between History and Archaeology*, held on 14–15 November 2003, at Cambridge University. For the changing (aesthetical) meaning of architectural works over time, see Dana Arnold and Andrew Ballantyne, *Architecture as Experience: Radical Change in Spatial Practice*, London and New York, 2004.
13 Eve Blau, 'A Question of Discipline: Plenary Address, Society of Architectural Historians Annual Meeting, Richmond, Virginia, 18 April 2002', *Journal of the Society of Architectural Historians*, 62: 1, March 2003, 125.

14 Blau, 'A Question of Discipline', 125.
15 For an influential critique of narrative in relation to history, see Hayden White, 'The Value of Narrativity in the Representation of Reality', in *The Content of the Form: Narrative Discourse and Historical Representation*, Baltimore, MD, 1990. For an argument about the indisposable nature of the short span (hence historical narrative) in addition to other time cycles, see Fernand Braudel, 'History and the Social Sciences, the *Longue Duree*', in *On History*, Chicago, IL, and London, 1980, 25–54.
16 Fischer Taylor, 'Architecture's Place in Art History'.

Part I
Boundaries

1
Art history and architectural history

Eric C. Fernie

Academic turf wars may be entertaining, but they are seldom productive. No one has rights, as a scholar, over any part of the historical record, and all evidence is open to all of us to use in pursuit of answers, regardless of our labels. That, however, is a privileged view, applicable to those with private means or very large grants. In the world of economic necessity, with its institutions, departments and funding streams, teaching makes unavoidable demands for boundaries, and research, with an increasing stress on collaborative projects and centres, even in the humanities becomes more institutionalized; and of course there is the matter of where the graduates get jobs, what might be called the reception theory of academic survival. In choosing the taxonomy of knowledge as its theme for the year, CRASSH (Centre for Research in the Arts, Social Sciences and Humanities, Cambridge University) called attention to both these aspects of the academy, the ideal and the real so to speak, concerning which I wryly noted that H. G. Liddel and Robert Scott, having given the meaning of *taxis* as 'disposition', add 'especially of military forces'.[1]

The main aim of the conference was to examine the place of the history of architecture in the taxonomy of knowledge, with particular regard to departmental contexts.[2] Architectural history is taught for the most part in departments of art history and schools of architecture, and to a lesser extent in departments of history, archaeology and architectural history. It is obvious that all departmental boxes have their own working assumptions, but let me illustrate the point. The booklet for the Leeds International Medieval Congress for 2003 contains a set of maps of the region, Leeds City centre, roads around the sites, the sites themselves and the individual buildings on them. These maps were provided by the School of Geography of the University and are excellent, except for one detail. All the diagrams have north lines, except for those of buildings; and, as some of the drawings are printed with a direction other than north at the top of the page, with some buildings it is almost impossible to find your bearings. So there is a professional quirk: diagrams of buildings are plans, not maps, and plans do not need, perhaps do not deserve, north lines. Even if this is the fault of one illogical geographer, it nonetheless illustrates the existence of mental categories based on disciplines.

That brings me to the aim of this essay, which is to assess the value of studying architectural history in the particular box of the history of art, and, I should immediately add, this is what I have always seen myself as doing. To provide a focus for this assessment, I am going to offer a brief account of a building, namely the eleventh-century cathedral at Speyer. Its status is almost unrivalled in German political history, both at the time of its construction and after. This status is echoed by the chief item in its bibliography: Hans Kubach and Walter Haas's *Der Dom zu Speyer* of 1972; the text and plates volumes are each like a domestic brick, and the volume of drawings, at 30 cm by 43, is almost the same size as a Roman sesquipedalian tile, that is, 1 ft by 1½, or 29.6 cm by 44.4. The text volume has 1,142 pages, and the plates volume 1,699 photographs.[3]

The city of Speyer is situated on the west bank of the Rhine, on the stretch of the river running north from France to the Netherlands. The present form

Figure 1.1 Speyer Cathedral from the south-east. (Hans Kubach and Walter Haas, *Der Dom zu Speyer*, 3 vols, Munich 1972, plate 125.)

of the cathedral is largely as it was built from 1030 by the German emperor Conrad II (emperor 1024–39) and refurbished in the late eleventh and early twelfth centuries by Henry IV (emperor 1056–1106), though with extensive restorations. It is vast, with six towers and a profile imposing even by the standards of the industrial age (Figure 1.1). The crypt contains the tomb of Conrad, making the building the mausoleum for the Salian royal house and putting it in the same category as St Denis and Westminster Abbey. The sources and meanings of Conrad's building are almost all to do with the Roman Empire, using both non-Christian and Christian precedents, such as the fourth-century basilica at Trier for the elevation, and the contemporary church of St Peter in Rome for the plan of the crypt.

It is the same with Henry's work. The *Vita Bennonis Osnabrugensis* records that, in or shortly before 1082, Bishop Benno of Osnabrück, 'well versed in the art of architecture, was brought to the city of Speyer by order of the King' to repair the building, which had been erected 'with too little caution [up to] the bank of the River Rhine'. Henry took the opportunity to refurbish the building, most notably adding the groin vaults in the nave and probably the rib vaults in the transepts (the dates of the vaults have been much debated, at times somewhat chauvinistically). There are Roman sources for both: thermae of the third century such as those of Caracalla or Diocletian in Rome for the groins, and the sixth-century Hagia Sophia in Constantinople for the ribs. And of course the Corinthian capitals have a Roman source. There are also features from contemporary Italy, such as the sculpture around the windows of S. Abbondio in Como, dedicated in 1095, which make it look as if everything from Italy was thought of as 'Roman', even if it was clearly contemporary. Thus, while problems with the damp courses and water ingress may have been the immediate reason for the work, this relentless aggrandizing and stress on classical sources make it difficult, despite the counter arguments, to ignore the fact that the work started within a few years of the investiture contest of 1077, and Henry's humiliating defeat at Canossa at the hands of Pope Gregory VII.

While they could not even be outlined within the scope of this essay, a proper study could also include, among other things, how the building was designed, especially the geometry used, how it was built, including the masonry techniques, how it was funded and how it affected the region in which it stands.

The later history of the building is equally interesting. Additions and alterations in the gothic style are nugatory, from which one can conclude that the romanesque building was probably considered special. Our knowledge of successive German invasions of France since 1871 tends to obscure the fact that before that date the relationship between the two states was reversed. Louis XIV's seizure of Alsace and Lorraine in the late seventeenth century brought the boundary of France to within a few miles of Speyer. When the town was sacked in 1689 Louis XIV commanded that the cathedral be spared, but fire still engulfed it, destroying much of the nave. In 1772 the west front was rebuilt by Ignaz Michael Neumann (son of Balthasar). A noteworthy aspect of this is that Neumann respected the romanesque style of the original. Apart from Christopher Wren's fragment at Ely, this sort of approach is hard to parallel anywhere at this time.

In the 1790s, when the French again occupied the town, their view of the cathedral was explicit: it represented the imperial German past and had to go, so they drew up a plan to turn it into a parade ground, using the western massif as a triumphal entrance arch. The plan was vetoed by Napoleon. After Waterloo, the Germans decided to remove the eighteenth-century west front and build one on the lines of the original romanesque design, with the Bavarians here playing the same role in the German *renovatio* as the Prussians with the cathedral in contemporary Cologne. After the Second World War General de Gaulle followed in the spirit of 1689 and 1792 in demanding that the Franco-German boundary north of Alsace be moved to the Rhine, which would have made Speyer a French city. It is possible that embarrassment on the part of the United States over having rejected de Gaulle's demand contributed to their agreeing to France being given a seat on the Security Council of the United Nations in the same deliberations.

Turning now to an assessment of the value of an art-historical context for the history of architecture, and starting by identifying the wide range of disciplines involved in this study of Speyer Catheral, those that appear to be necessary for using the textual evidence include the disciplines of those loosely called historians, that is, those for whom palaeography and languages are essentials, and who concentrate on various overlapping specialisms, such as the political, constitutional, social, economic and ecclesiastical. For the material evidence there are the disciplines of archaeologists, scientists (such as chemists and petrologists), architectural historians, cultural historians, architects, engineers and geographers.[4] Architectural history has, therefore, as one would expect, a central role to play among these disciplines. The question is, can it fulfil that role if it is studied in an art-historical context?

Thinking of the weaknesses and strengths of the history of art as a discipline, and starting with the weaknesses, the most obvious is the concentration on the individual artist. This is the biography industry, producing monographs on the life and work of Leonardo, Rembrandt, Frank Lloyd Wright, Picasso, etc. – works that tend to ignore contexts, be self-contained, discussing the authentication of objects and the so-called development of the artist's work. Hence Dana Arnold's comment, when we were organizing the conference, that art history encouraged searches for authorial authenticity. This does not make sense to a medievalist as there is only a tiny handful of names to choose from and those are cardboard characters (like Benno of Osnabrück). There is, however, a partial parallel in medieval studies, in the concentration on buildings as individual objects, like pieces in an exhibition.

Concerning style, what Nikolaus Pevsner is often and rightly accused of overemphasizing, this is the chief tool of art history, the *Kunstgeschichte* of Johann Joachim Winckelmann and Heinrich Wölfflin, and what Marvin Trachtenberg has referred to as a 'mythical Kunstwissenschaft', which is 'inherently asocial in its abstraction'.[5]

There is also a practical problem, that of recognition, in that 99 per cent of the population sees architectural history as separate from art history: art is painting and sculpture, architecture means buildings, as the arrangements of bookshops indicate. Organizations that ignore the distinction, such as the Royal Academy, are likely to be continuing a traditional view.

These points constitute a strong case against the relevance of the history of art for the history of architecture, and doubtless there are many more. It is also true that art historians are their own worst enemies, as I do not know of any other discipline that so assiduously plays down and even attacks its worth: I am not an art historian, I am a cultural historian, an archaeologist, a historian of visual culture, or a social historian; art history is only about connoisseurship, let's discuss the end of art history, etc. And yet, a good case can be made that taking full account of the individual work of art and using stylistic analysis can also be strengths, leading to insights that would be difficult to obtain in other ways.

The chief point about the work of art is that it is not necessary for art historians to restrict themselves to authentication and the treatment of the object as a work of art: I have tried to illustrate a much wider approach in my thumbnail sketch of Speyer Cathedral. But it is equally important that we should also, where appropriate, treat the building as a free-standing work of art, because at least some of the patrons, architects and users themselves appear to have done so, meaning that we have a reason, indeed a duty, for doing so as well. I think, for example, of the exterior of the thirteenth-century late romanesque abbey church of St George at Limburg-an-der-Lahn on the Rhine, where the reconstructed painted exterior surfaces are absolutely distinguished from the ground at the base of the walls; or Norman Foster's Swiss Ré building in St Mary Axe in the City of London, in the twenty-first century, which makes no acknowledgement of the surrounding buildings or even the ground on which it stands. Why was all that money spent on buildings like these if they were not intended to be seen and appreciated as individual objects?

While the criticisms of style analysis described earlier are all justified, as with the work of art there is another side to the question. One of the most revealing aspects of a culture or society lies in what it considers good style, or, to put it at its most ephemeral, stylish. If one wants an indication of the social importance of style one need only think of the six-year-old required to attend school wearing socks that they think are either too long or too short for the peer-group norm, or the minute differences in cut and colour that determine whether a shirt is a teenager's object of extreme desire or the epitome of the naff. At the other end of the cultural scale, one can recall the status of the original romanesque form of Speyer for later generations, in the gothic period, for Neumann, and in the nineteenth century. Style is an invaluable tool for understanding societies. Thus, while Trachtenberg's description of style-based criticism as asocial in its abstraction may be right in some and even the majority of cases, it is not inherently so.

Even connoisseurship, despite having been so roundly condemned, can be shown to be indispensable. Connoisseurship deserves to be rejected as a historical tool when it is used to support the notion of absolute standards of beauty, but there are two other ways of using it. First, it is necessary for an understanding of someone else's standards of beauty, that is, for understanding why a design or composition might have been considered successful by contemporaries. Second, it is also a necessary tool for attempting to distinguish the authentic from the inauthentic where there is no other kind of evidence, as with the telling example noted by the anthropologist William Fagg with regard to African sculpture.[6]

To conclude I would like to return to the distinction between the real and the ideal in the division of knowledge. In the case of the real, the practical, the question is, can the history of architecture be usefully studied in the context of the history of art? I have tried to present a defence of this context and I would say that it is no more confining than any other academic context and may be less so than some: thus, while a department dedicated solely to architectural history has many advantages, not least in terms of visibility, it runs the risk of creating narrower confines for the subject than those likely in a wider context, such as the art-historical (though of course the same could be argued about the history of art lying outside departments of history!).

In the end, however, I think the departmental question is secondary to the conclusions concerning the ideal. I have two, very obvious, ones. First, the basic questions are: what do you want to understand, and what disciplines do you need to do so? Second, if we want to define territories we should only do so for ourselves and not for others. In other words, our definitions of our territory do not exclude other investigators; they merely describe what we think we are doing. It is the questions that should drive our investigations, not the kinds of scholars we are or think ourselves to be.

Notes

1. H. G. Liddel and Robert Scott, *A Greek–English Lexicon*, Oxford: Oxford University Press, first published 1935.
2. This is a reference to the conference organized by Dana Arnold, Robin Osborne and me as part of the CRASSH events pursuing the theme, 'taxonomies of knowledge', and entitled *Architectural History: Between History and Archaeology?*, November 2003.
3. Hans Kubach and Walter Haas, *Der Dom zu Speyer*, 3 vols, Munich, 1972.
4. Mentioning petrologists, one of them provided me with my favourite footnote: the identification of the source of the stone for the carving of a bishop at Norwich Cathedral, which depended on distinguishing between mature female and adolescent male ostracods.
5. Marvin Trachtenberg, 'Some Observations on Recent Architectural History', *Art Bulletin*, 70, 1988, 208–41.
6. William Fagg, 'In Search of Meaning in African Art', in Anthony Forge (ed.), *Primitive Art and Society*, Oxford, 1973, 151–68.

2
Buildings archaeology
Context and points of convergence

Roger H. Leech

Some twelve years ago the late lamented Royal Commission on the Historical Monuments of England (RCHME) held a one-day meeting on Recording Historic Buildings.[1] What occasioned that meeting would not be immediately evident if one was not familiar with a then recent paper by Ian Ferris in *Vernacular Architecture*.[2] In brief this paper had argued for buildings to be recorded in the way that was by then the norm in Britain for archaeological sites. Ferris, a member of BUFA, Birmingham University's commercially based Field Archaeology Unit, set out the rationale for this and presented the BUFA recording forms as a new standard for the recording of buildings. With single-context recording objectivity would be ensured – in an area all too prone to interpretative excesses. With developer funding for the completion of separate recording forms for all identifiable units – walls, windows, doorframes, doors – this would have been bonanza and boom time for archaeological units across the land. The Vernacular Architecture Group responded with vigour, with two rejoinder papers in the same volume,[3] and one in the volume for the next year.[4] In the latter John Bold quoted Sir Flinders Petrie via Martin Carver: 'In recording the first difficulty is to know what to record. To state every fact about everything found would be useless ...'. Perhaps fearing the introduction of a PPG15 emulating the archaeological PPG16,[5] the RCHME responded with a conference to complete the kill.

Though I would count myself as an archaeologist, I was and am in broad agreement with the response of architectural historians on this issue. My first encounter with the detailed archaeological recording of buildings was in Bristol, where the then museum-based Archaeology Unit had in the late 1970s embarked upon building recording. The building being recorded was an early seventeenth-century lodge of hall-parlour plan. The chosen scale was 1:20, requiring two separate drawing sheets to cover each floor. Later twentieth-century wash basins were planned in consummate detail, including even the plugholes, plugs and their chains. But the overhead moulded and stopped ceiling beams, vital evidence for the original plan form of the building, were omitted altogether – it is not simply that archaeologists look down not up. This was a case of not understanding what questions needed to be asked – and therefore not understanding what needed to be recorded. Nicholas Molyneux provided similar examples in his paper to the RCHME conference.[6]

Detailed recording using drawing frames or other devices, applying techniques normally used for below-ground archaeology, does of course have a role, particularly in the conservation process. Examples of best practice in this area include, for instance, the work of the former Lancaster University Archaeology Unit at Bolton Castle and Furness Abbey.[7]

The papers in *Recording Historic Buildings* agreed that the search for objectivity, the BUFA goal, was a chimera, and set out cogently the case for building recording to be question led. But the authors were less concerned explicitly with context and the interdisciplinary approach to architectural history. Perhaps as a former RCHME employee I can hazard a guess that there was an underlying belief in the primacy of the architectural or material data – and that everything else was secondary. I do not agree with this approach. In many instances questioning the documentary evidence can bring us to conclusions quite different from those that we would reach if only the architectural data survived.

'Buildings Archaeology' is now a recognised branch of archaeology. The Institute of Field Archaeologists has its own 'Buildings Archaeology Group (BAG)' and a recent issue of its journal *The Archaeologist* (Winter 2005) was devoted entirely to Buildings Archaeology. University archaeology departments, for instance Bristol and York, now offer MA degrees in Buildings Archaeology and at least one book, by Richard Morriss, is devoted entirely to the subject.[8] Jason Wood has identified Warwick Rodwell's general guide to analysis of buildings using churches as examples and the long-term fabric surveys set up by English Heritage from the mid 1980s, the establishment of IFA's Buildings Special Interest Group and the resulting conferences, day schools and other events as 'important milestones in Buildings Archaeology'.[9]

The development of Buildings Archaeology has owed much to the long tradition in British archaeology of studying buildings, most especially those of medieval or earlier date. The misleadingly named British Archaeological Association has in recent years devoted its programme and publications largely to architectural history, most often focused on medieval religious buildings, its annual meeting devoted to a succession of cathedral cities, and venturing abroad to Angers, Utrecht and Rouen for the occasional wider context. The contents of the *Antiquaries Journal*, *Archaeologia* and the *Archaeological Journal* reflect the long interest of their parent societies and membership in architectural history.

From my own experience as an archaeologist studying buildings I see no divide between the two disciplines called history and archaeology. Another now widely recognised branch of archaeology is 'historical archaeology' part of which I would see as concerned with the archaeology of buildings. The historical archaeologist studying buildings will work as an architectural historian placing buildings in their physical and topographical contexts, within their own craft and design tradition, but also in their wider political and social context. I can best resort to demonstrating that this is so by reference to projects in which I have been personally involved.

The first of these was a study of early industrial housing in Frome, Somerset. In 1974, together with Professor Mick Aston, then County Archaeologist for Somerset, I was responsible for the production of a study of the archaeological implications of future development in the historic towns of Somerset.[10] Mick was to study the towns in the west of the county, I those in the east. It was our practice to perambulate each town to be studied and one day in 1974 we looked at Frome. On the north-west side of the town the later nineteenth-century map showed a regular suburb, which we took to be probably a Victorian suburb added to the earlier town. Walking down these streets we rapidly realised that they were lined by houses of the seventeenth century, largely refronted in the nineteenth century. Pinned to the doors of many of the houses were compulsory purchase orders presaging their planned demolition. Our response to this situation was rapid. The Regional Archaeological Unit took on the archaeological survey of the entire area to be demolished as a project, with funding from the RCHME.[11] The freshly completed new list of buildings of historic interest, which had inexplicably omitted a hundred or more surviving seventeenth-century houses, was rapidly revised. The decision was then made that the seventeenth-century suburb would be retained with the houses modernised to serve as new local authority housing. The restored housing was then given a ministerial reopening, with the minister being presented with a copy of the RCHME published survey of the seventeenth-century houses only recently scheduled for demolition and now listed as being of historic interest.

Early Industrial Housing: The Trinity Area of Frome, Somerset was based on what might be called an archaeologically informed survey. Buildings were placed in their physical and topographical contexts: the development of the street plan was traced through time, in *c*.1665, *c*.1685, *c*.1705 and *c*.1725; the building process was mapped in topographical context for five of the streets; the distribution of plan types was mapped across the area studied. The classification of plan types owed its inspiration to the then recently published study of vernacular housing in Wales.[12] The use of aerial photographs, normal for archaeological survey, was innovative in the area survey of a historic housing development. Here it enabled the identification retrospectively of the characteristics and plan forms of buildings in the half of the Trinity Area demolished in the 1960s. Also normal for archaeological survey was the preparation of new plans of the structures within the study area. These revealed many of the complexities in the relationships between adjoining houses, contributing further to the understanding of the building process (Figure 2.1).

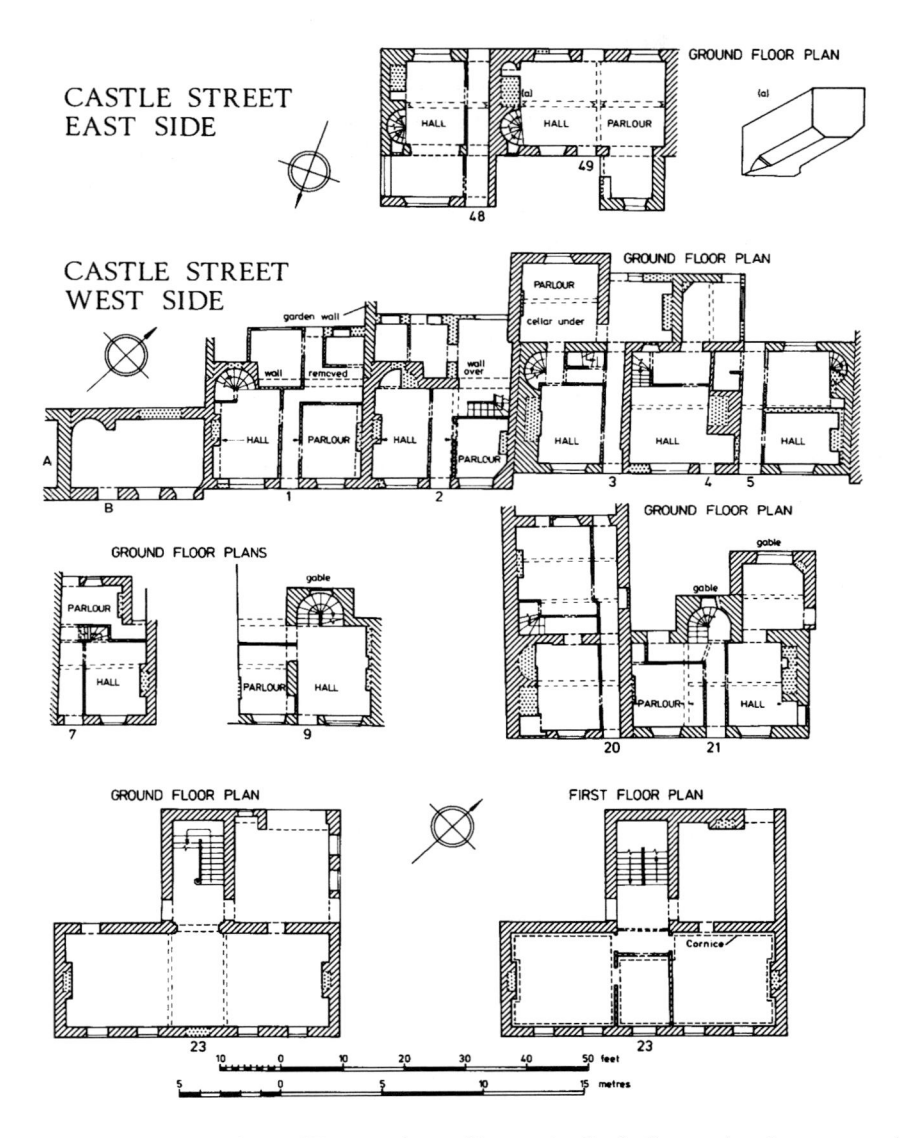

Figure 2.1 Trinity Area of Frome: plans of houses in Castle Street, showing structural relationships.

The archaeological research was fully complemented by research based on documentary sources, from the Public, Somerset and Wiltshire Record Offices, from the local authorities for the properties that they now owned, and from some private sources. These provided a historical context to the building process and enabled the identification in the Public Record Office of the only probate inventory surviving for any of the houses, all others having been destroyed in the wartime bombing of the Devon Record Office.

The second study to which I can usefully refer was of a development of similar extent but of two hundred years earlier. In assisting colleagues from the Colonial Williamsburg Foundation in searching for parallels to the row houses being built in Jamestown, Virginia, in the early seventeenth century, it made sense to look for any new housing developments of this period in London. One area that stood out as worthy of investigation was the site of St Bartholomew's Fair, highlighted by John Schofield.[13]

Here too there was a focus on the physical landscape context. From the surviving street plan and houses and from documentary sources it was possible to map the redevelopment of the fair from 1598 to c.1616, by when some 400 or more fairground booths had been replaced by about 175 houses (Figure 2.2), possibly the largest single development scheme in London in the three centuries preceding the development of Covent Garden.[14] Here too new plans were prepared of the original houses still surviving within the study area. These provided information on room sizes and construction. Original houses of c.1598 survived at nos. 74 and 75 Long Lane. The first-floor chambers of these houses were of near identical size to those provided at nos. 23–4 Clothfair, built c.1614. In each, the principal ceiling beams were of Baltic pine, the pegs for the subsidiary beams visible on the underside of the main beam; dendrochronology may confirm the date and source of the timber used.

A third study focused on an entire urban landscape was of the St Michael's Hill precinct of the University of Bristol, commissioned by the University of Bristol from the author's consultancy, 'Cultural Heritage Services', and then republished by the Bristol Record Society.[15] Building survey, aerial photography and documentary sources were combined to show the landscape of the precinct at different points in time. Successively these were the medieval and early post-medieval landscape, the Civil War and the Royal Fort, garden and gentry houses (Figure 2.3) and finally residential streets and larger houses in the eighteenth century.

In the seventeenth century the term 'garden house' was synonymous with both 'lodge' and 'summer house'.[16] These were terms used to describe a house that was a place of retreat from the city, a house that was seen as at one with its garden, the seventeenth-century predecessor of the Georgian villa. Such houses stood most often within one corner or at one side of a high-walled garden. The house was best seen from the garden, or from afar. The view from the house was first of the garden and then into the distance.

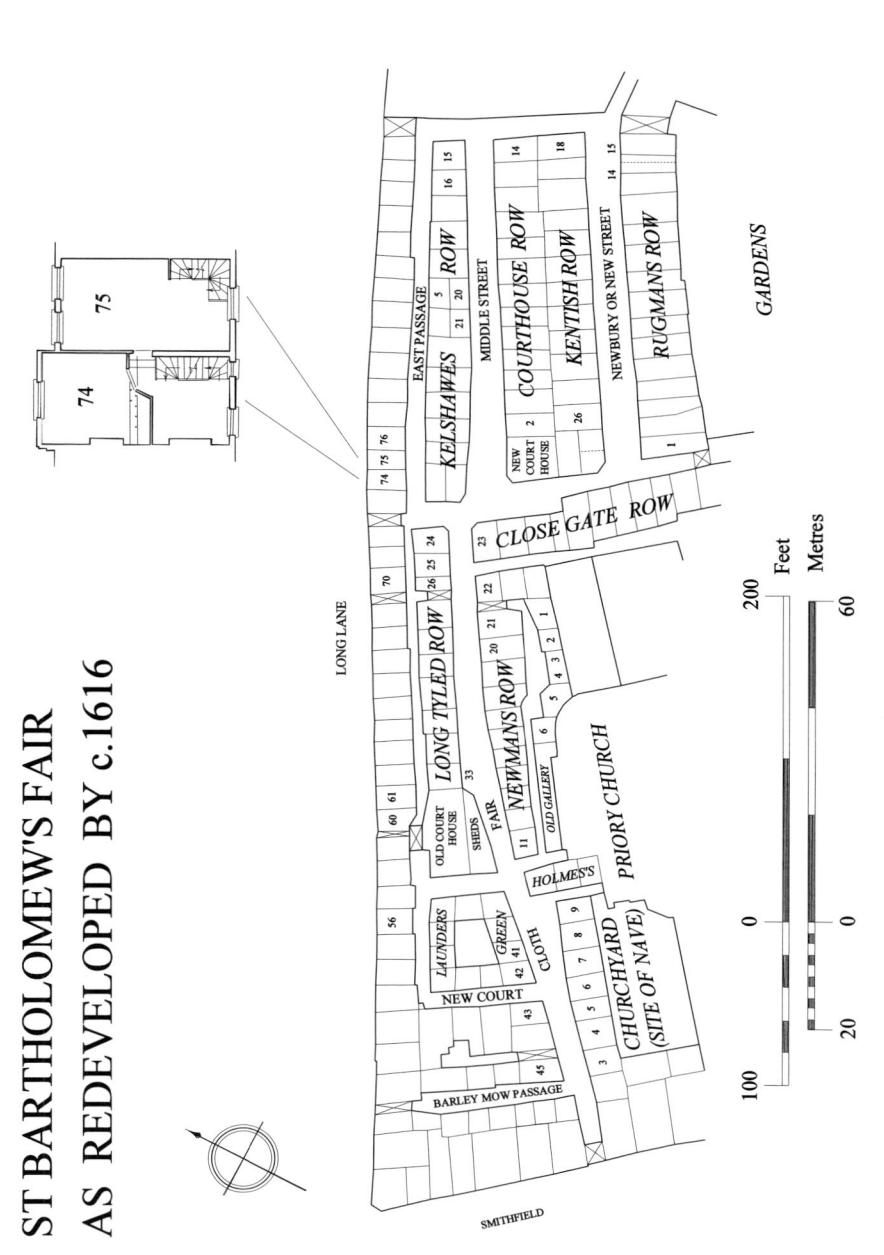

Figure 2.2 The redevelopment of St Bartholomew's Fair, London, *c.*1598–*c.*1616.

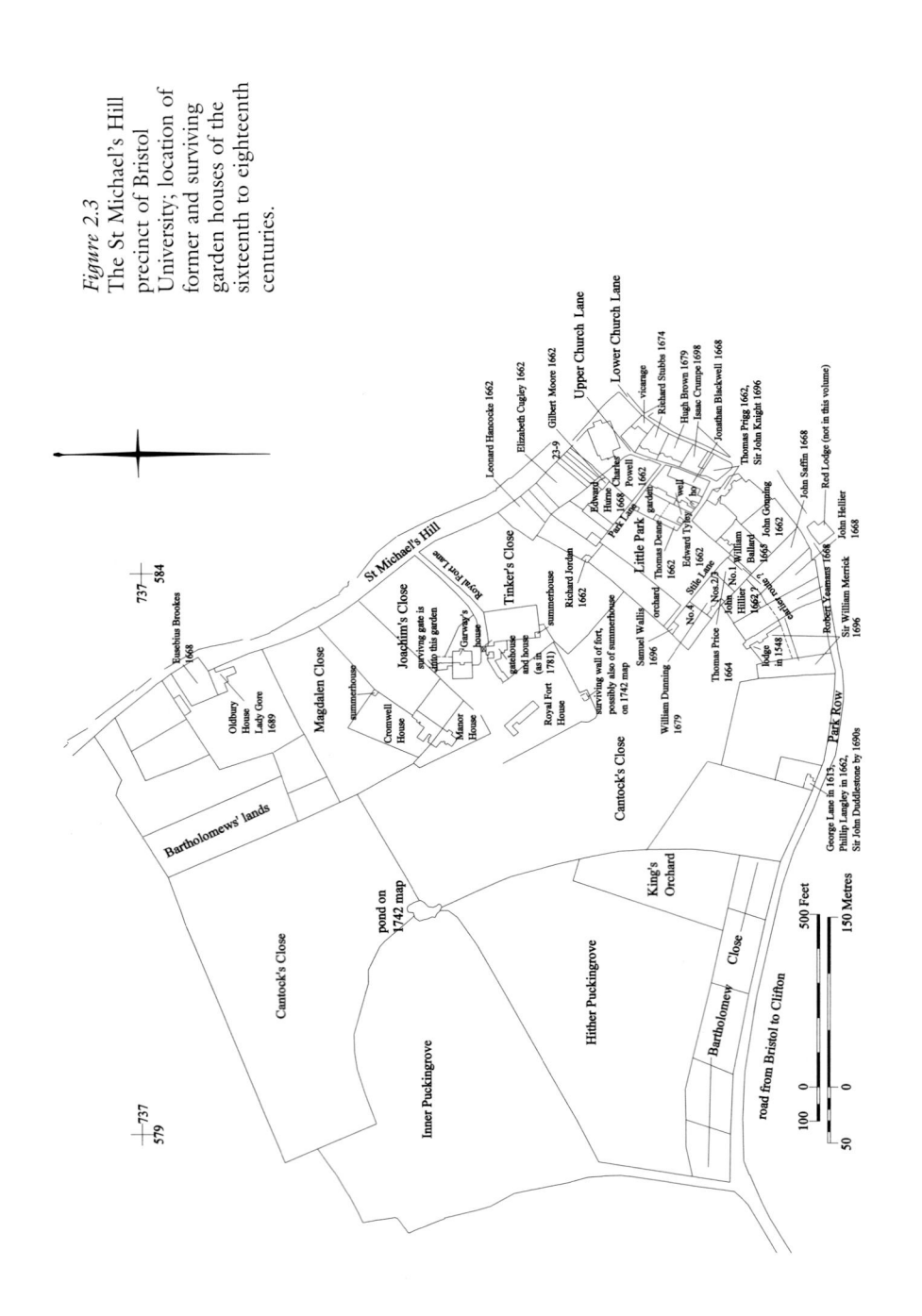

Figure 2.3
The St Michael's Hill precinct of Bristol University; location of former and surviving garden houses of the sixteenth to eighteenth centuries.

Such houses were emphatically different in their setting from houses built in continuous rows, such as the four houses on St Michael's Hill immediately above St Michael's church (Figure 2.3, nos. 23–9). As an addition to a residence elsewhere in the city, such houses were owned by the wealthier citizens. Most of the smaller garden houses on St Michael's Hill were owned by citizens who lived in the wealthiest city-centre parishes, notably that of St Werburgh, centred on Small Street. This survey was literally of buildings archaeology, buildings that for the most part now consisted solely of below-ground remains.

Clifton Wood House in Clifton, Bristol, was built around one such garden house. It had been argued that the house was built c.1723.[17] Detailed planning and survey showed that the house of c.1723 was an extension eastwards of an earlier house, of c.1690–1710, characterised by chamfered and stopped ceiling beams and by Baroque stone hood moulds over the windows, similar in its setting to the garden houses on St Michael's Hill.

Detailed survey and analysis of structural relationships have underpinned recent research in the English Caribbean. The invitation to undertake a study of the plantation house at Alleynedale, Barbados, followed a project re-examining the well-known seventeenth-century house of St Nicholas Abbey, owned from the seventeenth century until recently by a family closely associated with the City of Bristol. Detailed survey of Alleynedale provided sufficient data to hypothesise a sequence of plantation houses from the early seventeenth century to the present (Figure 2.4).[18] In this exercise the positioning of ceiling beams and cellar windows was critical. For the later phases, the information provided by documentary sources was equally essential.

Early plantation houses on Nevis have also been a focus of research utilising detailed survey and analysis of structural relationships, as part of the University of Southampton's Nevis Heritage Project.[19] At the Hermitage Plantation Inn, buildings survey combined with archaeological excavation has enabled identification of the Hermitage as a timber-framed house of post in the ground or earthfast construction, a building type very familiar to architectural historians working in Virginia and the Tidewater regions of the eastern United States. The Hermitage is probably the best preserved house of this mode of construction to be found now in the Western Hemisphere. Archaeological survey has enabled the identification of a much smaller house of similar construction at Fenton Hill on Nevis, the presence of the former posts here evidenced by their matrices in later stonework.

Detailed survey and analysis of structural relationships underpinned the survey of two complexes of major public buildings on behalf of the City of Bristol: the Exchange and St Nicholas Markets and the Guildhall in Broad Street. Survey of John Wood's Exchange, completed c.1740, showed that it was not completed to the plan shown in his account of the Exchange: that remained an ideal.[20] As finished, it encapsulated alterations required by the City authorities as its building proceeded, with several of the houses fronting the side streets remaining uncompleted. In the south range detailed survey

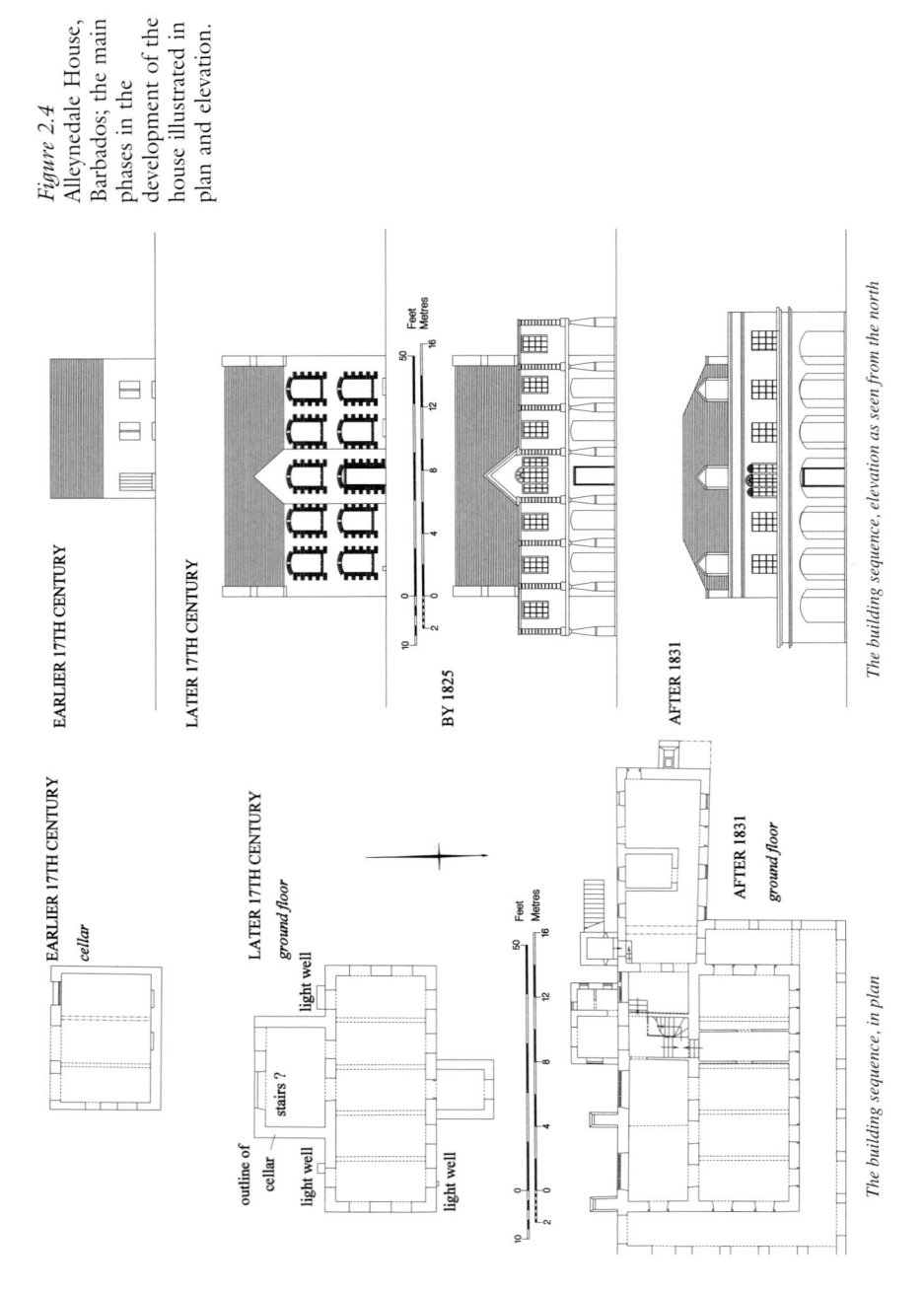

Figure 2.4 Alleynedale House, Barbados; the main phases in the development of the house illustrated in plan and elevation.

of repositioned folding partitions revealed Wood's original intention to provide on the first floor a multi-purpose space, for the use of both the Rummer Inn and the City's offices.

In the surveys of the Exchange Markets, the Guildhall and the university precinct in Bristol, aerial photographs again played a critical role. The date of the roof over St Nicholas markets (part of the Exchange Markets) was confirmed by aerial photographs as following its destruction in the Second World War.[21] An aerial photograph of 1935 provided the only view of the Guildhall courts complex prior to partial destruction in the 1939–45 war.[22] This informed the overall analysis of the development of the Guildhall complex. An aerial photograph provided the only view of a now demolished lodge on St Michael's Hill, no. 10 Park Row, first mentioned as 'le Lodge' in 1548.[23]

The research in Bristol is contributing to a study of urban housing in Bristol being prepared for English Heritage.[24] The historical context for many of the houses being studied is set out in the two volumes published to date of property holdings and topography.[25] Many of the houses long demolished are illustrated in the rich collections of paintings, drawings and photographs held by the City Museum and Art Gallery. The town houses of Bristol can then be set within a context rarely achieved elsewhere, notable exceptions being London and Lincoln.

Concluding this very personal account of Buildings Archaeology, I would agree with Richard Morriss's defining words on the same:

> It cannot be separated from the other aspects that make up the wider study of architectural history: documentary research, the history of design and the development of structural technology to name just three. The multi-disciplinary nature of architectural history is both inevitable and apt.[26]

In short, Buildings Archaeology is and can be architectural history. I have attempted to show here how archaeological methods form a vital part of this process: these include consideration of the physical landscape, the detailed analysis of structural relationships and the use of archaeological survey methods, both in the field and through aerial photographs. The use of documentary sources to provide a wider historical context is essential.

To end at my starting point, one outcome of the concerns that lead to the RCHME Recording Historic Buildings Conference was the publication of *Recording Historic Buildings: A Descriptive Specification*.[27] This reached its third edition prior to RCHME becoming part of English Heritage, and has now been reissued by English Heritage as *Understanding Historic Buildings: A Guide to Good Recording Practice*.[28] In its revised form these guidelines are in effect an aide-memoire for Buildings Archaeology. The principal activities that may be combined to create a record are stated to be documentary research, investigation, survey and drawings, photography and the written account.[29]

Notes

The author thanks Pamela Leech for her help in the preparation of this paper.

1. John Bold (ed.), *Recording Historic Buildings: A Symposium Organised Jointly by RCHME England and the Society of Architectural Historians of Great Britain*, London, 1991.
2. I. M. Ferris, 'The Archaeological Investigation of Standing Buildings', *Vernacular Architecture*, 20, 1989, 12–17.
3. Bob Meeson, 'In Defence of Selective Recording',*Vernacular Architecture*, 20, 1989, 18–19.
4. John Bold, 'The Recording of Standing Buildings', *Vernacular Architecture*, 21, 1990, 16–17.
5. Planning Policy Guidance notes issued by the Department of the Environment on historic buildings (PPG15) and archaeology (PPG16).
6. Nicholas Molyneux, 'English Heritage and Recording: Policy and Practice', in Bold (ed.), *Recording Historic Buildings*, 24–30.
7. Jason Wood (ed.), *Buildings Archaeology Applications in Practice*, Oxford, 1994.
8. Richard Morriss, *The Archaeology of Buildings*, Stroud, 2000.
9. Jason Wood, 'Buildings Archaeology: Problems and Opportunities', *The Archaeologist*, 55, 2005, 20–1.
10. Michael Aston and Roger H. Leech, *Historic Towns in Somerset*, Bristol: Committee for Rescue Archaeology in Avon, Gloucestershire and Somerset, 1977.
11. Roger H. Leech, *Early Industrial Housing: The Trinity Area of Frome, Somerset*, Royal Commission on Historical Monuments Supplementary Series No. 3, London, 1981.
12. Peter Smith, *Houses of the Welsh Countryside*, London: HMSO and Royal Commission on Ancient and Historical Monuments in Wales, 1975.
13. John Schofield, *The Building of London from the Conquest to the Great Fire*, London, 1984.
14. Roger H. Leech, 'The Prospect from Rugman's Row: The Row House in Late Sixteenth- and Early Seventeenth-century London', *Archaeological Journal*, 153, 1996, 201–42.
15. Roger H. Leech, 'The St Michael's Hill Precinct of the University of Bristol: The Topography of Medieval and Early Modern Bristol, Part 2', *Bristol Record Society*, 52, 2000, 1–133; and Roger H. Leech, 'The Garden House: Merchant Culture and Identity in the Early Modern City', in Susan Lawrence (ed.), *Archaeologies of the British: Explorations of Identity in Great Britain and its Colonies 1600–1945*, One World Archaeology Series, vol. 46, London, 2003, 76–86.
16. Leech, 'The St Michael's Hill Precinct', 22–6; and Leech, 'The Garden House'.
17. Timothy Mowl, *An Identity Within the City: University of Bristol Architectural Trail*, Bristol, 1992, 23.
18. Roger H. Leech, 'Alleynedale Hall, Barbados: A Plantation House of the Seventeenth Century', *Journal of the Barbados Museum and Historical Society*, 48, 2002, 123–41.
19. Roger H. Leech, 'Impermanent Architecture in the English Colonies of the Eastern Caribbean: New Contexts for Architectural Innovation in the Early Modern Atlantic World', in *Perspectives in Vernacular Architecture 10*, Knoxville, TN, 2006.
20. Roger H. Leech, *An Historical and Architectural Survey and Analysis of the Exchange, Corn Street, Bristol*, Bristol, 1999, copy in Bristol Record Office.
21. Roger H. Leech, *An Historical and Architectural Survey and Analysis of the Exchange Markets and their Environs, Bristol*, Cultural Heritage Services

Report 121, Bristol, 2001, copy in Bristol Record Office.
22 Roger H. Leech, *An Historical and Architectural Survey and Analysis of the Guildhall, Broad Street and Small Street, Bristol*, Cultural Heritage Services Report 167, Bristol, 2005, copy in Bristol Record Office.
23 Roger H. Leech, 'The St Michael's Hill Precinct of the University of Bristol', 111–12.
24 Roger H. Leech, *Town Houses: Capitalism, Slavery and the Streets of Bristol* (commenced for the Royal Commission on the Historical Monuments of England and now in preparation for English Heritage), forthcoming.
25 Roger H. Leech, *The Topography of Medieval and Early Modern Bristol, Part 1: Property Holdings in the Early Walled Town and Marsh Suburb North of the Avon*, Bristol Record Society, 48, 1–220, 1997; and Roger H. Leech, *The St Michael's Hill Precinct of the University of Bristol: The Topography of Medieval and Early Modern Bristol, part 2*, Bristol Record Society, 52, 1–133, 2000.
26 Morriss, *The Archaeology of Buildings*, 8.
27 RCHME, *Recording Historic Buildings: A Descriptive Specification*, London, 1990.
28 English Heritage, *Understanding Historic Buildings: A Guide to Good Recording Practice*, Swindon, 2006.
29 English Heritage, *Understanding Historic Buildings*, 4.

3
Architecture as evidence

Andrew Ballantyne

Buildings, especially when they are aggregated into cities, are the largest artefacts, and their importance to archaeologists is without doubt. If we think of buildings in connection with the life that produces them, then we can see that when we look at the ruins of buildings we are looking at powerful and incontrovertible evidence of *something*; but evidence of what? It is often difficult to say. Buildings are produced as the result of complex interactions of social and economic forces that put some decisions within our reach, while leaving others beyond our control or escaping our consideration. If we are to understand the ruins of buildings of cultures that have long vanished, we need to know something about the cultures by way of sources other than the buildings – perhaps from texts, or from other, smaller, artefacts. Architecture is gesture – gesture made with buildings. In order to understand any gesture we need to see it in its cultural context, and once we have contextualized it then it can be highly expressive and accurate; but without context the meaning is adrift and is not to be relied upon. We can measure and describe the form of a ruined building, but without a culture to locate it in it remains meaningless. If we cannot find the evidence to reconstruct the outline of a culture then we are highly inclined to imagine one and to project our own experience and intuitions on to the remains that we see. The theme that informs this chapter is a matter of wondering how we decide what is important when we write about architecture. What values inform our judgement when we decide what it is that is most important to write about? And what is it that we choose to say about the buildings we decide to include in our histories?

A building takes shape in an ethical milieu where many sets of forces can operate, but the most telling are those that relate to the distribution of resources. On one hand this is a question of the politics of the society – how are resources distributed? Who controls the distribution? On the other hand it is a question of systems of value. I might aspire to live in a palace, but be in a position in society where that is beyond my means. Alternatively I might see how to acquire the means but feel that it would involve too great a sacrifice of something that I value – too much effort, too much time away from my family, too much loss of self-respect, too many corpses. The system of values may not be absolutely uniform across a society, but the choices made and acted upon by the different individuals will contribute to the overall impression of what that society is like. What people say they care about, in their conversation or in their books, is one kind of evidence for the system of values in a society, but a better guide to what they really believe is to look at how they act. Buildings that are actually built tell us a good deal about the value-system of the society that produced them. This is because buildings are always expensive. Their cost is nearly always significant for the person who commissions them, so they are only very rarely frivolous. The decision to build is nearly always a decision that is taken seriously. There are ideas for all sorts of extraordinary buildings, most of which remain as unrealized flights of the imagination, but those that are actually built are nearly always in a fairly narrow range of 'the ordinary'. Even the most utilitarian building usually seems expensive for the person who pays for it, but utilitarian buildings are not usually what people choose when they can afford something more than the basic. Buildings can be used as a way of raising our status in a society, and this use of buildings as a form of cultural capital usually goes hand-in-hand with the buildings costing a good deal more than the most utilitarian alternative. Buildings that elevate our status in a society can be very expensive, indeed they must be more extravagant than the norm if they are going to have the effect of enhancing status. Buildings can also elevate the status of a whole society, and such buildings are very expensive indeed. For example, there is a recent building in Edinburgh, built to the designs of a Catalan architect, Enric Miralles, for the new Scottish Assembly. It was a bold choice, and an experimental design, which was calculated to position Scotland as a forward-looking country with a place in international culture. The building's costs are high, but it has attracted international attention and will have a level of prestige that it would not have done had the decision been taken to house the Scottish Assembly in standard commercial accommodation. Somebody took the decision that money spent in this way would be spent appropriately and well.[1]

There is a passage by Georges Bataille (1879–1962) that expresses very concisely the close relation between monuments and the power to command resources. 'Architecture,' he says,

> is the expression of the very being of societies, just as human physiognomy is the expression of individuals. Yet this comparison especially refers to the physiognomy of officials (prelates, magistrates, admirals). In fact, only society's ideal being (that which authoritatively orders and prohibits) is expressed in actual architectural constructions. Thus great monuments rise up like dams, opposing all disturbed elements to a logic of majesty and authority. This is in the form of cathedrals and palaces through which the Church or the State addresses and imposes silence on the multitude.[2]

This straightforward assertion is complicated by the fact that Bataille was, and felt himself to be, a disturbed element in the social order, so his feelings about architecture were not those of an architect who was trying to act as the conduit through which these idealized aspirations of the state became actualized as buildings – the aspiration, that is, of the state and of those who had power within it. On the contrary, Bataille felt himself to be part of the multitude that is coerced and oppressed by buildings. The state's institutions and its worthier citizens are housed in settings that give them authority and make it impossible to argue successfully with them. The beggar in the street can rant and shout, and will not undermine the dignity of the respectable bourgeois who will at some point phone for the police if the noise in the street persists. It is clear whose side the building is on. Of course, once it has been built, the building can be used in ways that the original client did not have in mind. The door could be left open, and people could be welcomed in off the street; but, if an architect were to design a house that did not permit its occupant to retreat into privacy and to keep a few belongings safe from theft, then it is highly unlikely that the architect would find someone to commission the house. Why would someone spend money on such a dwelling? It would not be impossible, or unimaginable, but equally we can be sure that in our society it would not normally be done. Houses that are built follow certain codes. We can easily imagine alternatives, but no one chooses to adopt them. Similarly, when an organization like the Salvation Army decides to shelter the homeless, it can mobilize the means to erect a building; but, even when the building in question is by as celebrated an architect as Le Corbusier, we find it relegated to an obscure quarter of Paris: it is not on the Champs Elysées.[3] If it were – if we imagine a refuge on axis, for example where the Louvre is now – then we imagine a state with a system of values that is very different from the one we actually have, where such a thing has not actually happened. It would not be an impossibility – it can easily be imagined, and unproblematically there are the techniques to build it – but it is an option that the society as a whole selects against, and that tells us something about the society's values.

I set a student project a while ago, where I asked the students to design a house that expressed the way we live now – or should aspire to live. The idea was that this should be a sort of exhibition house with a strong gestural content. The lack of an identifiable client and schedule of accommodation was experienced by some students as a welcome freedom, but some others were clearly uncomfortable with this lack of direction – the need to determine a direction from their own analysis of how we live and how we should be living. One way in which this group of students showed themselves that they were avoiding self-indulgence was by providing endless flexibility, so that responsibility for as many design decisions as possible were devolved on to the absent client. There was one student, I remember, who – when I asked what material she had in mind for the house's structural framework – explained that it could be steel (which would make it possible to make large open spaces in the house) or it could be timber (which would suit people who were concerned with green issues). And this took my breath away. If I imagine myself as the client: here I am being offered a house – with principles, or without – whichever I would prefer. The student was not being naive, and she was in her way declaring her values. She saw her role as being to serve the client, not to try in a futile way to propose impossible idealisms.

There are times when we like to think of architects as heroic figures, but more often the sensible architect who wants a steady supply of work will be happy to do the client's bidding. It confirms Bataille's assertion that it is the state's view that is expressed in its architecture. There is no room for transgression against the agenda that the client cares about. There are plenty of willing architects, so to cast oneself in the role of the transgressor as an architect is to see oneself supplanted from the job. Philip Johnson, acknowledging the subservience of the architect's role, declared himself willing to work for the devil himself – if it enabled him to do a good building.[4] He was far from being alone in this, though others might be more reticent in voicing the view. What we see here, though, is an idea that the building is good or not as something quite independent of the client's agenda. If the client is the devil, who is definitively bad, then the building would be commissioned with the aim of achieving something bad; but even such a building can nevertheless, by the architect's agenda, be a good buiding. The client normally is not the devil, but nevertheless the architect's agenda for the building is likely to be distinct from the client's. A persuasive architect will be able to redescribe the building in different ways in order to show how it meets different sets of needs. It will house the client, perhaps, and it might advance the art of architecture without the client quite realizing it. Architects are comfortable discussing the practicalities of building, but the admiration of practical ingenuities is traditionally given a lower status than is aesthetic appreciation. We are well supplied with architectural histories that assume that all practicalities are adequately dealt with, and that the consideration of matters stylistic and aesthetic properly exhausts what needs to be said about the buildings. For example, the buildings that are discussed in Heinrich Wölfflin's *Principles of Art History* were first of all selected for their ability to illuminate a particular discussion (the problem of the development of style) and then discussed in relation to a set of very particular themes (linear and painterly expression, plane and recession, closed and open form, multiplicity and unity, clearness and unclearness).[5] Wölfflin's discussion is concerned with the Renaissance and Baroque, and his exemplary buildings are fine creations: churches and palaces, all of them with a high level of artistic accomplishment. We can admire the Palazzo Borghese in Rome or the Palais Holnstein in Munich without being invited to wonder where people on average incomes lived, or what they cared about when they decorated their homes. We need not worry about the ways by which the Borghese family came to have the means to live so splendidly, but can admire their discernment in having commissioned so fine an edifice.

Most architectural history continues to treat social and economic history as something altogether alien, so that even to draw attention to the extravagant costs of building, or the political situation of the rich and powerful people who commission these buildings, seems to be a breach of etiquette that places one outside the properly polite discourse that is architectural history. Diane Ghirardo has drawn attention to the way in which architectural histories that give priority to fine aesthetic achievement while turning a blind eye to the politics that underpin the buildings' production can result in a state of affairs that seems deceitful.[6] However, it is unusual for it to be an architect or a historian's intention to deceive in their work. They would be more likely to feel that they were conforming to the proprieties of their situation. To take Ghirardo's example: it would be wrong to suppose that there was a conspiracy at work in nineteenth-century Manchester, working to hide the squalid dwellings of the poor well behind the prosperous-looking facades of the buildings that lined the main thoroughfares into the city. There was a shared sense of decorum in the society that meant that the situation arose without there being a need to impose artificial controls to make it happen. In the same way with historiography, if one makes it a point of methodology to distance oneself from considering the political, then the result is that we find ourselves producing and consuming architectural histories that are dominated by buildings made for the exceedingly rich and powerful. As these are the people whom we might expect to be able to command the finest buildings, this result need not take us by surprise. What is surprising is how rarely it is commented upon. It is a silence that can easily be mistaken for a conspiracy, but we know that it is nothing of the sort. It is the result of a shared sense of the right way to do architectural history.

In the English translation of Gilles Deleuze and Félix Guattari's work of ethics *Anti-Oedipus*, there is a preface by Michel Foucault where he distils a set of ethical principles from the text. The most exacting of these principles – perhaps it is impossible for an ambitious architect to follow it – is the last one: 'do not become enamoured of power'.[7] Architects keep falling in love with power. What are they to do? They can't help it. It is never a matter of falling in love with power for its own sake, but because it seems to be the surest route to securing the commissions that will make possible the maximum level of freedom in the play of the aesthetic agenda that is prized so highly by architects and historians alike. It is necessary to have access to large sums of money if one is to make a mark as an architect, and there is always the hope that the great commission will make an imperishable reputation. Sir Christopher Wren would not have secured the commission to rebuild St Paul's cathedral had he not been a friend of King Charles II. He was given the project when he had only a few university buildings to his name, and when the businessmen in the city were inclined to favour Edward Jerman, all of whose buildings have now disappeared, along with his reputation.[8] Albert Speer had a close rapport with Hitler and the monument-building side of his imagination, and his reputation is consequently beyond repair. But Speer was not uniquely evil among the German architects of the 1930s – he was just the most successful in understanding and projecting the leader's vision and architectural ambition. The dynamic tension between the prospect of opportunity and a repugnant political order was played out uncomfortably and visibly in the career of Mies van der Rohe. His reputation is tainted by the fact that he did not emigrate from Germany until after it had become apparent that Hitler was not going to commission buildings from him. He was unsuccessful there, and successful in America, and his architecture became the image of mid-century corporate capitalism – another source of immense wealth and power – more diffused, and now of course networked globally. The relation between architects and power is close, and if we want to make architects into heroes then it is an uncomfortable relation, as it becomes clear that it is never the designer who has the real power in a society. What the architect does is to give expression to certain things by way of the design of a building. An architect as a private individual can commission a building that plays to his or her own personal agenda, but the prominent buildings in a city are always more expensive than an ordinary individual could afford to consider building. The architects of these buildings are always in the service of something that is in some way more powerful than them – usually something impersonal (institutional or abstract) and always formless until it has been given an embodiment in building. The architect does not have power as a right, but is allowed to exercise power in the service of the client, working to the client's agenda. It is this that makes buildings especially valuable for archaeologists. They are evidence of the will of a society, and point to that society's ethos and to where the real power lies. However, the evidence is ambiguous. There is a famous passage in Thucydides' account of the Peloponnesian War – an account written by an Athenian in Athens' Classical age – the fifth century BC. Athens was at war with Sparta, and Thucydides contrasted the appearance of the two cities:

> Suppose, for example, that the city of Sparta were to become deserted and that only the temples and foundations of buildings remained. I think that future generations would, as time passed, find it very difficult to believe that the place had really been as powerful as it was represented to be. Yet the Spartans occupy two-fifths of the Peloponnese, and stand at the head not only of the whole Peloponnese itself but also of numerous allies beyond its frontiers. Since, however, the city is not regularly planned and contains no temples or monuments of great magnificence, but is simply a collection of villages, in the ancient Hellenic way, its appearance would not come up to expectation. If, on the other hand, the same thing were to happen to Athens, one would conjecture from what met the eye that the city had been twice as powerful as in fact it is. We have no right, therefore, to judge cities by the appearances rather than their actual power.[9]

Each city had its own government, and its own laws; and it is a further irony that Athens is now the capital of Greece – something that it had never been before the nineteenth century – on account of the literature, the philosophy and the monuments that were produced at Athens, and that were not produced at Sparta, despite it having greater military power. Before independence Greece was part of the Ottoman Empire, run from İstanbul, which before 1453 had been Constantinople, the capital of the Greek-speaking Byzantine Empire, with Athens a provincial outpost. The idea of Greek independence found support in western Europe mainly on account of the cultural importance of the Classical past with Athens as its clearest embodiment. Incidentally the Romans had visited Sparta as a tourist destination, to see people living frugally and exercising ferociously. They saw in Sparta a prefiguring of the Roman military culture. Where the Athenians were building monuments, the Spartans took pride in not having them. There was no need for a city wall at Sparta because the Spartan army was so effective that enemies were annihilated without the need for a wall to hide behind. Each city had its own ethos; its own ethics. Had a Spartan prince commissioned an Athenian temple then he would have forfeited the respect of the citizens who would have seen it as an extravagant luxury that weakened and depleted the patron, whereas in Athens Pericles' reputation was made imperishable by the decision to rebuild the monuments on the Acropolis.

In commissioning its extravagant new parliament building, Edinburgh continues to be 'the Athens of the north'. The important point to be made here is that the ethics are not to be isolated in the individual architect, but are diffused through the society of which the architect is a part. If I were a Spartan then I could not expect to act like an Athenian and win respect in Sparta. If I were an architect and had the choice in that world, then I would have chosen to move to Athens, where the opportunities would have been greater. There might have been some scope to live in Sparta by an agenda that differed from that of the generality of society, but the scope would have been very limited. In a more liberal society there is less coercion to a normative agenda, and that finds expression in a wider range of possibilities for buildings. So, for example, buildings with eccentric forms or apparently subversive functions do not challenge but give expression to the real values of the society. Radical practice – practice that would actually challenge the values of a society, not just its conventional expectations – is scarcely possible. If we confine our attention to actual buildings, rather than fantastical ideas – then there is scope only for the few elements of radicalism that the society is willing to sponsor. Given a sponsor, one can test the limits of that freedom, but if we find a new monument being built in a place of national prominence, then we know to read it as the announcement of the arrival of a new power, a new establishment, or a new housing for the same old power. The Swiss Ré building in St Mary Axe, for example, has some novelty in form and technique, but is clearly not going to do anything to undermine the commercial power of the City of London. It would be wrong to expect it to do that, however piously one might hope for it, because an architect who had such an agenda would have been removed from a position of influence, or at least would have been unable to act on the transgressive agenda. Yet the commercial power is the real power here, and if we are to look for radicalism then that would be the power we would be looking to see challenged. The stylistic novelty is a side issue that impresses people who are interested in such things, but it does not raise any important issues for the people who commissioned the building – unless they also happen to be interested in the way the building looks as well as in the way that it performs. 'Radicalism' in architecture, if the term is to retain any useful meaning, cannot be allowed to identify buildings that have novel forms but that do nothing to reorient the dominant agenda. In the commercial world the dominant agenda is to turn a profit. Buildings with clear identites can be marketed at a premium, and work perfectly well within the dominant agenda.

Nevertheless, architects often like to think of themselves as radicals and free spirits, and there is a cultivation of 'hidden' agendas that might be recognized by other architects, and can win the respect of other architects. Architects, for example, tend to be more interested than are their clients in such issues as the resolution of form, in proportion, or in the expressive qualities of a building. The architects' hidden agendas normally remain hidden, but sometimes come into sight when architects write about buildings. My favourite example of a personal agenda is from one of Peter Eisenman's buildings – a convention centre in Columbus, Ohio, where the sinuous spaces with slightly sloping floors and off-vertical walls had an unsettling effect, and made people feel queasily sea-sick, and even made them vomit. This is alarming enough, but the really interesting thing about the story is that it turns out not to be true.[10] The building did no such thing. So how did the story start? It turned out to have been a story invented by the ever-creative imagination of the architect; which is fascinating – because it is a story that one would have thought would have made him seem to be a rather poor architect. By the practical standards of the Spartans, this was a building that worked reasonably well, and the architect was saying that it did not. We need to suppose that the architect was working to a different agenda, and by a different scale of values for the spreading of this story to make any sense. Also we need to know that the story was spread in the first instance among architecture students. What it tells us is that this architect is special because he has been able to escape from the everyday agendas of practicality and economy, and to work some mischief into the building. If the architect is doing something that the person who pays the bills could not possibly want, then it shows that the architect's volition has not been exterminated. But if we examine the source of the will that is at work here – the will to transgress the client's will – then we can see that it is a long way from being the will of someone who can freely exercise power. On the contrary, its perversity and its hidden agenda reveal very clearly that this is driven by an ethic of *ressentiment*. It acknowledges that the real power lies elsewhere, and the architect is pushed into the position of finding a trivial ethic of resistance, by doing funny shapes, or making up stories, that escape the notice of the client and – since they are of no real concern – are allowed to happen. The illusion of free will is maintained, and the architect can believe in his or her role as a creative individual. The Eisenman example is extreme and amusing, and need not be taken too seriously; but it is very normal indeed for architects to have their own agendas, which I suggest is a way of holding on to a sense of personal power and freedom. The various aesthetic agendas of architects, which correlate with the agendas in architectural historiography, are agendas of this type.

If we restrict ourselves to the hard-nosed commercial world for the moment – the architect's freedom to select and to express is confined to elements of the building that are insignificant to the corporate client. This can be seen in the normal commercial buildings of our cities – now dominated by facilities for shopping and parking that have a sameness wherever we go; they are even the same shops selling the same goods most of the time. They are in slightly different configurations from place to place, but the ethos that they express is that of our society working collectively, not that of the individual architects who worked on the designs. There is a concern to have the maximum of effect for the lowest price. It is seen to be worth paying more if the development becomes highly visible and therefore attracts more custom. This contrasts with the thinking involved in a non-commercial building with a function to represent civic dignity – such as the grandiose Victorian town halls in places like Manchester and Bradford – from the days when these cities were at the height of their prosperity. These buildings were very expensive when they were built, so that the citizens could feel proud to belong to such splendid towns; and it is to be hoped that the Scottish Assembly building will prove in the end – once the bills have been paid – to be similarly a source of quiet national pride for the Scots.

Am I saying, then, that there is no scope for architects to have an ethos? Certainly not. Architects have their systems of value – their ethics – and draw on them whenever they take decisions. There are codes of professional conduct – professional ethics.[11] However, the concern in this essay is the kind of ethics that sets priorities when we are faced with a decision between one desirable thing and another. For example, nowadays everybody wants green buildings. But we (as a society) also want our buildings to be good commercial investments. So, given the way the money-markets work, and the way that shareholders move their money around if one company is outperforming another, the commercial values tend to win out, and our buildings are only as green as the market can tolerate. We still see buildings with air-conditioning systems, when they are not technically necessary to keep people comfortable, because air-conditioning has come to connote 'high status' in commercial buildings, and therefore higher rentals can be charged. The green building that does away with the need is still seen as having a lower status – though there is hope that things are changing. However, the change is not something that an individual architect can bring about; it needs a shift in the general culture of those who use and commission commercial buildings – a shift that is brought about not through technical developments, or logical argument, but by shifting attitudes in the popular mass-media. But, as we are dealing here with a mobile globalized culture, it is not a culture whose ideas are easily shifted.

The individual architect's ethos tends to end up giving a high value to the things that an individual architect can control, such as the use of novel methods of construction, arresting combinations of colour, form and texture in a building, or the ways in which the form is brought out with sympathetically ingenious lighting; or style. These are the things that are discussed in the architecture journals, and also in most architectural histories, where the world of commerce is systematically excluded from consideration. Equally the discourse of architects is like a foreign language to the developers who commission nearly all of the buildings in our cities. If I try to form a view of the built world by reading architecture journals and architectural histories then I can see little contact between that view and the world that I encounter when I set foot outside my door. To take a recent substantial publication: *The Phaidon Atlas of Contemporary World Architecture*[12] mentions no editors' names and so gives an illusion of objectivity, as if there is no personal opinion here to argue with. But it does not tell us what the buildings of today are actually like. It selects 'the most notable' buildings, which is to say the most extraordinary buildings. It also follows the neutron-bomb tradition of architectural photography, in which any view of a person is excluded from the images. The system of values that keeps being presented to us from the architecture-media is one in which the formal qualities of inventively unusual buildings are to be considered as so much more important than the impact on people's lives, that the lives are excluded from view. Elsewhere in our culture there is plenty of discussion about the way people – especially famous people – live in surroundings that they have had designed for them, but not in the architecture press. Even if architects insist that they want their buildings photographed with people in them, the photographers and picture editors have a different vision of what looks well on the page. This could look like a conspiracy, but it is not a conspiracy – it is the working out of a set of values that is never quite declared but that quickly becomes apparent once we start looking for it. The historiography repeats it back to us, but, if we have learnt our values and our ways of looking at buildings from that same historiographic tradition, then we find that its conventions are transparent for us, and we look right through them without seeing how they refract our view.

Similarly, we need to pay attention to the systems of value that we see operating in the world around us. There is no doubt that when we walk through a British city most of the buildings and the biggest of the buildings will be the product of commerce in one way or another. As aficionados of architecture we have on the whole taught ourselves not to notice them. We seek out the rare and the extraordinary and say that this is what really counts.

What does that say about our system of values? If we can read in buildings where the real power lies in a society (as Bataille asserted) and if we see in them a representation of the ethics of a society (as Thucydides explained) then what sort of society are we living in? What are the values that we really have? As a society we seem to like the sound of high-minded principles and fine artistic achievements, and treat such things with respect, but actually we would rather spend our money on shoes, plasma screens and holidays. Our buildings reflect that – and so do the buildings in resorts around the world. The architect whose ethics cannot accept this state of affairs can flourish only in the margins – outside our normal commercial activity – and, while that is something that many might aspire to, it is something that only relatively few can achieve.

To take a historical example: consider the Cistercian monks of the twelfth century. They were a reform movement within monasticism, and they set up communities in remote places where the monks lived on the fruits of their labours. It would be possible to describe them as constituting a counter-culture that was critical of the mainstream culture of the day; but normally they are described as a vital part of the social fabric of their day. It is difficult to look at the ruins of buildings as impressive as those of Fountains Abbey in North Yorkshire and see this movement as an attempt to overturn secular medieval society, with which it was in fact in contact, trading its produce and accepting gifts of money and land. The Cistercians were endorsed by mainstream society, which saw the monks as doing something that had value. This state of affairs came to an end during the reign of Henry VIII, when the influence of the monasteries was seen to be in opposition to the interests of the state. At that point the monasteries became truly radical; but it was at that point that they were 'dissolved', which is to say sacked and plundered. The state made it very clear where the real temporal power lay. Had the monasteries been allowed to continue their operations, then we would be able to infer something quite different about the value-system of the state at the time – we would see it as having been more liberal, as it would have been able to tolerate powerful organizations with value-systems quite different from its own. The buildings are, one way or another, an index of the value-system of the society in which they flourished or were destroyed. The size of the original buildings is an indication of the power and wealth of the monastery. The ruinous condition is an indication of its suppression by the temporal state. However, in the absence of historical evidence it would be impossible simply by looking at the building to infer the reasons for its condition. Where there is little more than the remains of a great building as evidence about which to speculate, we find conditions for a creative ferment of interpretation. Stonehenge on Salisbury Plain would be a case in point here. It is one of the most ancient of human monuments, and is sufficiently prominent to have attracted the attention of antiquarians across the ages. It has been thought of variously as a magical place with healing properties, brought by Merlin from Ireland (where it had been assembled from stones brought from Africa), as a Roman temple, as a burial place for Viking monarchs, as a place for Druidic sacrifices, and as an observatory.[13] The interpretations tell us much about the interpreter and the obsessions of the age when the interpretation was made, and perhaps a little about the arresting and evocative stones.

I conclude with a passage from Alexis de Tocqueville (1805–59), whose meditation on the great city of Washington DC has strong overtones of Thucydides about it. Both writers were considering the buildings of their own day in relation to the ruins of the past. Tocqueville argued that, in democratic America, the individual did not come to embody greatness and did not build great monuments. However, the state came to be seen as very important indeed, and its monuments were correspondingly magnificent. Here is Tocqueville:

> On the site they wanted to make their capital Americans have placed the precincts of an immense city which today is still scarcely more populated than Pontoise, but which according to them will one day contain a million inhabitants; they have already uprooted trees for ten leagues around lest they should become inconvenient to the future citizens of this imaginary metropolis. In the center of the city they have raised a magnificent palace to serve as the seat of Congress, and they have given it the pompous name of Capitol.
>
> [...]
>
> if the Romans had known the laws of hydraulics better, they would not have raised all the aqueducts that surround the ruins of their cities, and they would have made a better use of their power and wealth. If they had discovered the steam engine, perhaps they would not have spread to the extremities of their empire the long artificial rock masses named Roman roads.
>
> These things are magnificent testimonies to their ignorance at the same time as to their greatness.
>
> A people that left no vestiges of its passage other than some lead pipes in the earth and iron rods on its surface could have been more a master of nature than the Romans.[14]

Buildings are very powerful evidence because they are so closely implicated in the social and economic processes that provided the means to build them. However, they are also very complex pieces of evidence, because their production is mediated by societal and aesthetic agendas that are quite separate and independent. Our historiography is not neutral, and nor is it uniform. The discipline of architectural history has tended to exclude economic and political considerations from its discussions, but buildings have importantly informed the work of archaeologists, sociologists and other commentators who have had occasion to notice effects of the buildings other than their fine aesthetic effects. Moreover, there is much to be learnt from the great mass of buildings that are not beautiful or striking to look at. A society might make great social progress that might be made manifest in the fact that the housing of the poorest members of the society improved markedly. There could be an improvement from absolute squalor to general decency without there being anything significantly novel in the plane of formal invention and such a development would then fall entirely outside the scope of traditional architectural historiography. It would be for archaeologists and social commentators to remind us of such buildings' value for humanity. Equally, the most dazzling technical inventions and formal ingenuities, if they can be deployed only in amusing the jaded tastes of the super-rich, might seem astonishingly novel and important for a traditional architectural history, but might be insignificant in the plane of a history of the society's development. The point to be made here is that a multiplicity of narratives intersect in any building, and it is important for our understanding of them to realize that any single narrative will be seen to be reductive if it is claimed as the only narrative that really matters. For buildings to be given their proper due as evidence, they need to be included in narratives that are constructed in ways that allow for multiple perspectives. Each perspective generates its own architecture from the building, as the long-standing building's gestures come to be understood in ways that may be old or new.

Notes

1 The costs of this building are, at the time of writing, controversial in Scotland.
2 Georges Bataille, 'Architecture', in *Oeuvres completes*, 12 vols, Paris, 1971–88, vol. 1, 171–2; translated by Michael Richardson as 'Architecture', in Michael Richardson (ed.), *Georges Bataille: Essential Writings*, London, 1998, 37. The article is included in the volume of the complete works that covers the period 1922–40. It remained unpublished during Bataille's lifetime. Reprinted in Andrew Ballantyne, *Architecture Theory: A Reader in Philosophy and Culture*, London, 2005, 16.
3 Le Corbusier's Cité de Refuge for the Armée du Salut, 12 rue Cantagrel, in the 13th *arrondissement*, was built in 1929. It is very well known among architects, but is not part of the mainstream tourist agenda.
4 Philip Johnson in conversation with J. W. Cook and H. Klotz, in J. W. Cook and H. Klotz, *Conversations With Architects*, New York, 1973, 36.
5 Heinrich Wölfflin, *Kunstgeschichtliche Grundbegriffe* (1929), translated by M. D. Hottinger, *Principles of Art History: The Problem of the Development of Style in Later Art*, New York, 1932.
6 Diane Ghirardo, 'The Architecture of Deceit', in Andrew Ballantyne, *What Is Architecture?*, London, 2002, 63–71.
7 Michel Foucault, in Gilles Deleuze and Felix Guattari, *L'Anti-Oedipe*, Paris, 1972, trans. Robert Hurley, Mark Seem and Helen R. Lane, *Anti-Oedipus: Capitalism and Schizophrenia*, New York, 1977, xiv.
8 Helen Collins, *Edward Jerman 1605–1668: The Metamorphosis of a Master-Craftsman*, London, 2004.

9 Thucydides (460–400 BC), trans. Rex Warner, *History of the Peloponnesian War*, Harmondsworth, 1972, 41.
10 Michael Pollan, *A Place of My Own: The Education of an Amateur Builder*, New York, 1997, 68n.
11 See Tom Spector, *The Ethical Architect*, New York, 2001.
12 *The Phaidon Atlas of Contemporary World Architecture*, London, 2004.
13 Andrew Ballantyne, 'Misprisions of Stonehenge', in Dana Arnold and Andrew Ballantyne (eds), *Architecture as Experience*, London, 2004, 11–35.
14 Alexis de Tocqueville, *De la démocratie en Amérique*, 2 vols, 1835 and 1840, Paris, 1990, trans. Harvey C. Mansfield and Delba Winthrop, *Democracy in America*, Chicago, IL, 2000, book 2, ch. 12, 'Why the Americans at the Same Time Raise Such Little and Such Great Monuments', 443–4.

4
Program and programs
Christian F. Otto

Histories of architecture and urbanism are taught at Cornell University as part of the five-year Bachelor of Architecture requirements, and as a graduate course of study leading to both MA and PhD degrees. A graduate program in the history of architecture was initiated in 1961 within the Field of Architecture,[1] and a decade later was established as a separate Graduate Field in the History of Architecture and Urban Development.[2] The Field was promoted and administered by Stephen W. Jacobs, who defined its purpose in relation to the study of architectural design at both the undergraduate and graduate levels: then and still today, Cornell's flagship curriculum is its BArch program; a graduate curriculum offers a specialized, second degree in design (MArch II[3]), and a new, three and a half-year graduate program in design (MArch I) was started in 2004–5.[4]

The study of history for Jacobs was a 'significant means of gaining insight' into design issues.[5] History would provide students with a 'basis for personal formulation', it would assist their 'judgment of quality', and potentially it would offer a philosophical base for 'activities and hopes'. Furthermore, familiarity with architecture history might help students effectively 'approach particular communities or architectural situations' by providing case studies of historic instances that could enable them, when in practice, to argue successfully the merits of their designs in various political, social, and economic circumstances.[6]

Toward these ends, Jacobs identified the task of history as recognizing 'regional tradition and the special problems and solutions of particular climatological areas', and revealing the 'artistic and expressive potential' of historical continuities, 'of real sites and situations, and of real life'. History scholarship, he contended, should also explore the motivations and 'rationales of existing solutions' by addressing the material character of works of architecture and highlighting the 'attitudes and messages of consumers and producers in the past'. In these ways, he wished to replace an architecture history based on period styles with one based on the model set out by James Ackerman, with whom he had taught at Berkeley in the later 1950s. In Jacobs' summary of Ackerman's position, history would

> provide a large fund of knowledge – of facts, impressions, and appreciations of existing large-scale social artifacts – but it [would] also provide an adequate exposure to the range of ideas, aesthetic effects, technical solutions, social formulations, and specialized traditions which form our architectural heritage.[7]

Jacobs extended these propositions about history into the graduate program, whose purpose as he defined it was to train 'scholars sympathetic to the atmosphere and disciplines of the professional schools'. Thus graduate study possessed a pragmatic character, similar to the undergraduate curriculum, since it was to train 'qualified, creative, and productive architectural historians able to make a contribution of high scholarly caliber to the . . . educational scene' in professional schools.[8]

Jacobs' positions about history reveal his efforts to integrate the scholarship of a new generation of American architectural historians with a design curriculum. The nature of this work by emerging scholars would be summarized by Spiro Kostof in his 1985 text, *A History of Architecture*.[9] In the first chapter of the book, entitled 'The Study of What We Build', he discussed four premises that comprise the discipline of architecture history:

> First, the material aspect of every building should be looked at in its entirety. Second, the building should be thought of in a broader physical framework and not just in terms of itself. Third, *all* buildings of the past, regardless of size or status or consequence, should ideally be deemed worthy of study. And finally, the extramaterial elements that affect the existence of buildings should be considered indispensable to their appreciation.

Propositions such as these had been under discussion by some scholars for decades; they had determined as well Jacobs' 1979 publication on *Wayne County: The Aesthetic Heritage of a Rural Area*.[10] This 'Catalogue for the Environment', as he termed it, grappled with the nature of significance, and inclusively embraced the aesthetic heritage of the area, including natural patterns, and social and economic development. The text also reflected Jacobs' involvement with preservation concerns, which included establishing a Masters program in preservation in 1970 as part of the graduate field in the History of Architecture and Urban Development. Pedagogically and intellectually this area of study was never effectively linked to either history or design, however, and, several years after Jacobs' death in 1978, it was shifted to another graduate field.

Jacobs was the architecture historian of record at Cornell, but another faculty member was more influential: Colin Rowe determined the international reputation of architectural design at Cornell for decades, and in conjunction with it the presence of history.[11]

Rowe began his long tenure at Cornell in the fall of 1962.[12] To consider how he perceived the purpose of the history of architecture, and to suggest why his approach was so persuasive, the attitudes that inform his writings must be associated with his approach to design in studio.

Rowe promoted the history of architecture on the basis of his belief in precedent as invention, a heuristic position different from that of Jacobs' vision of history as a service discipline, although both advanced in their different ways the utility value of history for architectural practice. For Rowe, historical artifacts, architectural and urban, comprised the very core of architecture; they were the catalysts of the design process. He asserted, 'I am not able to comprehend how anyone can begin to *act* (let alone to *think*) without resorting to precedent.' He asked rhetorically: '[Is] it possible to conceive of any society, any civilization, or any culture without the provision of precedent?'[13] Historic precedents for him were evocative objects that promoted invention; they stimulated the mind and the eye; they could be mined and transformed. Without them there could be no architecture.

In the studio, Rowe did not guide students with a specific agenda intended to achieve a particular resolution; indeed, he did not seem to possess predetermined positions about how projects should develop. Instead, he steeped students in precedents to get them into motion; the more they drew on and reworked historic materials, toward ends they thereby continued to redefine, the more 'heavenly' the result.[14]

Rowe's authority, the basis of his international reputation, derived from four habits of mind, unique to him in their combination: the sharpness of his eye; his unexpected yet telling juxtapositions; his erudition, which effortlessly embraced literature and philosophy, diplomatic, social, and genealogical history, and social and cultural mores; and his writing, which combined a rich vocabulary and driving rhythm with lucid exposition.

For Rowe, precedent was architecture – just as history, theory, and criticism were inseparable to him and never discussed as distinct entities. He saturated his students with examples of historic buildings and sites, making these references vital in his manner of presentation. But his central interest was producing architectural objects, not writing history. He employed historical buildings as the medium for instruction in contemporary design.[15]

Rowe's approach to historical materials is fundamentally different from that followed by the historian. This assertion can only be proffered on the basis of a position about what historians do. In a short essay, it is not possible to review in any purposeful manner the vast literature on, and the many subtle and detailed discussions about, history and historical scholarship. Yet I cannot avoid the issue, since it is critical to my intentions of setting out distinctions and difference. Thus, what follows about what we do when we do history, though reductive to a fault, is intended less as a statement of action and more as a working indication of the historian's purpose.[16]

This purpose is to collect evidence pertinent to an investigation, or several interlocked investigations, about a building, site, designer, client, situation, event, or theme. This promotes the consuming interest among historians in assembling a preponderance of evidence on which to base an assessment. The historian attempts to understand artifact or phenomenon in terms of its making. Why does this building look like it does? Why did events occur as they did? How do these suggest meaning? And so on. Toward these ends, the historian accepts or devises means of collecting and assessing evidence to advance the most effective case. Methods may be modified or abandoned during the course of an investigation if they appear to be failing. None of the research is complete or objective, though scholarship works toward some definition of each. Mostly, historians investigate material on the basis of an agenda and with a certain audience in mind. Indeed, the very titles of some texts set out the purposes of their authors, such as Samuel John Klingensmith, *The Utility of Splendor, Ceremony, Social Life, and Architecture at the Court of Bavaria, 1600 – 1800*.[17] This does not, however, release them from the obligation of collecting material fully and responsibly, of applying standards of evidence to it, and of adhering to a conceptually rigorous method.

This was not Rowe's approach to precedent. To say this is not to make a value judgment – to privilege one sort of work over another – but to locate difference. Let me make this point on the basis of Rudolf Wittkower's *Architectural Principles in the Age of Humanism*.[18] First published in 1949, *Architectural Principles* was a pioneering history of Italian Renaissance architectural theory; scholars of the Italian Renaissance have interacted with it one way or another ever since. The design profession also celebrated the text, which Wittkower found flattering. In the preface to the revised edition of 1962, he wrote: 'The book is concerned with purely historical studies of the period 1450 to 1580, but it was my most satisfying experience to have seen its impact on a young generation of architects.'[19] I emphasize Wittkower's distinction between historical scholarship and use of the book by designers. For Wittkower, the value placed on the text by the architectural profession did not valorize his work, whereas the integrity of his research did. But for the sentence I quoted, the entire preface to the revised and expanded 1962 edition concerned the scholarly evaluation of the book since it was first published.

Wittkower wrote about the history of architectural theory. In the quarter century following World War II, his use of archival and published sources from the time to specify motivations that determined design and practice began to reconfigure the practice of architecture history, which had become more formulaic than based on difficult research and thought. Reams of writing, for example, considered what formal properties might constitute 'Baroque' in contrast to 'Rococo'.

In recent decades, the practice of architecture history has changed again, as speculative strategies have been imported wholesale into the field. Among these, to cite a summary by Irving Lavin, have been 'structuralism, deconstruction, semiotics, symbolic anthropology, patronage, rhetoric . . ., collective social history ("mentalités"), microhistory, new historicism, cultural studies, critical theory, reception theory, feminism, queer studies, multiculturalism . . .'.[20] Some of these approaches have provided us with powerful analytic instruments that have added importantly to our study of the built domain. Mostly, however, they have been employed for their own sake, not for the purpose of better understanding a body of material. The reflections of a particular writer – that of a Benjamin or Bourdieu – are applied to familiar material, providing a new package for a known product. Or a sequence of observations by several authors is strung like a series of colored light bulbs over a familiar text. These techniques too easily apply the practices of consumer capitalism to the world of the mind, staging spectacle rather than providing substance.

To return to Rowe: he did not employ architecture history to promote an architectural pedagogy; quite differently, he employed historic buildings to teach design. Making new buildings was the issue, not engaging a history of the built domain. This is a logical, appropriate, eminently sensible occupation in a school of architecture. It is also distinct from a pedagogy based on the history of architecture.

During the Jacobs and Rowe decades at Cornell, both the study of architecture history, and its position within architecture program curriculums, changed in the United States. We may observe an instance of this shift institutionally in the evolution of the Society of Architectural Historians (SAH), the national organization of record for the practice of architecture history. Founded in 1940 by a small group of teachers and students, by that decade's end the Society had been drawn into the orbit of the College Art Association; architecture history was defined as an area of study within the history of art, as it would continue to be for the next decades.[21] During the course of the 1970s, however, the history of architecture developed into an autonomous practice and the two organizations dissolved their institutional association. The SAH became an independent organization, holding its own annual meetings, developing its own regional chapters, supporting its own publications, and running its own domestic and foreign tours.[22]

Membership as well as the presidency of the SAH were dominated from the outset by scholars whose interest was lodged in the practice and dissemination of scholarship. Advocacy of architectural history within schools of architecture was very much part of the aim of the Society. Already in 1942, for example, the Association of Collegiate Schools of Architecture (ACSA), meeting together with the Association for the Advancement of Architectural Education, invited the Society to hold a symposium on 'The Function of Architectural History in the Modern Professional Curriculum'. And in 1978, to cite a later instance, SAH members attending an ACSA convention introduced a resolution 'to encourage and strengthen the teaching of architectural history in schools of architecture'.[23]

Events such as these reveal an interest by Society members in promoting the study of architecture history as part of architectural design. This was not the practice at Cornell. When its graduate program in architecture history and urbanism was founded in 1970, it was a pioneering effort at establishing a disciplinary praxis with an independent identity, a graduate field that was separate and distinct from both the degree programs in architecture and art history. Fifteen years later, the SAH *Guide to Graduate Degree Programs in Architectural History*[24] listed thirty-two institutions of higher learning where the history of architecture could be studied in the United States. Of these, three-quarters existed within Art History departments; of the remaining quarter, only Cornell offered training and advanced degrees as a program in its own right.[25] Thus, by the mid-1980s, an institutional disciplinary praxis of architecture history had been established, but almost entirely within the purview of architecture: identity without independence.

Given the status of the Cornell program, consideration of its intellectual trajectory since the Jacobs–Rowe era offers another perspective on historiographical inquiry. At the outset, however, it must be recognized that an academic program is seldom an intellectually coherent project; it is rather an administrative organization, perhaps a curricular framework. What constitutes the program intellectually is a collection of individuals who do not act in concert. A case in point is the history of the Bauhaus curriculum, as differently understood by the various masters during the Gropius years.[26]

Both faculty and students in the Cornell History of Architecture and Urbanism program draw on the intellectual resources of the university. This is not an interdisciplinary pursuit but rather an exploration of what other disciplines might contribute intellectually and methodologically to the enterprise. Supported by a small number of faculty and students, this very condition necessitates that the program must function within the larger territory of the university. Recognizing as well that we as scholars are no longer able to maintain notions of a core in architecture history – that is neither the possibility nor advisability of a collection of major monuments as a commonly agreed upon body of material that should be studied according to a short list of standards – students are encouraged to engage the rich potential of courses of study and research at the university. This enables them to pursue their individual agendas in challenging and innovative ways.

Diversity and multiplicity, however, become profitable if engaged from a center. The conceptual center for the Cornell History of Architecture program, as I see it, is a renewed interest in society and culture, as pursued in recent decades by scholars such as Lynn Hunt, Caroline Bynum, and William Sewell, Jr. Some of these historians work with methods appropriated from the social sciences, primarily sociology, and anthropology. This has generated considerable activity, but the particular lines of inquiry, focused on politics and economics and social issues, do not probe the visual world, which is the primary purpose, and uniqueness, of architecture history as a discipline.

More purposeful for me is work on culture, for which Clifford Geertz's *Interpretation of Cultures* of 1973 is a foundation piece.[27] 'Believing,' he wrote, 'with Max Weber, that man is an animal suspended in webs of significance he himself has spun, I take culture to be those webs, and the analysis of it to be ... an interpretive one in search of meaning.' He interrogated symbols, rituals, events, historical artifacts, social arrangements, and belief systems as part of a meaning complex. The dilemma here, as Bonnell and Hunt have noted, is that if analyses of culture depend 'on the interpretation of meaning ..., then what serve[s] as the standard for judging interpretation? If culture ... entirely permeate[s] the expression of meaning, then how [may] any individual or social agency be identified?'[28]

Thus, we find in history scholarship an emphatic return to the vexing issue: what is culture? An aspect of life, such as society or politics? Or a way of defining a set of beliefs and practices? William Sewell, Jr has attempted to work past the many meanings of culture found in anthropological, sociological, and historical scholarship:

> He argues that culture is most fruitfully conceptualized as a dialectic between system and practice. It is a system of symbols and meanings with a certain coherence and definition but also a set of practices, thus the symbols and meanings can and do change over time, often in unpredictable fashion.

He also insists, however, on practice, arguing for 'a necessary tension between system and practice, a tension often erased in the polemics about culture'.[29] The built domain is an ideal subject precisely for investigations of this kind.

Of critical importance to these considerations is the matter of narrative. A series of occurrences become an event by means of a story, as we have seen the story of modern architecture emerge and evolve during the course of the twentieth century.[30] 'Narrative,' again citing Bonnell and Hunt, 'is an arena in which meaning takes form, in which individuals connect to the public and social world, and in which change therefore becomes possible. Narrative ... provides a link between culture as system and culture as practice.'[31]

These concepts about culture, society, and narrative become effective when they are explored with a disciplinary rigor: not architecture history among the disciplines, but rather the energetic and intellectual and committed pursuit of a disciplinary praxis that draws on appropriate methodologies toward specific purposes. Historians of architecture and cities who engage study in this manner are not easily integrated into pedagogies of architectural design. When this difficult tension becomes productive, however, it can provoke compelling work in both domains.

Notes

1 Graduate study at Cornell is organized by fields of study, defined by the *Code of Legislation of the Graduate Faculty* as:

> voluntary groupings of members of the graduate faculty who have academic interests in common and who wish to exercise shared responsibility for an area of inquiry and for the admission, education, and, as appropriate, financial support of graduate students. Fields are independent of traditional college or department divisions, so they may draw together faculty members from several colleges, departments, and related disciplines in accordance with scholarly interests.

2 Listed for years in Field publications and web sites as the History of Architecture and Urbanism, the official name of the program remains the History of Architecture and Urban Development.

3 The four-semester program is presently being changed to a summer and two semesters.

4 The MArch I program is intended for students who already have a bachelor's degree in any subject, and who wish to obtain a professional degree in architecture.

5 My essay on 'Orientation and Invention: Teaching the History of Architecture at Cornell', in Gwendolyn Wright and Janet Parks (eds), *The History of History in American Schools of Architecture, 1865–1975*, New York, 1990, 111–22, offers a more detailed consideration of the history program.

6 The citations in this and the following paragraph are from Stephen W. Jacobs, 'History: An Orientation for the Architect', in Marcus Whiffin (ed.), *The History, Theory and Criticism of Architecture*, papers from the 1964 AIA–ACSA Teacher Seminar, Cambridge, MA, 1965, 47–69; see specifically 48–51 and 67. This statement followed soon after Jacobs arrived at Cornell and introduced a new history program, suggesting that it presents his philosophic underpinning for the Cornell curriculum.

7 Jacobs, 'History: An Orientation', 68. For Ackerman's position, see James S. Ackerman, 'Western Art History', in James S. Ackerman and Rhys Carpenter, *Art and Archaeology*, Englewood Cliffs, NJ, 1963, 123–231.

8 *Faculty Minutes of the College of Architecture*, vol. 1960–69, specifically February 14, 1961, 476–7, 'Proposed Graduate Program in Architectural History', 478d–e. The initial proposal for a revised undergraduate curriculum had been advanced as, *inter alia*, providing 'the opportunity of offering a graduate program in History of Architecture', October 11, 1960, 467.

9 Spiro Kostof, *A History of Architecture: Settings and Rituals*, New York, 1985, ch. 1, 3–19, quote on 8.

10 Stephen W. Jacobs, *A Catalog for the Environment. Wayne County: The Aesthetic Heritage of a Rural Area*, photographs by David Plowden, Wayne County Historical Society, 1979 (Architecture Worth Saving in New York State).

11 The practice of architectural history at Cornell was a more complex enterprise than the activities of Jacobs and Rowe, both members of the Department of Architecture. Theodore Brown, trained as an architect and historian, with Rietveld as a special research area, also taught modern architecture in the Department of the History of Art. His colleague in that department, Robert Calkins, taught and published on medieval architecture. In the Department of City and Regional Planning, one of the three departments that

comprise the College of Architecture, Art + Planning, John Reps was the pre-eminent figure in the history of American physical planning. The dysfunctional relationship among these individuals is a story for another time.

12 Rowe had a degree in architectural design from Liverpool, a Master's in history from the Warburg and Courtauld Institutes, London, and a Master's in architecture from Cambridge. For his appointment at Cornell, see *College Minutes*, October 9, 1962, 530.

13 Colin Rowe, letter to the editors, *The Harvard Architectural Review*, 5, 1986, 188.

14 A favorite term of Rowe's in conversation.

15 It is difficult to assess Rowe's design pedagogy, since he did not write about it. His essay, 'Architectural Education in the USA', *Lotus*, 27, 1980, 43–6, is not about education, but a meditation on modern architecture, which he would develop more fully in *The Architecture of Good Intentions: Towards a Possible Retrospect*, London, 1994. Without Rowe's thoughts on how a design studio might be run, we are left with the experiences of those who studied with him from which to extrapolate his pedagogical attitudes. The most balanced and thorough discussion of these experiences is: Alexander Caragonne, *The Texas Rangers: Notes from an Architectural Underground*, Cambridge, MA, 1995, especially 237–49 on the studio.

16 An excellent consideration of the historian's purpose is: Mark Richard Ashton, 'Purpose and Purposes in the Study of Art', dissertation, May 1981, Cornell University.

17 Edited for publication by Christian F. Otto and Mark R. Ashton, Chicago, IL, 1993.

18 Rudolf Wittkower, *Architectural Principles in the Age of Humanism*, 3rd com. rev. edn, London, 1962. The Cornell connection to Wittkower is that Rowe studied with him in the mid-1940s, as did I in the mid-1960s.

19 Wittkower, *Architectural Principles*, 163. The reference here was presumably to the Smithsons, and the role they played in establishing Team X.

20 Irving Lavin, 'The Crisis of "Art History"', *Art Bulletin*, LXXVIII: 1, March 1996, 13–15. Specifically for architecture history, see the editorial by Nancy Stieber, *Journal of the Society of Architectural Historians*, 62: 2, June 2003, 176–7.

21 Marian C. Donnelly, *A History, Society of Architectural Historians 1940–1995*, Eugene, OR, 1998, ch. 2

22 Donnelly, *A History*, 39–45.

23 Donnelly, *A History*, 10; the ACSA information is on p. 43.

24 *1986 Guide to Graduate Degree Programs in Architecture History*, prepared by the SAH Education Committee, Dora Wiebenson, Chair, and distributed by the Society of Architectural Historians.

25 Administratively, the PhD programs in architecture at Columbia, MIT, Princeton, Berkeley, and UCLA are located within architecture departments.

26 Despite an extensive literature in recent decades, this issue is best discussed in Hans M. Wingler, *Das Bauhaus: 1919–1933 Weimar Dessau Berlin und die Nachfolge in Chicago seit 1937*, Bramsche, 1962, with later revised and expanded editions.

27 Clifford Geertz, *The Interpretation of Cultures: Selected Essays*, New York, 1973. The following quotation is from p. 5.

28 Victoria E. Bonnell and Lynn Hunt, *Beyond the Cultural Turn: New Directions in the Study of Society and Culture*, Berkeley, CA, 1999, 9.

29 Bonnell and Hunt, *Beyond the Cultural Turn*, 12.

30 Architects' conversation of the 1920s told this story, which was then scripted in a series of publications, beginning with Adolf Bruno Behne, *Der moderne Zweckbau*, written 1923, published Munich, 1926, and continuing with texts such as: Gustav Adolf Platz, *Die Baukunst der neuesten Zeit*, Berlin, 1927; Sigfried Giedion, *Bauen in Frankreich: Eisen, Eisenbeton*, Leipzig, 1928; Henry Russel Hitchcock, *Modern Architecture: Romanticism and Reintegration*, New York, 1929; and on through the 1930s and 1940s.

31 Bonnell and Hunt, *Beyond the Cultural Turn*, 17.

5
Hercules at the roundabout
Multidisciplinary choice in the history of architecture

Fikret Yegül

Among the models available for a multidisciplinary approach to architectural history the 'discipline of architecture' itself is a fundamental one. The complementary relationship that exists between these two overlapping fields makes it natural, even inevitable, that the principles and concepts of design – such as composition and order, space and mass, solid and void, surface and texture, light and shadow, and many others – serve as the basic tools in understanding and analysing current and historical architecture. Architectural history stands to be enriched by exploiting the design-based methodologies of its parent before looking afar to distant disciplines and methods. Apparent shortcomings of understanding design through an architectonic, and essentially formalistic, approach could be balanced by architecture's own humanistic and re-creative component sustained by the experience and subjective assessment of the built and lived-in environment.[1] In short, whether we apply the abstract and formalistic principles of design analysis, or real and humanistic methods of experientialism, buildings, as the principal objects of our inquiry, should come first.

The openness of architectural culture in admitting the input of other disciplines is astonishing and remarkable. After all, the wide variety of subjects and skills an architect was expected to command – from drawing to arithmetic, from history to accounting, from philosophy to music – is the critical opening discourse of *De architectura*, Vitruvius' famous treatise. In underlining the importance of this formidable multidisciplinary programme prescribed for the education of an architect, Vitruvius declared that it is 'by [the architect's] judgment that all work done by *other* arts is put to test' (I.1.1). Although this is an exaggerated, idealized, academic and unrealistic view (even Vitruvius recognized that), the point is well taken that the assessment of architecture and architectural history benefits from a wide variety of approaches and disciplines. Like Hercules at the crossroads, the architect and the historian, too, are offered choices, some more redeeming than others.[2]

Our hero's list of choices cannot be easily subsumed in simple dualities, the hard and steep road leading to virtue and fame, the soft and easy one to vanity and vice. The possibilities of method and discipline offered at the 'roundabout' are diverse, difficult to define, and often require multiple journeys. We could start with technology. The science of building is unique in its ability to bring a logical, objective and measurable basis for viewing and evaluating architecture – an antidote to methods that emphasize subjective and emotive evaluations. The understanding of the structural underpinnings of architecture, their effectiveness and efficiency, is paramount to understanding its nature and syntax, even its ethical basis.[3]

History and language share important methodologies with history of architecture. In a more focused way, history of architecture offers a disciplinary umbrella that covers relevant concerns, such as questions of text and record, politics and patronage, or economy and power, all useful in analysing motives and meanings in architecture. The politics of architecture, or the architecture of politics, focusing on the reciprocating relationships between power, ideology and the built world, are valid concerns for ancient as well as modern societies alike. As manifestations of the arts of persuasion and propaganda, they cross cultural and temporal borders with alarming ease. Likewise, an economic, and essentially Marxist, critique of architecture operates within universal cross-disciplinary, cross-cultural models for the production and commodification of objects of art and architecture, and has been a particularly relevant concern during the early part of the twentieth century. The latter part of that century, on the other hand, seems to have been engrossed and enthralled by questions of post-colonial cultural studies and the politics of ethnicity and identity. These approaches not only provide engaging perspectives of regional architecture, but transform architecture itself into an effective tool in illuminating larger cultural agendas and relationships. Perhaps one could claim, with Nikolaus Pevsner, that all architecture, private or public, a bicycle shed or the Lincoln Cathedral, is a reflection of the urge to put a human face on building.

This is only a redacted and impressionistic view of the interaction of architecture and architectural history with a few selected overlapping fields. My intention is not a full discussion, or even a comprehensive overview, of theories and methodologies: these can be found in any number of dictionaries, anthologies, compendiums and specialized articles.[4] However, I would like to highlight as an exemplar one particular approach employing the methods of psychological analysis. Lately, I have been working on a psycho-biographical reading of Vitruvius, an architect and theoretician who lived at the end of the Roman republic and the beginning of the empire, and is solely known for his important architectural treatise, *Ten Books on Architecture* (*De architectura*).[5]

Whether we view Vitruvius' masterpiece as a useful manual of building, or a learned treatise drawing upon a vast store of practical and theoretical knowledge of past ages, depends very much on our view and understanding of

Vitruvius – the man, the military engineer, the architect and the scholar. Was Vitruvius a competent technician and a sound builder suspicious of architectural creativity and experimentation whose long service as a military engineer stunted his imagination and restricted his vision? Can we view his historicizing and antiquarian treatise as the bitter fruit of a mediocre mind?

Rereading *De architectura* with the specific purpose of searching for psychological clues might shed light on the complex personality and intentions of Vitruvius and his work. The text, closely read, particularly the fantasy constructions of the 'introductions' to each 'book', offer rich insights into the author's personality and inner world. The margins of plausibility invested in his fantasy constructions appear appropriate for psychological investigation and provide a link between the externalized power of the world and the internalized life of its author. The introduction to the second book, addressed to Augustus – a psychodrama rich in meaning and overtones – is the one I chose to share with you among several others. Dinocrates, a handsome and creative Macedonian architect, seeks audience with Alexander the Great in order to present a project for a very interesting and unusual city. With his tall and fine physique, semi-nude and oiled to resemble Hercules, lion skin over his shoulder, club in his right hand, he has no difficulty attracting the attention of the busy king. He proposes to shape Mount Athos into the statue of a man, the left hand holding a fortified city, a basin in the right hand receiving waters from the streams of the mountain. Alexander first compliments this interesting scheme, but when he asks where the farmlands and corn fields to feed the city are located Dinocrates is unable to give an answer. Thus demonstrating that even the most imaginative idea is worthless if it cannot come to terms with reality, Alexander nonetheless decides to retain the architect in his service. 'This is how Dinocrates, recommended only by his good looks . . . came to be famous,' wistfully observes Vitruvius. It is not hard to find the real personalities behind the protagonists of this story. Dinocrates is Vitruvius' alter ego. A young, creative genius with striking appearance, he is the opposite of the stunted, elderly architect, an ideal that combines his love and hate. Augustus speaks through the mouth of Alexander: knowledge and experience gained over years is more valuable than lofty ideas and undisciplined genius. An intelligent but unimaginative autodidact, a capable but unexceptional architect left on the margins, Vitruvius must have known the yearning of the half-talented. He sought to achieve the fame and recognition that eluded him in getting important commissions during that first and exceptionally creative era of Augustus' early empire by writing a scholarly and comprehensive treatise that aimed at collecting all there was to know about architecture. The 'wholeness' he sought by the power of the word granted him the wholeness that eluded him in person.[6]

Any attempt to use the psychological analysis primarily involves a deeper understanding, or the remaking, of the artist or the architect. Therefore, the process is essentially re-creative: it involves the dismantling and reconstruction of the author's personality in order to reach a deeper level of understanding his work, his desire. Consequently, psychoanalytical method opens the door dangerously wide to the theories of deconstruction, an approach that many now believe disproportionately dominated the discussion on humanities and arts in American academic circles during the last few decades.[7]

Deconstruction believes that history is defined by meta-narratives that are open to gross distortions because they depend for their meaning on the inherently unstable and arbitrary medium of language. Architecture, however, has little use for traditional, written text, and can be considered to be relatively free of textual distortions. Dealing directly with the raw material of building, it evades such linguistic instabilities of meaning, or, as Jacques Derrida has put it, 'the absence of presence'.[8] But while the primary source material for architecture is 'itself', that for the history of architecture, which often deals with historicized records of buildings, is mediated by linguistic text, thus is open to the same uncertainties and the same 'absences'. Like history, it is subject to logocentrisms, or the masking of meaning through the writing or reading of a text. Furthermore, even historic architecture physically 'present' depends on cultural and temporal semiotics, and, to be properly understood, assumes a familiarity with its symbols and metaphors. The past is a foreign country.

As art historian Keith Moxey comments, the inevitable and widely discussed solution to this conflict is the 'realization that the historian necessarily invests language with absent meaning that history is not found but constructed'.[9] New construction fills the absence and makes the unfamiliar familiar. Understanding and interpreting architecture, too, has to do not with values of the past, but those of the present, not with the architect, but the historian. Thus, the deconstruction argument cannot invalidate the historical meaning of architecture, but it infects it with an overused, and questionable concept of cultural relativism – which squarely assumes that our reading of the past is solely determined by the context of the present.

One problem with this picture is that deconstruction agendas focus more on the social and political ideas that generate architecture, and its representational value, rather than its inherent double realities: the physical/structural and the human one. And in retelling its story deconstruction is more interested in 'taking apart' than putting together even though Derrida himself maintained that the process is not destructive; rather, it is an affirmative questioning.[10] Stripping and unmasking the institutions of the past, one of the sacred charges of deconstructivist analysis, is suspect because the unmasking is controlled – or tainted – by current agendas. Often, the historian/critic operates from an unarticulated, but still transparent a priori political platform. Nonetheless, even if the mechanisms of our critique of these masternarratives are flawed, not criticizing – paramount to replacing one politically charged interest with another – is not an option.[11]

If narratives – even the circumscribed, individual, psychoanalytical ones – cannot represent the truth and are subject to logocentrisms, then 'are we not placed in a situation where we possess no rationale for preferring one historical interpretation to another?' Moxey asks.[12] If there is no historical truth to be found, the question is moot, as your truth is as good as mine, and one is back again on that easy road that leads to the pleasures of cultural and temporal relativism (Hercules, take heed!). Can truth bargain with its powers? Or, to put a more positive face on it, could the existence of multiple truths lead to meritorious pluralism? Pluralism, as a kind of intellectual licence to include several perspectives at one time, subsumes the essence of multidisciplinarity and espouses ambiguity. The protean face of ambiguity – at least, in its intellectual postmodern guise, with its partial truths, layered reasons, learned conundrums, word games, tropes, tropics, shifts in temporality, complexities and contradictions – appears to be good. Perhaps, truth in this sense can bargain with its powers and still remain in control. Such pluralism allows for a dynamic and reciprocating scale of time that intentionally blurs the boundaries between the past and the present (perhaps, the past after all is no longer a foreign country). With such a powerful intellectual tool one could bring the past to the present, and, in the words of Dominick LaCapra, 'let the past interrogate us as much as we interrogate the past'.[13]

Some might argue that, since historic truth exists only in illusion, we could start building new meanings by resorting to fictive truths. Perhaps, this is the road Derrida and his fellow travellers wished us to take. At any rate, in the post-Derrida world many judge that deconstruction is not enough. Rather, we should strive to make deconstruction the basis of a new *construction* and *reconstruction*, not only taking apart but also putting together in order to invent fresh meanings, create new truths, complete new tasks and, as soon as these are fulfilled, like Sisyphus, start over again to 'roll our rock' to the top of the mountain and overcome our punishing gods and assert our humanity. In Camus' penetrating vision, Sisyphus' victory is his identification with the hopelessness of his task, the consciousness of his condition, and the acceptance of a world with gods ('who have preference for human suffering') that he can scorn, as he toils eternally, the earth below, the sky above, and the centre he fills with his rock.[14] Perhaps, in defeating the nihilistic agenda with its empty core as served to us by the gods of deconstruction, we could reach out for a belief that puts the human being in the centre, conscious of and hence superior to his fate as Sisyphus is with his rock. It has to be a belief that accepts the primacy of the physical world as the *topos* for human destiny. The individual must be *there present* to the end, clinging to his/her world-rock or the rocky shores of his/her world-island as the last erupting volcano shakes it and pushes it below the sea, or tending his/her last rose-bush as his/her dime-sized planet whirls in a forgetful universe – and asking with Rilke: 'Are we perhaps here to say: house, bridge, fountain, gate, jug, fruit tree, window . . . column, tower?'[15]

Sisyphus' destiny takes us to Martin Heidegger's philosophy of phenomenology, which starts from the acceptance of the world of physical realities – the unabashed 'thingness' of things. As the opposite of the cultural relativity and nihilism of deconstruction, phenomenology is characterized by its inherent architectural nature, its manifest tangibility and human presence. It is a system that accepts the rock and places Sisyphus squarely between the sky above and the earth below. Robert Mugerauer, who questions Derrida's sceptical view of 'objective reality', in which architecture – columns, houses, the pyramids, indeed, the whole world of connected things – is seen not as a 'presence' but a web of references, or representational texts for semiotics, asks if there is a way in our time 'to recover genuine belonging with reality and truth'. He concludes that, if there is, it would have to come from overcoming the textual world of deconstruction in favour of the 'thingness' world of phenomenology, or through establishing 'a genuine belonging with what-is-given-to-us'. In this approach, architecture is privileged 'as a primal mode of interpreting the world, bringing forth order [and] setting out an individual's place in nature and the community'.[16]

Christian Norbert-Schulz credits Heidegger for leading us out of the 'impasse of scientific abstraction and back to what is concrete, that is, to the things themselves'.[17] In Heidegger's thinking it is essentially the physical objects that reveal and manifest the world – not ideas. It is helpful to recall Heidegger's analogy of the bridge, which '*gathers* the earth as landscape around the stream'.[18] The bridge does not simply connect the banks that are already there, but gives presence to a 'place'; it gathers, it does not take apart. Likewise, architecture gathers, or makes manifest, the physical and cultural elements and reveals the world. Its material presence – walls, columns, sheltering roof, smoke through its chimney – creates and bears witness to an inhabited landscape, an inhabited human core between the earth and the sky, as proudly and poetically as the vision of a labouring Sisyphus. Since architecture makes a site a *place*, it follows that it is up to the architect and the historian of architecture to uncover 'the meanings potentially [and already] present in the given environment'[19] – a charge that is not a mere individual choice but almost a sacred duty, just as identifying the 'privileged situations' embedded in life's messy, random course, and transforming them into 'perfect moments', that was perceived as a moral obligation by the late existentialist philosopher Jean-Paul Sartre.[20] As current interests increasingly take into account the larger environment and ecology as the proper context for architecture, an appropriate point of departure may be found in reviving the old Roman concept of *genius loci*, 'the spirit of place', or, in Louis Kahn's famous dictum, 'what a thing or a place wants to be'.[21] Arbitrarily placing the individual between the earth and the sky is not sufficient then, there should be a quest for a *place*; architecture should be able to make him/her *dwell* there meaningfully and poetically. Phenomenology here transcends its material core to reach to the realm of values. Norbert-Schulz contends that this can be done 'by means of buildings which gather the properties of the place [like the bridge gathering the material world around it] and bring them close to man' – make the place inhabited or dwelt-in.[22] In other words, it seems that the task of the architect and the historian is to find and express the identity and poetics of place.

Poetics of place should not be confused with its valuable, but more mundane, cousin of general regionalism and simple contextuality. Just over two decades ago a number of architects and architectural historians, including Kenneth Frampton, Alexis Tzonis, Liane Lefaivre and Karsten Harries, introduced the concept of critical regionalism as 'one of the alternatives to a clearly aging modernism and post-modernism's younger but prematurely aging sibling, deconstruction'.[23] Indeed, the subtlety of the 'new critical regionalism' is invested in its inherently elusive nature. Its protagonists, architects, historians and philosophers are at pains to point out that this is no ordinary nostalgic yearning for local culture and colour; no chasing after the memories of an irretrievable past; no apology for the creation of commercial settings to tweak populist romanticism. It has nothing to do with regionalist architectural pastiches such as the white-lace concrete screens of Minoru Yamasaki or Edward Durell Stone that were supposed to have been inspired by local climate, but more with the Scandinavian vision of Alvar Aalto or the Venetian one of Carlo Scarpa. Nor should the new critical regionalism be confused with the kind of sentimental vernacular produced, say in both southern and northern California early in the twentieth century, by the so-called 'regionalist schools', which sought to fuse 'the combined interaction of climate, culture, myth and craft'.[24] Frampton considers prosperity, political savvy, cultural independence and, most importantly, an awareness and desire for local identity as the preconditions for the emergence of critical regionalism. There is more than a little elitism here.[25]

Tzonis and Lefaivre, on the other hand, emphasize the notion of criticality as a response to the general sense of miasma created by unfettered globalization. By means of a cycle of perpetual self-evaluation, critical regionalism tries to achieve 'de-familiarization' as the antidote against the kind of easy familiarization valued by romantic and commercial regionalism.[26] Tzonis and Lefaivre's formulation of the architectural characteristics of critical regionalism is intellectually engaging and deserves full quoting:

> [Critical regionalism] selects regional elements for their potential to act as support, physical or conceptual, of human contact and community, what we may call 'place-defining' elements, and incorporates them *strangely* rather than *familiarly*.... It makes them appear distant, hard to grasp, difficult, even *disturbing* [my italics].... It disrupts the sentimental 'embrace' between buildings and their consumers, 'de-automatizing' perception and thus 'pricking the conscious'.... Hence, through highly appropriately chosen poetic devices of defamiliarization critical regionalism makes the building appear to enter into an imagined dialogue with the viewer.[27]

These powerful and evocative words open up a wide world of ideas, but, architecturally, what does the landscape of critical regionalism really look like? I would like to imagine that this landscape could include some of the best buildings of Aalto that merge local materials, colours, craftsmanship and light 'layered and inlaid into their sites'; or it could be described by the sensitively crafted, austere and abstract landscapes and 'enclosures' of the Mexican architect Luis Barragan, devoid of all traces of populist photogenic imagery ('a plaza is a "façade" that mirrors the sky') (Figure 5.1); or it could be like a detail by Carlo Scarpa, in which Kahn perceived 'the adoration of Nature ... which makes manifest the wholeness of [architectural] Form' (Figure 5.2).[28] In attempting to respond to the almost insurmountable and paradoxical quest for 'becoming modern and returning to sources' (without pandering to populist and photogenic forms of the vernacular, on the one hand, and the technologically seductive globalizations, on the other), some of the sensitive and regionally inspired architects, such as Joseph Esherick, Mario Botta, Tadao Ando and Renzo Piano, stand as promising leaders.[29] Lesser-known but equally important contributions to the landscape of critical regionalism are the ideas and the selected projects by a handful of architects from countries where an uneven but critical dialogue between tradition and innovation (read 'international modernism') still exists: Dimitris and Susana Antonakakis from Greece, Sedad Hakkı Eldem and Turgut Cansever from Turkey, Geoffrey Bawa from Sri Lanka and, of course, Hassan Fathy from Egypt (Figures 5.3 and 5.4).[30] As visualized by Karsten Harries, the quest for critical regionalism should start with a community dedicated to recovering the human's place on earth and giving him a dwelling.[31] Such a quest could place ethical and philosophical burdens on architecture, forcing it to shed its aesthetic, formalist and theoretical garments and return to the modesty of good design espoused by common sense. This brand of critical regionalism, too, espouses its own kind of elitism, but one that is based on artistic sensitivity, craftsmanship, intellectual rigour and sophistication, and above all a true sense for place. The promise of this para-discipline is mainly due to its overwhelming investment in the culture of architectonics – that is, its decision to put at centre forward the visceral, intoxicating, design-based visions and prerogatives of architecture itself. The fusion of physical reality and human ethos informs architecture with the identity, meaning, memory and the poetry of a lived-in place. Such a process of visualizing and reconstituting place is immensely exciting but transitory and impermanent: people are gone and so are the gods who dwell in their houses and cities. Like Italo Calvino's Despina, a 'border city' between the desert and the sea, the perception and re-creation of a city very much depend on whether the camel driver or the sailor is viewing it.[32]

Continuing interest in critical regionalism is substantiated by the recent session entitled 'Beyond Critical Regionalism: The Local and Global in Post-World War II Architecture', at the 58th Annual Meeting of the Society of Architectural Historians in Vancouver, 2005.[33] The participants for the most part presented new case studies rather than analysed the precepts of the 'new' critical regionalism as explored and defined in the 1980s and 1990s by Frampton, Tzonis and Harries. The new examples and the architects

Figure 5.1 Luis Barragan: San Cristobal Stables and Egerstom House, Mexico City, 1968 (photograph by the author).

Figure 5.2 Carlo Scarpa: main door of the Banca Popolare di Verona, Verona, 1973 (photograph by the author).

Figure 5.3 (above)
Sedad Hakkı Eldem,
Şark Kahvesi
(Oriental Café),
İstanbul, 1948
(photograph by
the author).

Figure 5.4
Fikret Yegül: Country
House, Gölcük-
Ödemiş, Turkey,
1999 (photograph
by the author).

associated with them (such as the formation of *Free Town Christiana* near Copenhagen, or the work by Geoffrey Bawa in Sri Lanka) expand and articulate the ongoing significance of the subject. They also sharpen our perception of the putative disjunction between local and global identities and question their future relevance. They ask if in a global world the restrictive polemics of cultural oppositions need to be replaced by total immersions in participatory policies and hybrid possibilities.

An important question for future studies in critical regionalism is whether the post-Second World War modernism and the globalization concerns of the last few decades are essentially one and the same thing with similar universalizing, destructive tendencies. Or, if globalization is – especially as shaped by its recent, economy-driven agenda – a beast that should be accepted on its own terms, tamed and put to work on our behalf. After all, even the much larger concerns of environmental protection (of which architecture and the creation and preservation of culturally determined *places* are small parts) seem to be more effective when working with market forces than against them. Turning traditional Marxism on its head, such a market-based approach defines a very real, and for some quite chilling, prospect of a methodology.

It is not easy to choose among the roads offered to this generation's architectural Herculeses. Like all choices there are ethical consequences between the stern and the fair, and the possibility of failing to choose wisely is always there, but like all choices even the wrong choice must be seen as a privilege.

Notes

1 Functionalist and formalist ordering of early modern architecture was established by eighteenth- and nineteenth-century French academics and theorists such as J.-D. Leroy and J.-N.-L. Durand and A. C. Quatremere de Quincy, whose positivist views of architecture as a science of measurable and definable aesthetic doctrine influenced architectural theory until the late nineteenth century. Formal analysis of painting, sculpture, but less so architecture in paired visual categories, was identified by Heinrich Wölfflin in his epoch-making *Principles of Art History* in 1915 (trans. M. D. Hottinger, 1932) and the extension of these ideas expressed in Paul Frankl's *Principles of Architectural History* (original 1914, trans. James O'Gorman, 1968). Echoes of this formally and visually based approach to design theory and analysis can be traced as a strong background in shaping the thinking and education of many modern architects, city planners and historians. Some of the most effective applications of this method can be seen in the works of Sigfried Giedion, Gyorgy Kepes and Kevin Lynch.

2 Offered a choice by two women at crossroads between the easy road leading to pleasure and delight and the steep, rocky one leading to honour and virtue, Hercules decides to take the latter, establishing a powerful humanistic metaphor for the rewards of virtue gained through hardship and self-sacrifice – or, in Panofsky's words, the difference 'between ascetic

moralism and hedonistic evolutionalism (65)'. The theme of Hercules' choice, articulated in Xenophon (*Memorabilia* 2.1.20–34), inspired generations of Western artists and musicians. Erwin Panofsky, *Hercules auf dem Scheidewege und andere antike Bildstoffe in der neueren Kunst*, Studien der Bibliothek Warburg 18, Leipzig, 1930; *Studies in Icology*, New York, 1962 (original 1939), 64–5; Karl Galinsky, *The Herakles Theme*, Oxford, 1972, 198–9.

3 Gyorgy Kepes (ed.), *Structure in Art and Science*, New York, 1965; R. J. Mainstone, *Developments in Structural Form*, Cambridge, MA, 1975; Robert Mark, *Light, Wind and Structure: The Mystery of the Master Builders*, Cambridge, MA, 1990; Robert Mark (ed.), *Architectural Technology up to the Scientific Revolution*, Cambridge, MA, 1993. See also Geoffrey Scott, *The Architecture of Humanism*, Garden City, NY, 1924 (original 1914), esp. ch. 4.

4 Among the many I could mention: H.-W. Kruft, *A History of Architectural Theory*, Princeton, NJ, 1994; K. Michael Hays (ed.), *Architecture Theory, Since 1968*, Cambridge, MA, 1998; Kate Nesbitt (ed.), *Theorizing a New Agenda for Architecture: An Anthology of Architectural Theory, 1965–1995*, New York, 1996; Keith Moxey, *The Practice of Theory: Poststructuralism, Cultural Politics, and Art History*, Ithaca, NY, 1994; I. Borden and D. Dunster (eds), *Architecture and the Sites of History*, New York, 1995; J. Ockman (ed.), *Architecture Culture: A Documentary Anthology*, New York, 1993; Elizabeth B. MacDougall (ed.), *The Architectural Historian in America*, Studies in the History of Art 35, Washington DC, 1990; T. M. Greene, *The Arts and the Art of Criticism*, Princeton, NJ, 1940; B. C. Heyl, 'The Critic's Reasons', in *Aesthetic Inquiry: Essays on Art Criticism and the Philosophy of Art*, Belmont, CA, 1967, 231–40; Manfredo Tafuri, *Theories and History of Architecture*, New York, 1976; Dana Arnold, *Reading Architectural History*, London and New York, 2002, esp. 1–33.

5 The bibliography on Vitruvius is vast and growing. For a straightforward assessment of the elusive author and his relation to the architecture of his times: Frank E. Brown, 'Vitruvius', in Adolf Placzek (ed.), *Macmillan Encyclopedia of Architects*, vol. 4, New York, 1982, 334–42; 'Vitruvius and the Liberal Art of Architecture', *Bucknell Review*, 2, 1963, 99–107; Axel Boethius, 'Vitruvius and the Roman Architecture of His Age', in *Dragma: Martino P. Nilsson*, Acta Instituti Romani Regni sueciae 1, Lund, 1939, 114–43; B. Baldwin, 'The Date, Identity and Career of Vitruvius,' *Latomus*, 94, 1990, 425–34; Fikret Yegül, 'Vitruvius ve *De architectura*', in *Vitruvius, Mimarlık Üzerine On Kitap*, trans. Suna Güven, Ankara, 1990, xi–xvii. See also, H. Geertman and J. J. Jong (eds), *Munus non ingratum: Proceedings of the International Symposium on Vitruvius' De architectura and Hellenistic and Republican Architecture*, Bulletin Antike Beschaving, supplement 2, 1989. Recent translations of and commentaries on *De architectura* include: Ingrid D. Rowland and Thomas N. Howe, *Vitruvius, Ten Books on Architecture*, Cambridge, 1999; Thomas G. Smith, *Vitruvius on Architecture*, New York, 2003; Indra K. McEwen, *Vitruvius: Writing the Body of Architecture*, Cambridge, MA, 2003.

6 Yegül, 'Vitruvius', xvii.

7 The recent death of Jacques Derrida occasioned the growing concern and unease about the validity and effectiveness of the impenetrable language and the obscure logic preferred by the followers of deconstruction and Derrida

himself, whose influence was waning among French academics already in the 1980s. The obituary in the *Economist* (23–9 October, 2004, 89) is typical and instructive. Twenty years ago, in a delightfully witty and whimsical article, John Onians speculated on the play between strong architecture and flimsy theory: 'The Strength of Columns and the Weakness of Theory', in Susan C. Scott (ed.), *The Art of Interpreting*, Papers in Art History from the Pennsylvania State University IX, 1995, 31–9.

8 Among the relevant sources on Derrida's philosophy on language and meaning are: *Writing and Difference*, trans. Alan Bass, Chicago, IL, 1978; *Of Grammatology*, trans. Gayatri Spivak, Baltimore, MD, 1976; David Wood (ed.), *Derrida: A Critical Reader*, Cambridge, MA, 1992; Peggy Kamuf (ed.), *A Derrida Reader: Between the Blinds*, New York, 1991. See also 'History, Theory, Cultural Politics', in Keith Moxey, *The Practice of Theory*, London, 1994, 1–19.

9 Moxey, *The Practice of Theory*, 8.

10 Raoul Mortley, *French Philosophers in Conversation: Derrida, Irigaray, Levinas, Le Doeuff, Schneider, Serres*, London, 1991, 96–7.

11 One possibility is to replace the broad historical/institutional masternarratives with restricted, personal and 'imaginary' ones. According to Lacanian psychoanalytical theory such personal narratives ultimately empower the individual through a more direct understanding of the world he inhabits. Hayden White, 'The Value of Narrativity in the Representation of Reality', in *The Content of Form: Narrative Discourse and Historical Representation*, Baltimore, MD, 1987, 1–25, esp. 20–1.

12 Moxey, *The Practice of Theory*, 13.

13 Dominick LaCapra, *Rethinking Intellectual History: Texts, Contexts, Language*, Ithaca, NY, 1983, 29–30.

14 Albert Camus, 'The Myth of Sisyphus', in *The Myth of Sisyphus and Other Essays*, New York, 1955, 88–91.

15 Rainer Maria Rilke, '9th Elegy', in *The Divine Elegies*, New York, 1972.

16 Robert Mugerauer, 'Derrida and Beyond', in Nesbitt (ed.), *Theorizing*, 184–97, 196; Karsten Harries, 'Thoughts on a Non-Arbitrary Architecture', *Perspecta: The Yale Architectural Journal*, 20, 1983, 10–20.

17 Christian Norbert-Schulz, 'Heidegger's Thinking on Architecture,' *Perspecta*, 20, 1983, 61–8, 68.

18 Martin Heidegger, *Poetry, Language, Thought*, New York, 1971, 152; Norbert-Schulz, 'Heidegger's Thinking', 64–5.

19 Christian Norbert-Schulz, 'The Phenomenon of Place', *Architectural Association Quarterly*, 4, 1976, 3–10.

20 Jean-Paul Sartre, *Nausea*, New York, 1964, 195–9.

21 Louis I. Kahn, 'Order Is', *Perspecta: The Yale Architectural Journal*, 3, 1955, 59; Kahn, *Conversations with Students: Architecture at Rice* 26, Princeton, NJ, 1969, 22–4, 28. See Norbert-Schulz's essay, which explores and interprets the theoretical basis of Kahn's writings and links them to Heidegger: 'Kahn, Heidegger and the Language of Architecture', *Oppositions*, 18, 1979, 29–47; Christian Norberg-Schulz, *Genius Loci: Towards a Phenomenology of Architecture*, New York, 1980, 197–8.

22 Norbert-Schulz, 'The Phenomenon of Place', 426.

23 Alexander Tzonis and Liane Lefaivre, 'Why Critical Regionalism Today?', *Architecture and Urbanism*, 236, May 1990, 22–33, 25.

24 Kenneth Frampton, 'Prospects for a Critical Regionalism', *Perspecta*, 20, 1983, 147–62, 148. See also by Frampton, 'The Isms of Contemporary Architecture', in *Modern Architecture*

and the Critical Present, New York, 1982, 61–82.

25 Distancing the new critical regionalism from the populist, modernist and historicist rhetoric of architecture, Frampton explains in 'Critical Regionalism', 148–9:

> Critical Regionalism is a dialectical expression. It self-consciously seeks to deconstruct universal modernism in terms of values and images which are locally cultivated, while at the same time adulterating these autochthonous elements with paradigms drawn from alien sources.... Critical Regionalism recognizes that no living tradition remains available to modern man other than the subtle procedures of synthetic contradiction. Any attempt to circumvent the dialectics of this creative process through the eclectic procedures of historicism can only result in consumerist iconography masquerading as culture.

26 For the concept and technique of 'de-familiarization', or promoting and emphasizing perception in art and architecture by 'making the familiar seem strange', see Victor Shklovsky, 'Art as Technique', in Lee T. Lemon and Marion J. Reis (eds), *Russian Formalist Criticism: Four Essays*, Lincoln, NE, 1965, 3–24; Tzonis and Lefaivre, 'Why Critical Regionalism?', 29. See also by the same authors: *Classical Architecture: The Poetics of Order*, Cambridge, MA, 1986, 273–87.

27 Tzonis and Lefaivre, 'Why Critical Regionalism?', 31.

28 Marco Frascari, 'The Tell-The-Tale Detail', in Nesbitt (ed.), *Theorizing*, 500–14. See also Maria A. Crippa, *Carlo Scarpa: Il pensioro, il disegni, I progetti*, Milan, 1984; Bianca Albertini and Sandro Bagnoli, *Carlo Scarpa: l'architettura nel detaglio*, Milan, 1988; Francesco Dal Co and Giuseppe Mazzariol (eds), *Carlo Scarpa: The Complete Works*, New York, 1985. For Kahn's admiration of Scarpa, see *Accademia Olimpico: Carlo Scarpa*, Vicenza, 1974, 1. For Barragan, see Federico Zanco (ed.), *Luis Barragan: The Quiet Revolution*, Milan, 2001; Antonio R. Martinez, *Luis Barragan, Mexico's Modern Master, 1902–1988*, New York, 1996; Raoul Rispa (ed.), *Barragan: The Complete Works*, Princeton, NJ, 2003.

29 K. Frampton, 'Critical Regionalism', 147–62. See also P. Ricoeur, 'Universal Civilization and National Cultures', in *History and Truth*, Evanston, IL, 1961, 276.

30 For Dimitris and Susana Antonakakis, see Alexander Tzonis and Liane Lefaivre, 'The Grid and the Pathway: An Introduction to the Work of Dimitris and Susana Antonakakis', *Architecture in Greece*, 15, 1981, 164–78. For Sedad Hakki Eldem, see Sibel Bozdoğan *et al.*, *Sedad Eldem: Architect in Turkey*, Singapore, 1987, and London, 1991. For Geoffrey Bawa, see Brian B. Taylor, *Geoffrey Bawa*, New York, 1995. For Hassan Fathy and New Gournia, see *Architecture for the Poor*, Chicago, IL, 1973.

31 Karsten Harries, *The Ethical Function of Architecture*, Cambridge, MA, 1997; Harries, 'Thoughts on a Non-Arbitrary Architecture', 10–20. See also J. Bruner, *Actual Minds, Possible Worlds*, Cambridge, 1986.

32 Italo Calvino, *Invisible Cities*, New York, 1972, 17–18.

33 Session chaired by B. McLaren and V. Prakash. The abstracts of the papers will be published in a forthcoming issue of the *Journal for the Society of Architectural Historians*.

6
Frontiers of fear
Architectural history, the anchor and the sail

Suna Güven

When allied bombing sliced away the medieval and modern housing from the hill-side town of Palestrina (Roman Praeneste) in 1944, the hitherto unknown architecture of the Sanctuary of Fortuna Primigenia was unexpectedly revealed for investigation by archaeologists and architects. Through this accidental recovery a new and important chapter was opened in the study of Roman Republican architecture. By a similar feat of catastrophic revelation the receding waters of the recent *tsunami* in December 2004 removed many centuries of accumulated sand, bringing to light well-preserved sculpted temples in the Far East.

Whether the bonus of serendipity, or the reward of unflagging intellectual resolve in scientific exploration, there is no question that the body of historic architecture is continually growing. New stock is unremittingly replenishing an already gargantuan corpus with fresh discoveries in different parts of the world. By the same token, there is certainly no abatement in the creation of new architecture. Buildings are continuously being built in every part of the globe from rural backwaters to metropolitan hubs. As both novel and more-tested formulations of the man-made environment are generated at an accelerating rate in response to pressures of urbanization and heterogeneous demands, the new buildings keep mushrooming in great quantity and variety with no end in sight.

Once built, every construction is a potential member of the club of architectural history that sometimes includes unbuilt or unrealized projects too. No matter how recent, due to the fact that they constitute a product of architecture physically completed in what is already the past, the new buildings of the present get added to the already enormous data of architectural history. Not surprisingly, these newcomers are currently accumulating faster than the architecture of past centuries.

Yet there exists another dimension beyond inflation in numbers that needs to be reckoned with and which poses a further complication in grasping the material range of architectural history. Added to the hard-core statistics is the question of multiple lives in buildings. Adaptive reuse, the heyday of occupation, and periods of oblivion, demolition and rebuilding are all building blocks in the creation of the master narrative in architectural history even though, taken on their own, each episode might not be equally significant or similar in duration. In terms of physical being, therefore, there is no vacuum or break in the extant life of buildings since each time capsule is linked through architectural continuity. Moreover, the active role of the perceptual dimension is yet another major instrument in building the narrative text. This is because the time of the maker and different users together with the historical consciousness of successive beholders all fuse in the present, which is renewed with each reading of the architectural object. In such an overlapping and hybrid act of mapping, every building becomes inscribed accordingly, acquiring a new age and meaning. As a result, each reading is valid at the time the reading is accomplished, that is, in its own present.[1] Hence, the physical and perceptual boundaries concerning the architectural object become porous, resulting in the transmutation of space and time and layered narratives. Attempting to harness this ever-increasing data of architecture of the distant or more recent past and the present is simply daunting by any standard and presents serious challenges for understanding the epistemological nature and production of architectural knowledge.

The challenge appears to be two-fold: on the one hand, sheer quantity and variety are storming the traditional stronghold of established canons. Who decides what to include or exclude, and how much? Is there a limit to the canon? If we regard the canon as a container, can the canon 'burst'?[2] In reverse, is it possible to have an architectural history without a canon? However, abolishing the canon implies replacing it with a workable substitute that has been lacking so far. Yet, given the present conjecture in architectural history, the grip of an organizing canon appears tighter than it actually is. While there is no blueprint for a history of world architecture, there are no strong taboos either. In the English-speaking world, the material limits became delineated in a fairly consistent armature simply because they were within the intellectual and geographical grasp of the western, and masculine, mind. Interaction with other mindsets usually occurred in the form of the dominating idiom becoming translated in a one-way traffic. Opening up physical boundaries globally has now begun easing conceptual boundaries toward greater equity with expanded representation although the latter appears to be the more difficult of the two and the results remain to be seen.

On the other hand, in tandem with the upward-swing of the material spectrum, the way of dealing with this corpus has itself become the focus of animated methodological controversy. This has led to the peculiar conundrum whereby theory sometimes tends to subsume the very material that it was originally meant to put in order, explain and rationalize in a conceptual framework. While the end of architectural history does not appear in sight, the discourse on its method and range as a discipline in its own right has grown almost as much as the main object of the field. Absolute emancipation from methods of inquiry borrowed from other fields toward a solely architectural way of thinking remains a desideratum. Yet, as architectural history simultaneously appropriates and trespasses porous boundaries in diverse fields, it is said to undermine its own legitimacy as an independent discipline. For some, such as Mark Jarzombek, the fuddled position of architectural history is indicated by bracketing 'architectural' within history.[3] If indeed there never was absolute autonomy, this is understandable. Losing ground in what never was would not mean much. However, relegating architectural history to simply another category of history like the history of plants, coins, food, automobiles, airplanes, etc. would be an oversimplification. From this standpoint, the distinction between 'history of architecture' and 'architectural history' is not a twisted way of saying the same thing but carries a more profound implication. Both labels imply a mapping of the past with architecture as the main object. In the former, architecture is classified in the same way as the other objects in question by using a linear and probably evolutionary sequence. Less clear is the latter 'architectural' brand of thinking about the past. While it is differentiated from the former in terms of method, its hybrid nature embedded in a cross-section of disciplines evades a clear and sharp definition to everyone's satisfaction.

In this hybrid nature, standing out as innate to architecture are the components of visuality and space. Visual history and spatial history each constitute a self-referential equation peculiar to the architectural brand of history. Although visuality and space are inseparable bed-fellows in art history too, the object of art history is often a subordinate element of architectural, and in a wider sense, environmental space. However, reducing the art object into a mere object of contemplation devoid of social and cultural function is neither tenable as articulated by Richard Leppert,[4] nor the issue here. Yet, while the autonomy of the art object is not to be denied, in spatial terms, the direct immediacy of a more comprehensive contextual experience is often missing. In wishing to penetrate the hearts and minds of the people for ideological purposes, Benito Mussolini manipulated precisely this over-reaching feature of architecture. His conviction in the powers of architecture is crystal clear: 'In my opinion, the greatest of all arts is architecture, because it comprises them all.'[5] In contrast to architecture, therefore, experiencing the space of an art work involves a secondary gear since it is generally perceived in a piecemeal fashion, through representation or within the larger context. Compromised autonomy of a similar sort may be an inherent danger in architectural history also, especially when the dimension of history gains ascendancy at the expense of its object. When this happens, architecture becomes merely the space of history, providing a stage for its events, and loses its capacity as an active agent in forming history. It then follows that recording, explaining and then reading the architectural object with a balanced historical view and with the requisite sensitivity toward spatial and visual dynamics, which are both contained and generated by architecture, constitute the essence of architectural history. On the other hand, since history involves plotting human actions and establishing salient relationships in their causality, the historical dimension of architecture inevitably intersects with the humanistic disciplines. Thus, in reading the past, finer tuning in territorial definition has emerged as a pressing question in recent scholarship. Among others, Dana Arnold has advocated 'unpacking' the terms of 'history' and 'architecture' in order to understand what architectural history really is.[6] Yet, in all fairness, one has to admit that architectural history is feeling the pinch of upheavals in an arena transcending its own disciplinary boundaries. The crisis in the humanities[7] has had its toll also in architectural history.

Looking at the course of architectural history in the twentieth century, however, one thing is tantalizingly clear: the state of the field has been anything but stagnant. New approaches in scope and method have always injected a certain momentum, if not catapulting spirit. The body of architectural history has expanded spherically and not in a single direction, all the time pushing the limits of the field centrifugally outwards. In this expanded panorama there are stepping-stones that stand out more than others in their relatively early interdisciplinarity. For example, Lewis Mumford's *Sticks and Stones: A Study of American Architecture and Civilization* was first published in 1924. When Mumford wrote a preface to the second edition thirty years later, he justified his 'lack of generous emendations' by the pioneering nature of the original version:

> Such a book could have been written only by a young man, with no reputation to risk, with no vested interest to protect, bold to the point of recklessness, and ready to intrude where professors, if not angels, would fear to tread. Doubtless if I had a better sense of the difficulties or of my own limitations, I should have left the field alone.[8]

What instigated such trepidation and a certain sense of lament on Mumford's part was not only his choice of subject matter but his way of treating it. As a trailblazer, Mumford opened new ground because his examination of American architecture was not based on forming an exhaustive catalog of buildings with their isolated histories; it was important to relate the buildings to their urban or rural setting and to do so required broaching other fields, such as city and regional planning and geography. More than half a century later, William MacDonald hailed Spiro Kostof as a 'master interpreter' of architecture and urbanism, praising his acute eye and intimate knowledge in weaving together settings and rituals in the writing of architectural history.[9] Doors opened by Mumford and Kostof have never closed. In fact, doors to many other fields, new and old, have exponentially multiplied, although the dust coming from outside has occasionally obscured what is within.

Naturally, writing architectural history and writing about architectural history share some common denominators that confront those engaged in their production. Not unlike Mumford, Marvin Trachtenberg felt he was 'skating on thin ice' when he was invited to compile his observations on the field of architectural history as a whole. Faced with the enormity of the undertaking, his 'main reaction' at the outset was one of 'apprehension' but he was not overwhelmed by it. Interestingly enough, despite the proliferation of architectural publications, the lack of an overview of architectural history comparable to areas like art history caught his eye, leading him to remark about architectural historians:

> too much of their writing is heavy, obscure, or pretentious, and often concerned with technical matters understandably unpalatable or irrelevant to readers devoted to drawings, paintings and sculptures. Architecture is a subject not without difficulties, and a great deal – too much – of its literature fails to make this less so.[10]

The formidable range and the complexity of method to manage architectural history is not a new phenomenon of an age where the rate in the production and dissemination of information and knowledge has reached explosive proportions. Through the thick lens of two thousand years, Vitruvius appears as a besieged intellectual, bombarded by the changes in architecture and circumstance that he was unwilling and, to a certain extent, unable to absorb. Vitruvius was a man of his age and not ours. However, it would not be an exaggeration to claim that, not unlike Mumford and Trachtenberg, he also approached the task of compiling his *Ten Books on Architecture* (*De architectura libri decem*) with a certain feeling of trepidation and fear. Ironically, his style of writing – like some of his modern counterparts – suffers from stilted and obtuse language that has tormented his translators. Apart from the validity of the theoretical premise today, there are those who still find that Vitruvius' ideas 'perennially return to invigorate architecture'.[11] Whether considered of instrumental value for architectural production or possessing more theoretical universal validity, Vitruvius' relevance nowadays is attested by the new editions that keep coming.

Although Vitruvius' underlying incentives may have been different, his aim was to reconcile theory (*ratio*) and practice (*fabrica*) in order to assemble the body of architectural knowledge.[12] Translated in modern terms, this is nothing else than bringing together the worlds of the architect and the historian, which are increasingly floating away from each other. For some, there are 'two architectural histories, one based in monuments and linked to art history and archaeology, and the other based in ideas and linked to architectural practice' that need to be brought together.[13] Yet the territorial limit of where these 'ideas' are to come from and how they can be internalized for the purposes of architectural history is a challenge akin to what Vitruvius was facing. Even though Vitruvius' avowed task was to formulate a conceptual framework for the field of architecture at large, it is to be understood that writing about architecture or its products requires a clear idea of the polyvalent mechanisms that are intimately related in the creation of both. For Vitruvius, this entailed a working knowledge of nearly a dozen fields, including writing, drawing, geometry, optics, arithmetic, history, philosophy, physics, music, law, medicine and astronomy. However, this did not mean acquiring the thorough knowledge or know-how of a practicing expert in each area. In other words, one need not be a doctor, lawyer or climatologist to comprehend the importance of salubrity, ethics and proper setting, just as one does not have to be a trained semiologist or cultural anthropologist in dealing with architectural history today. Vitruvian dictum deemed it sufficient to have an overall common sense and rationality derived from many current fields in shaping architectural production and understanding. Any understanding of process therefore is a laborious undertaking and involves reconstructing the mental frames that are instrumental in the formation of the architectural product. Once formulated, this reconstruction is above temporal and geographical distance. So, when dealing with Roman, Ottoman or Turkish Republican architecture, or even the present (which incidentally becomes the past as it is talked about), what changes is not the mental processes used in the reconstruction but rather the nature of the evidence used and its varying degree of accessibility and availability. Of course, the mental processes themselves are not entirely static and bear a cultural stamp.

Toward the end of her mission as editor of the *Journal of the Society of Architectural Historians*, Zeynep Çelik concluded her open forum on the teaching of architectural history globally.[14] Her results show that, like flowing water finding its course, architectural history is adapting to changing conditions – as it has done in the past – and is more vibrant and intellectually stimulating than ever. Navigating in uncharted waters naturally brings with it fears of the unknown and the yearning for a compass. In reaching for new horizons, the sight of land might sometimes disappear. But with strong oars and a sturdy hull the safety of familiar land will provide anchor until it is time to sail again (Figure 6.1). This metaphor is enhanced by another borrowed from John Lewis Gaddis and reused here. It is based on Caspar David Friedrich's painting *The Wanderer Above the Sea of Fog*, where a man with his back turned to us faces a scene at once mysterious, turbulent and tranquil. Perched on a rock, his stance appears heraldic. If there is fear and awe, it is not openly revealed. Gaddis has used this image as a metaphor for the 'landscape of history', remarking that it is not easy to determine whether the gaze is directed forward, or backward, to the landscape of the past or the future.[15] But does it really matter, since one cannot go back without going forward? From what may be discerned, taking issue with adherents of doomsday for architectural history seems as remote as a snowball in fire.

Figure 6.1 Vitruvius: figure at the end of Book 5, *Vitruvius*, Rusconi edition, Venice, 1590. (Bodo Ebhardt, *Vitruvius*, Ossining, NY, 1962, 29.)

Notes

I would like to thank Chris Otto for introducing me to the wonderful book *The Landscape of History* by John Lewis Gaddis.

1 Mary Hesse, 'Past Realities', in Ian Hodder and Michael Shanks (eds), *Interpreting Archaeology: Finding Meaning in the Past*, London and New York, 1998, 45–7; Geoffery R. Elton probes the issue of identity in 'Putting the Past Before Us', in Stephen Vaughan (ed.), *The Vital Past: Writings on the Uses of History*, Athens, GA, 1985, 42.

2 The metaphor is borrowed from Christopher Steiner, 'Can the Canon Burst?', *The Art Bulletin*, 78: 2, June 1996, 213–17. Although Steiner utilizes marginalized African slingshots to make his point in the field of art history, he stresses that he is challenging not the category formation but the social structure of the canon.

3 Mark Jarzombek, 'The Disciplinary Dislocations of (Architectural) History', *Journal of the Society of Architectural Historians*, 58: 3, September 1999, 488–93.

4 Richard Leppert, *Art and the Committed Eye: The Cultural Functions of Imagery*, Boulder, CO, 1996.

5 A. E. Ludwig, *Colloqui con Mussolini*, Milan, 1932, 203, quoted in Luisa Quartermaine, 'Slouching Towards Rome: Mussolini's Imperial Vision', in Tim Cornell and Kathryn Lomas (eds), *Urban Society in Roman Italy*, London, 1996, 211.

6 Dana Arnold, *Reading Architectural History*, London and New York, 2002, 3.
7 Belgin Turan, 'The Crisis in the Humanities and the Writing of History: A Tentative Inquiry via Althusser', *METU Journal of the Faculty of Architecture*, 17: 1–2, 5–13.
8 Lewis Mumford, *Sticks and Stones: A Study of American Architecture and Civilization*, 2nd rev. edn, New York, 1955, v.
9 William L. MacDonald, 'Spiro Konstantinos Kostof 1936–1991', *Society of Architectural Historians Newsletter*, June 1992, 2–3.
10 Marvin Trachtenberg, 'Some Observations on Recent Architectural History', *Art Bulletin*, 70: 2, June 1988, 208.
11 Thomas Gordon Smith, *Vitruvius on Architecture*, New York, 2003, 7.
12 John Onians, *Bearers of Meaning: The Classical Orders in Antiquity, the Middle Ages, and the Renaissance*, Princeton, NJ, 1990, 33.
13 Nicholas Adams, 'History in the Age of Interpretation', *Journal of the Society of Architectural Historians*, 53: 1, March 1994, 6.
14 Zeynep Çelik, 'Editor's Concluding Notes', *Journal of the Society of Architectural Historians*, 62: 1, March 2003, 121–3. Although the role of requirements in teaching has been, and still is, a primary factor in the production of architectural history, the discussion of the subject has been deliberately left out of this essay.
15 John Lewis Gaddis, *The Landscape of History*, New York, 2002, 1, 151 and cover. Perhaps it should be noted here that, in using this image, Gaddis was in turn inspired by Paul Johnson, who also used the painting on the cover of his book *The Birth of the Modern*.

Part II
Critical engagements

7
Questions of Ottoman identity and architectural history

Tülay Artan

Was there really such a thing as 'Ottoman' architecture? Did it possess (or represent), always, everywhere and at all levels, a universal common language? The question itself has been repeatedly posed, and neither is my first approximation to an answer going to sound entirely original.[1] The central canon that was established in the capital for the public, monumental embodiments of imperial institutions was disseminated virtually everywhere through a whole array of mosques and tombs, baths, khans or caravanserais, bridges, hospices and graveyards.[2] As ultimate icons of the imperial legacy, Ottoman mosques seemed to reach for and to emulate the heavens with their domes and minarets, and, within their sacred interiors, royal loggias looked upon stately ceremonies extolling the grandeur of the patrimonial, absolutist dynastic state[3] – whose sovereign, as captured in his idealized sixteenth-century portraits,[4] became a patron of the arts for all times. The most sumptuous among these mosques were lavishly decorated with blue-and-white wall tiles, red or crimson silks and carpets, and woodwork and metalwork that bore the insignia of the court workshops. Under the patronage of Süleyman I (d. 1566), a genius like Sinan (d. 1588) played a crucial role in both the iterative making and the transmission of a readily accessible Ottoman identity, magnified and inscribed in stone, which separated the Ottoman realm from the rest of the world.[5]

This imperial identity also constituted an ideal for the lesser members of the Ottoman ruling elite.[6] As a plethora of state officials, in their capacity both as military bureaucratic or provincial governor-patrons, and as artists and architects, were incorporated into 'the Ottoman way', certain archetypes and artistic canons, as well as rituals, ceremonies, codes and manners, designed at the court and developed at the capital, were transported to the provincial centres, serving to spread the imperial image, to co-opt provincial elites, and to legitimize Ottoman rule. So successful was this 'Ottoman-ness' that, even when the grip of the central administration began to weaken, the established artistic and cultural order continued to serve as an instrument of consensus.

Thus, some forces that would emerge or be labelled as 'centrifugal' in later centuries, such as powerful landholders, self-aggrandizing local dynasties, or communities in search of autonomy, were not as comprehensively excluded or self-excluded as is commonly thought, but came to participate in various power-sharing arrangements with the central government.

The conventional picture: decline, decentralization and loss of imperial identity

Much as I agree with some of the key components of this vision, there are a few elements with which I take issue. The first has to do with a certain dichotomy that is established between public monumentality and the sphere of daily, private or residential use, a distinction that concerns architecture in particular. The second has to do with the long-term dynamics emanating from this 'classical' stasis. Furthermore, both weak links are interconnected in various ways.

The notion of an imperial canon limited to the sphere of the state and hence to monumental architecture is too restrictive. The dearth of residential architecture in Ottoman lands, of which only a very few eighteenth- and nineteenth-century examples have survived, plays a dual role in this approach. First, it enhances the position of (mostly, but not entirely religious) monumental architecture as the sole representative of Ottoman aesthetic/visual identity, which seems to swallow and subsume all the rest. Second, as it heightens the conventional understanding of the extant, omnipresent public buildings as 'Ottoman', at least in Turkey residential architecture comes to be contraposed to this as 'Turkish'.[7] This is a manifestation of Republican nationalist ideology built around the rejection of a hated *ancien régime*, coupled with an ethnocentric identity thought to be suitable for the nation-state. By the same token, elsewhere in the nation-states that were born in the process of the disintegration of empire, we are also supposed to have Greek, Bulgarian, Albanian, Serbian, Syrian, Egyptian, Lebanese, etc. 'national styles' embedded in their residential architecture(s).

Furthermore, what are generally regarded as the outstanding examples of the vernacular architecture of the Ottoman lands, whether in the eastern or the western provinces of the empire, are made to fall neatly within the current (eroded, but still dominant) historical paradigm that sets up a 'Classical Age' to be followed by 'Decline' and then 'Collapse': (1) as the centre became weaker, the lesser gentry are said to have taken over not just in politics but also in artistic patronage; (2) faced with military defeats and economic setbacks, both the centre and the provinces are perceived to have given in to modernization and westernization; and (3) the ruling elite is believed to have retreated into hedonism. The assumed demise of both the 'genius' and the 'patron' has resulted in a shallow neglect of, and even disdain for, post-sixteenth-century aesthetics and patronage. This has led to a treatment of all forms of Ottoman cultural expression, including literature, music, painting and the decorative arts, as undergoing a process of disintegration, of a relapse into disunity and incoherence, from which the loss of an artistically constructed imperial identity emerges as running parallel to and echoing the break-up of empire.

The challenges of a new historiography

The reappraisals currently underway in seventeenth- and eighteenth-century Ottoman historical studies are, unfortunately, largely bypassed in this overall approach. Debates around the formation of the modern state prior to the Tanzimat era, for example, or the redefinition of the relationship of the centre with the provinces, extending to the contraposition of a notion of the 'reconquest' of those provinces to the earlier and much more traditional idea of 'decentralization', as well as new perspectives on cycles of rebellion, repression and reinvention – these and other scholarly developments have been largely overlooked by art and architectural historians.[8] This is a pity, for only if the idea of a certain reconsolidation (re-centralization) of collective rule en route to modern state-formation is fully taken into account, does it become possible to capture, fully and thoroughly, the post-classical cultural struggles that it entailed both at the Ottoman court and throughout the empire. Conversely, a fresh analysis of what was happening in the cultural sphere is capable of further explaining and elaborating political-institutional developments.

The standard historical view suggests that, from the early seventeenth century onwards, a process of partial breakdown followed by an (also partial) reconstitution of the power bloc ruling the Ottoman empire was set in motion. As various socio-economic conflicts surfaced among sub-groups of the one and only ruling establishment, their increased proclivity for contestation was reflected in a fierce cultural competition within the same class (which now included provincial notables as well as a new, non-hereditary but close-knit network of dignitaries at the centre). Thus there set in a deepening factional competition, which – it is true – initially made it more difficult to sustain a single corporate identity, a relatively homogeneous Ottoman-ness, because of all the changes that were taking place in the composition of the ruling elite (both at the centre and in the provinces). Instead, there developed a more open kind of intra-elite power struggle, which was waged in both real-political and cultural-symbolic terms.[9]

This first phase of partial breakdown and decomposition, however, neither lasted forever nor resulted in complete and irreversible disintegration. Rather, it eventually led into a newly coalescing realignment. By way of their artistic and architectural patronage, the newfangled provincial elites of the later Ottoman centuries strove to insert themselves into a new kind of 'imperial' identity that was no longer so loaded with patriarchalism or absolutism (of the centre). It is this process that tends to be obliterated from two different ends by two diametrically opposed points of view. Thus, while it passes unnoticed by Turkish art and architectural historians adhering to the 'decline' paradigm, it is also implicitly rejected by non-Turkish nationalist discourses that cling to the notion of their local renaissances – national 'awakenings' said to have been preceded by the absence of any internal dynamics of significance. Traditionally, the former have sought comfort in the ephemeral brilliance of the so-called 'Tulip Age' and 'Ottoman Baroque' (both of which I regard as a misnomer), while the latter have chosen to ideologize and promote their respective national or regional styles. In between, there is supposed to be nothing but darkness and bleak stagnation.

The relevance of Arel's studies of Aegean magnates' architectural patronage

To this conventional picture, a thought-provoking challenge has been mounted by the architectural historian Ayda Arel in her study of the architectural patronage of the Cihanoğulları, a provincial dynasty in Aydın.[10] Arel describes the Cihanoğulları as having fostered a novel style marked with baroque and rococo embellishments of the so-called Italian school, but mixed with anachronistic gothic forms. Attributing the initiation of the hybrid style in question to Greeks fleeing to western Anatolia before and after the Morean revolt of 1770, Arel characterizes it as a 'family style' embodied both in the mosques and the mansions commissioned or used by the House of Cihan. In other studies on the fortified (*müstahkem*) estates or manors (*çiftlik*) of western Asia Minor, Arel explores the indigenous medieval roots of a particular type of walled-in residential complex featuring 'towers' (or keeps or donjons), and convincingly argues for such mansions as constituting a 'local type'.[11]

It is true that, despite their distinctively local decorative vocabulary, certain easily recognizable archetypes, such as ablution fountains (*şadırvan*), porticoes (*revak*) or royal loggias (*mahfil*), continue to mark provincial Aydın mosques (and their annexes) as 'Ottoman'. However, the fortified mansions of western Anatolia are a class apart. Structurally comparable to European manor houses (if not full-fledged castles), or even to convents, but, at the time, part and parcel of thriving agricultural estates, they stand out as a conscious choice complementing the more mosque-based 'official' canon. In the absence of war or other major threats such as Celâlî-type insurgent activity, this raises the question of whether this particular choice represents a degree of continuity with a late medieval Turkish-Ottoman *state* tradition. This cannot be easily answered. But it is clear that, in terms of scale, there was no cash-supported effective demand or social patronage that could have aspired to and achieved comparable grandeur before the eighteenth century. The architectural type/style in question displays an unexpected degree of novelty and creativity simply because it is employed by (if not entirely new, then at least) freshly resurgent groups of provincial gentry and notables that are now coming out of the woodwork to reclaim a reconfigured place for themselves within the imperial matrix. Arel writes:

Since it is impossible to find a place for these building types in our established inventory of Ottoman architectural typologies, it becomes facile to regard them – superficially – as either regional innovations or anachronisms. Actually, however, they should be perceived as paradigms of local culture that were breathing relatively easily as pressure from the central administration slackened – as sedimentary layers of a cultural legacy that were just coming to the surface.[12]

Thus, she retrieves the study of the provincial, vernacular architectures of the Ottoman Empire from a 'what is monumental is Ottoman, what is residential is local-national' type of dichotomy, and provides such studies with a much more socio-political, i.e. much more *historical*, and therefore potentially more fruitful, theoretical-methodological basis.

Ottoman geography reconsidered

One reason why Arel's work has not received the attention it deserves may be that the geography whose architectural output she has been studying falls within the borders of contemporary Turkey (even though she traces the origins of the decorative vocabulary of the Cihanoğlu 'family style' to Chios, once a major trading emporium in the Aegean Sea). It is a case of not being able to please anyone: within the 'decline' paradigm of Turkish architectural historians, there should be no room for innovation in (western) Anatolia in the late eighteenth century, while, for nationalists elsewhere, the links that Arel suggests between fortified mansions in Asia Minor and comparable examples of residential architecture in many Balkan locations (ranging from Kamenicë in Albania through Melnik in Bulgaria to Mani in the Morea),[13] are an anathema – in each and every case, these diverse local styles are supposed to be connected only vertically to specific medieval (read: *national*) precursors, and not horizontally to any shared Ottoman experience that might force nationalist historians to look for undesired parallels, offshoots or collaterals in the Ottoman 'heartlands' in Anatolia.

But where, really, were these Ottoman 'heartlands'? How did the Ottomans themselves conceive of their geography, including their various regions? What did Rumelia and Anatolia mean for them? Was Anatolia itself fully and completely Turkish-Ottoman? Where was Turkistan?[14] What was there beyond Rumelia and Anatolia, and what did the architectural traditions of all these diverse lands entail for the elite(s) of the Ottoman empire?

For any definition of separate regions with distinct architectural traditions, an understanding of the aspirations and scope of patronage, as well as of the ways and waves of transmission or dissemination of a given artistic vocabulary, are crucial.[15] To judge from the cases of the Cihanoğulları as well as the Karaosmanoğulları or Katiboğulları in western Anatolia,[16] at least some local dynasties would seem to have sought to relate to and to utilize (and therefore also to revive and to recycle) the available resources and traditions of their own area in their quest for autonomy. The preferred legacies and patronage networks of comparable (provincial) power groups in Rumelia, too, as well as most other parts of the empire, have yet to be investigated in the fashion set out by untiring Arel.

An additional, complicating factor is that not everything begins and ends with the leading families of the gentry and notables as mentioned above. Even within a relatively small sub-region like the Aegean coastal zone, a multiplicity of architectural types/styles is very much in evidence, ranging from the Italianate villas (built in faultless ashlar masonry with bands of red limestone) of the wealthy merchants of Kampos on Chios,[17] through the fortified complexes of timber mansions and rubble-stone towers of the Aydın dynasty at Koçarlı, to the wooden multiple-storey residential complexes of prosperous tax-farmers or revenue-sharers at Birgi, Mudanya, Datça, Milas or Fethiye. All of these bear witness to what was going on behind the imperial façade: the interplay between the supply and the demand sides of vernacular architectures – between the building materials (and corresponding local skills) provided by the various micro-climates of the Mediterranean, and the varying tastes and ambitions at work in provincial communities.

The 'Turkish' house with an open hall: a contested patrimony

One among all these styles is the last of the above-named examples: the multiple-storey wooden house, characterized by an open hall (*hayat*), courtyard (*avlu*) and projections (*çıkma*), which we encounter in many localities, particularly in Rumelia/Rum-ili.[18] Parallel to this wide geographical spread, it has been singled out as encapsulating the 'Ottoman way' in non-monumental architecture, and hence *the* Ottoman house type. Virtually in the same breath, therefore, it has also become a contested patrimony, variously nationalized (along with coffee, with *sarma/dolma* and many other aspects of Ottoman culture) as (originally and authentically) Turkish, Greek, Serbian, Bulgarian or Albanian.

As against this retrospective parcellization of an imperial legacy, I would like to argue, first, that, although it may not have been a single type of house, and certainly not a single type of house that 'travelled' or was disseminated only outward from a single cultural centre, but, more correctly, a set of relatively coherent resemblances dictated both by patronage and by production conditions, and, while it had its material foundations in the life-style of Rumelian landlords,[19] the 'Ottoman house' in question *also* accommodated an elite, Rûmî identity (of which more below) bestowed on these landlords by the state, i.e. from above. Let me note, even at this early point, that this entails not just a purely-from-the-centre, nor, conversely, a purely-from-below view, of this type of residential architecture. Instead, it proposes to address its formation in terms of a Bakhtinian circularity between the centre and the periphery, between the high culture of the Ottoman court and the lower or outlying (but interconnected) culture(s) of the provinces. Second, even given this loose definition of a common language in vernacular architecture, it is all the more striking to note that, as one crosses the straits to proceed east-southeast, all semblance of such commonality seems to disappear long before one arrives in the Arab and Iranian lands.

For there, there is no such thing as a typical (wooden) 'Ottoman house' that marks the old quarters of Urfa, Diyarbakır, Antep, Mardin, Aleppo, Cairo or San'a.[20] The connective tissue of a common vernacular makes way for many different localisms, against which the element of unity residing in the imperial canon of monumental religious architecture radiating outward from İstanbul stands in starker contrast. Nevertheless, even here, within this broader range and variety of localisms, there are certain convergences to be perceived. As virtually autonomous local dynasties kept investing in architecture as a means of constructing an identity of their own, in contrast to the Rumelian type, a single-storey stone house, incorporating Georgian, Armenian, Arab or Iranian building traditions and decorative repertoires, seems to have emerged and to have come to symbolize provincial power. In a way, this is the common denominator between the tripartite İshak Paşa Palace of the Çıldıroğulları crowning a hilltop in Doğu Beyazıd,[21] and the palatial urban residences of the provincial centres of upper Mesopotamia.

Further afield, this single-storey stone house or palace, too, disappears, but a comparable socio-political use of architecture remains. Thus, the 'kethüda style' in eighteenth-century Cairo, too, testifies to a conscious turning to a pre-existing architectural stock in search of a more independent assertiveness.[22] Even in far-away provinces such as Tunisia, local gentry came to invest in residential architecture as a means of constructing an autonomous identity.[23]

The beginnings of a Rûmî consciousness

This overall view, involving a multiplicity of residential types inhabiting small areas, with these small areas then making up two or three big regional patterns, comprising at least (a) the Balkans and western Anatolia, (b) eastern and south-eastern Anatolia, and perhaps also (c) even more distant, outlying territories, all of them conceived in varying degrees of emancipation from the centre, does not really comply with architectural historians' accepted norm. It is true that, to a certain extent, its main (north-west and west vs. south and south-east) division coincides or overlaps with a geo-specific and climate-specific split between stone and timber architecture that has been identified as constituting, and accounting for, the two main zones of 'Ottoman architecture'.[24] But, useful as this notion might be, it also embodies a certain material-technical determinism that does not fully take into account the cultural problems and choices involved. More specifically, it does not do justice to the extent to which the Ottoman elite of the imperial centre was not neutral or equally balanced between its north-west and south-east – that is to say, to the true scope of Rumelia and the Rûmî identity that the Ottomans tailored for themselves, and which provided a ground to build Ottoman-ness upon.

Between being named from the outside and naming themselves, where did the Ottomans stand? From the twelfth century onwards, it was as 'the land of the Turks' that neighbours or adversaries came to regard this geography.[25] Nevertheless, this terminology was not appropriated by its referents. First, the Greater Seljukids, in contact and conflict with Byzantium before and after Manzikert (1071), regarded Anatolia as '*Bilad al-Rûm*', that is to say the land of the Romans. Then the Seljuk main line's Anatolian offshoot came to be called the Seljuks of Rûm. At another step along the same line, the Ottomans, too, were denoted as Rûmî – that is, peoples of the lands of (eastern) Rome – both by themselves and those closest to them:

> This was primarily a geographic appellation [says Cemal Kafadar], indicating basically where those people lived, but it did not escape the attention of the geographers and travellers that the Turco-Muslim populations of Rûm, a frontier region from the point of view of the central lands of Islam, had their own peculiar ways that distinguished them from both the rest of the Muslim world and from other Turks.[26]

The conquest of Constantinople, through which the Ottomans staked out their claim to world power, was followed by expansion both east and west, all of which had ushered in an overbearing, all-consuming dynastic self-confidence by the sixteenth century.[27] It was at this time, too, that dynastic designations for the state, such as *Âl-i Osman*, *devlet-i Âl-i Osman* or (referring to the well-protected domains of the Ottoman dynasty/state), *memleket/memâlik-i mahrûse (-i Osmanî[ye])*, were formulated.[28] Sounding a majestic note, the *Âl-i Osman* version was abridged into *devlet-i Âliye*, which as *devlet-i ebed-müdded* was also pronounced eternal. Simultaneously, formulations emphasizing Islam *(memâlik-i İslam[iye])* and the Roman legacy *(memleket/memâlik-i Rûm/diyâr-ı Rûm/mülk-i Rûm/bûm-i Rûm/iklîm-i Rûm/kurûm-Rûm)* continued to be employed to refer to the Ottoman lands,[29] but their small-time, faith-specific or geography-specific use reveals that, at this stage, at least, it was the (all-encompassing) imperial claim of the dynastic state that mostly defined and identified the Ottoman polity.

Nevertheless, the sultan was frequently referred to in terms of the territories that he ruled over, as in *sultan-ı rûm*, *padişah-ı rûm* or *han-ı rûm* (pl. *mülûk-i rûm*), which was also the case when it came to speaking of elite identities, such as *şuarâ-yı rûm* for the poets, *udebâ-yi rûm* for the belle-letristes, *ulemâ-yı rûm* for the religious scholars and *zurefâ-yi rûm* for the genteel people, of the lands that had been inhabited by the Romans. Hence, too, the historian Selânikî (d. after 1600) spoke easily of the state and the reign as *devlet-ü saltanat-ı Rûm*,[30] as did the bureaucrat and intellectual Gelibolulu Mustafa Âli (d. 1600) of its capital: *pay-i taht-ı Rûm*, i.e. İstanbul.

In terms of his political-ideological concerns, Âli was preoccupied with articulating and examining the ideals and realities of the 'Ottoman way' embodied in *kanun-i Osmanî*, the Ottoman code. He regarded *kanun* as governing matters ranging from taxation to court ceremonial, or from officials' salaries to the paths by which they might be promoted. For Âli, as well as for his peers, *kanun* was prescriptive as well as descriptive; insofar as it defined the structure of government and the nature of Ottoman society, it was *kanun* that enshrined the empire's ideals and made it distinctively Ottoman.[31] Hence, it becomes all the more striking for him, too, to refer to many other aspects of imperial rule (including the throne and the capital) on the basis of Rûm. In fact, there is only one other area to which this general Rûmi inclusivity did not extend, and that has to do with language.

What was it that the Ottoman elite spoke and wrote most of the time? Only on the eve of the Tanzimât did it evolve into *lisân-i Osmanî*.[32] Before (and even after) the pressing demands of the 1800s, the official language of the state, of its ruling house and household, was not called Ottoman but Turkish. Overflowing with borrowings from the neighbouring (Muslim) cultures – i.e. Persian and Arabic – but ultimately based on West Turkish and Çagatay, *lisân-ı Türkî* defined the linguistic identity of the political elite.[33] Not only the state papers, but Ottoman literary production, too, was in *lisân-ı Türkî*. Although other terms like *lisân-ı Rûmî*, *Rûmî sohbet*, *zebân-ı Rûmî* or *Türkî-zebân*, or even the composite *lisân-ı Türkî-i Rûm*[34] were also in use, when it came to language the ethnonym of a singular ethnicity, contrary to all other practices of the empire, seems to have been preferred over the others.

The exorbitation of 'Turkishness' from language to other spheres of culture

In time, and in manifold, complicated ways, this has led to an invalid or misleading ethnic characterization of phenomena outside the sphere of language. Ottoman poetry was one of the channels of the creation and dissemination of such confusion. As already indicated, it was written in *lisân-ı Türkî*. At the same time, however, it borrowed enormously from Persian poetry – including all sorts of clichés about the male homosexual beloved (*mahbub*) as an unruly Turk. As a result, these and other derogatory remarks regarding Turks have come to abound in Ottoman poetry, giving rise to a confusing, contradictory situation, and eventually triggering nationalist reactions of all kinds. One option has been to try to explain away such pejoratives as purely political, or tactically motivated in a short-term situation.[35] Another has been to regard such imperial contempt for Turks as a sign of external pollution or contamination. A third has been to extend the Turkish dimension implied by the use of *lisân-ı Türkî* to retrospectively Turkify the various non-linguistic elements or dimensions of Ottoman society.

Both the second and the third options may be seen to be at work in certain archetypal interpretations of both Ottoman poetry and architecture. The perception that Ottoman poetry was a foreign (meaning Persian) accretion, and the product of a small elite, had already taken root among late Ottoman intellectuals of the Tanzimat era in the nineteenth century. Building on and elaborating this view, first E. J. W. Gibb,[36] and then Fuad Köprülü, attuned to Kemalist Republicanism, were certain that court poetry did not concern itself with the human condition in general – with the daily circumstances, the pains and tragedies, and the spiritual wounds of broader sections of society. When it came to 'folk' (or non-court) literature, of course, Köprülü was a pioneer in terms of regarding it as part and parcel of 'social history'.[37] In doing so, however, he rejected the Rûmî identity of court poets writing in *lisân-ı Türkî*. Instead, he reserved this Rûmî identity only for Anatolian Turks, projecting this supposedly pure and uncontaminated 'folk' as the true repository of Turkish identity.[38]

The same Republican insistence on Turkishness as against Ottoman-ness also leads the architectural historian Doğan Kuban to comprehensively ethnicize, Anatolianize and Turkify key elements or dimensions of Ottoman vernacular architecture.[39] He first takes the multiple-storey wooden house and simply names it a Turkish house, more specifically the *hayatlı Türk evi*, or 'the Turkish house with an open hall' (or with an extended, covered upper floor balcony) – thereby identifying its basic form and layout as peculiarly and distinctively Turkish. Second, he locates its heartlands in Turcoman (i.e. unadulterated) Anatolia. Third, he relates its presence in Rumelia, too, purely to the spread of Turkish settlement. In the end, therefore, we do get something like a common language in vernacular architecture, but one that is focused on Anatolia (as indeed the modern Turkish state came to be), and identified not with Ottoman-ness but with Turkishness.[40] This then becomes an influential paradigm. In her recent study of the subject, the architectural historian Nur Akın, for example, uses 'Ottoman' rather than 'Turkish' in her title, but throughout her text keeps equating Ottoman with Anatolian-Turkish.[41]

Identity through shared characteristics vs. identity through exclusion

'The worst consequence of continuing this ethnicization of the Ottoman tradition,' says Kafadar, 'is that it masks the imperial character of Ottoman history.'[42] Yes, particularly in the heyday of the Ottoman empire, this imperial character had come to be embodied in a certain Rûmî identity that at the outset had been more narrowly geographical, but which by the sixteenth century had come to be embraced by the ruling class(es) of a much larger area – stretching from Yemen to the Crimea, from Bosnia to Basra, and from Morocco to the Caucasus. It imparted a high sense of belonging, and also required the full acceptance and observance of imperial norms and customs, from both the members of the ruling house and its servants, as well as the population at large. And, yes, this is important enough in itself; it is a necessary safeguard against the historian's cardinal sin of anachronism, which in this case manifests itself as a retrospective nationalism. But, by the same token, it is also in the nature of a negative, cautionary measure. Should we stop there? In a more positive, exploratory or investigative sense, was this all there was to the definition, the formation or crystallization, of Ottoman identity?

It is worth noting, in this connection, certain methodological insights being provided by the current state of the art in Cultural Studies. Thus, Stuart Hall, for one, differentiates between a naturalist conception of identity as 'a recognition of some common origin or shared characteristics with another person or group', and 'a discursive approach that sees identification as a construction always in process'. He continues:

> Although a constant continuity of construction does not necessarily suggest that identities can be lost or won at any time, it indicates a state of conditional existence. On the other hand, the conditions under which identities are sustained depend on difference and exclusion, rather than internal sameness. Therefore, they are constructed not outside, but through difference, through a relation to what they are not; and this process should be understood as the product of specific times and specific discursive formations. That is to say, while identities are formed through a process of closure, the norms that determine the exclusion of the other and the different are subject to historical change.[43]

Applied to Ottoman historical studies, this line of thinking would mean that 'Ottoman-ness/*Rûmîlik*', first discussed and hypothesized in the course of the Köprülü–Wittek debate, and further elaborated through the contributions of Halil İnalcık, Norman Itzkowitz, Cornell Fleischer, Gülru Necipoğlu, Cemal Kafadar, Michel Balivet and, most recently, Salih Özbaran, can no longer rest on the understanding of only those elements that were woven into a transcendent dynastic identity. In the long run, a more refined, more pluralistic approach to the multiple socio-cultural and historical determinants of Ottoman identities is needed.

Looking below the surface: the sub-cultures and hybridities of Ottoman society

Presently, however, we are still suffering from a scarcity of research concerning the various sub-cultures and the corresponding identity constructions of Ottoman society. We do have lots of clues concerning a complex, criss-crossing web of ascriptions and descriptions lurking beneath the surface, but we have yet to take a good, long, systematic look at them. We know, for example, that people living inside the Ottoman empire thought a lot in terms of religious or ethno-religious groups, as indicated by denominations like

(*Sünni*) Müslüman, Ermeni, Ysevî/Naserî/Mesihi(yye), Yehudi, Kıptî, Dönek, Kızılbaş, Çingâne, Tatar, Kürd, Bulgar, Çepni or Habeş. With regard to *mütemekkin* urban elites in particular, they also referred to individuals' home towns through adjectives like Bursevî, Birgivî, Konevî or Selânikî. (Other nicknames could extend to (original) profession, to literacy, to eating and drinking habits, or to physical shape, height or obesity.)

Together with references to class, gender, dress codes or rules of etiquette, these could gel into certain broadly regional identities that both coexisted with, and were counterposed to, the dominant Rûmî self-perception and the set of values and obligations that it entailed. The uncouth Turks (*el-etrâk*)[44] constituted one such contraposition, as well as the Arabs and the Acems, who were regarded as foreigners (*ecnebî*), or not belonging to the group (*ecânib*) over the fourteenth–seventeenth centuries.[45] This is also reflected in the inscription on the Sultan's Pool fountain in Jerusalem, which refers to Süleyman I (r. 1520–66) as the *sultan al-rûm wa'l-arab wa'l-ajam*.[46] Ruler of the lands of Rûm, of Arabia and of Persia: this phrase serves well to identify the lands and peoples beyond Rûm-ili (including Anatolia) that the Ottomans brought (sometimes) under their jurisdiction, but which they continued to regard as distinct and not part of the core of that overarching sovereignty.

On the whole, this was also a situation hugely suitable to the emergence and projection of what have come to be regarded, through Cultural Studies but also, and especially, through Post-colonial Studies, as *métissages*: hybrid or patchwork identities. Something like the colonial or post-colonial approach may also provide fruitful insights in the case of the outlying provinces of the Ottoman Empire. Take the case of the famous poet Fuzûlî (d. 1556). He was born, and lived virtually all his life, in the town of Kerbela close to Baghdad; he was emphatically a Shiite; absolutely fluent in Persian, Arabic and Ottoman Turkish, and writing in both Persian and *lisân-ı Türkî*, he achieved fame as Fuzûlî of Baghdad – though hardly any of these crucial facts are adequately accounted for in Turkish textbooks on Turkish literature. Yet they are absolutely indispensable for a proper understanding of Fuzûlî, who alternately eulogizes Shah Ismail Safevid and (after the Ottoman capture of Baghdad in 1534) Süleyman I and his leading dignitaries – who, in his yearning for the capital and the court-city of İstanbul, the lands of the *zârifan* or *zurefâ-yı Türk*, displays the high esteem of provincial intellectuals for the centre, and simultaneously keeps referring to Turks in a derogatory fashion. This is neither political survival skills nor schizophrenia, but a genuine case of multiple identities.[47]

Marginalization of Turks and Turkishness extending into the eighteenth century

Apart from dimensions of hybridity, a particular point that comes out of all this is the extent to which the peoples of the *vilayât-ı şark* or the *diyâr-ı şark* (the Arab and Acem lands), including ethnic appellations like Turks or Turcomans, or urban groups referred to as Diyarbekirlüs or Baghdadîs, were often set in, or set themselves in, opposition to those of the Rûmî lands.[48] With the sole exception of linguistic usage, the inclusion of Turks in this broad group served to emphasize that the civilizing imperial culture, of Rûmî identity, perceived the non-elite as suspicious and 'low'.[49]

Such contempt or dislike actually grew from the sixteenth into the seventeen and eighteenth centuries. As tensions increased between the different factions of the ruling elite (and their supporters in and out of İstanbul), the competition for elite identity also intensified. Discordant sounds were heard more frequently. To some extent, Turks appear to have been caught in between, as not only provincials like Fuzûlî or Nâbî,[50] but even official chroniclers at the centre, or eyeing the centre,[51] began to put them down in a more comprehensive, more strident manner. Thus the *Risâle-i Garibe*, an eighteenth-century Book of Manners (or Curses), lists various clichés through which İstanbuliote Turks were looked down upon as belonging to the lower classes. As such, opprobrium was said to attach not only to them but also to all those who mingled with them. Simultaneously, Turks from central and western Anatolia, from Madanşar (?), Karaman, Siga(la) or Gerede, were castigated for speculation and profiteering.[52] Turks were, however, only one of those races, faiths or classes that could be recognized by their bad manners. But it was not all one way. For example, since the Turkish language still played a pivotal role in determining and allocating elite status, those who did not learn Turkish, or had still not perfected their Turkish pronunciation, or those who, while fluent in Turkish, immediately reverted to their own mother tongue whenever they saw one of their own (unbeliever) kind, were all harshly criticized.[53]

In both its anti-Turkish dimensions and its defence of *lisân-ı Türkî*, the *Risâle-i Garibe* may be said to reflect the view from the top, though it contains no direct reference to any code of Ottoman-ness. Moreover, in the seventeenth and eighteenth centuries, in either court or folk poetry, any explicit references to an Ottoman identity are purely negative in tone, identifying it only in the context of reproaches and laments targeting the state or the ruling elite as oppressors. Before the advent of nationalism(s), in other words, it is difficult to come across manifestations of an all-inclusive cultural Ottoman-ness, which seems to have developed only in a defensive context en route to *Tanzimat* modernization.

The search for a new idiom from mode to style

Referring to a comment in Tursun Beg's *Târih-i Ebü'l-feth* that, after the conquest of Constantinople, architects and engineers came from the lands of *Arab-u Acem-ü Rûm* to work for Mehmed II, Gülru Necipoğlu rightly took Rûm as referring to the existing Ottoman territories.[54] Tursun Beg also happens to mention an 'Ottoman mode' in architecture as early as the 1460s.

Speaking of the pavilions built in the outer gardens of the Topkapı Palace, he identifies the only surviving one (the present Çinili Köşk) as

> a 'tile palace' (*sırça saray*), constructed in the mode of Persian kings (*tavr-ı ekâsire*); the other, across from it, was a pavilion (*kasr*) constructed in the Ottoman mode (*tavr-ı Osmanî*). This last one was a 'wonder of the age', embodying the science of geometry.[55]

At the end of the sixteenth century, we find that 'building style and essential image (*tarz-ı binası ve resm-i esası*)' of mosques built in Cairo during the rule of Ottoman sultans were not in the style and image of the mosques of Arab lands; but they were 'in the style and image of Ottoman mosques (*diyâr-ı Rûm cevâmi tarz ve resminde*)'.[56] In Cafer Efendi's 1614 *Risâle-i Mimariyye*, the only Ottoman treatise on an architect (namely, the life and works of Sedefkâr Mehmet Ağa), which is also a treatise on the science of geometry and a compilation of trilingual (Arabic, Persian, Turkish) terms having to do with architecture, there is only a single reference (as *resm-i Osmanî*) to any kind of Ottoman manner or style in any branch of the arts, and then only in the context of the paging of a monumental Koran.[57] Later in the seventeenth century, Evliya Çelebi referred to congregational mosques in the provinces, sponsored by Ottoman sultans and governors, as in the 'Ottoman style' *(tarz-ı Rûm)*.

This is why, in the heyday of Ottoman architectural grandeur (when there was no need to engage in any comparisons with 'foreign' influences), the *tavr-ı Osmanî* was rarely acknowledged as it came to be rivalled by localisms only in a very few cases.[58] Its sway was so complete that the court itself felt free to experiment with vernacular styles without perceiving of them as such. This was the case with the Baghdad Kiosk (1635) and the Revan (Erevan) Kiosk (1638), put up to commemorate Murad IV's (r. 1623–40) conquest of the cities after which they were named. In opting for the differing architectural modes of the domains that he had newly conquered – says Necipoğlu – Murad IV was following in the footsteps of Mehmed II, who had not only incorporated new kingdoms into his world empire but had also incorporated their artistic representations, as garden pavilions, into the grounds of his new palace.[59]

So this was all safely within the bounds of tradition. When further change came, however, it was duly noted. On the same marble terrace of the Fourth Courtyard occupied by the Baghdad and Revan Kiosks, Murad's successor İbrahim (r. 1640–8), too, decided to build in 1641–2.

> He ordered a lofty and high pavilion to be made
> In an new, joyful manner that should not be in the old style,

says the relevant inscription in the present Circumcision Room,[60] attesting to a consciously innovative intention. The further pursuit and unfolding of this intention over the next fifty years or so, however, becomes difficult to demonstrate through concrete examples simply because architectural output over the rest of the much-troubled seventeenth century diminishes in terms of both numbers and real grandeur while routinely (and dully) repeating the established imperial idiom.

The dynasty's return from Edirne to İstanbul

In the seventeenth century the long-cherished Persianate aesthetic was finally exhausted, leading to the formulation of a more clearly and explicitly Ottoman way in music, literature or the decorative arts.[61] Simultaneously, patronage systems were also becoming more pluralistic, with members of a new elite of high-ranking dignitaries coming to participate more and more in what had hitherto been a virtual monopoly of the sultans. Also, over the second half of the seventeenth century, the sultan and his court had been sojourning in Edirne, where they had been forced to take refuge in 1658. This self-exile also amounted to a hiatus in royal rituals and architectural patronage – until 1675. Then there came yet another, protracted crisis, punctuated by the two disasters of defeat at Kahlenberg (1683) and the Edirne Incident (1703). Their cumulative impact was such as to force the court to return, albeit reluctantly, to İstanbul. By then, a new oligarchy was in positions of power. The ruling elite's self-image had become blurred, and the monolithic (Rûmî) identity that had been adopted and projected since the sixteenth century seems to have lost its definitional distinctiveness. The dynasty was faced with the massive problem of a major reconfiguration and re-legitimation of power.

The challenges of re-inscribing the dynasty into the space and society of the old imperial capital, and of re-creating its symbolic rites of power, had implications for architecture. What immediately emerges is, first, an emphatic reaffirmation of the desire for novelty, for a new style or manner as first implied by İbrahim I sixty-odd years earlier, and, second, a drive to move outside the Topkapı Palace in order to render the sultan and other key members of his household increasingly visible to the populace of İstanbul. The chronicler Râsid testifies to Ahmed III's preference for residential as opposed to monumental religious architecture, as well as for ephemeral timber as opposed to more durable stone construction.[62]

With the court ensconced once more in the urban matrix of İstanbul, a fusion of the monumental and the residential was realized in the waterfront palaces of the royal princesses who were often married to leading dignitaries. But what were the social (and perhaps also cultural) dynamics behind this new, enhanced role accorded to residential architecture, to the point of bestowing on it a degree of monumentalization? In court poetry, over a few centuries there had been a growing number of voices calling for a simpler language, for a *Türkî-i basit*, though it was only with Nedim that they finally won the day at the court. Was residential architecture coming to play the same role of a modernity-related simplification and vernacularization? Or, as in music, which had been largely emancipated from Persian models and repertoires, was architecture in both the capital and the provinces turning to local resources to create a new but still imperial idiom that would suit the need for re-legitimation in the eyes of rising power groups, including the new dignitaries at the centre as well as the provincial gentry and notables?[63] I would argue that it was both – and that this fusion of the monumental and the residential corresponded to, and reflected, something that I hypothesized earlier: a partial breakdown followed by (also partial) reconstitution of the power bloc ruling the Ottoman empire.

Not Anatolia but a broader Rumelia as the core area of the Ottoman empire

This can be taken as yet another manifestation of the extent to which the richest heartlands of the Ottoman Empire were in Rumelia. In various ways, the Ottoman ruling elite was in and of Rûm-ili.[64] The early Ottoman principality expanded primarily into Rumelian space, where they learned to tax sedentary peasantries as they went along, and where the *timar* system grew and developed through successive amalgamations of previous or contemporary land régimes. Simultaneously they absorbed *bashtina* and *pronoia* into their *mukataa* units, just as they absorbed particularly the lesser but numerous elements of the Christian warrior nobilities into their *sipahi* caste or class. Between Edirne and Belgrade, Muslim and Christian (or former Christian) lords alike acquired (or retained) their best and largest holdings, which they tried to privatize and render hereditary as much as possible in the form of *mülks*, *mülk timars* (freeholds) or *vakıfs* (pious foundations). Then, after the court settled in İstanbul, the *devşirme* system, too, got going in this same region, establishing a new channel for recycling 'Byzantino-Balkan aristocrats into grand viziers',[65] though as numerous names or nicknames would suggest (e.g. Sokolovic/Sokollu), local affinities were never entirely erased through such attempted *kapıkulu* deracinations. Still later, royal women and their high-standing husbands, as well as a host of lesser dignitaries, started competing with one another for the lucrative *çiftliks* and tax-farms of the Balkans. And as the *iltizam* (tax-farm) and *malikâne* (life-farm) systems of the seventeenth and eighteenth centuries could operate only through chains of intermediaries extending from the capital all the way down into the provinces, both *voyvodas* and *kocabaşıs* started travelling increasingly frequently between the centre and its Rûmelian periphery as part of the whole process of local factions acquiring patrons in the capital and İstanbuliote factions looking for allies among the gentry and notables.[66]

Shortly after the introduction of *malikâne* in 1695, established as an attempt to cope with the century-long crisis of tax-farming, the most lucrative lands or revenue-districts were redistributed among the female members of the royal family. Hadice the Elder was the sister of Ahmed III. A complete register of this Hadice's revenue-districts (or *appanages*) provides a relatively full account of the revenues accruing to her from some thirty tax-farms in Thrace, western Anatolia and south-east Anatolia over 1713–30.[67] This list, indicative of the long-lasting Ottoman interest in the agricultural and other revenues of Thrace and the Balkans and beyond, would be repeatedly assigned and reassigned to other royal women in decades to come.

The correlation between royal tax-farms and the Rûmî vernacular of 'the Ottoman house' in southeast Europe

Even at first sight, there seems to be a rather striking correspondence between a provisional map of such royal and sub-royal tax-farms, on the one hand, and an equally provisional map of the spread of a common language of vernacular architecture, on the other. In other words, that distinctly recognizable vernacular architecture that we encounter again and again in Rumelia (in Chios and Rhodes in the Aegean, in Shkodra, Ergeri and Berat in Albania, in Thessaly and the Morea, in Skopje, Monastir, Ochrid, Melnik and Plovdiv, in Yenişehir/Larissa, Kavala, Karaferye/Verria or Kesriye/Kastoria, etc.), to the point where it has come to be called 'the Ottoman house' and then to be claimed as their very own by Turkish and other, rival, nationalisms, as repeatedly explained above, is precisely the vernacular architecture the spread and coverage of which turns out to be quite closely correlated with the spread of royal and sub-royal tax-farms over that same Rûmelia. For all of the towns or cities named above were located in districts where the most remunerative *mukataas* coveted by princesses, grand viziers and other high-ranking bureaucrats were located.[68] As the same revenue districts or tax-farms kept passing from one royal woman to another, this picture speaks very strongly for the importance of elite patronage, and of chains and movements of administrative, tax-farming intermediaries in transmitting cultural patronage between the imperial centre and the provinces.

It is difficult to avoid the conclusion that the royal women in question succeeded one another as absentee/rentier overlords at definite localities. In short, the Ottoman royal and sub-royal elites mainly coveted, competed for, and were relatively firmly enracinated in the Balkans, where they also exercised a culturally much more interactive kind of patronage – interactive not only between İstanbul and the provinces, but also between different ethno-religious communities or elements. Here Ottoman Turkish could develop for a time into a lingua franca; here, too, Muslim as well as non-Muslim townsmen or landholders could commission Greek, Serbian or Turkish architects to build their houses using Bulgarian stonemasons and Albanian workers. Ultimately, combined with a particularly strong patronage focus, it was this mobility and interchangeability that created and sustained a common language of vernacular architecture – which, for want of a better word, we can only call Rûmelian or Rûmî – that also spread to Bursa, Mudanya, Göynük, Konya, Kula, Ankara, Beypazarı, Amasya, Tokat, Kastamonu, Safranbolu, Muğla, Datça, or İzmir where, apparently, the royal house was in search of alliances of various kinds.

By the same token, it was these two fundamental, social dimensions of architecture that appear to have been missing beyond *Rûm-ili*, including Anatolia. That the new Turkish nation-state came to be Anatolian-centred should not cause any retrospective, anachronistic confusions in this regard. Neither should one be misled by the relative Turkish-Islamic continuum extending into Anatolia. Such homogeneity does not connote dynamic interaction, and – to repeat – what we are talking about here are not the national blocs of a later era but the court vs. provinces juxtapositions of a traditional empire. Thus, first, royal holdings became less and less frequent in going from west to east within and especially beyond Anatolia, and, second, the postings and prebendal allotments here were much more temporary in nature; the interactions between local elites and the servitors of the Porte were both looser, and did not allow so much scope to the latter as transmitters of the capital's influence.[69]

Ottoman architectural history vs. the history of Ottoman architecture

In conclusion, I would argue that we do face a real choice between talking about Ottoman architectural history and talking about the history of Ottoman architecture. It is the second phrase that is the more problematic, tending as it does to posit a single 'Ottoman architecture' as a cohesive entity. This is also loaded with imperial aspirations of the so-called Classical Age, namely with patriarchalism, absolutism and relative centralization. The first phrase, on the other hand, is potentially looser and more flexible, capable of being understood as the historical study of the totality of architectural output within the Ottoman Empire. It is capable of better coping with critical notions that are mentioned but then decidedly kept in the background in the more orthodox approach – notions about the extent to which 'the imperial cultural tradition was polymorphous, a juxtaposition more than a coherent blending of elements from the traditions out of which it had been forged'.[70]

It is not difficult to understand the whys and wherefores of such suppression or self-censorship. Having, from the late 1920s onwards, proclaimed something of a cultural revolution against the Ottoman *ancien régime*, even when they were moving beyond their most Jacobin, most nihilistic phase, the Kemalists (or Kemalist ideology) could not admit of a direct and frontal reconciliation with *Osmanlılık, Ottomanitas,* the Ottoman way. Instead, they had to resort to special channels, excuses or pretexts. Basically, they dealt in differential fashion with two main groups of phenomena: what could be regarded as really and truly past, and therefore treated as a historical category, and what was still a living legacy. 'Ottoman miniatures', for example, were 'dead', and hence there was no danger in referring to them as *Ottoman* miniatures.

It was the same with literature.[71] But music was alive,[72] and so was residential architecture. Both, therefore, had to be explained and named as other than Ottoman. In the case of residential architecture, this has meant referring it to this or that 'folk' identity. It is time for it, too, to be re-explained on the basis of a new sociology of empire.

Notes

Earlier versions of this paper, provisionally called 'The Imperial vs the Local in Ottoman Architecture. Patronage: What Difference?', exploring the localisms in Greece and Bulgaria respectively, were presented in: *Localities and Empire–Approaches to Ottoman/Greek Civilization*, Chios Workshop organized by the Program in Hellenic Studies, Princeton University, 23–26 September 2000; and *Economy, Society and Culture: XVIIth–XXth Centuries*, Workshop on the Balkan Provinces of the Ottoman Empire, University of Sofia, St Kliment Ohridski, 5–7 October 2001. The present text has been read and commented upon by Halil Berktay, Hakan Erdem, Suraiya Faroqhi and Metin Kunt, for which I am grateful, though responsibility for what remains is entirely mine.

1 This essay takes as its starting point a congress held in 1999, and a corresponding volume published by the Chamber of Architects of Turkey. This was on the occasion of the so-called 700th anniversary of the founding of the Ottoman Empire, and the theme in question was *Seven Centuries of Ottoman Architecture: 'A Supranational Heritage'* (N. Akın, A. Batur and S. Batur, İstanbul, 1999). It is interesting to note that, while the organizers and editors prudently qualified only the legacy as 'supranational', such niceties would seem to have been lost on quite a few participants, who were not able to refrain from talking of the historical reality itself as – anachronistically – 'supranational'. And yet, to some extent this danger is present whenever we abide by the custom of talking, not of the architecture(s) of the Ottoman lands, but, in a much more homogenizing, reifying way, of the totality of 'Ottoman architecture'.

2 G. Necipoğlu, 'The Süleymaniye Complex in İstanbul: An Interpretation', *Muqarnas*, III, 1985, 92–120; G. Necipoğlu, 'A Kanun for the State, A Canon for the Arts: Conceptualizing the Classical Synthesis of Ottoman Art and Architecture', in G. Veinstein (ed.), *Soliman le Magnifique et son temps*, Paris, 1992, 195–216; G. Necipoğlu, 'Challenging the Past: Sinan and the Competitive Discourse of Early Modern Islamic Architecture', *Muqarnas*, X (*Essays in Honor of Oleg Grabar*), 1993, 169–80.

3 H. Crane, 'The Ottoman Sultan's Mosques: Icons of Imperial Legacy', in I. A. Bierman, R. A. Abou-el-Haj and D. Preziosi (eds), *The Ottoman City and Its Parts: Urban Structure and Social Order*, New York, 1991, 173–243.

4 G. Necipoğlu, 'Word and Image: The Serial Portraits of Ottoman Sultans in Comparative Perspective', in *The Sultan's Portrait: Picturing the House of Osman*, İstanbul, 2000, 22–61.

5 G. Necipoğlu, 'Anatolia and the Ottoman Legacy', in M. Frischman and H. Khan (eds), *The Mosque: History, Architectural Development and Regional Diversity*, New York and London, 1994, 141–56. See also note 2.

6 R. Ousterhout, 'Ethnic Identity and Cultural Appropriation in Early Ottoman Architecture', *Muqarnas*, VII,

1995, 48–62; Ç. Kafescioğlu, '"In the Image of Rûm": Ottoman Architectural Patronage in Sixteenth Century Aleppo and Damascus', *Muqarnas*, XVI, 1999, 70–95.

7 A. Arel, 'Inaccuracies, Commonplace Statements and Marginality: The History of Ottoman Architecture Revisited', in N. Akın, A. Batur and S. Batur (eds), *7 Centuries of Ottoman Architecture: A Supranational Heritage*, İstanbul, 1999, 30–3.

8 R. Abou-el-Haj, *Formation of the Modern State: The Ottoman Empire, Sixteenth to Eighteenth Centuries*, Albany, NY, 1991; B. Doumani, *Rediscovering Palestine: Merchants and Peasants in Jabal Nablus, 1700–1920*, Berkeley, CA, 1995; D. Ze'evi, *An Ottoman Century: The District of Jerusalem in the 1600s*, Albany, NY, 1996; D. Khoury, *State and Provincial Society in the Ottoman Empire: Mosul, 1540–1834*, Cambridge, 1997; J. Hathaway, *The Politics of Households in Ottoman Egypt: The Rise of the Qazdağlıs*, Cambridge, 1997; M. L. Meriwether, *Family and Society: The Kin Who Count in Ottoman Aleppo*, Austin, TX, 1999; J. Hathaway, *A Tale of Two Factions: Myth, Memory, and Identity in Ottoman Egypt and Yemen*, Albany, NY, 2003; A. Salzmann, *Tocqueville in the Ottoman Empire: Rival Paths to the Modern State*, Leiden, 2004.

9 See various articles by R. Abou-el-Haj, as well as his *Formation of the Modern State*, 14 and note 19.

10 A. Arel, 'Cincin Köyünde Cihanoğulları'na Ait Yapılar', in *V. Araştırma Sonuçları Toplantısı*, Ankara, 1988, 43–55, figs 1–37; Arel, 'Belgesel İçerikli Bir Yapı: Cihanoğlu Mehmet Ağa Camii', *Müze-Museum*, 4, Ankara, 1990–1; Arel, 'Aydın ve Yöresinde Bir Âyân Ailesi ve Mimarlık: Cihanoğulları', in *Osmanlı'dan Cumhuriyet'e: Problemler, Araştırmalar, Tartışmalar. I. Uluslararası Tarih Kongresi, 24–26 May 1993* (Ankara), İstanbul, 1998, 184–221.

11 A. Arel, 'Image architecturale et image urbaine dans une série de bas-reliefs de la région égénne', *Turcica*, XVIII, 1986, 83–101, figs 1–24; Arel, 'Arpaz'da Beyler Konağı', *Tarih ve Toplum*, 69, 1989, 174–81; Arel, 'Une ferme dominiale d'Arpaz à Aydın', in *V. Milletlerarası Türkiye Sosyal ve İktisat Kongresi Tebliğler*, Ankara, 1990, 787–96; Arel, '18. ve 19. Yüzyıl Ege Dünyasında İkonografik İzlek ve Kalıplar', in *Sanat Tarihinde İkonografik Araştırmalar: Güner İnal'a Armağan*, Ankara, 1993, 21–9, figs 1–9; Arel, 'Gothic Towers and Baroque Mihrabs: The Post-Classical Architecture of the Aegean Anatolia in the Eighteenth and Nineteenth Centuries', *Muqarnas*, X (Essays in Honor of Oleg Grabar), Leiden, 1993, 212–18; Arel, 'Menteşe Beyliği Mimarisinde Latin Etkileri', in *VII. Uluslararası Osmanlı Öncesi Türk Kültürü Kongresi (20–21 Mart 1993)*, İstanbul, 1998, 9–31; Arel, '18. Yüzyılda İzmir Civarında Mimari Ortam', in *18. Yüzyılda Osmanlı Kültür Ortamı*, İstanbul, 1998, 9–31; Arel, 'Ege Bölgesi Ayânlık Dönemi Mimarisi: 1986–1991 Çalışmaları', in *X. Araştırma Sonuçları Toplantısı*, Ankara, 1993.

12 Arel, 'Aydın ve Yöresinde Bir Âyân Ailesi ve Mimarlık', 195.

13 P. Thomo, 'Village Houses, Kamenicë, Albania', in S. Curcic and E. Hadjitryphonos (eds), *Secular Medieval Architecture in the Balkans, 1300–1500 and Its Preservation*, Thessaloniki, 1997, 246–7; S. Boiadzhiev, 'The Great House, Melnik, Bulgaria', in S. Curcic and E. Hadjitryphonos (eds), *Secular Medieval Architecture*, 258–61.

14 With reference to Koçi Bey, Hakan Erdem argues that it was the vicinity of İstanbul that was known as Turkistan

as early as the mid-seventeenth century: H. Erdem, 'Türkistan: Nerede, Ne Zaman', *Toplumsal Tarih*, 58, Eylül, 1998, 38–44, after A. K. Aksüt (ed.), *Koçi Bey*, Koçi Bey Risâlesi, İstanbul, 1939, 28.

15 In addition to the numerous articles by both authors, see: D. Behrens-Abouseif, *Egypt's Adjustment to Ottoman Rule: Institutions, Waqf, and Architecture in Cairo, 16th and 17th Centuries*, Leiden, 1994; M. Kiel, *Studies on the Ottoman Architecture of the Balkans*, Aldershot, 1990.

16 Y. Kuyulu, *Kara Osmanoğlu Ailesine Ait Mimari Eserler*, Ankara, 1992; Y. Nagata, *Tarihte Âyânlar: Karaosmanoğulları Üzerine Bir İnceleme*, Ankara, 1997; Nagata, *Studies on the Social and Economic History of the Ottoman Empire*, İzmir, 1995. For comparison: G. Veinstein, '"Ayan" de la région d'İzmir et le commerce du Levant (deuxième moitié du XVIII siècle)', *Études Balkaniques*, XII: 3, 1976, 71–83.

17 F. Aneroussi and L. Mylonadis, *The Kampos of Chios in its Heyday: Houses and Surroundings*, Nea Smyrni, n.d., includes, among the villas and mansions that it deals with, that of the Mavrocordatos family in the eighteenth century, a family of the most influential official court translators.

18 Rûm-ili refers here not to the Ottoman administrative unit, eyâlet or province, which in the sixteenth century included Thrace, Macedonia, Epirus, Thessaly, Albania, southern Serbia and western Bulgaria, but to a wider geography comprising the lands of the previous Roman empire.

19 T. Stoianovich's work, compiled in four volumes, sheds light on the material foundations, culture and mentalités of the Rumelian landlords: T. Stoianovich, *Between East and West*, vols I–IV, New York, 1992–5.

20 For a social history of the Ottoman house in Aleppo: A. Abdel Nour, *Introduction à l'histoire urbaine de la Syrie Ottomane (XVIe–XVIIIe siècle)*, Beirut, 1982. See also: H. Z. Watenpaugh, *The Image of an Ottoman City: Imperial Architecture and Urban Experience in Aleppo in the 16th and 17th Centuries (Ottoman Empire and Its Heritage)*, Leiden, 2004.

21 Built in 1784, next to the modest, but typically 'Ottoman', mosque of Selim I (1514), the İshak Paşa Palace incorporates Georgian, Armenian and Iranian building traditions and decorative repertoires: Y. Bingöl, *İshak Paşa Sarayı*, İstanbul, 1998.

22 D. Behrens-Abouseif, *Azbakiyya and Its Environs – from Azbak to Isma'il, 1476–1879*, Cairo, 1985; Behrens-Abouseif, 'The Abd al-Rahman Katkhuda Style in 18th Century Cairo', *Annales Islamologiques*, XXVI, 1992, 117–26. B. Maury, A. Raymond, J. Revault and M. Zakarya, *Palais et Maisons du Caire II : Epoque Ottomane (Xve–XVIII siècles)*, Paris, 1983.

23 J. Revault, *Palais et résidence d'été de la région de Tunis (XVIe–XIXe siècles)*, Paris, 1974.

24 D. Kuban, 'Türk Ev Geleneği Üzerine Gözlemler', in *Türk ve İslam Sanatı Üzerine Denemeler*, İstanbul, 1995 [1982], 226–7; G. Necipoğlu, 'Anatolian Legacy', 144.

25 R. Zirinski, 'How Did the Ottomans Become Ottman? The Construction of an Imperial Brand Name in the Time of Cultural Big Bang', *Archivium Ottomanicum*, 22: 2004, 125–58.

26 C. Kafadar, *Between Two Worlds: The Construction of the Ottoman State*, Berkeley, CA, 1995, 1–2. That these Turks were different, and were differentiated from the orthodox Sunni Muslims of the larger Islamic realm, is attested to by terms such as *abdalan-ı Rûm/gaziyan-i Rûm*, referring to the

colonizing heterodox sufi dervishes inhabiting the frontier zones: A. Y. Ocak, *Osmanlı Toplumunda Zındıklar ve Mülhidler (15.–17. Yüzyıllar)*, İstanbul, 1998, 80–1.

27 C. H. Fleischer, *Bureaucrat and Intellectual in the Ottoman Empire: The Historian Mustafa Âli (1541–1600)*, Princeton, NJ, 1986, 253–72.

28 C. Neumann, 'Devletin Adı Yok: Bir Amblemin Okunması', *Cogito*, 19 (Osmanlılar Özel Sayısı), Yaz, 1999, 269–83.

29 Not to be confused with the Eyalet-i Rumeli (Rûm-ili), an administrative unit: see S. Özbaran, *Bir Osmanlı Kimliği. 14.–17. Yüzyıllarda Rûm/Rûmî Aidiyet ve İmgeleri*, İstanbul, 2004, 49.

30 Selânikî Mustafa Efendi, *Târih-i Selânikî*, M. İpşirli (ed.), İstanbul, 1989, vol. 1, 64, 196, 224, 312, 429.

31 Fleischer, *Bureaucrat and Intellectual in the Ottoman Empire*, 93–4: Celâlzâde and Ramazanzâde, fully educated, worldly, pre-eminent littérateurs, distinguished themselves in the service of the state by virtue of their learning and devotion to codifying and creating the 'Ottoman way'.

32 And even then it was known that Ottoman was not an all-inclusive language, but a certain 'dialect', or only one of the languages that the peoples of the empire spoke. Hence 'Lehçe-i Osmanî' was the name given by Ahmed Vefik Paşa to his dictionary published in 1872–3. See also: F. Köprülü, 'Saz Şairleri, Dün ve Bugün', in *Edebiyat Araştırmaları*, Ankara, 1986, 199; B. Lory, 'Parler le turc dans les Balkans au XIXe siécle', in F. Georgeon and P. Dumont (eds), *Vivre dans l'Empire ottoman: Sociabilités et relations intercommunautaires (XVIIIe–XXe siécles)*, Paris, 1997, 237–49; J. Strauss, 'La conversation', in F. Georgeon and P. Dumont (eds), *Vivre dans l'Empire ottoman*, 251–318.

33 For Âli's description of 'the astonishing language current in the state of Rûm': Fleischer, *Bureaucrat and Intellectual in the Ottoman Empire*, 22–3.

34 Özbaran, *Bir Osmanlı Kimliği*, 110.

35 For a critique of those who have argued that linguistic scorn for Turks was no more than a reflection of Ottoman–Safavid conflict, see: Özbaran, *Bir Osmanlı Kimliği*, 109–14. For an exhaustive coverage of offensive words used for Turks in Ottoman poetry see: M. Kalpaklı, 'Osmanlı Edebi Metinlerine Göre Türklük ve Osmanlılık', in *Tarih ve Milliyetçilik. I. Ulusal Tarih Kongresi*, Mersin Üniversitesi, 1997, 75–90. Pejoratives of the same kinds and frequency can also be found in the chronicles. Taş Köprülüzade's *Mevzûat-ı Ulûm*, a biographical history, is a case in point. For various other uses of 'Turk' as an ethnonym in early Ottoman chronicles see: H. Erdem, 'Osmanlı Kaynaklarından Yansıyan Türk İmaj(lar)ı', in Ö. Kumrular (ed.), *Dünyada Türk İmgesi*, İstanbul, 2005, 13–26.

36 It was Gibb again who, in the introduction of his 1901 *History of Ottoman Literature*, formulated a periodization of the old (Ottoman) and the new (Turkish) literature, and, while devaluing the 'old' (Persianate) mode, glorified the 'new', post-nineteenth-century (western) models. For a resurrection of Gibb's premises, see: T. S. Halman (ed.), *Turkey: From Empire to Nation. Review of National Literatures* (series ed. A. Paulucci), New York, 1973. For a critique of Gibb, see: V. R. Holbrook, *The Unreadable Shores of Love: Turkish Modernity and Mystic Love*, Austin, TX, 1994, 28–31.

37 For the image of Ottomans in folk poetry, see: Kalpaklı, 'Osmanlı Edebi Metinlerine Göre Türklük ve Osmanlılık', 88–90.

38 Köprülü, 'Saz Şairleri, Dün ve Bugün', 198–9; F. Köprülü, 'Milli Edebiyat

Cereyanının İlk Mübeşşirleri', in *Edebiyat Araştırmaları*, Ankara, 1986, 290–2. For the making of the court poet and the tension between those of Arab and Acem, as well as those at the centre, see: H. İnalcık, *Şair ve Patron*, Ankara, 2003.

39 Doğan Kuban has always insisted on the ethno-cultural origins and subsequent spread of a dominant type that he calls 'the Turkish Anatolian [and not the Ottoman] house'. For his antagonistic criticism of Ayda Arel and Sedat Hakkı Eldem's preference of 'Ottoman house', see: D. Kuban, *Türk Hayat'lı Evi*, İstanbul, 1995, 22–3.

40 For historians ranging from Mustafa Akdağ to Michael Winter, or linguists from Andrea Tietze to literary historians like Fuat Köprülü or Orhan Şaik Gökyay, all of whom have read 'Rûmî' as Turkish, see: Özbaran, *Bir Osmanlı Kimliği*, especially 89–108, 109–14. The modern claim for the Turkishness of the dynasty and the state rests on such mistaken or careless readings, further coloured at times by Republican ideological preferences for the negation of Ottoman inclusiveness. Equally misleading is the reading of the term as referring to Greeks. In the same section referred to above, Özbaran cites examples from: A. Singer, *Palestinian Peasants and Ottoman Officials: Rural Administration around Sixteenth-Century Jerusalem*, Cambridge, 1994, 127, 189; H. Lowry, 'Süleyman's Formative Years in the City of Trabzon: Their Impact on the Future Sultan and the City', in H. İnalcık and C. Kafadar (eds), *Süleyman the Second and His Time*, İstanbul, 1993, 22–4; H. Gerber, 'Palestine and Other Territorial Concepts in the 17th Century', *IJMES*, 30: 4, 1998, 568.

41 Akın, *Balkanlarda Osmanlı Dönemi Konutları*, İstanbul, 2001.

42 C. Kafadar, 'The Ottomans and Europe', in T. A. Brady, H. A. Oberman and J. D. Tracy (eds), *Handbook of European History 1400–1600: Late Middle Ages, Renaissance and Reformation*, Leiden, 1994, 619–20.

43 S. Hall, 'Who Needs "Identity,"', in Paul du Gay, Jessica Evans and Peter Redman (eds), *Identity: A Reader*, London, 2000, 16–18; N. Elias, 'Homo Clausus and the Civilizing Process', in P. Gay, J. Evans and P. Redman (eds), *Identity: A Reader*, 294 and 295; R. G. Dunn, *Identity Crises: A Social Critique of Postmodernity*, Minneapolis, MN, 1998, 3; E. P. Thompson, *Customs in Common: Studies in Traditional Popular Culture*, London, 1993, 2, 6.

44 U. W. Haarmann, 'Ideology and History. Identity and Alterity: The Arab Image of the Turks from the Abbasids to Modern Egypt', *IJMES*, 20, 1988, 177, 191.

45 Fleischer, *Bureaucrat and Intellectual in the Ottoman Empire*, 253–72.

46 A. Singer, *Palestinian Peasants and Ottoman Officials: Rural Administration Around Sixteenth-century Jerusalem*, Cambridge, 1994, 127, 189.

47 İnalcık, *Şair ve Patron*, 13–14, 38–9.

48 Özbaran, *Bir Osmanlı Kimliği*, 112, after H. Tolasa, *Sehî, Latifî, Aşık Çelebi Tezkirelerine Göre 16.yy'da Edebiyat Araştırma ve Eleştirisi*, İzmir, 1983.

49 Özbaran, *Bir Osmanlı Kimliği*, 106–8.

50 This is not to say that all provincials were anti-Turkish. Nâbî (d. 1712) for one, a court poet originally from Urfa, strove not only to make a career in İstanbul, but yearned to be able to write poetry in 'Türkî'. Just as he expressed his dislike for Arabic, he was also complaining for having been forced to spend twenty-five years of his life in Aleppo. Nâbî exemplifies the world of his contemporaries, and establishes a link with the eighteenth century, when an even larger set of multiple identities was established. Never-

theless, Turks continue to be denigrated in seventeenth- and eighteenth-century court and folk poetry. See: Kalpaklı, 'Osmanlı Edebi Metinlerine Göre Türklük ve Osmanlılık', 75–90.
51 Even the official chronicler Nâima, like many Arab-speaking provincial notables and litterati, looked towards İstanbul, though he continued to speak Arabic while he wrote in Ottoman. See: S. Faroqhi, *Subjects of the Sultan: Culture and Daily Life in the Ottoman Empire*, New York, 2000, 80, 81.
52 H. Develi, *XVIII. İstanbul'a Dair Risale-i Garibe*, İstanbul, 1998, 34, 32, 23, 41.
53 Develi, *XVIII. İstanbul'a Dair Risale-i Garibe*, 41, 22, 33.
54 Necipoğlu, *Architecture, Ceremonial and Power*, Cambridge, MA and London, 1991, 14.
55 Necipoğlu, *Architecture, Ceremonial and Power*, 210. Necipoğlu also cites Angiolello with reference to the pavilions in questions. Angiolello identified the first of these as being in the Persian mode (alla Persiana), decorated in the mode of the country of Karaman, and covered with wattle and daub; the second as being in the Turkish mode (alla Turchesca); and the third as being in the Greek mode (alla Greca), and covered with lead.
56 Ç. Kafescioğlu, '"In the Image of Rûm"', 70; after Mehmed Âşık bin Ömer Bayezid, *Menazirü'l-Avalim*, Süleymaniye Library, Halet Efendi 616, fol. 228r.
57 H. Crane, *Risâle-i Mimariyye: An Early-Seventeenth-Century Ottoman Treatise on Architecture*, Facsimile with translation and notes, Leiden, 1987, 36.
58 For the Mamluk-inspired decoration in the 1523–4 complex of Çoban Mustafa Paşa, see: Y. Altuğ, *Gebze Çoban Mustafa Paşa Külliyesi*, Ankara, 1989.
59 Necipoğlu, *Architecture, Ceremonial and Power*.
60 Necipoğlu, *Architecture, Ceremonial and Power*, 194.
61 T. Artan, 'Arts and Architecture', in S. Faroqhi (ed.), *The Cambridge History of Turkey*, vol. III, Cambridge, 2006, 408–80.
62 Mehmed Râsid Tarih-i Râsid, vol. III, İstanbul, 1282 (1865), 307. For an illuminating study of pre-eighteenth-century İstanbul houses, see: S. Yarasimos 'Dwellings in 18th Century İstanbul', in S. Faroqhi and C. Newman (eds), *The Illuminated Table, the Prosperous House*, İstanbul, 2003, 275–300.
63 Some local musical genres continued to exist independently of the centre, while others were direct borrowings of the new experientialism at the court. Some local changes took place in indiscernible fashion, while others were striking. Nevertheless, closer links between the music of the centre and the provinces were established. The Anatolian mode (makam), called Hüseynî (Kürdî), became predominant at the court together with several popular local rhythms.
64 K. Kreiser, 'Üben den Kernraum des Osmanischen Reiches', in K.-D. Grothusen (ed.), *Die Türkei in Europe*, Goettingen, 1979, 53–63.
65 H. W. Lowry, *The Nature of the Early Ottoman State*, Albany, NY, 2003, 115–30.
66 J. Chr. Alexander, *Brigandage and Public Order in the Morea 1685–1806*, Athens, 1985; T. Artan, 'Periods and Problems of Ottoman (Women's) Patronage on the Via Egnatia', in *Proceedings of the Second International Symposium of the Institute for Mediterranean Studies: Via Egnatia Under Ottoman Rule, 1380–1699*, 9–11 January 1994, Rethymnon, 1997, 19–43.
67 Başbakanlık Archives, MAD 7137 (1125–1142).
68 T. Artan, 'Boğaziçi'nin Çehresini Değiştiren Soylu Kadınlar ve Sultanefendi Sarayları', *İstanbul Dergisi*, III,

69 İstanbul, October 1992, 109–18 (republished in English as: 'Noble Women Who Changed the Face of the Bosphorus and the Palaces of the Sultanas', in *Biannual İstanbul*, I, İstanbul, January 1993); Artan, 'From Charismatic Rulership to Collective Rule: Introducing Materials on Wealth and Power of Ottoman Princesses in the Eighteenth Century', *Toplum ve Ekonomi*, IV, İstanbul, 1993, 53–94; Artan, 'Gender Problems of Legalism and Political Legitimation in the Ottoman Empire', in *Proceedings of the Sixieme congres international d'histoire economique et sociale de l'empire Ottoman et de la Turquie (1326–1960), 1–4 June 1992*, Aix-en-Provence, 1995, 569–80.

69 Exceptions in this regard are Cairo, Aleppo and Damascus, where we do get town houses of a distinctive character. And, on closer inspection, these turn out to be the rather monumentally imposing town houses of local families founded by members of the capital's *devshirme* elite who settled here for good, so that the case of the 'Arab house' is likely to be the proverbial exception that proves the rule.

70 Very probably the same is also true of the suggestion embodied in Nancy Stieber's contribution in this volume, which seems to weigh in favour of a 'Cultural History of the (Ottoman) Built Environment'.

71 In addition to 'divan literature', terms such as 'Classical Ottoman literature', 'Ottoman elite literature', 'Ottoman upper-class literature', 'medieval Ottoman literature', 'Ottoman court literature', 'Ottoman court poetry' or 'Islamic Turkish literature' are often used.

72 Names given range from *alaturka musiki* (music *alla turca*) to 'Turkish Music', 'Classical Turkish Music', 'Traditional Music' and, finally, the absurdly vacuous 'Turkish Art Music' (*Türk Sanat Müziği*).

8

In Ordinary Time
Considerations on a video installation by Iñigo Manglano Ovalle and the New National Gallery in Berlin by Mies van der Rohe

Edward Dimendberg

What escapes analysis in architectural history? The question is a fair one, for even the most robust historical methodology necessarily disregards alternative approaches and leaves many questions unanswered. In their concern with typologies, the formal languages of buildings, and developments in technology, architectural historians frequently ignore the lived experience facilitated by the built environment, from the single-family dwelling to the metropolis. Forms of movement, modes of habitation, and even more intangible kinesthetic and emotional responses to architecture are frequently ignored, or at best reconstructed after the fact through surveys and questionnaires.

Here audio-visual media such as film, video, and newer digital technologies hold great promise as means of increasing understanding of how built spaces are inhabited and used. By directing attention to the role of the body in architecture, these tools portend new advances in architectural history by sensitizing scholars to lived space and proposing new ways to account for its transformation over time. Perhaps no European city has a greater lead in this process than Berlin, for already in the classic documentary *Berlin: Symphony of a Great City* (Walther Ruttmann, 1927) the daily lives of ordinary people, their routines and occupation of public spaces, are explored in a detailed cinematic record of incalculable value for historicizing life in this metropolis.

Throughout the twentieth century Berlin has been identified with the modern movement in architecture and long regarded as a key city for its development and popularization. While this reputation is generally associated with the decade before the 1914–18 war and the Weimar Republic, a growing body of scholarship has begun to treat a period in the history of the city of equal significance to the diffusion of modernism, if far less studied: the post-1945 years, in which modern architecture played a decisive role in Germany's national redefinition and reckoning with the Third Reich and in the unique status of Berlin as the front line of the cold war.[1] No single building constructed in West Berlin during the period from 1945 to 1989 better embodies these aspirations and tensions than the New National Gallery by Mies van der Rohe, whose construction commenced in the Fall of 1965. Three years later, it opened its doors on September 15, 1968. Mies died on August 19, 1969, and this public museum soon became recognized as among the most significant of his late works.

Two retrospectives devoted to the architecture of Mies in 2001 have directed renewed attention to his achievements.[2] Yet one of the most striking recent engagements with this legacy is found in three video installations by the Chicago-based artist Iñigo Manglano Ovalle (born 1961 in Madrid). In *Le Baiser/The Kiss* (1999), *Climate* (2000), and *Alltagszeit/In Ordinary Time* (2001), Ovalle selects three of the most iconic buildings by Mies – the Farnsworth House in Plano, Illinois (1949), the apartment high rises at 860–80 Lakeshore Drive in Chicago (1952), and the New National Gallery in Berlin (1968) – as sites for filming activities that provocatively question the modernity and significance of his architecture in the present. In *The Kiss* Ovalle the artist himself plays a window washer who lovingly, if fetishistically, cleans the windows of the Farnsworth House. A series of disconnected images of men wearing headsets, guns, and the Lakeshore Drive apartments comprise the action in *Climate*. Both installations involve video projections on aluminum channel structures, as if to realize architecture within the gallery space.

It is the third video installation in what has become known as Ovalle's 'Mies trilogy', *In Ordinary Time*, that I wish to consider here, especially its trenchant investigation of a specific building by Mies in relation to the surrounding urban environment. Playing upon the transparency of his New National Gallery, Ovalle's video explores its overlap between internal and external space and demonstrates how each functions simultaneously as symbolically and socially organized. Like his other two video installations, it is an exercise in site specificity involving the reconnaissance and surveying of a specific place. But, as its title conveys, it is also an investigation of temporality and the imbrication of architecture with both the time of lived human experience and the longer cycles of history that lend the built environment its meaning.

Historians have noted the debt of Mies to the Berlin architectural tradition, especially the austere neoclassicism of its greatest nineteenth-century architect, Karl Friedrich Schinkel.[3] Like Schinkel, Mies specializes in the deft manipulation of geometric volumes whose flat surfaces and lack of ornament responded to the call for *Sachlichkeit* (objectivity) among architects during the 1920s. Mies employs numerous techniques favored by Schinkel, such as the siting of a building on an elevated viewing platform (evident in the latter's design of 1822 for the Neues Museum). Schinkel's design for the Berlin Charlottenburg pavilion of 1824 provided an important precedent for Mies, who also sought to establish a strong connection to the surrounding environment by building on an axis to existing structures. Yet his greatest inspiration from Schinkel may well have been his ability to recreate what critic Paul Westheim called Schinkel's 'remarkable feeling for masses, relationships, rhythms, and form melodies'.[4]

Mies commenced his second career in Berlin several years before he was approached to design the New National Gallery, intended to house under a single roof the city of Berlin's holdings of twentieth-century art and the Prussian Cultural Heritage Foundation's collection of modern art. By the Spring of 1961, Rolf Schweder and Werner Duettman, the heads of the construction and planning senates, had convinced Mies to undertake a new project in the metropolis where he had lived, worked, and built from 1906 to 1937. At once renewing the connection of Berlin to its Weimar modernist past, the gesture of inviting the exile Mies back to the country from which he emigrated to the United States in 1938 also implied an effort to repair a history truncated by National Socialism.[5]

Coming less than six months before the appearance of the Berlin Wall in August 1961, the selection of Mies also suggests an effort to position Germany as a patron of the postwar international modernism. Nowhere had this style more vigorously established itself than in the United States, thanks in large measure to the prominence of his best-known projects, such as the Chicago Lakeshore Drive apartment buildings (1951), Crown Hall at the Illinois Institute of Technology (1956), and the New York Seagram Building (1958). By selecting Mies as an architect, Berliners could simultaneously build a bridge to their own architectural history while identifying with the globally ascendant American cultural style, if not the political and economic might of the United States.[6]

Before finally agreeing to design the New National Gallery, Mies was invited to consider two other possible commissions, a museum on the grounds of the Charlottenburg Palace and an extension to the Free University. When both of these failed to materialize, he accepted the offer to design the New National Gallery on the Kemperplatz. So great was the architect's prestige and the desire of the Berlin authorities for him to build there, that he was granted an unprecedented degree of creative autonomy and the promise of minimal interference from local building administrators. Thus, even before Mies had submitted a design, the New National Gallery had become imbued with his persona.

Located but a short walk from Potsdamerplatz, once home to Erich Mendelsohn's Columbus House (1931) and among the busiest urban intersections in the world before the 1939–45 war, the site of the museum comprises an integral element of its meaning. In close proximity to a synagogue destroyed during Kristallnacht and the Reichstag, it is also a short distance from what once was the site of Albert Speer's Reich Chancellery. Speer's presence comes even closer to the New National Gallery, for its building site contained the ruins of the Runder Platz, one of the few realized segments of his Germania masterplan.[7] It was demolished in 1966 to accommodate the museum, whose aspiration to provide a new foundation for postwar German culture is literally grounded in its site and obliteration of the National Socialist past.

Sanctioned by Mies, despite his awareness of the ruins of Speer's project, the siting of the New National Gallery may thus be viewed as a radical exercise in modernist decontextualization.[8] Located less than 100 meters from the former office of Mies, the site of the museum is bordered on its South side by the Reichpietsch Ufer, adjacent to the Landwehr Canal where the bodies of Karl Liebknecht and Rosa Luxemburg were dumped by the Freikorps in 1919, an event acknowledged by Mies in his monument of 1926 to the November Revolution. To the North lies the St Matthews Church of 1846 by Friedrich August Stüler, a pupil of Schinkel. The Southwest side of the Museum is on an axis with James Stirling and Michael Wilford's Science Center (1988). And, to the East, just beyond the Potsdamer Strasse and the City Library by Hans Scharoun (1966–78), lay the Berlin Wall until its demolition in 1990.

Scharoun's Library and his Philharmonic Hall (1956–63) together with the New National Gallery were to be the center pieces of the Kulturforum whose gestation emerged in the context of the founding of Prussian Cultural Heritage Foundation in 1957 and the Berlin Capital City international design competition of 1957–8. Intended to plan for the day when the city would again be the seat of the German government, the competition's emphasis on East–West circulation routes led many, including Scharoun, to conceive of a cultural band to begin at the 'Museum Island' in the Eastern sector and to conclude at the Charlottenburg Palace. In 1962 the Prussian Cultural Heritage Foundation formulated the plan to build a museum complex at the Kemperplatz, so as not to be overshadowed by the Museum Island, now cut off from the Western sector of the city by the Berlin Wall. Centered in one location, Scharoun's expressionist designs of the Philharmonic and City Library and the New National Gallery of Mies thus became synonymous with the cultural identity of Berlin during the cold war.[9]

Designed in the shape of a square, measuring 177 feet in circumference with 25,000 square feet of temporary exhibition space on its main level, the New National Gallery is a perfectly symmetrical modular grid. Its 1,250-ton, 210-square foot welded steel roof is suspended twenty-eight feet above the gallery floor by eight cruciform-shaped perimeter columns located outside of the building. With the exception of two marble-clad non-load-bearing service structures stretching from floor to ceiling, two elevators, two cloakrooms, and two stairways leading to the 100,000 square feet of exhibition space for permanent collection on the lower level, the main floor is a totally unobstructed expanse. Open to many possible uses, it exemplifies the notion of a programmatically flexible and infinitely expandable 'universal space' that Mies began exploring in his unrealized designs for the 50 × 50 House (1952) and Chicago Convention Hall (1954).[10]

The glass and steel box of the museum continues the exploration of architectural transparency and reflectivity commenced by Mies in the Farnsworth House, Crown Hall, and the Seagram Building. Situated atop a 124,000-square foot elevated pedestal, it updates Schinkel's aspiration in his Neues Museum to realize a classical temple of culture. By aligning the Northwest corner building of the museum terrace on an axis with the St Matthews Church, Mies brings the two structures into dialogue, as if to propose the New National Gallery as a spiritual edifice of its age.

This association is powerfully conveyed by *In Ordinary Time*, produced in September 2000 by Ovalle as a commission for the *Mies in America* exhibition organized by the Canadian Centre for Architecture, for which he also provided the exhibition design. Its German title was selected by the artist to translate 'in ordinary time', the phrase for those periods of the Catholic calendar punctuated by common daily rituals rather than major holidays. The decision by the organizers of a retrospective on the architect's North American work to commission a video work set in the New National Gallery suggests the degree to which the building embodies the late American style of Mies, despite its location in Germany.

In Ordinary Time (Figures 8.1 and 8.2) depicts the passage of a single day in the museum, commencing before sunrise and concluding at sunset. Filmed on 35 millimeter film stock and later transferred to video, it was recorded with two cameras. One was fixed in a stationary position facing the West side of the building and recorded a single frame of film every two seconds. The other was moved to various points around the museum to capture cut-aways and close-ups of the actors and interior and exterior views from different positions. Radiant light bathes the museum, and long shadows creep across floor, eventually culminating in the darkness with which the film began. Just as Mies conceived of the museum's space as a neutral frame open to many possible uses, Ovalle's video suggests temporality as an equally pliable correlate to the universal space of Mies.

The video begins and concludes with a single man facing the Western window of the museum. Other figures of different ages, genders, and ethnicities also appear, frequently filmed in shots of closer range and in corners of the building. The two marble-clad service structures located on its North and South ends provide the principal means of spatial orientation for spectators and actors alike. Wherever the latter walk, the modular grid of the museum, evident in welded sections of its roof and the linear blocks of the floor, seems to impress itself upon their movements.

Much of the film depicts the actors engaged in a limited range of directional movements, walking closer or farther away from the camera, from one side of the frame to the other, or from one corner to another. Frequent shots

Figure 8.1 Iñigo Manglano Ovalle: *In Ordinary Time*, 2001; video installation, frame enlargement (courtesy of the artist).

Figure 8.2 Iñigo Manglano Ovalle: *In Ordinary Time*, 2001; video installation, frame enlargement (courtesy of the artist).

of St Matthews Church and the often solemn gait of the figures in the museum underscore the relation between the museum building and the church as social institution. It suggests the political functions of modernism, a key element in the cultural legitimation of West Germany, if not the central article of its official state culture, from the Hochschule für Gestaltung in Ulm to Gunter Behnisch and Frei Otto's Munich Olympic grounds to Norman Foster's Reichstag renovation.

Coordinating the time-lapse camera that recorded the central span of the museum with the second mobile camera entailed a detailed choreography of directional movement plotted out on a plan of the building's interior. Introducing these constraints implicitly challenges the description of the New National Gallery by Mies as a building that permits 'freedom of movement within a space that does not dictate'.[11] All architecture, of course, constrains the body, dictating how and where it can occupy a structure or circulate within it. Yet choreographing movement within a structure whose free plan deliberately avoids directing its occupants in particular directions is not simply a perverse gesture but rather should be understood as an attempt to highlight modalities of constraint irreducible to limitations of circulation.

Traversing the interior of the New National Gallery, the figures in *In Ordinary Time* appear to embody the very distance of the space they inhabit, often alone, sometimes clustered in pairs, but never gathering together or forming larger groups, as if to celebrate their romanticized isolation, not unlike the panels suspended from the ceiling on which art in the museum is displayed. Ovalle's video suggests their freedom comes at the cost of a social separation, perhaps the inner resoluteness and resistance to external distractions necessary to lead a spiritual life. The artist has admitted the film *Playtime* (Jacques Tati, 1967) provided an initial inspiration for his work. Yet the contrasts between them are revealing. For, while in the earlier film architecture provides material resistance in the form of the glass walls and windows with which its characters constantly collide, in Ovalle's video architectural transparency allows for the seepage of history and urban context in and across interior space.

> Writing of Kulturforum, the architect Oswald Matthias Ungers observed the two contradictory spirits, the classical and the extravagant, personified in Mies and Scharoun, visualized in the New National Gallery and the Philharmonic, emerged once again in the interplay of feelings and opinions. The Apollonian National Gallery with its simple square form, its cheerful pose, and its rational clarity is confronted by the dynamic Philharmonic Hall with its ecstatic rapture, its fundamental sensuality, its emotionality and irrationality . . . . It is the image of a city in which buildings do not communicate with each other across the spaces between them to form a third component, a kind of negative space, as it were, but rather a city in which the buildings simply exist in their sublime solitude.[12]

This 'sublime solitude' and 'negative space' also vividly convey the distance between the people in *In Ordinary Time*, and it becomes possible to read their isolation as mirrored in the surrounding built environment and vice versa. Yet the description by Ungers of the urban fabric of the Kulturforum seems far-fetched, aestheticizing as it does a vast, disconnected, and uninviting expanse, virtually without public space. These limitations are only further exacerbated by the recent tawdry redevelopment of Potsdamer Platz and the American-style shopping mall in its center, and may well represent the low point of postwar planning in Berlin. To label this district sublime, even a variant of the urban sublime, is to circumvent a confrontation with its real failures.

The romanticization of the Kulturforum's haphazard and poorly coordinated development, a product of political and historical events as well as architectural decisions, can also be discerned in the discourse around the New National Gallery. Its universal space and glorification of social distance were also reflected in such contemporaneous cultural staples of the 1960s as abstract expressionism and jazz that soon became associated with Mies's building. Employing a debased vocabulary of existentialism, the rhetoric around the New National Gallery occludes historical and political preconditions, while overlooking its shortcomings as an art museum, especially the dark and cramped spaces of the basement in which its permanent collection is housed.

While Mies spoke of the open expanse of the museum as 'certainly nothing that can be calculated or measured. It is always something imponderable, something that lies between things', other contemporary observers were less charitable in their judgments.[13] Writing shortly after the opening of the New National Gallery, one commentator claimed:

> The scale of the museum is a worrying thing. It sits on its too-vast plaza in a too empty neighborhood like a serene piece of sculpture. It appears much smaller than it is, and desperately needs the constant swirl of human habitation to give it scale and life. Taken simply by itself, it is an extraordinarily ambiguous thing: a large and vacant 'anonymous' envelope designed to receive works of art, but at the same time a monument in itself and perhaps the most prestigious work of art in the whole collection. It cannot be wholly one or the other, and winds up, unfortunately, being neither. It remains a very interesting piece of architectural history made flesh, and of course, as usual, of godly details for effete collectors. It is exquisite, pleasurable to behold, but with little relavance for the turmoil of Berlin life or, perhaps, even for the turmoil of today's art.[14]

Just as Ovalle's video reveals two separate temporalities, the time-lapse scenes with their sped-up motions, and the cut-away shots filmed in real time, Mies's New National Gallery also presents two temporal regimes. The passage of time conveyed by the rising and setting of the sun in the main floor area for temporary exhibits represents what we might call ordinary time. Its dilation and acceleration by the film is conveyed by Jeremy Boyle's soundtrack, an electronically manipulated and distended version of the first and last notes of Beethoven's 'Moonlight Sonata'. Architecture is 'the spatially apprehended will of the epoch', and this oft-cited dictum of Mies suggests a second temporal register that we might call the imperceptible temporality of the *Zeitgeist*.[15]

The great conceit of his architecture remains the presumption of its inherent timelessness, the tension between its ability to serve continuously new functions while nonetheless embodying the deep structure of the age, held by Mies to be manifest in technology. Building in his later period almost exclusively with glass and steel, the materials he thought most modern, Mies understood his architecture to express his age by virtue of its sophisticated engineering and embrace of modern construction technology and typologies such as the skyscraper.

By documenting the passage of ordinary time in the museum, Ovalle questions its transcendental aspirations and recontextualizes this work of modernism, now shown to be as fully mired in the passage of time and aging as any other building. He allows us to perceive the New National Gallery, and by implication the Kulturforum, as no longer new, and sensitizes us to their simultaneously enframing and framed character, their achievements no less than their histories and incompleteness. Here the museum itself, rather than its objects, is put on display, interrogated and revealed to be as embedded within historical time as an insect within a block of amber. Removed from the heroic temporality of modernist rhetoric, the New National Gallery is reinserted into the 'ordinary time' of daily life.

Mies believed in universal space as an indivisible and infinitely expandable whole, a quasi-logical form in which particulars matter less than the expression of a Hegelian essence of history. This idea was ideally suited to bolster the rhetoric of cold war universalism, and, situated but several hundred meters from the former site of the Berlin Wall, the New National Gallery became a powerful architectural emblem of western capitalism.

To gaze upon it and the other buildings of the Kulturforum today is to discern their relation to contemporaneous postwar urban projects such as the master plan of Wallace Harrison for the Lincoln Center in New York (1962–8) and the almost talismanic force that the notion of the revitalized urban cultural center radiated during this period worldwide.[16]

It is also to acknowledge the fundamentally different political, economic, and cultural situation in which Berlin today functions as capital of a unified Germany and to remain open, in the spirit of modernism, to the architectural and urban forms best suited to its evolving identity. Writing new histories of modern architecture sensitive to the lived appropriation of space, the cultural politics of built form, and the urbanistic role of particular buildings within the city comprises an urgent task if the built environment of the twenty-first century is to benefit from the lessons of the previous one. *In Ordinary Time* suggests how technologies of the moving image hold great promise as research tools capable of illuminating space, time, and movement in the lives of buildings whether ordinary or extraordinary.

Notes

For comments on an earlier version of this essay, I am grateful to Nora Alter, Alexander Alberro, Gertrud Koch, Scott Nygren, Maureen Turim, and the other participants in the conference 'Beyond/After the Screen: The Impact of Documenta X on Contemporary Film and Video Practices', held April 10–12, 2003 at the University of Florida, Gainesville. Daniel Herwitz also provided valuable comments. Iñigo Manglano-Ovalle kindly answered my queries and requests.

1 On this history see the essays collected in Thorsten Scheer, Josef Paul Kleihues, and Paul Kahlfeldt (eds), *City of Architecture/Architecture of the City: Berlin 1900–2000*, Berlin, 2000.
2 These were *Mies in America*, organized by the Canadian Centre for Architecture, and *Mies in Berlin*, organized by the Museum of Modern Art.
3 For this analysis I am indebted to Barry Bergdoll, 'The Nature of Mies's Space', in Terence Riley and Barry Bergdoll (eds), *Mies in Berlin*, New York, 2001, 66–105, esp. 73–85.
4 Paul Westheim, 'Schinkel und die Gegenwart', *Der Baumeister*, 11, January 1913, B83, quoted and translated in Bergdoll, 'The Nature of Mies's Space', 79.
5 On the architect's activities during these years see the essays in Phyllis Lambert (ed.), *Mies in America*, Montreal, 2001.
6 On the relation of German modernism to the United States see Paul Betts, *The Authority of Everyday Objects: A Cultural History of West German Industrial Design*, Berkeley, CA, 2004.
7 On Speer's Berlin plans see Hans J. Reichhardt and Wolfgang Schäche, *Von Berlin nach Germania: Über die Zerstörungen der Reichshauptstadt durch Albert Speers Neugestaltungsplanungen*, Berlin, 1998, and Stephen D. Helmer, *Hitler's Berlin: The Speer Plans for Reshaping the Central City*, Ann Arbor, MI, 1985.
8 For a discussion of the building's proximity to Speer's work see Mark Jarzombek, 'Mies van der Rohe's New National Gallery and the Problem of Context', *Assemblage*, 2, 1987, 32–43.
9 On this point see Gabriela Wachter (ed.), *Mies van der Rohe's New National Gallery in Berlin*, trans. Peter Craven, Berlin, 1995, and Bettina Vismann and Jürgen Mayer H., 'The Perspiration Affair, or the New National Gallery Between Cold Fronts', *Grey Room*, 9, 2002, 80–9.
10 For the notion of universal space see Franz Schulze, *Mies van der Rohe: An Intellectual Biography*, Chicago, IL, 1985, 267–9, and Peter Serenyi, 'Mies' New National Gallery: An Essay on Architectural Content', *The Harvard Architecture Review*, 1, 1980, 180–9.
11 Phyllis Lambert, 'Mies Immersion', in *Mies in America*, 499.
12 Oswald Matthias Ungers, 'Schönheit ist das Glanz des Wahren', in Andres Lepik and Anne Schmedding (eds), *Architektur in Berlin: Das XX Jahrhundert – Ein Jahrhundert Kunst in Deutschland*, Cologne, 1999, 74, quoted and translated in Martin Kiren, 'The 1960s: The Legacy of Modernism – Curse or Blessing', in Scheer, Kleihues, and Kahlfeldt (eds), *City of Architecture*, 293.
13 Mies van der Rohe, 'Build Beautifully and Practically! Stop this Cold Functionality' (1930), in Fritz Neumeyer (ed.), *The Artless Word: Mies van der Rohe on the Building Art*, trans. Mark Jarzombek, Cambridge, MA, 1991, 307.
14 See 'Mies Monument', *Progressive Architecture*, November 1968, 108–13. For a more positive review see Peter Blake, 'Mies's Berlin Museum',

The Architectural Forum, 129, October 1968, 35–47.

15 Mies van der Rohe, 'Building Art and the Will of the Epoch' (1924), in Neumeyer (ed.), *The Artless Word*, 245–7.

16 On the history of Lincoln Center see Victoria Newhouse, *Wallace Harrison, Architect*, New York, 1989, 186–98.

9

Reopening the question of document in architectural historiography
Reading (writing) Filarete's treatise on architecture for (in) Piero de' Medici's study

Sevil Enginsoy Ekinci

> It seems to me that there are, in any case, at least three types of pleasure of reading.... According to the first mode, the reader has a fetishist relation with the text being read: he takes pleasure in the words, in certain words, in certain arrangements of words.... According to the second mode, ... the reader is drawn onward *through* the book's length by a force always more or less disguised, belonging to the order of suspense: the book is gradually abolished, and it is in this impatient, impassioned erosion that the delectation lies. ... Then there is a third adventure of reading (I am calling *adventure* the way in which pleasure comes to the reader): that of Writing; reading is a conductor of the Desire to write ...; not that we necessarily wanted to write *like* the author we enjoy reading ...: we desire the desire the author had for the reader when he was writing, we desire the *love-me* which is in all writing.
>
> (Roland Barthes, 'On Reading')

Over the past several decades, architectural historiography has been engaged in reflecting on its own disciplinary grounds vigorously. It has undergone a radical transformation by reviewing and expanding its fields of inquiry theoretically, methodologically, thematically, chronologically and geographically. Rather surprisingly, however, what has remained largely unexplored in this self-critical activity is the question of document. Considering the related theoretical developments in other sub-fields of historiography,[1] I would admit that to address this question today may seem an oddly belated endeavour. Nevertheless, I also believe that it is still worthy of taking this risk.

In this essay, my basic concern is not to provide an extensive overview of this question, but rather to sketch a frame that stimulates possible readings of written documents, and, accordingly, possible rewritings of architectural history. In doing this, I draw on the selected discussions that lie outside architectural historiography but that, in one way or another, present invaluable insights into how the discipline can critically revise its established ways of reading documents.[2]

So, my sketch begins with a criticism, as articulated by Dominick LaCapra, which problematizes the treatment of a document 'purely and simply as a quarry for facts in the reconstruction of the past'.[3] When a document is read in such a 'reduced' way of 'synoptic content analysis',[4] LaCapra adds, 'the dimensions . . . that make it a text of a certain sort with its own historicity and its relations to sociopolitical processes . . . are filtered out'.[5] Ultimately, this results in a failure to see that 'documents are themselves historical realities that do not simply represent but also supplement the realities to which they refer'.[6] Therefore, it is crucial to inquire into 'how [documents] do what they do – how, for example, they may situate or frame what they "represent" or inscribe',[7] meaning how documents 'rework' or 'process' realities, as LaCapra argues, by 'mak[ing] a difference in the sociopolitical and discursive context in which they are inserted'.[8]

In a similar vein, Roger Chartier claims that 'no [document] . . . entertains a transparent relationship with the reality that it apprehends'.[9] As he defines, a document is 'a system constructed according to categories, schemas of perception and appreciation, rules of functioning and of writing that go back to the very conditions of its production'.[10] So, Chartier emphasizes that '[t]hese categories of thought and these principles of writing must be brought to light before one attempts any "positive" reading of the document'.[11] In this way, he adds, '[t]he real then takes on a new meaning: what is real, in fact, is not (or is not only) the reality aimed at by the text, but the very manner in which the text aims at it in the historicity of its production and the strategy of its writing'.[12]

Resting on this theoretical frame, my essay centres on the reading, or rather the rereading, of a specific document for a specific space, that of Filarete's treatise on architecture for Piero di Cosimo de' Medici's study. I argue that any historiographical approach that confines itself only to the content analysis of a few passages in Filarete's treatise with the goal of extracting simply factual information about the physical qualities of Piero de' Medici's study fails to perceive how the treatise as a whole represents the study as a social and cultural space; and, accordingly, how it re-presents this space in relation to its own conditions and motives of production, and in the final analysis, to its own historicity. So, in my reading, where the study appears as the site of convergence of the relations between Filarete, the writer/architect, the treatise and Piero de' Medici, the dedicatee/potential reader/potential patron/owner of the study, I also juxtapose my frame with the one formulated by the history of the book and the history of reading.[13] Accordingly, this frame situates Filarete as an actor whose role in the textual production of his treatise was fabricated within a network of social, cultural and economic processes; the treatise as a textual form, a material object and a socio-cultural commodity; and Piero de' Medici as an active figure who did not necessarily receive the treatise in the way that Filarete expected.

Finally, what I suggest in this essay is that reading a document is not simply a technical issue, but a practice that can encompass the 'three types of pleasure of reading', defined by Roland Barthes.[14] More particularly, it is the third type, the one that arouses 'the desire to write', that can provide new lenses for viewing the reading of a document not as an instrumental, but as a stimulating practice that initiates the activity of writing history. It is, then, in this sense that the pleasure of reading a document corresponds to the pleasure derived from the 'adventure' of writing history.

Piero di Cosimo de' Medici's study in the Palazzo Medici, Florence, was a distinguished example of its kind in early modern Italy. Finished probably around the mid-1450s,[15] the room ceased to exist during the substantial alterations that the Palazzo underwent after its sale to the Riccardi in 1659.[16] In light of research of the past several decades, what is known about Piero de' Medici's study today is that it was located on the *piano nobile* of the Palazzo Medici and next to Piero's chamber in his apartment.[17] Measuring approximately 4 × 5.5 metres, the room was probably covered by a barrel vault, decorated by twelve glazed terracotta roundels with the *Labours of the Months*, now preserved in the Victoria and Albert Museum, London. In addition to these roundels, Luca della Robbia, a well-known Florentine sculptor of the time, executed the floor decoration by glazed terracotta tiles.[18] Yet, the decoration was not only limited to the ceiling and the floor but also possibly extended to the walls in the form of intarsiated panels[19] and/or frescoes.[20] Presenting such physical qualities, the study was the space where Piero de' Medici collected his gems and other precious objects together with his valuable manuscripts.[21] While those manuscripts were possibly kept flat on forward-sloping shelves, other items were probably stored in intarsiated cupboards.[22]

Filarete's treatise on architecture, written in the first half of the 1460s, has been recognized as revealing significant information on the possible original layout of Piero de' Medici's study. In Book XXV, which is devoted exclusively to the praise of the building activities of Cosimo de' Medici and his sons, Piero and Giovanni, Filarete describes Piero's study in a passage while discussing the Palazzo Medici, and, more specifically, the *piano nobile* of the Palazzo. He starts this passage by explaining Piero's apartment as consisting of a chamber and a study, or, in his own words, a '*studietto*', 'decorated with books and other noble things'.[23] Filarete then tells us that the 'pavement of the study [is also] most ornate, as is the ceiling with glazed terra-cotta made in fine figures', and adds that the 'master of these glazed terra-cottas was Luca della Robbia'.[24] What is remarkable here is that Filarete describes the *studietto* by emphasizing its ornamental value in reference not only to its floor and ceiling but also to its collection. Furthermore, he connects this visual quality of the room to its use by Piero in such a fashion as to cause 'greatest admiration in anyone who enters it'.[25] In line with other documentary information that records the visits of some distinguished figures of the time to Piero's study,[26] what can be suggested here is that Filarete's description helps one imagine the *studietto* as a space of spectacle that Piero shows his guests to declare his wealth, civility and refined taste.[27]

However, this is not the only scene where Piero de' Medici's study appears in Filarete's treatise on architecture. In another passage, also in Book XXV, Filarete mentions the room again, but this time he calls it a 'studio', instead of a '*studietto*'. As another difference, he emphasizes that what he discloses in this passage is second-hand information, narrated to him by 'an intimate of [Piero's], Nicodemus by name, a worthy man, secretary and friend of the most illustrious Francesco Sforza, fourth duke of Milan'.[28] Moreover, Filarete cites this information in a totally different context, which revolves around the theme of Piero's suffering from gout. He explains that, as a relief from this illness, '[Piero] has himself carried into [either] the buildings that [Piero and the other members of his family] are building, . . . [or] into a studio'.[29] Filarete then adds:

> When [Piero] arrives [in this studio], he looks at his books. They seem like nothing but solid pieces of gold. . . . He has so many different kinds that not one day but more than a month would be required to see and understand their dignity. Let us leave aside the reading and the authors of these books. It is not necessary to list them, because he has them in every discipline, whether in Latin, Greek, or Italian, so long as they are worthy. He has honoured them . . . with fine script, miniatures, and ornaments of gold and silk. . . . [And] he runs over all these volumes with his eye for his pleasure, to pass time and to give recreation to his sight.[30]

In this passage, Filarete defines the room as a space of spectacle, as well, by emphasizing, again, the ornamental value of its manuscript collection. But this time, the room offers visual pleasure only to its owner.[31]

As Filarete explains further, this visual pleasure is similar to the one that Piero derives from looking at his collection of other valuable objects, including 'effigies and portraits of all the emperors and noble men . . . made in gold, silver, bronze, jewels, marble, or other materials', 'jewels and precious stones', 'vases of gold, silver, and other materials made nobly and at great expense' and 'other noble things that have come from different parts of the world, [and] various strange arms for offence and defence'.[32]

Yet, regarding Piero's manuscript collection in particular, Filarete also adds that it is a source not only of visual but also of aural pleasure, since, at other times, aside from looking at or reading the books himself, Piero 'has them read' to him.[33] So, in contrast to the previously mentioned passage in which Filarete describes the study as a space of display where Piero welcomes his guests to impress them, here he presents the room as a space of retreat and healing that Piero enjoys only by himself.[34] In other words, in these two different scenes Filarete depicts two different practices, corresponding to Piero's use of his study as a public space and a private space, respectively.

Despite their differences, these two depictions of Piero de' Medici's study actually complement, rather than conflict with, each other by alluding to a notable characteristic of the early modern study in Italy. Shared especially by the courtly examples, that was the characteristic of functioning as both a public and a private space, meaning that, while exhibiting, through its contents and physical aspects, the owner's social, cultural and economic power to prestigious visitors, the study in early modern Italy was reserved to its owner's retreat, contemplation and learning, as well.[35] Filarete's treatise is, therefore, an important document on Piero de' Medici's study, not only because of what it tells us about the physical qualities of the room, but also because of how it relates these qualities to Piero's use of this room and, accordingly, how it renders a frame to envision this specific example within the context of the early modern study in Italy.

To attribute such a documentary role to Filarete's treatise on architecture brings to the fore, inevitably, the question of by which means Filarete reached the information on Piero de' Medici's study. A tentative answer lies in the treatise itself: while presenting the study as a public space, on the one hand, Filarete gives the impression that this information derives from his own observation, and, while discussing it as a private space, on the other hand, he cites a particular name as his source of information. However, it is not known whether he actually visited the study or not, and whether what his source told him was simply a rumour or not. In other words, it is not known to what extent Filarete's documentation of Piero de' Medici's study is a product of his and/or others' imagination. In any case, what really matters here is that, in both passages, the way Filarete delineates Piero's study reflects the panegyric tone of Book XXV by enriching the portrait of Piero that Filarete draws as a learned patron of architecture with refined tastes.[36]

This indicates that, in any attempt to interpret Filarete's documentation of Piero's study, these two passages should be read in relation not only to each other but also to Book XXV, in which both are embedded. Such a reading offers a much broader view by juxtaposing the question of what Filarete records with that of how he records, and, accordingly, by casting light on the possible conditions and motives of this very practice of recording itself. Then, what I contest is that the panegyric tone of Filarete's record of the study is directly related to the issue that, after dedicating and presenting a copy of his treatise to Francesco Sforza, Duke of Milan, Filarete dedicated and presented a revised copy of his treatise to Piero de' Medici with the hope of finding a place for it in Piero's study and on a shelf in his prestigious library. This means that Filarete did not record just any study, but particularly one that he imagined as the ultimate destination of his treatise on architecture. Remarkably, this imagination unfolds itself not only in the specific literary character of Book XXV but also in some other textual features that concern the production of the treatise as a whole.[37]

In the preface, Filarete presents his treatise to his dedicatee by explaining that it is written in the vernacular, or, in Filarete's own words, in the '*volgare*'. He seems quite conscious about the requirement that, as a treatise dedicated to such an illustrious figure, namely Piero de' Medici, it should have been written in Latin, not in the vernacular. As an excuse, he asks his dedicatee to 'take [his treatise] not as written by Vitruvius nor by other worthy architects', but by Filarete himself.[38] In other words, he asks Piero not to compare his treatise with these works, but to evaluate it on its own merits. Accordingly, he tries to convince Piero that the use of vernacular language in his treatise is a merit, not a deficiency, since, as he remarks: 'there are [already] enough [works] to be found in Latin by most worthy men'.[39] So, Filarete implies that its language in the '*volgare*' distinguishes his treatise from the others written in Latin, and that his treatise, simply at least for this reason, deserves a place in his dedicatee's prestigious library, holding copies of works in Latin in great number,[40] and perhaps next to the copy of Vitruvius' *De architectura*.[41] Here, Filarete possibly hints at, and accordingly, relies on Piero's interest in vernacular language, and also on his manuscript collection displaying this very interest.[42]

But, more than its language, what Filarete trusts about Piero de' Medici's reception of his treatise is its inclusion of many drawings and Piero's consequent derivation of particular pleasure from looking at architectural illustrations. In Book XXV, while delineating Piero's study as a private space, Filarete mentions the drawings of 'the buildings of Rome and other places', executed by masters, as among Piero's sources of visual pleasure, and then reveals his hope that '[Piero] will sometime derive pleasure from [his treatise]', too.[43] Actually, Filarete expects from his dedicatee to receive his treatise by deriving aural pleasure as well. He explains this expectation in the preface by requesting of Piero: 'If it does not displease you, read this book on architecture or have it read to you.'[44] He then adds that his treatise, hopefully, 'will give a certain amount of pleasure to [his dedicatee's] ears'.[45] While revealing this intended reception of the treatise, Filarete also assumes that Piero will follow Filarete's own depiction of Piero's usual practice in his study, that is, of reading his books or having them read to him.[46]

Yet, if the treatise was written not only to be read and looked at, but also to be listened to, is it possible to trace this particular intended reception in the textual production of the treatise? First of all, the use of the literary form of dialogue in the treatise, a form suitable for reading aloud, is a particularly salient feature. Second, this dialogue form is embedded in a narrative structure that presents digressions due to the incorporation of some secondary narratives into the primary one. The treatise narrates basically the building of an ideal city, Sforzinda, but deepens this narration by articulating it with other narrations and by covering topics of great variety. Although these secondary narratives or digressions are interpreted by some scholars as the main source of weakness in Filarete's treatise, they actually allude to a typical aspect of works written to be listened to as well as to be read silently. Moreover, the secondary narratives in this structure serve to entertain the audience, an essential function when a work is intended to be received aurally. Finally, within this narrative structure, nearly every book in the treatise opens with a summary of the preceding one and ends with an introduction of the following book. This technique is especially prevalent in long literary works written to be read aloud in many sessions. In short, the adoption of this technique in Filarete's treatise indicates that it was probably written to be listened to book by book, one book for each session of reading aloud.[47]

It appears that Filarete wrote, dedicated and presented the revised copy of the treatise to Piero de' Medici by imagining that Piero would place the copy in his study, display it on a shelf among other manuscripts, as the only architectural treatise of the time written in the vernacular and illustrated extensively, read it, look at it and listen to it.[48] From this point of view, the treatise appears as documenting its own modes of production. The important point here is that this documentation overlaps with that of the study in the treatise. Or, to put it another way, while constructing an image of the study, the treatise reflects that image through its own textual construction as well. In this sense, to perceive the study as drawn in the treatise calls for a broader perspective that embraces the production and, accordingly, the historicity of the treatise itself.

Filarete wrote his treatise at a time when the architectural profession emerged through the definition of the architect as a practitioner of a liberal art or as an artist whose practice required theory and, accordingly, whose profession and social status were distinct from the craftsman's.[49] In this emergence of the architectural profession, the transformation of architectural patronage in relation to the change in moral and intellectual attitudes towards wealth and its use, the rise of a new wealthy class, and the use of architecture as a tool for converting economic power into political, social and cultural power played a crucial role.[50] Concomitant with these developments in the architectural profession and its patronage, it was also the time that witnessed the appearance of an architectural literature written by architects and addressed to both architects and patrons.[51]

Filarete's treatise was not only a product of this historical context but also an active agent in it, in the sense that it contributed significantly to the emergence of the architectural profession, as well as to the transformation of architectural patronage.[52] Moreover, as one of the pioneering examples of the early modern architectural literature, it was addressed to both architects and patrons, and, more specifically, to Francesco Sforza and Piero de' Medici, two celebrated patrons of the time, to whom it was successively dedicated around the mid-1460s. As such, it was also an example of the early modern practice of dedication. Especially for the works written in the form of manuscripts, this practice paved the way for reaching a more or less general audience, and also for gaining popular approval by means of the circulation of their copies derived from the ones originally presented to dedicatees. Alongside this, it served, for the writers of such works, to receive or improve the patronage of dedicatees, too.[53]

But, quite significantly, Filarete's treatise was also an example of how the practice of dedication did not always guarantee such favourable results. Although the dedication of the treatise to Francesco Sforza and Piero de' Medici may have been effective in the recognition of the treatise among a group of architects and patrons of the time,[54] it could not have performed its expected role successfully in Filarete's effort to enhance his relations with the dedicatees themselves, corresponding to his actual and potential patrons. In other words, it seems that the dedication of the treatise failed to help Filarete adequately improve his position as the court architect of Francesco Sforza, which he eventually left. Moreover, it also probably fell short of helping him realize his hope of working for another patron, who had been influential in his employment by Sforza, namely Piero de' Medici.[55] One possible reason for such a failure may have been related to the issue that the early modern practice of dedication was contingent upon a delicate exchange between writers and dedicatees. While writers presented works to dedicatees, hoping to receive or improve their patronage, dedicatees accepted those works by expecting them to be valuable enough to be shelved in their studies.[56] As I have already mentioned, the early modern courtly studies were spaces of both reading and displaying, and, therefore, what determined the value of those works was not only their contents but also their material qualities.[57] This, then, shows that the chance of Filarete's protection and employment by the dedicatees may have been dependent considerably upon the potentiality of the presentation copies of the treatise to perform as objects to be read as well as to be displayed in the dedicatees' studies.

Today, little is known about the copy presented to Sforza, in particular, and, to a certain extent, about the one presented to Medici.[58] What is known, however, is that these copies were not listed either in the inventory of Sforza's study, dated 1469,[59] or in the ones of Medici's study, dated 1464/5 and 1495.[60] This indicates the possibility that the presentation copies of the treatise may not have been received by the dedicatees as favourably as Filarete expected, and, therefore, may not have been placed in their studies. In the first case, regarding the copy presented to Sforza, the reasons for such a failure remain uncertain. But, in the second case, it seems that the copy presented to Medici probably fell short of fulfilling a crucial requirement of his study. Medici's study was a compact room and, therefore, more than the size and the scope, what distinguished his manuscript collection among the others of the time was its high material quality, reflecting his taste for luxuriously bound and finely decorated copies.[61] Filarete's manuscript was possibly copied on paper, not on vellum; thus, lacking in luxuriousness, it was probably not placed in the study, but in some other location in the Palazzo Medici.[62]

However, this does not necessarily show the complete exclusion of Filarete's treatise from Piero de' Medici's study, because, I would argue, the treatise had already inscribed itself within this space through its historicity, whether it was actually placed there or not. Therefore, what is crucial in reading Filarete's treatise vis-à-vis Piero's study is to trace not only the study in the treatise, but also the treatise in this space. Such a reading makes it possible to see the history of the study through the lens of a version that imagines the study as a space that collected the marks left by the works that were not actually placed there.[63] Accordingly, it is this version of the history of the study that makes visible the treatise in terms of the conditions and motives of its textual and material production, and also of its intended and actual reception. Finally, what I would suggest by referring to Dominick LaCapra is that the documentary value of Filarete's treatise lies in setting one's 'historical imagination' in motion in the sense of 'seeing' Piero de' Medici's study 'differently or [of] transforming [one's] understanding of it through reinterpretation', rather than of 'throwing new light' on this space through 'the discovery of hitherto unknown information'.[64]

Notes

This essay is a revised and extended version of the papers that I presented at the 2003 Society of Architectural Historians' Meeting in Denver, Colorado, and 2004 International Conference of 'Rethinking Architectural Historiography' at Middle East Technical University, Ankara. I am grateful to Dana Arnold, Elvan Altan Ergut and Belgin Turan Özkaya for their invaluable efforts in realizing the project of publishing this book. I owe additional thanks to Belgin and Elvan for their careful reading and insightful comments and, moreover, for their constant support throughout the process of writing and revising this essay. I am also indebted to Davide Deriu for his helpful suggestions.

1 Here, I am considering particularly the developments in cultural history, history of the book, history of reading and intellectual history that have emerged parallel to the ones in cultural and literary criticism.
2 As an example from architectural historiography, see Dana Arnold's *Reading Architectural History*, London and New York, 2002. Although it does not deal specifically with the question of reading documents, it presents a suggestive general outlook for the practice of reading itself as a critical and self-conscious enterprise that is contingent upon the context not only of what is read, but also of who reads it, and how, why and when s/he reads it.
3 Dominick LaCapra, 'Rethinking Intellectual History and Reading Texts', in *Rethinking Intellectual History: Texts Contexts Language*, Ithaca, NY, and London, (1983) 1994, 31; see also his *History & Criticism*, Ithaca, NY, and London, (1985) 1992, 62. For a similar criticism as part of a general criticism of positivist and empirical historical writing, see also Philippe Carrard, *Poetics of the New History: French Historical Discourse from Braudel to Chartier*, Baltimore, MD, and London, 1995, 149–66; and Alun Munslow, *The Routledge Companion to Historical Studies*, London and New York, 2000, 1–20.
4 LaCapra, 'Rethinking Intellectual History', 33.
5 LaCapra, 'Rethinking Intellectual History', 31.
6 LaCapra, *History & Criticism*, 62.
7 LaCapra, *History & Criticism*, 38.
8 LaCapra, *History & Criticism*, 19, 141.
9 Roger Chartier, 'Intellectual History or Sociocultural History? The French Trajectories', in Dominick LaCapra and Steven L. Kaplan (eds), *Modern European History: Reappraisals and New Perspectives*, Ithaca, NY, 1982, 39.

10 Chartier, 'Intellectual History or Sociocultural History?', 39.
11 Chartier, 'Intellectual History or Sociocultural History?', 40.
12 Chartier, 'Intellectual History or Sociocultural History?', 40.
13 See especially Guglielmo Cavallo and Roger Chartier (eds), *A History of Reading in the West*, Amherst, MA, 1999; Roger Chartier, 'Laborers and Voyagers: From the Text and the Reader', *Diacritics*, 22: 2, Summer 1992, 49–61; Roger Chartier, *The Order of Books: Readers, Authors and Libraries in Europe between the Fourteenth and Fifteenth Centuries*, Oxford, 1994; Robert Darnton, 'History of Reading', in Peter Burke (ed.), *New Perspectives on Historical Writing*, University Park, PA, 2001, 157–86; and Donald Francis McKenzie, *Bibliography and the Sociology of Texts*, London, 1986. For a discussion that points out the relevance of the methodological models developed by the history of reading and the history of the book in architectural historiography, and that hints at how these models can be adopted in the case of study and in terms of author, book and reader as its basic components, see Sarah McPhee, 'The Architect as Reader', *Journal of the Society of Architectural Historians*, 58: 3, September 1999, 454–61.
14 Roland Barthes, 'On Reading', in *The Rustle of Language*, Oxford, 1986, 39–41.
15 Francis Ames-Lewis, *The Library and Manuscripts of Piero di Cosimo de' Medici*, New York and London, 1984, 14.
16 Wolfgang Liebenwein, *Studiolo: Storia e tipologia di uno spazio culturale*, Modena, 1988, 55.
17 See especially Wolfger A. Bulst, 'Die urspruengliche Aufteilung des Palazzo Medici in Florenz', *Mittilungen des Kunsthistorischen Institutes in Florenz*, 14, 1970, 368–92; and Liebenwein, *Studiolo*, 55–7.
18 See especially John Pope-Hennessy, *Luca della Robbia*, Oxford, 1980, 42–5; and Dora Thornton, *The Scholar in His Study: Ownership and Experience in Renaissance Italy*, New Haven, CT, and London, 1997, 49. Thornton points out the possibility that Luca della Robbia may have also co-worked with Michelozzo Michelozzi, the architect of the Palazzo, in the creation of the study as a whole.
19 Rab Hatfield, 'Some Unknown Descriptions of the Medici Palace in 1459', *Art Bulletin*, 52, 1970, 235–6; Thornton, *The Scholar in His Study*, 58–9.
20 Ames-Lewis, *The Library and Manuscripts*, 13–14.
21 On Piero de' Medici's collection, see especially Ames-Lewis, *The Library and Manuscripts*; and also Liebenwein, *Studiolo*, 57–65.
22 Ames-Lewis, *The Library and Manuscripts*, 14, 34.
23 *Codex Magliabechianus*, Fol. 190r (hereafter, I shall refer to this codex by its folio numbers); Antonio Averlino detto il Filarete, *Trattato di Architettura*, Anna Maria Finoli and Liliani Grassi (eds), Milan, 1972, 696 ('uno studietto ornato di degnissimi libri e altre cose degne'); *Filarete's Treatise on Architecture, Being the Treatise of Antonio di Piero, Known as Filarete*, New Haven, CT, and London, 1965, 325.
24 Fol. 190r; Filarete, *Trattato*, 696 ('è così il suo studietto: ornatissimo il pavimento, e così il cielo, di vetriamanti fatti a figure degnissime. . . . El maestro di questi invetriamenti si fu Luca della Robbia'); Filarete, *Treatise*, 325 (added words in brackets are John R. Spencer's, the translator of the English edition).
25 Fol. 190r; Filarete, *Trattato*, 696 ('chi v'entra dà grandissima ammirazione'); Filarete, *Treatise*, 325.

26 Among those visitors, I can cite Cardinal Francesco Gonzaga (Thornton, *The Scholar in His Study*, 50), Galeazzo Maria Sforza, Francesco Sforza's – duke of Milan – son and count of Pavia (Hatfield, 'Some Unknown Descriptions', 232–49), and Ippolita Sforza, Francesco Sforza's daughter and Alfonso's – King of Naples – wife (Thornton, *The Scholar in His Study*, 91).

27 For a similar interpretation of this use of the study by Piero de' Medici, see also Lisa Jardine, *Worldy Goods: A New History of the Renaissance*, New York and London, 1996, 183.

28 Fol. 186v; Filarete, *Trattato*, 686 ('uno suo intimo, il quale Nicodemo si chiama, uomo degno, segretario e amato dallo illustrissimo Francesco Sforza, duca quarto di Milano'); Filarete, *Treatise*, 319 (added word in brackets is mine).

29 Fols 186v–187r; Filarete, *Trattato*, 686 ('quando in quelli loro edificii che fanno si fa portare, e di questo piglia sommo piacere e diletto; quando altri tempi fussino che occupazione avesse, o di tempo che nol comportesse, lui mi dice che piglia piacere e passatempo in questo: che si fa portare in uno studio'); Filarete, *Treatise* 319–20 (added words in brackets are mine).

30 Fol. 187r; Filarete, *Trattato*, 686–7 ('il quale quando accadrà . . . vedrà e suoi libri: non altrimenti a vedergli in suo aspetto che una massa d'oro paiono . . . e di questi n'ha tante varie ragioni, che nonché uno dì, ma più d'uno mese bisognerebbe a uno a vedere e intendere la degnità loro, lasciamo stare il leggere. E anche gli auttori degli detti libri non bisogna narrare, perché di qualunque facultà, o in latino, o in Greco, o in vulgare, pure che degno sia, lui l'ha voluto e onoratogli . . . e di scrittura e di minii, e sì d'ornamenti d'oro e di seta. . . . Poi, quando in uno dì voglia con l'occhio trascorrere per suo piacere tutti questi volume, per passare il tempo e solo per dare alla vista recreazione'); Filarete, *Treatise*, 320 (added words in brackets are mine).

31 For a discussion of this topic in general terms, see also Caroline Elam, *'Studioli' and Renaissance Art Patronage*, MA report, Courtauld Institute of Art, London, 1970, 59; Ernst H. Gombrich, 'The Early Medici as Patrons of Art: A Survey of Primary Sources', in Ernest Fraser Jacob (ed.), *Italian Renaissance Studies*, New York, 1960, 302–3; and Liebenwein, *Studiolo*, 61.

32 Fol. 187r; Filarete, *Trattato*, 687–8 ('l'effigie e le imagine di quanti imperadori e d'uomini degni . . . : chi d'oro e chi d'argento, e chi di bronzo e chi di pietre fine, e chi di marmi e d'altre materie', 'gioie e pietre fini', 'vasi d'oro e d'argento e di varie materie fatti, di degna e grande spesa', 'altre cose degne, venute di varii e diversi luoghi del mondo, e varie armadure strane da offendere e da difendere'); Filarete, *Treatise*, 320 (added word in brackets is mine).

33 Fol. 187r; Filarete, *Trattato*, 686 ('E così quando uno e quando un altro si legge o fa leggere'); Filarete, *Treatise*, 320.

34 For a similar interpretation of this use of the study by Piero de' Medici as a space of healing, see also Ames-Francis, *The Library and Manuscripts*, 6; and Liebenwein, *Studiolo*, 61–2.

35 On the study as both a public and a private space in early modern Italy, see Thornton, *The Scholar in His Study*, and also Paula Findlen, *Possessing Nature: Museums, Collecting, and Scientific Culture in Early Modern Italy*, Berkeley and Los Angeles, CA, and London, 1996, 101–29.

36 For the panegyric characteristic of Filarete's treatise, regarding especially Book XXV, see also Hatfield, 'Some Unknown Descriptions', 238.

37 As I shall explain below, there could have been some common textual

features between the copy dedicated and presented to Piero de' Medici and the one dedicated and presented to Francesco Sforza. However, the codex Palatinus, the copy derived from the lost or destroyed original Sforza manuscript but lacking considerable content, does not give any information about Sforza's study. Therefore, it is not possible to read Filarete's treatise vis-à-vis Sforza's study, another well-known example of the time, built in his *Castello* in Milan in the early 1460s, and modelled possibly on Medici's (Thornton, *The Scholar in His Study*, 90–1).

38 Fol. 1r; Filarete, *Trattato*, 4–5 ('Come si sia, pigliala, non come da Vetruvio, né dalli altri degni architetti, ma come dal tuo . . . architetto Antonio Averlino fiorentino'); Filarete, *Treatise*, 3 (added words in brackets are mine).

39 Fol. 1r; Filarete, *Trattato*, 4 ('in latino se ne truova da degnissimi uomini essere fatte'); Filarete, *Treatise*, 3 (added words in brackets are Spencer's, the translator of the English edition).

40 Fol. 1r; Filarete, *Trattato*, 4 ('in latino se ne truova da degnissimi uomini essere fatte, *de le quali credo ne sia copioso*') (emphasis mine.) Curiously, Spencer's translation omits this significant part of the sentence that expresses Filarete's implication. See also Filarete, *Trattato*, 4, n. 4.

41 For the description of the copy of Vitruvius' *De architectura* in Piero de Medici's library, see Ames-Lewis, *The Library and Manuscripts*, 243.

42 For Piero de Medici's interest in the vernacular, see Ames-Lewis, *The Library and Manuscripts*, 7. For a discussion of the language of the treatise in a more general framework, see also Ayşe Sevil Enginsoy, *The Visuality/Orality/Aurality of Filarete's Treatise on Architecture*, PhD thesis, Cornell University, Ithaca, NY, 2002, 48–50. The preface of the codex Palatinus (Filarete, *Trattato*, 8, n. 1; Filarete, *Treatise*, 4, n. 5) does not give any information about such a relationship between the language of the treatise and its intended reception by Francesco Sforza.

43 Fol. 187v; Filarete, *Trattato*, 688 ('nello edificare n'ha piacere intendere, e fattone disegnare. Sì che lui ha voluto da bonissimi maestri gli sieno stati ritratti gli edificii di Roma e d'altri luoghi, e in questi disegni molte volte si diletta in essi. Sì credo ancora che di questo mio libro . . . alcuna volta piglierà piacere'); Filarete, *Treatise*, 320–1 (added words in brackets are mine). In the preface of the codex Palatinus, Filarete (*Trattato*, 8, n. 1; *Treatise*, 4, n. 5) invites Francesco Sforza, rather vaguely, to receive his treatise visually. However, this copy is illustrated in a very limited number; and, furthermore, there is even a possibility, pointed out by Mario Carpo (*Architecture in the Age of Printing: Orality, Writing, Typography, and Printed Images in the History of Architectural Theory*, Cambridge, MA, and London, 2001, 135), that the original presentation copy may not have been illustrated at all. On the intended visual reception of the treatise, see also Enginsoy, *The Visuality/Orality/Aurality*, 83–95.

44 Fol. 1v; Filarete, *Trattato*, 7 ('Sì che non ti rincresca alcuna volta leggere o fare leggere questo architettonico libro'); Filarete, *Treatise*, 3.

45 Fol. 1v; Filarete, *Trattato*, 7 ('questo architettonico libro, nel quale, com'io ho ditto, troverrai, varii modi di edificari, e così varie ragioni di edifizii in esso si contiene. Per la qual cosa, credo, daranno alquanto di piacere a'tuoi orecchi'); Filarete, *Treatise*, 4 (added words in brackets are mine).

46 In the preface of the codex Palatinus, Filarete (*Trattato*, 8, n. 1; *Treatise*, 4, n. 5) explains his intention as to give pleasure to Francesco Sforza's ears. So,

it is possible to suggest that the textual production of the copy originally presented to Sforza was also related to its aural reception. On the intended aural reception of the treatise, see also Enginsoy, *The Visuality/Orality/Aurality*, 75–81.

47 On the relation between the aural reception and textual production of an early modern work, see especially Peter Burke, 'The Renaissance Dialogue', *Renaissance Studies*, 3: 1, 1989, 8; Guglielmo Cavallo and Roger Chartier, 'Introduction', in Cavallo and Chartier (eds), *A History of Reading*, 4; Chartier, 'Laborers and Voyagers', 53 and 58; and William Nelson, 'From "Listen, Lordings" to "Dear Reader"', *University of Toronto Quarterly*, 46: 2, Winter 1976/1977, 110–24. On this relation in Filarete's treatise on architecture, see Enginsoy, *The Visuality/Orality/Aurality*, 75–81; and John R. Spencer, 'Introduction', in Filarete, *Treatise*, xix–xx.

48 Here, I am well aware of the complexity of the visuality, orality and aurality of the treatise, and I do not intend to oversimplify this issue by reading the treatise only in relation to Piero de' Medici's study. So, what I am trying to do is just to focus on one possible way of reading it. For a comprehensive discussion that deals with this complexity by juxtaposing this specific reading with some other possible ones, see Enginsoy, *The Visuality/Orality/ Aurality*.

49 Leopold D. Ettlinger, 'The Emergence of the Italian Architect during the Fifteenth Century', in Spiro Kostof (ed.), *The Architect: Chapters in the History of the Profession*, New York and London, 1986, 96–123; Mary Hollingsworth, 'The Architect in Fifteenth-Century Florence', *Art History*, 7: 4, 1984, 385–410; and Catherine Wilkinson, 'The New Professionalism in the Renaissance', in Kostof, *The Architect*, 124–60.

50 See especially Richard A. Goldthwaite, *Wealth and the Demand for Art in Italy 1300–1600*, Baltimore, MD, and London, 1995, 176–224; Magali Sarfatti Larson, 'Emblem and Exception: The Historical Definition of the Architect's Professional Role', in Judith R. Blau, Mark La Gory and John S. Pipkin (eds), *Professional and Urban Form*, New York, 1983, 53–4, 59; and Magali Sarfatti Larson, 'Patronage and Power', in William S. Saunders (ed.), *Reflections on Architectural Practices in the Nineties*, New York, 1996, 130–2, 134.

51 For a general overview of this architectural literature, see especially Vaughan Hart and Peter Hicks (eds), *Paper Palaces: The Rise of the Renaissance Architectural Treatise*, New Haven, CT, and London, 1998.

52 See especially Enginsoy, *The Visuality/Orality/Aurality*, 105–34, 146–78.

53 Roger Chartier, *Forms and Meanings: Texts, Performances and Audiences from Codex to Computer*, Philadelphia, PA, 1995, 41.

54 Carpo, *Architecture in the Age of Printing*, 134–5; Anna Maria Finoli, 'Nota al testo', in Filarete, *Trattato*, cviii, cxii–cxiii; Deborah Howard, *Jacobo Sansovino: Architecture and Patronage in Renaissance Venice*, New Haven, CT, and London, 1975, 152, n. 97; Alessandro Scafi, 'Filarete e l'Ungaria: l'utopia universitaria di Mattia Corvino', *Storia dell'arte*, 81, 1994, 140; Peter Tigler, *Die Architekturtheorie des Filarete*, Berlin, 1963, 13–15.

55 On Filarete's biography that covers specifically his years in Milan and also his attempt to move to Florence, see especially Evelyn S. Welch, *Art and Authority in Renaissance Milan*, New Haven, CT, and London, 1995, 145–66.

56 Chartier, *Forms and Meanings*, 42.

57 Cavallo and Chartier (eds), *A History of Reading*, 20; and Dorothy M.

Robathan, 'Libraries of the Italian Renaissance', in James Westfall Thomson (ed.), *The Medieval Library*, New York, 1967, 524.

58 In contrast to a generally accepted view, Ames-Lewis (*The Library and Manuscripts*, 473, n. 1) and Finoli ('Nota al testo', cvii) explain that the well-known *Codex Magliabechianus*, now preserved in the Biblioteca Nazionale, Florence, is not the original one presented to Piero de' Medici, but only its copy, since the watermarks date it at around the late 1480s.

59 Elisabeth Pellegrin, *La Bibliothèque des Visconti et des Sforza, ducs de Milan, au XV-siècle*, Paris, 1955.

60 Ames-Lewis, *The Library and Manuscripts*.

61 Ames-Lewis, *The Library and Manuscripts*, 42, 137–8.

62 Ames-Lewis, *The Library and Manuscripts*, 49, 468, n. 38, 473, n. 71. Aside from this, there is no information whether Piero de' Medici ever read, looked at or listened to the treatise, as Filarete intended.

63 Another similar example is Francesco Filelfo's *Sforziade*, which was dedicated successively to Francesco Sforza and Piero de' Medici, and failed to be received favourably by the dedicatees, and to be placed in the latter's study, since it was probably copied on paper, not on vellum (Ames-Lewis, *The Library and Manuscripts*, 49–50, 468, n. 38, 473, n. 71).

64 LaCapra, *History & Criticism*, 18.

10
From architectural history to spatial writing

Jane Rendell

I started out as an architectural designer and came later to architectural history. From there I moved into teaching art and writing art criticism. More recently I have returned to architecture, and to history, but my journey through art changed me and the way I write architectural history. This essay tracks the transformation in my own architectural history writing as a microcosm of a larger shift, a change in the role of critical theory in practising architectural history. It locates architectural history in an interdisciplinary context, between history, theory and practice, and argues that architectural history can no longer only be understood as a form of research that locates the researcher as a disinterested observer. Rather, drawing on the work of post-structuralist feminist theory, I demonstrate how architectural history is a spatialized practice, a mode of writing, which constructs, and is constructed by, the changing position of the author. This is not so much an essay then, as an outline of an approach, my changing approach to the practice of architectural history.[1]

Interdisciplinarity

The term interdisciplinarity is often used interchangeably with multidisciplinarity, but I understand the terms to mean quite different things: multi-disciplinary research refers to a way of working where a number of disciplines are present but maintain their own distinct identities; interdisciplinary research is where individuals operate at the edge of, and between, disciplines and in so doing question the ways in which they usually work. In exploring questions of method or process that discussions of interdisciplinarity inevitably bring to the fore, Julia Kristeva has argued for the construction of 'a diagonal axis':

> Interdisciplinarity is always a site where expressions of resistance are latent. Many academics are locked within the specificity of their field: that is a fact . . . the first obstacle is often linked to individual competence, coupled

with a tendency to jealously protect one's own domain. Specialists are often too protective of their own prerogatives, do not actually work with other colleagues, and therefore do not teach their students to construct a diagonal axis in their methodology.[2]

Engaging with this diagonal axis demands that we call into question what we normally take for granted, that we question our methodologies, the ways we do things, and our terminologies, what we call what we do. The construction of 'a diagonal axis' is necessarily a difficult business. Kristeva's 'expressions of resistance' refers to problems we encounter when we question the disciplines we identify with. And Homi Bhabha has described the encounter between disciplines as an 'ambivalent movement between pedagogical and performative address'.[3] It is precisely for this reason that I am a passionate advocate for interdisciplinary research, because such work is often a transformational experience, combining critical engagement with the emergence of new forms of knowledge.

Much of my research has involved working as part of a multidisciplinary team. In *Strangely Familiar: Narratives of Architecture in the City*, an exhibition, symposium and catalogue, the working group included architects, graphic designers, film makers and multimedia artists. Our response to an invitation to curate and design an architectural exhibition was to reject the notion of architectural history written only by architectural historians, consisting of boards on walls describing the work of famous architects. Instead we invited academics from disciplines outside architecture to provide a short narrative about a specific place in a city and an object related to that place. Each interpretative stance revealed a place that was 'strangely familiar', familiar because certain aspects were already known, strange because they were being revealed in new ways. For *The Unknown City*, the book that followed *Strangely Familiar*, we invited practitioners from art, film and architecture, as well as theorists from geography, cultural studies and architectural and art theory, to comment on the relationship between how designers make and how occupants experience the city.[4]

The edited book offers a good site for developing interdisciplinary debates. The process involves identifying a new area of study, often located at the meeting point between previously distinct and separate areas of thought. This was the case for *Gender, Space, Architecture: An Interdisciplinary Introduction*, a collection of seminal texts that examined the relationship between feminist theory and architectural space, and *InterSections: Architectural Histories and Critical Theories*, a set of specially commissioned essays, where each author was asked to address the relationship between critical theory and architectural history in their own work.[5] In the introduction to *InterSections*, 'From Chamber to Transformer: Epistemological Challenges and Tendencies in the Intersection of Architectural Histories and Critical Theories', Iain Borden and I set out to conceptualize the various different methodologies adopted by authors in negotiating the relationship between critical theory and architectural history. We saw these as nine approaches: Theory as Object of Study, New Architectures, Framing Questions, Critical History, Interdisciplinary Debates, Disclosing Methodology, Self-Reflexivity, Re-Engagement with Theory, and Praxis

For me, theory, specifically critical theory, is what demands and also allows the historian to make explicit their interpretative agenda. The term 'theory' is often understood to refer to modes of enquiry in science, either through induction, the inference of scientific laws or theories from observational evidence, or deduction, a process of reasoning from the general overarching theory to the particular. Critical theory however does not aim to prove a hypothesis nor to prescribe a particular methodology, instead it offers in a myriad of ways self-reflective modes of thought that seek to change the world: 'A critical theory, then, is a reflective theory which gives agents a kind of knowledge inherently productive of enlightenment and emancipation.'[6] The term is usually used to refer to the writings of those of the Frankfurt School; however, I extend the term to include the work of later theorists, post-structuralists, feminists and others, whose thinking is also self-critical and desirous of social change. For me, this kind of theoretical work provides a chance to reflect upon what is there but also to imagine something different, to question and transform rather than describe and affirm.

Critical theory itself is instructive in offering many different ways of considering practice, and the relationship between theory and practice. Binary systems operate around models of sameness, A and not-A, rather than difference, A and B. It is in dialectical thinking, the art of clarifying ideas through discussion, or the exposure of contradiction through debate, where we find a relation between two. Where Georg Wilhelm Friedrich Hegel's dialectic took the form of thesis, anti-thesis and synthesis, and emphasized the direction of movement from spirit to matter, Karl Marx's historical materialism turned Hegelian dialectics on its head, starting from material circumstances and moving to ideational concept.[7] Jacques Derrida's deconstruction is also a critique of binary logic; his writing questions the terms of binary distinctions and puts into play deferrals and differences, which instead suggest undecidability and slippage of meaning.[8] The radical move deconstruction offers in this direction is to think in twos, to think 'both/and' rather than 'either/or'.

But it seems that, of all critical theorists, the work of Gilles Deleuze and Felix Guattari has, in recent years, offered the most seductive way of negotiating the relationship between theory and practice. Their appeal is in no small part due, I suspect, to their way of writing, where thinking operates as a mode of practice. Through 'figures' or 'models' such as the rhizome, the assemblage and the abstract machine, Deleuze and Guattari offer an attempt to go beyond dialectics and deconstruction, providing instead possibilities for imagining spatial relationships between two in terms of 'beside' and 'next to'.[9]

In a fascinating conversation between Deleuze and Michel Foucault that took place in 1972, Deleuze revealed much more directly a 'new relation between theory and practice'. Rather than understanding practice as a consequence of or the inspiration for theory, Deleuze suggests that the 'new relationships appear more fragmentary and partial'.[10] He discusses this process most clearly in terms of 'relays':

> Practice is a set of relays from one theoretical point to another, and theory is a relay from one practice to another. No theory can develop without eventually encountering a wall, and practice is necessary for piercing this wall.[11]

Although the notion of relays at first appears symmetrical, the suggestion that theory needs practice to pierce the wall it encounters is not accompanied by a similar such statement on what practice might need. This may well be because, for Deleuze, theory is 'not for itself':

> A theory is exactly like a box of tools. It has nothing to do with the signifier. It must be useful. It must function. And not for itself. If no one uses it, beginning with the theoretician himself (who then ceases to be a theoretician), then the theory is worthless or the moment is inappropriate.[12]

It is this proactive and inventive aspect to Deleuze, his thinking about what theory can do, that lends itself most to practice, and perhaps here comes close to Marx's term praxis, an action or activity that produces and changes the world. Praxis is what brings theory and practice together into transformative action. In their edited collection, *The Point of Theory*, Mieke Bal and Inge E. Boer put forward a useful way of considering the relationship, that theory is a way of 'thinking through the relations between areas' and 'a way of interacting with objects':[13]

> 'Theory' only makes sense as an attitude; otherwise the generalization of the very concept of 'theory' is pointless. Part of that attitude is the endorsement of interdisciplinarity, of the need to think through the relations between areas where a specific theory can be productive, and of the need to think philosophically about even the most practical theoretical concepts, so-called 'tools'.[14]

My own individual research has investigated the relationship between feminist theory and architectural history, examining the ways in which feminist theory questions the methods of architectural historical enquiry, the subjects and objects we choose to study and the ways in which we study them. In my pursuit of historical knowledge, to understand architecture and gender in early nineteenth-century London, two texts seduced me, one a feminist polemic, the other an urban narrative from the 1820s.[15] These two created an intersection, a dialectical site of methodological struggle, where alternating questions of theoretical and historical knowledge were raised.

The first time I read the French feminist psychoanalyst and philosopher Luce Irigaray's essay 'Women on the Market'[16] I was inspired. Irigaray's text was a critical and poetic expression of the anger I felt about women's oppression. Her writing fired me as it has many others. For me, 'Women on the Market' served as a political manifesto, a source of creative inspiration and a theoretical tool-kit. I read it in the park, on the bus, in bed. The more I read Irigaray, the more I felt I knew about the way in which space was gendered in nineteenth-century London. Yet I had not looked at a single piece of primary evidence.

Starting with Marx's critique of commodity capitalism, Irigaray argues that women can also be understood as commodities in patriarchal exchange. In Irigaray's version of patriarchy, men and women are distinguished from each other through their relationship to property and space: men own property/women are property; men own and occupy spaces and women/women are space. Irigaray's work suggested to me a way of thinking about the gendering of space that was dynamic, where the spatial patterns composed between men and women as they occupy space, both materially and metaphorically, could be considered choreographies of connection and separation, screening and displaying, moving and containing.

I discovered Irigaray through passion, but, as I read, a more distanced and abstracted stance emerged. Irigaray's 'theory' told back to me what I already knew, but in a different language, one which seemed to speak objectively rather than subjectively. Unlike my own, her voice held weight within academia, and so could reasonably influence the way I knew and understood events in the past, the way I did history. Before I had looked at any primary documents, Irigaray allowed me to speculate – in theory – about the gendering of architectural space in early nineteenth-century London.

The second text that held my attention was Pierce Egan's *Life in London* (1820–1), an example of an early nineteenth-century ramble.[17] In the early nineteenth century rambling was defined as the pursuit of pleasure, specifically sexual pleasure.[18] In *The Pursuit of Pleasure* I looked briefly at the cartography of the ramble in London overall and then focused on a particular part of the ramble, London's St James's, an area bounded by Pall Mall, Piccadilly, St James's Street and the Haymarket.[19] Represented as the most élite upper-class or, more precisely, aristocratic neighbourhood in London, and, from the late eighteenth century onwards, a predominantly masculine district, St James's offered a highly specific urban site through which to explore ideas of gender and space.[20] My investigation took me to a number of architectural spaces – streets, clubs, assembly rooms, opera houses and theatres – all places of upper-class leisure.

Methodologically, the sites of ramble, the activity of rambling and figures such as the rambler provided me with new objects of study for architectural history through which I could develop alternative theoretical models for organizing historical enquiry and architectural analysis. I argued that typically architectural history had dealt with form, style, physical modification and spatial typology, but, if we considered the production, reproduction and representation of urban space through rambling, then we could create a new conceptual and physical map of the city, placing urban locations in temporal and sequential relations. In search of pleasure, in constant motion, rambling represented the city as multiple sites of desire, redefining architecture as the space of related social and gendered interactions rather than as a series of isolated and static objects.

My pursuit of pleasure worked in two directions, from the theoretical to the historical and from the historical to the theoretical, from Irigaray's 'Women on the Market' to 1820s London, and from *Life in London* to the gendering of architectural space through rambling. Irigaray's theoretical work suggested to me that the discipline of architectural history should be extended to consider the gendered and spatial relations of movement and vision; *Life in London* in particular, and rambling texts in general, allowed me to situate and explore some of these broader theoretical issues in more specific terms.

Spatial writing

But let us not generalize the relationship between theory and practice; each historical moment and specific context offers a different set of conditions for making connections between them, and each historian adopts their own specific angle. I trained and worked first as an architect or practitioner, and later as an historian and theorist. This greatly influences the place I occupy between theory and history. However, although I was educated first as a spatial practitioner, it was reading theory that changed my world – allowed me to know things differently.

Numerous post-structuralist and materialist feminists have argued for the positional and situated nature of knowledge. New ways of knowing and being are discussed in spatial terms – 'mapping', 'locating', 'situating', 'positioning' and 'boundaries'. Employed as critical tools, spatial metaphors constitute powerful political devices for examining the relationship between identity and place, subjectivity and positionality. *Where* I am makes a difference to what I can know and who I can be. Such feminist theories provide an account of subjects constructed in relation to others, whose knowledges are contingent and partial rather than 'all knowing'.[21] For example, Donna Haraway's 'situated knowledges', Jane Flax's 'standpoint theory' and Elsbeth Probyn's notion of 'locality' all use 'position' to negotiate such ongoing theoretical disputes as the essentialism/constructionism debate. In particular, Rosi Braidotti's notion of the 'nomadic subject' provides an important 'theoretical figuration for contemporary subjectivity'. The nomad describes an epistemological condition, a kind of knowingness (or unknowingness) that refuses fixity, that allows us to think between or 'as if', to articulate another reality.[22] My own recent research has taken up such concerns to question the very position that the author holds in relation not only to theoretical ideas and architectural objects, but also to the materiality of writing as a critical and spatial practice.

When Jonathan Hill asked me to contribute a chapter about DIY (Do It Yourself) for a book he was editing called *Occupying Architecture*, I decided to write about a place in which I had previously lived. My co-habitant of that house, Iain Hill, had been making our living space through an unusual mode of DIY, much of which involved the removal, rather than the addition, of building elements, as well as the use of objects for purposes for which they had not been designed:

> On a leafy street in Clapham, minutes from the common, is a terraced house which was my home for two years. Scattered all over London, all over England, all over the world, are other homes, houses where I once lived. In some still standing, I return and revisit past lives and loves. Others have been destroyed, physically crushed in military coups, or erased from conscious memory only to be revisited in dreams.
>
> Through its fragile structure this house physically embraced my need for transience, and it was perhaps this unhomeliness, which made it feel more like home to me than any other.[23]

In my previous work in architectural history, in 'taking a position', I had used theory to elucidate a certain approach to the definition of the site of research and the interpretation of archival material in historical methodology. I referenced theoretical texts and ideas to perhaps justify my own position. This was the first piece of writing where I referred to my life as the subject matter for theoretical reflection and where I started to experiment with different personal voices, from the experiential to the intellectual. This incorporation of the personal into the critical had different kinds of effect depending on the reader. Other academics and artist friends loved the piece – they liked it because I was so 'present' in the work. But my retelling of events had disturbed two important people in my personal life. My mother was upset by my description of this house, as 'more like home to me than any other' and my description rendered the house unrecognizable to Iain Hill.

The responses I received made me aware that words do not mean the same thing for writer and reader and raised many questions about storytelling. While the subject matter and subjective stance of a personal story may upset and destabilize the objective tone of academic writing, as was my intention, the presentation of such events was uncomfortable for those involved in the story. Unlike the fiction writer, who may use friends and family in novels, but who provides a disguise through a character, my writing offered nowhere to hide. Although I was writing about the transitory nature of a house in which I once lived and the questionable DIY of my housemate, I was not simply recounting a series of events in my life, I was doing so in order to question the authorial position of the architect and the permanence of architecture assumed by the profession. So, here, the telling of a personal story is a critical act. This piece of writing, architectural theory as others have called it, is the first of what I have now come to call my 'confessional constructions'.

Mieke Bal has pointed out that the story a person remembers is not identical to the one that happened, but that it is the 'discrepancy' itself that becomes the dramatic act.[24] And, for bell hooks, it is the lack of distinction between 'fact and interpretation of fact' in our remembering of the past that has influenced her own thinking about autobiography:

> Audre Lourde – introduced to readers the concept of biomythography to encourage a move away from the notion of autobiography as an exact accounting of life. Encouraging readers to see dreams and fantasies as part of the material we use to invent the self.[25]

Having read this commentary on Lourde by hooks, I misremembered Lourde's term 'biomythography' as 'biomorphology', or in my mind 'the shape a life takes', reflecting my interest in autobiography as a kind of spatial writing.

At the BookArtBookShop in London, artist Brigid McLeer was invited to curate the outside wall in 2002. As part of 'LLAW', she asked me to write a 'page' that would be pasted to that wall for a month. Initially I wanted to research the history of the construction of the building and insert a text that suggested connections between the material construction of the wall and the ways in which we make our own edges as people. But Brigid made it clear to me that, as a curator, she was less interested in the physical construction of the text and more concerned with the ways in which I might explore my own position as the subject of my own writing. How would the public placing of the 'page' on the wall influence what I might write?

Through discussion with Brigid a new way of working emerged that changed my understanding of the possibilities for the layout of the text on the page and my place within it. A confession was interwoven with reflections upon what it means to confess. I placed the footnotes down the side of the page, numbered from bottom to top, to read upwards as one builds a wall. These contained architectural specifications by an architect friend, Deborah Millar, about how to construct walls and openings that touched upon my own interest in how the 'confessional construction' was both a revealing and a masking of the self. I had previously considered autobiographical writing to be a process of revelation, one that uncovered the truth beneath. Uncovering for me involved being prepared to lose or at least question authorial control. But, once a story is repeated, I discovered, the fear dissipates and the confessional voice reclaims an authorial position.

The way a writer positions herself in her writing is architectural and has implications for the way in which the writer meets the reader. Certain forms of writing make walls, others create meeting points; some stories close down possibilities for discussion, while others invite participation. Italo Calvino has explored the relationship the writer has to his/her writing in terms of his/her position inside and/or outside a text,[26] as well as the places writers occupy in terms of their different identities as subjects or 'I's.[27] In a collection of critical essays, A. S. Byatt examines her fascination with 'topological fictions', fictions where the term topological means 'both mathematical game-playing, and narratives constructed with spatial rather with temporal images'.[28] Byatt names certain works by Primo Levi, Italo Calvino and George Perec as the most interesting examples of this kind of writing.[29] For me, these authors have different ways of making topological fictions, or spatial writing. While Calvino often uses combination and permutation as strategies for constructing the shape of stories, Perec's playfulness in the ordering of observations and descriptions of existing places produces new imaginative spaces. Discussing his own interest in 'topological fictions', Calvino refers to a review by Hans Magnus Enzensberger of labyrinthine narratives in the work of Jorge Luis Borges and Robbe Grillet, where Enzensberger describes how, by placing narratives inside one another, these authors make places where it is easy to get lost.[30]

This essay ends with such a place, one where it is easy to get lost. When I read out my 'confessional construction', pasted to the wall of the BookArtBookShop, as one would read a page – from left to right, from top to bottom – I transformed my relation to the page and its contents. What has been created through this process, by accident it seems, is a series of encounters with walls that only the sound of my voice can carry you through.

In 1989, on the way from Austin, Texas

FACEWORK:

Protect against damage and disfigurement, particularly arises of openings and corners.

I've always considered autobiographical writing to be confessional, part of a process of revelation, one that uncovers the truth beneath. But recently

14

to Tikal, Guatemala, I met a Chicano

BASIC WORKMANSHIP:

Store bricks/blocks in stable stacks clear of the ground. Protect from inclement weather and keep clean and dry.

I've come to realise that a confessing is not a revealing, but a constructing (of ourselves). 2 Writing about myself is a making of myself. 3 Although

13

artist, who gave me a book, *The*

POLYETHYLENE DAMP PROOF COURSE:

Joint sheets with continuous strips of mastic between 150mm overlaps and seal with tape along the edge of the upper sheet, leaving no gaps. Ensure that sheets are clean and dry at the time of jointing.

the writing professes, confesses, to be a window or an opening to an

If sheets cannot be kept dry, double welted joints may be used, taped to hold in position prior to laying concrete.

interior, 4 it might better be described as a mask, 5 or a wall, 6 a boundary

12

***Passionate Nomad.* The book was the**

Lay neatly and tuck well in angles to prevent bridging. Form folded welts at corners in upstands.

between myself and another. 7 As such it is a form of physic architecture.

11

diary of Isabelle Eberhardt, a young

SECOND HAND LONDON STOCK FACING BRICKWORK:

Bricks: Second hand London Stock bricks, to match existing, free from deleterious matter such as mortar, plaster, paint, bituminous materials and organic growths. Bricks to be sound, clean and reasonably free from cracks and chipped arises.

Some bricks can be salvaged from demolitions C10/5–7. As far as possible these should be re-used for making good reveals to same, in order to achieve best possible colour match.

Sometimes I draw others into my stories – my father, my mother, even my lover. 8 sometimes it is without their consent. 9 They are an integral part of

10

ALTERATIONS/EXTENSIONS:

Except where a straight vertical joint is specified, new existing facework in the same plane to be tooth bonded together at every course to give continuous appearance.

woman from an affluent French family

Where new lintels or walling are to support existing structure, completely fill top joint with semi-dry mortar, hard packed and well rammed to ensure full load transfer after removal of temporary supports.

my confessional construction. 10 If they are the building materials, then who is

9

the architect? 1

ALTERATIONS/EXTENSIONS:

Arrange brick courses to line up with existing work.

Brick to brick: 4 courses high at 8 course centres.

Brick to block, block to brick or block to block: Every

who spent the later part of her short

alternate block course.

Bond new walling into pockets with all voids filled solid.

8

My love of writing is generated through a desire for encounters. I often tell stories about myself to make a place to meet my reader.

FIRE STOPPING:

Fill joints around joist ends built into cavity walls with mortar to seal cavities from interior of building.

Ensure a tight fit between brickwork and cavity barriers to prevent fire and smoke penetration.

Life disguised as an Arab man wander-

7

In telling you about myself, I reveal aspects of myself, make myself vulnerable. 11 But am I really revealing?

FACEWORK:

Keep courses evenly spaced using gauge rods/ set out carefully to ensure satisfactory junctions and joints with adjoining or built-in elements or components.

ing the North African deserts. She died

6

Is it not that I am showing you my vulnerability, showing you who I am? 12

FACEWORK:

Select bricks/blocks with unchipped arises. Cut with a masonry saw where cut edges will be exposed to view.

5

aged 28, on 20.10.1904 in a flash flood at

TIMBER WINDOWS:

To BS 644: Part 1

Manufactured by a firm currently registered under the British Woodworking Federation Accreditation Scheme.

Materials generally: To BS EN 942.

Are my stories walls or windows? 13

When not predrilled or specified otherwise, position fixings no more than 150mm from each end of jamb, adjacent to each hanging point of opening lights and at maximum 450mm centres.

4

Ain-Sefra. Her diary is one of my

BASIC WORKMANSHIP:

Bring both leaves of cavity walls to the same level at

– Every course containing rigid ties.

– Every third tie course for double triangle/butterfly ties.

– Courses in which lintels are to be bedded.

*What does psycho-analysis say about boundaries? * What do walls say about*

Do not carry up any one leaf more than 1.5m in one day unless permitted by the CA.

self-protection?

3

favourite books. I too have had addictive

BASIC WORKMANSHIP:

Build walls in stretching half lap bond when not specified otherwise.

Lay bricks/blocks on a full bed of mortar; do not furrow. Fill all cross joints and collar joints: do not tip and tall.

Rack back when raising quoins and other advance work. Do not use toothing.

Are architectural and psychic elements, processes and structures analogous? 14

2

relationships with food and travel.

* On the corner of Charles Street and Pitfield Street, she found a bookshop, one that she had not noticed before. She walked in. On the left-hand wall, lying on the floor, quite close to the wall, she saw a book. When she bent down to pick it up, she saw it was a copy of Sigmund Freud, *The Essentials of Psycho-analysis*, London, 1986. She turned to page 11. Crouching there, close to the floor, head almost touching the wall, she started to read: 'Our hypothesis (. . .)'. She read for 41 seconds.

I opened this essay arguing that critical theory provides an important contribution to architectural history, challenging the discipline to make explicit its thought processes and modes of operation. In closing, I note that such theorized histories are spatial practices – writings – material structures constructed by and for embodied subjects that position, and are positioned by, reader and writer.

Notes

1 Parts of the essay have been previously published in the following places: Jane Rendell, *The Pursuit of Pleasure: Gender, Space and Architecture in Regency London*, New Brunswick, NJ, 2002; Jane Rendell, 'Between Two: Theory and Practice', *Journal of Architecture*, 8, Summer 2003, 221–37; Jane Rendell, 'Architectural History as Critical Practice', in Elizabeth Tostrop and Christian Hermansen (eds), *CONTEXT: (Theorizing) History in Architecture, Proceedings of Historicity in Architecture and Design, the Annual Nordic Research Conference*, Oslo School of Architecture, 2003, 17–29; Jane Rendell, 'Writing in Place of Speaking', in Sharon Kivland (ed.), *Transmission: Speaking and Listening*, Sheffield, 2003.
2 Julia Kristeva, 'Institutional Interdisciplinarity in Theory and Practice: An Interview', in Alex Coles and Alexia Defert (eds), *The Anxiety of Interdisciplinarity, De-, Dis-, Ex-*, vol. 2, London, 1997, 3–21, 5–6.
3 Homi K. Bhabha, *The Location of Culture*, London, 1994, 163.
4 Iain Borden, Joe Kerr, Alicia Pivaro and Jane Rendell (eds), *Strangely Familar: Narratives of Architecture in the City*, London, 1996.
5 Jane Rendell, Barbara Penner and Iain Borden (eds), *Gender, Space, Architecture: An Interdisciplinary Introduction*, London, 1999, and Iain Borden and Jane Rendell (eds), *InterSections: Architectural History and Critical Theory*, London, 2000.
6 Raymond Geuss, *The Idea of Critical Theory: Habermas and the Frankfurt School*, Cambridge, 1981, 2.
7 See for example, G. A. Cohen, 'Images of History in Hegel and Marx', in *Karl Marx's Theory of History: A Defence*, Oxford, 1978, 1–27. See also Karl Marx, 'Critique of Hegel's Dialectic and General Philosophy', in David McLellan (ed.), *Karl Marx: Selected Writings*, Oxford, 1977, 96–109.
8 See for example, Jacques Derrida, *Of Grammatology* (1967), trans. Gayatri Chakravorty Spivak, Baltimore, MD, 1976, 6–26, and Jacques Derrida, *Dissemination* (1972), trans. Barbara Johnson, London, 1981.
9 See for example, Gilles Deleuze and Felix Guattari, *A Thousand Plateaus: Capitalism and Schizophrenia*, London, 1988, 25, 88, 90.
10 'Intellectuals and Power: A Conversation between Michel Foucault and Gilles Deleuze' (1972), in *Language, Counter-memory, Practice: Selected Essays and Interviews*, Ithaca, NY, 1977, 205–17, 205. This text came to my attention at a seminar conducted by Andrew Ballantyne at the University of Nottingham.
11 'Intellectuals and Power', 206.
12 'Intellectuals and Power', 208.
13 Mieke Bal and Inge E. Boer (eds), *The Point of Theory: Practices of Cultural Analysis*, Amsterdam, 1994, 8–9.
14 Bal and Boer (eds), *The Point of Theory*, 8.
15 Rendell, *The Pursuit of Pleasure*.

16 Luce Irigaray, 'Women on the Market', in *This Sex Which Is Not One* (1977), trans. Catherine Porter with Carolyn Burke, Ithaca, NY, 1985, 170–91.

17 Pierce Egan, *Life in London; or, the day and night scenes of Jerry Hawthorn, Esq, and his elegant friend Corinthian Tom, accompanied by Bob Logic, the Oxonian, in their Rambles and Sprees through the Metropolis*, London, 1820–1.

18 See *Oxford English Dictionary*, CD-ROM, 2nd edn, 1989, and Eric Partridge, *A Dictionary of Slang and Unconventional English*, London, 1964, 958. See also Francis Grose, *A Classical Dictionary of the Vulgar Tongue*, London, 1788, n.p., and Pierce Egan, *Grose's Classical Dictionary of the Vulgar Tongue, revised and corrected, with the addition of numerous slang phrases, collected from tried authorities by Pierce Egan*, London, 1823, n.p. Words such as rambling and the associated ranging featured in the titles of a large number of contemporary magazines concerned with sex. See, for example, *The Rambler's Magazine or the Annals of Gallantry, Glee, Pleasure, and the Bon Ton; calculated for the entertainment of the Polite World and to furnish a Man of Pleasure with a most delicious bouquet of amorous, bacchanalian, whimsical, humorous, theatrical and literary entertainment*, London, 1783–9; *The Ranger's Magazine or the Man of Fashion's Companion, being the XXXXX of the Month and general assemblage of Love, Gallantry, Wit, Pleasure, Harmony, Mirth, Glee, and Fancy, containing monthly List of Covent Garden Cyprians; or, the Man of Pleasures Vade Mecum*, London, 1795; *The Rambler's Magazine or Annals of Gallantry or Glee, Pleasure and Bon Ton*, London, 1820; *The Rambler's Magazine or Fashionable Emporium of Polite Literature*, London, 1822; *Rambler*, 1824; and *Rambler's*, 1828.

19 See, for example, F. H. W. Shepperd (ed.), 'The Parish of St. James's Westminster, Part 1, South of Piccadilly', in *The Survey of London*, London, 1960, 29; Shepperd (ed.), 'The Parish of St. James's Westminster, Part 2, South of Piccadilly', in *Survey*, 30; Shepperd (ed.), 'The Parish of St. James's Westminster, Part 1, North of Piccadilly', in *Survey*, 31; Shepperd (ed.), 'The Parish of St. James's Westminster, Part 2, North of Piccadilly', in *Survey*, 32.

20 See, for example, P. J. Atkins, 'The Spatial Configuration of Class Solidarity in London's West End 1792–1939', *Urban History Year Book*, 17, 1990, 36–65, 38; Penelope J. Corfield, 'The Capital City', in *The Impact of English Towns 1700–1800*, Oxford, 1982, 66–81, 78; and Leonard D. Schwarz, 'Social Class and Social Geography: The Middle Classes in London at the End of the Eighteenth Century', *Social History*, 7: 2, 1982, 167–85, 178, 181.

21 See, for example, Donna Haraway, 'Situated Knowledges: The Science Question in Feminism and the Privilege of Partial Knowledge', *Feminist Studies*, 14: 3, Fall, 1988, 575–603, and Elspeth Probyn, 'Travels in the Postmodern: Making Sense of the Local', in Linda Nicholson (ed.), *Feminism/Postmodernism*, London, 1990, 176–89, 178.

22 Rosi Braidotti, *Nomadic Subjects*, New York, 1994, 22.

23 Jane Rendell, 'Doing it, (Un)Doing it, (Over)Doing it Yourself: Rhetorics of Architectural Abuse', in Jonathan Hill (ed.), *Occupying Architecture*, London, 1998.

24 Mieke Bal, *Looking In: The Art of Viewing*, Amsterdam, 2001, 47–8.

25 bell hooks, *Wounds of Passion: A Writing Life*, 1998, xix.

26 Italo Calvino, 'Literature as Projection of Desire', in *The Literature Machine*, London, 1997, 58.

27 Italo Calvino, 'Cybernetics and Ghosts', in *The Literature Machine*, London, 1997, 15.
28 A. S. Byatt, *On Histories and Stories*, London, 2001, 139–41.
29 See Primo Levi, *The Periodic Table*, London, 2000; Italo Calvino, *If on a Winter's Night a Traveller*, London, 1998; and Georges Perec, *Life: A User's Manual*, London, 1992.
30 Hans Magnus Enzensberger, 'Topological Structures in Modern Literature', *Sur*, May–June 1966.

11

Presenting Ankara
Popular conceptions of architecture and history

Elvan Altan Ergut

> The most important monument of Ankara is undoubtedly the tomb of Mustafa Kemal Atatürk, a magnificent classic building appropriately designed with sombre lines and set on a vast esplanade. Access to this, known in Turkish as *Anıtkabir*, is through a triumphant alley lined with granite lions. It is a fitting monument to the greatness of the founder of modern Turkey.[1]

As exemplified in this description from a tourist web site, *Anıtkabir*, the Mausoleum of Atatürk (Figure 11.1a), has become a symbol, and is reproduced in almost every popular image of Ankara, the capital of Turkey. Such images and words, as they circulate in various media, convey meanings about the built environment. Thus, different visions of a city are institutionalized: they are not the actual buildings but their reproductions in books, journals, exhibitions, web sites, etc. that affect how and why certain works are valued, establishing a 'canon of famous architecture'.[2] The diffusion of visual and verbal accounts of buildings in professional printed media has been well investigated and criticized.[3] Popular perceptions about architecture and the city, on the other hand, are mediated by wider means of communication such as films, souvenirs or tourist guides. Unlike historical and theoretical studies that address a professional audience, popular accounts of buildings reproduce architecture to be consumed by a broad range of publics, and necessitate thinking of architecture as 'a process of reception, representation, use, spectacularization and commodification'.[4]

The verbal and visual representations of Ankara in tourist guides,[5] prepared by private as well as governmental and administrative bodies such as the Ministry of Culture and Tourism, the Metropolitan Municipality and the Governor's Office, provide a framework of discussion on popular conceptions of architecture and history of the city. These accounts construct canonical visions of 'the city at a glance', by advertising 'highlights/attractions' as the

Figure 11.1a Anıtkabir, Mausoleum of Atatürk, in Ankara; Emin Onat and Orhan Arda, 1942. (Mehmet Hengirmen, Anakara, 2002.)

'sites of interest'. Through a general survey of such accounts, this essay aims to analyse the discourses that identify Ankara by defining certain buildings and places as 'sites to be seen' for tourists, to evaluate how and why these sites are (re)presented to the public, and to discuss the resultant paradigms of perception that attribute different meanings to the history of architecture of the city.

The 'national' city

In the brochure of the 'Miniaturk' (Figure 11.1b) – the miniaturized popular park of 'Turkish architecture' recently opened in İstanbul – the Mausoleum is also defined as 'the most important and the most meaningful building of the Republican period'.[6] The meaning of the Mausoleum of Atatürk is clear

Presenting Ankara 153

Figure 11.1b Model of *Anıtkabir* in Miniaturk, İstanbul. (*Miniaturk Rehber* (Miniaturk Guide), İstanbul.)

enough beyond its architectural significance because it is where the most sacred rituals of the nation-state are held in the name of its founder. The Turkish Republic was founded in 1923, signifying the ultimate breakdown of the Ottoman Empire. The formation of a new regime necessitated a new political centre to represent the awareness and acceptance of this historical event. The most significant strategy to demonstrate the intention of changing the entire social and spatial organization of a country is to relocate the capital city; and this was why the new Turkish Republic declared Ankara as the capital, instead of İstanbul – the capital of the Ottoman Empire.[7]

Most significantly, by declaring Ankara as the capital, the new state aimed to rid itself of all the reminiscences of a defeated empire. The remarks of a foreign tourist who visited Ankara at the time exemplify the general view about the new capital city: 'Ankara is a city of the future. İstanbul is a city of the past.... What a person who really wants to know Turkey of today and tomorrow should do, is to take the first train for Ankara.'[8] Once it was chosen as the seat of the national government, the construction of the new state was literally put into action by the construction of Ankara. A competition was held in 1927 for the production of a plan on which to develop the city. The winning design by a German planner, Hermann Jansen, proposed the growth of the city along the major north–south axis.

According to the plan, Ankara began to change and grow rapidly from the late 1920s onwards with the construction of various buildings, mainly to house the government, administrative, legal and economic facilities, and the increasing number of people who began to populate the new capital. The newly built environment, with its wide avenues, parks, shops, theatres and restaurants, provided and enlivened a new social life for the growing population of Ankara. The new capital city of Ankara thus developed away from the old one, towards the south where the buildings of the Parliament and the Presidential Palace were located.

Although not as frequently as *Anıtkabir*, the Parliament and the Presidential Palace are also among the cited 'attractions' in Ankara in tourist as well as official guides of the city, for such buildings are accepted to symbolize the new system of the Republic. The criteria for their inclusion in guides are determined with reference to their representative quality of a certain collective identity, i.e. the identity of the Turkish Republic in this case: what underlies the inclusion of these buildings in tourist guides, catalogues or web sites, are the ideological and political meanings attributed to the building of a nation-state. It is the common collectivist approach that chooses certain buildings as representative of 'Republican Turkish architecture' in Ankara. 'Capital cities exist not by virtue of their own size or economic importance, but because of their relationship to a nation-state', as symbolic national centres; and 'each capital city is seen as in some sense representative of its state and its characteristics'.[9] Similarly, the idea of Ankara as the symbol of the 'nation' has been the most significant among the canonical visions of the city since it was declared the capital of the new Republic.

Capital cities are (re)constructed as such on the assumption that buildings not only house but also represent a 'nation', as does the 'nation'-state in political terms. The assumption here is based on nationalist ideology, which accepts that the 'nation' is a real entity to be characterized by a homogeneous, unified and stable identity. Along these lines, as the large number of books on 'national' architectures demonstrates, architectural production is also defined – mostly unconsciously – in 'national' categories, and each 'nation' is accepted to have its own distinctive architecture that is evidence of, and implicitly supportive for, the powerful existence of the 'nation'. This provides ample evidence that the validity of a 'nationally' divided world is also present in architectural thought, and the concept of a unified 'national architecture' is often accepted as unproblematic. Hence, for example, two Turkish architects stated in the early 1930s:[10]

> It is certain that each country has its specific characteristics. Therefore, it is also natural that it will have an architecture specific to itself. As it is possible to differentiate a Chinese from a Frenchman, a German from a Turk, it should also be possible to differentiate architecture in Vienna from that in İstanbul, French architecture from Russian architecture.[11]

Instead of defining the 'national', contemporary scholars of nationalism deal with when, how and why 'national identity' is formulated, and hence they accept nationalism as a process rather than an ideology. As a process, nationalism creates, invents, imagines and constructs 'nations': they are not natural, given entities. As such, nationalism is a continuous process of 'nation'-building that generates 'national identity' specifically in time and place – always leaving aside, of course, what or who is unwanted in, or to be excluded from, the 'nation'.[12] These critiques have been effective in questioning the notions of 'nation', and consequently 'national architecture', as a given, i.e. as having synthetic and unchanging meanings. Taking into consideration the fact that the 'nation' is an ideological concept the reality of which requires a certain degree of construction and imagination, it can be said that the 'nation' is also conventionally 'imagined' as reflected in architecture throughout the process of 'nation'-building.

On the basis of nationalist processes lie the alleged oppositions between 'national' and 'international', 'past' and 'future', 'traditional' and 'modern', and 'East' and 'West'. On the one side, 'national identity' is based on the idea of a common culture that is accepted as having been rooted in common history. All 'nations' strive to establish their distinct cultural identity by referring to their supposed enduring tradition. Still, once the system of 'nation'-states has been founded, all 'nations' should also strive to satisfy the new 'rules' of being a unified 'nation'. It should be remembered that the desire to have such a distinctively defined 'national identity' is itself something 'modern', related to the 'nation'-state formation as a 'modern' phenomenon with its specific understanding of progress through the 'norms and forms' of the state. This underlying aim of a specific kind of progress thus makes the definition of 'national identity' explicable principally in terms of transforming the undesired traditional identities and foretelling new ones, the ones that are accepted as necessary in catching up the progress defined according to specific values, qualities and skills of the new age.

From the late eighteenth century onwards, Western European thinkers have promoted the idea of progress as part of the new 'modern' age. Consequently, Eurocentric evaluations have permeated studies of nationalism, attempting 'to correlate geographical, historical and social elements with an ideological distinction'[13] that derives from the standpoint and focus of the Western European experience, further complicating the issue of identity formation in 'non-western' contexts such as Turkey.

156 Elvan Altan Ergut

The seeming paradox of this kind of dual move towards both past and future, including elements attributed to both the 'tradition' of Turkey and the 'progress' of the 'West', becomes superficial when the move is understood as selective in order to construct the desired 'national identity'. What is significant here is that the framework for defining identity is constituted selectively by incorporating certain aspects of tradition that are taken to be relevant to how the future is formulated. Different and differing interpretations of traditional identities and those attributed to the 'West' have constituted the framework in which the identity of the new state is variously formulated in Turkey.

The 'modern' city

Once Ankara is envisioned as the 'symbolic centre of national identity', it is naturally trapped in between such dichotomies of nationalism. Accordingly, from the foundation of the Republic, one of the seemingly dominant constructs about the built environment in Ankara has been the vision of a 'modern' city that has been attempting to take its part in the western world. Hence, for example, the first tourist guide of the city, which was written by Ernest Mamboury and published in early Republican years, introduces the changes that the Republic has brought about in a celebratory tone (Figure 11.2), stating that, 'with the application of the plan of Jansen, who is a master of modern urbanism, Ankara will no more have anything to envy at European capital cities'.[14] Similar remarks still characterize the definitions of Ankara in popular accounts, which emphasize the western – i.e. European – attributes

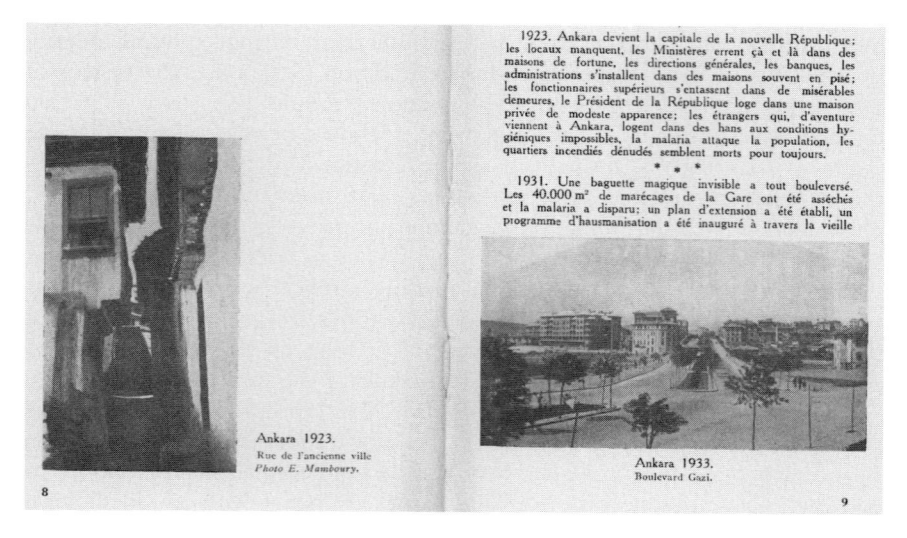

Figure 11.2 Photographs of Ankara in 1923 and 1933. (Ernest Mamboury, *Ankara Guide Touristique*, Ankara, 1933.)

of the city. In tourist web sites, for example, Ankara is praised as 'the only large urban centre in the interior of Turkey with a European appearance',[15] or as 'a sprawling urban mass thoroughly organized and well-planned and much [more] European in look than most of the cities in Turkey'.[16]

The construction of the capital city in the early Republican period was based on the idea that Ankara was to be a new city where a modern, contemporary and western way of life would emerge, in order to be exemplary for the development of other cities in the country, and also in order to symbolize the 'modernity' of the new Republic. The manner in which the construction of the new capital commanded the allegiance of people during the early period of the Turkish Republic exemplifies the representative and creative potency of architecture. Hence, a foreign tourist in Ankara during the early Republican years wrote:

> [T]he waiter who brings our breakfast inquires how we like 'his' new capital with a pride which makes us feel that he must have personally had a hand in its building. And so he has, for Ankara is a city built by the people of a living generation – by Atatürk and his followers. They wanted and they have for a capital an absolutely new city which would symbolize the breaking away from the old and which would demonstrate to themselves and their visitors what can be done in a hitherto backward Turkey. After breakfast as we drive along the wide boulevards passing magnificent, modern, light-filled schools, parks and government buildings which do credit to the best modern architects, we cannot help exclaiming over them. 'Well, of course it's all terribly new. We have only been building the city for fifteen years and there's a lot more for us to do', the taxi driver apologizes, but not without pride. 'You know we started practically from scratch'.[17]

'A radical break with the immediate past' was the significant characteristic of the new regimes founded during the period following the First World War. Eric Hobsbawm states that '[t]hey were not landlords of old buildings but architects of new ones'.[18] The Turkish Republic was founded as one of the regimes of the period that attempted to transform and reconstruct society in order to create a new order in the country; and the case of Ankara is illustrative for a better understanding of the creation of the 'new' in Turkey.

A determinist approach towards the history of the city is operative when Ankara is accepted as the ultimate embodiment of modernist production. In popular accounts, the dominant discourse tells the story of the 'backward' Ottoman town of Ankara 'in the centre of Anatolia on the eastern edge of the great, high Anatolian Plateau',[19] which 'had been a small provincial city lost in the middle of the steppe lands until in 1923 it was declared the capital of the Turkish Republic',[20] when it was modernized and almost magically transformed into the 'developed' capital of the new state. In such a discourse, the past of the country could not take on an active role but could only be appropriated and transformed in the museums opened during the early Republican years in Ankara – i.e. the Ethnographical Museum and the Museum of Anatolian Civilizations, which claim the ownership of the whole heritage of the country by displaying the past of Turkey in its very 'hearth'.[21] As a result of the perception of time in such developmentalist terms, the history of the city from the Bronze Age onwards – including the significant remains of the Roman, Byzantine, Seljuk and Ottoman times[22] – is preserved but only to be displayed in such museums and archaeological sites in the city, which are cited as the most significant tourist places to be visited in Ankara, where the 'museological past' could be compared to the present, and thus the idea of 'progress' of the contemporary city is better emphasized.[23]

It is not only the displays in museums but also the traditional city itself that is accepted as representing the past of the city (Figure 11.3). While the new parts of the city drastically changed after the plan of Jansen from the 1930s onwards, the way of life remained more or less the same in the old city inside and around the citadel.[24] Jansen's plan did not propose a transformation for the citadel area; it rather emphasized the need to preserve the place to form a 'visual centre' as 'the crown of the city'.[25] Jansen stated:

> the new urbanism require[d] to separate the construction of the new city from the sprawl of the old one. Theoretically, it [was] in fact necessary to cover the Old City with a glass frame so that it [would] be possible to easily follow its change and to protect it from harmful effects.[26]

Figure 11.3 Postcard showing *Hisar*, the citadel of Ankara.

This means the 'objectification' of the citadel area, whereby it is isolated from the life in the newly developing parts of the city; and, for the inhabitants of the new city as well as for tourists, the old city has become a 'site to be seen' to represent the 'traditional' as against the contemporary 'modern' city of Ankara. Therefore, in a tourist web site, it is stated that, today:

> Modern Ankara is really two cities, a double identity that is due to the breakneck pace at which it has developed since being declared capital of the Turkish Republic in 1923. Until then Ankara – known as Angora – had been a small provincial city, famous chiefly for the production of soft goat's wool. This city still exists, in and around the old citadel that was the site of the original settlement. The other Ankara is the modern metropolis that has grown up around a carefully planned attempt to create a seat of government worthy of a modern, Western-looking state. It's worth visiting just to see how successful this has been.[27]

Besides Atatürk's Mausoleum, the 'old' city in and around the citadel of Ankara is the most recommended site by tourist guides. Accordingly, 'most visitors head straight for *Hisar*' – the citadel as named in Turkish – to see the traditional houses, mosques and shops where local people continue their modest daily lives, while parts of the area have been transformed into tourist places such as cafés, restaurants and souvenir shops. 'A couple of km to the south is Atatürk's mausoleum, [defined as] a monumental building, spare but beautiful, that echoes the architecture of several great Anatolian empires'.[28] As such, *Anıtkabir* and *Hisar* stand as the most important tourist 'attractions' in Ankara, signifying the multiple meanings that are generated in popular conceptions about the city whereby the meaning of the built environment is invested in not only the 'past', the 'traditional', the 'national' and the 'East', but also the 'future', the 'modern', the 'international' and the 'West', and most importantly in between and beyond the two poles of such dichotomous constructs.

What could be the role and the place of such popular conceptions in the construction of an understanding of architectural production in Ankara? What could be their relation then to the writing of the history of architecture in the city? It is clear that conventional architectural historiography explains unique architectural works with reference to the a priori categories of styles that are mostly classified according to periodical divisions. In order to understand the architectural development, only those buildings that are accepted as the greatest examples of a style are studied. These 'chosen' examples form the canon of architectural works that are 'agreed to represent the greatest examples of a genre, and which hence [provide] a standard against which new work can be judged'.[29] The formation of the canon depends on a differentiation between building and architecture, which is what architects do. In popular accounts, on the other hand, architecture is neither explained with reference to styles nor is the architect of a building of particular concern. Moreover, contrasting with the 'neutron-bomb tradition' of architectural photography 'in which any view of a person is excluded from the image',[30] daily experiences of 'touring' people in and around buildings are also detailed in tourist accounts. *Hisar*, for example, is not the typical canonical work of architecture designed by a 'great' architect in a certain style, but exemplifies instead a built environment of different spaces that define the everyday life of the area from houses to religious buildings to the surrounding walls. For another example, although the competition process and the final choice of Emin Onat and Orhan Arda's project, as well as the style of *Anıtkabir*, brought about serious debates in contemporary architectural circles,[31] in none of the accounts that cite the complex as a tourist destination in Ankara are the names of the architects or the style of the building stated. Such an analysis may lead to the question of whether sites of tourist attraction have been defined beyond the limits of historiographical classifications of architecture, and hence whether they may provide possibilities to rethink architectural historiography from new perspectives.

Indeed, contemporary rethinking of historiography aims at such an expansion of limits, by questioning the basis of canon formation and hence asking why and how certain works are accepted as the most representative and 'valuable'. How *Anıtkabir* is praised in a tourist guide could be evaluated in these terms: defined as 'an impressive fusion of ancient and modern architectural ideas ... [that] remains unsurpassed as an accomplishment of modern Turkish architecture',[32] the Mausoleum of Atatürk is taken as exemplifying the ambiguous relationship of the new regime with both the 'traditional' and the 'modern': the basis for legitimizing the 'value' of the building depends on the nationalist framework of the modernizing 'nation'-state as explained above. With reference to the significant critique of historiography that the judgements to include certain works in canonical lists are not made objectively but under moral, political, economic and social influences, the inclusion of *Anıtkabir* or *Hisar* in lists of 'places to see' in Ankara exemplifies that the touristic presentation of the city cannot escape from, but is instead constrained by, conventional limits of canon formation:

> This helps us to interpret the act of visiting buildings and the reading and experience of its histories as a confirmation of an entire body of social, economic and aesthetic values that reinforce the dominant assumptions and the existing social structure of society.[33]

Popular accounts of architectural history also take on the collectivist and determinist approach in professional history writing, which accepts architecture as representing a certain collective – the 'nation' and the 'nation'-state in this case – and as presenting the ultimate level of the development of that collective in its material form.

The 'bureaucratic' city

Popular accounts define

> Ankara ... [as] the modern metropolis that has grown up around a carefully planned attempt to create a *seat of government* worthy of a modern, Western-looking state. It's worth visiting just to see how successful this has been, although there's not much else to the place.[34]

The idea of the 'bureaucratic' city of Ankara has accordingly resulted as another canonical vision of architecture in the city. In a tourist web page, for example, Ankara is defined – in an objective tone – as 'the city of bureaucrats with the President's residence, the parliament building, government offices and foreign embassies'.[35] Similarly, in a recent issue of *İstanbul* magazine, Ankara is defined as 'clumsy', 'official' and 'bureaucratic'.[36]

The critical vision of a 'bureaucratic' city has emerged in contemporary context of globalization, in which the modernist perspective of national formation has become obsolete. Once the celebrated new capital, Ankara seems to have already lost the 'significance' that it had in the early Republican period as the 'modern' symbol of the 'nation'. The centralized system of the nation-state is questioned in the globalizing world, disfavouring the capital city, and its role as a model for the modernization of Turkey.[37] This approach is also exemplified in the editorial introduction of a recent catalogue of twentieth-century buildings in Ankara, which states:

> some early indicators of [the new century] make us think that Ankara has also got used to the realities of market economy. A real 'private' sector of architectural production is born also in this city, no longer taking its aims as limited to providing inexpensive service to the public. ... Maybe Ankara has now begun to produce a 'civic' architecture that is not defined by direct access to state resources.[38]

Shopping malls are among such sites of 'civic' architecture in Ankara, adapting urban daily life to contemporary economic realities. *Atakule*, the complex of a tower and a shopping mall that was built during the 1980s on the highest hill in the southern part of the city, is the initial example of its kind in Ankara (Figure 11.4). The complex is most frequently cited in tourist guides as a successful 'modern shopping area', signifying the attempt to provide a new and 'marketable' image for Ankara, necessary if it were to take its place in the contemporary context of globalization. Despite the reference here to the role of the building in the economic life of the city that aspires to take its place in the developing global system, the fact that *Atakule* is named after Atatürk reminds us that it still symbolizes the prevalent effect of the nationalizing perspective.

Figure 11.4 Postcard showing *Atakule*, the tower and shopping mall in Ankara; Ragıp Buluç, 1986.

Atakule is also represented in the graphical symbol of the Ankara Municipality, whose dome is interpreted here as referring to the Ottoman past. The current Municipality began to use this symbol having replaced the solar disc of the Hittites – who are accepted to have created 'Anatolia's earliest known civilization'[39] – which had been used as the symbol of the city by earlier municipalities, and is still preferred by the Governor's Office of Ankara. The emphasis on traditional/religious references is similarly apparent on the choice of the new Kocatepe Mosque to rival *Anıtkabir* in popular photographs of the city.

Such symbolic features of the city, not only in graphical but also in built form, 'are sites of social conflict',[40] and have always brought about serious debates that are based on the differences among the multiple perspectives that define Ankara. The architectural and historical identity of the city is contentious, and it seems to be trapped in between the two sides of nationalist approach, i.e. tradition and modernity, whereby some emphasize the historical-traditional characteristics of the city while others celebrate its contemporary Republican features. For example, the web page of the conservative Municipality includes a building in the list of attractions in Ankara, naming it as the *Türk Ocağı* (Turkish Hearth) with reference to the original function of the building, which was constructed as the club of a social and cultural organization that had been the principal source of essentialist ideas of nationalism since the late Ottoman period.[41] Apparently, the Municipality preferred to use the original name because of such nationalist connotations. However, the building is currently the Museum of Painting and Sculpture – as referred to in most tourist guides – and, as such, it symbolizes the modernity of Turkey by housing the collection of art in the country since the late nineteenth century to the present.[42] Similarly, the Municipality lists many mosques and khans of the Ottoman period on its web page, while Republican buildings like the new and the old Parliament buildings, parks like the Atatürk Forest Farm and the Youth Park, and monuments like the *Ulus* (Nation) Monument, *Güven* (Trust) Monument and *Zafer* (Victory) Monument of the early Republican years form the majority of 'sites of interest' cited by the Ministry of Culture and Tourism.[43]

The definitions of Ankara as 'national', 'modern' or 'bureaucratic' show that popular perceptions of the city are the result of multiple perspectives. Nonetheless, these different perceptions seem to be still delimited with the same vision of the 'nation'-state, and thus attribute unified images to the city to symbolize the 'modern' Republican identity. In historiography, Ankara and the Turkish Republic are almost identified with each other, and both are defined as symbolizing the birth of the 'modern nation'.[44] As the dominant vision of 'modern' Ankara is criticized in the globalizing context, contemporary tourism cannot find much to consume in the historical heritage of the city.[45] Hence, the search in tourist guides for 'attractions' in Ankara may also result today in total failure:

Ankara Attractions

Research: **0** attractions in Ankara.
We currently do not have any Attractions
available in Ankara.
We add new features to MyTravelGuide
every day. Please check back soon.[46]

Contemporary critical perspectives provide the basis to question the limits and the problems of conceptualizing Ankara as the abstract geography of the 'nation'-state.[47] Nonetheless, the aim to produce a marketable image for the city to be consumed by heritage tourism should similarly be criticized, as the result then is 'a tyranny of a commodified, synchronic past, where all our yesterdays only exist as today's commodities. The heritage industry denies historical process, and radiates only historical surfaces'.[48] The understanding that is contended with the preservation of the traditional city as an 'object' of the past to be compared with the present, is only as questionable as recent attempts at gentrification that change the way of life in the area into a commodity to be served to tourists in old houses transformed into restaurants, cafés and shops,[49] as both define the architectural history of the city as unitary and unchanging. To overcome the problems of the formation of such canonical visions of a built environment to meet both ideological and touristic aims, historiography should be sensitive to differences and multiple meanings.[50] Only when a more inclusive approach is employed to analyse the built environment as a whole, could the conceptions of Ankara not be bounded by dichotomies of imagined identities that represent the city as 'new', 'modern' and/or 'bureaucratic' as against everything that represents the 'old'. Professional and popular conceptions of architectural history of Ankara could then be based on the real and multiple identities of the people of the city from the politicians in the very centre to the migrants who live in peripheral squatters.

In the face of the analysis undertaken in this essay on popular conceptions of Ankara, it seems that the writing of the history of architecture in the city needs to be revised in a similar inclusive approach: basically, the identification of Ankara with the modernizing Republican period should be reconsidered, and the history of the city should be rewritten not just to incorporate a chosen past but rather more inclusively to reach beyond nationalist limits. Nevertheless, this should not mean to support the contemporary neo-liberal aims of globalization and thus to accept all aspects of modernization as outdated;[51] on the contrary, the argument is that a more inclusive approach in historiography will give their due value to the multiple and changing characteristics of the city[52] – without having recourse to ideological or touristic justifications – in order to provide the necessary popular consciousness about, as well as legal protection of, buildings and sites produced in different periods, including the modern.[53]

Notes

1 www.letsgoturkey.com/regions/central_ anatolia/ankara/index.asp.
2 Kester Rattenbury, 'Introduction', in Kester Rattenbury (ed.), *This is Not Architecture: Media Constructions*, London and New York, 2002, xxiii. See also Michael Camille, 'Prophets, Canons, and Promising Monsters', *Art Bulletin*, LXXVIII: 2, 1996, 198.
3 See especially Beatriz Colomina (ed.), *Architectureproduction*, New York, 1988. Contemporary urban representations have also been the topic of theoretical and methodological analyses. See, for example, Anthony D. King (ed.), *Re-Presenting the City: Ethnicity, Capital and Culture in the 21st-Century Metropolis*, New York, 1996.
4 D. Medina Lasansky, 'Introduction', in D. Medina Lasansky and Brian McLaren (eds), *Architecture and Tourism*, Oxford and New York, 2004, 3.
5 The tourist guides investigated include printed brochures, books and catalogues, as well as web sites that provide information about Ankara. The commonly cited reference for a critical reading of tourist guides is: Roland Barthes, 'The Blue Guide', in *Mythologies*, New York, 1994 (1957), 74–7. For an analysis of the characteristics of 'guidebooks' in the context of architectural historiography, see Dana Arnold, 'The Illusion of Inclusion: The Guidebook and Historic Architecture', in *Reading Architectural History*, London and New York, 2002, 173–88.
6 *Miniaturk Rehber* (Miniaturk Guide), İstanbul, 5.
7 For detailed information on the development of the new capital, see Bilal Şimşir, *Ankara ... Ankara: Bir Başkentin Doğuşu* (The Birth of a Capital City), Ankara, 1988, 25; and İlhan Tekeli, 'Ankara'nın Başkentlik Kararının Ülkesel Mekan Organizasyonu ve Toplumsal Yapıya Etkileri Bakımından Genel Bir Değerlendirilmesi (A General Evaluation of the Choice of Ankara as the Capital City in Terms of its Effects on the Spatial Organization and the Social Structure of the Country)', in Enis Batur (ed.), *Ankara Ankara*, İstanbul, 1994, 147.
8 'Ankara İstanbul', *La Turquie Kemaliste*, 47, 1943, 38–9.
9 A. Sutcliffe, 'Capital Cities: Does Form Follow Values?', in J. Taylor, J. G. Lengelle and C. Andrew (eds), *Capital Cities*, Ottowa, 1994, 195.
10 For a detailed analysis of the relation between architecture and nationalism in Turkey during the early Republican period, see T. Elvan Ergut, *Making a National Architecture: Architecture and the Nation-State in Early Republican Turkey*, unpublished PhD dissertation, SUNY, Binghamton, NY, 1998.
11 'Her memleketin kendine mahsus bir karakteri olduğu muhakkaktır. Binaenaleyh kendine mahsus bir mimarisi olması tabiîdir. Bugün nasıl bir Çinliyi bir Fransızdan bir Almanı bir Türkten ayırmak kabilse; bir Viyana mimarisini bir İstanbul mimarisinden, bir Fransız mimarisini bir Rus mimarisinden ... ayırmak lâzımdır.' Behçet and Bedrettin, 'Türk İnkılap Mimarisi (Architecture of the Turkish Revolution)', *Mimar*, 9–10, 1933, 266.
12 For an understanding of the various aspects of the process of nationalism, which is taken as creating, inventing, imagining and/or constructing 'nations', see Eric J. Hobsbawm and Terence Ranger (eds), *The Invention of Tradition*, Cambridge *et al.*, 1983; Ernest Gellner, *Nations and Nationalism*, Ithaca, NY, and London, 1983; Benedict Anderson, *Imagined Communities: Reflections on the Origin and Spread of Nationalism*, London

and New York, 1983; and Eric J. Hobsbawm, *Nations and Nationalism since 1780: Programme, Myth and Reality*, Cambridge et al., 1990. On the other hand, a critique of this approach is that 'national identity' is not constructed but reconstructed with reference to some existing elements (selectiveness is still accepted as a base for 'national identity'); see Anthony D. Smith, 'The Myth of the "Modern Nation" and the Myth of Nations', *Ethnic and Racial Studies*, 11: 1, 1988, 1–26.

13 Anthony D. Smith, 'Nationalism: A Trend Report and Bibliography', *Current Sociology*, XXI: 3, 1973, 29.

14 'Avec l'application du plan Jansen, un des maîtres de l'urbanisme moderne, Ankara n'aura plus rien à envier aux capitales européennes.' Ernest Mamboury, *Ankara Guide Touristique*, Ankara, 1933, 84.

15 www.turkishodyssey.com/places/anatolia/ana3.htm.

16 www.travelershub.com/destination_guide/europe/ankara.html.

17 'Ankara İstanbul', *La Turquie Kemaliste*, 47, 1943, 41–2.

18 Eric J. Hobsbawm, 'Foreword', in *Art and Power, Europe under the Dictators 1930–45*, 1996, 11.

19 *Ankara and the Central Anatolian Region*, Republic of Turkey, Ministry of Culture and Tourism, İstanbul, 2004.

20 www.ankertravel.net/location.asp?_lctn=46.

21 'References to Ankara in official and popular publications of [the early Republican period] as "the heart of the nation" (*ulusun kalbi*) point to more than the geographical centrality of its location within the boundaries of modern Turkey. It was a powerful metaphor for the organic unity of the nation, as in the other nationalist slogan of becoming "one body, one heart".' Sibel Bozdoğan, *Modernism and Nation Building: Turkish Architectural Culture in the Early Republic*, Seattle, WA, and London, 2001, 68.

22 For detailed accounts of the history of settlements in Ankara, see Batur (ed.), *Ankara Ankara*; Ayşıl Tükel Yavuz (ed.), *Tarih İçinde Ankara* (Ankara in History), Ankara, 2000; and Yıldırım Yavuz (ed.), *Tarih İçinde Ankara II* (Ankara in History II), Ankara, 2001.

23 'Museums do not simply or passively reveal or "refer" to the past; rather they perform the basic historical gesture of *separating out of the present* a certain specific "past" so as to collect and recompose (to *re*-member) its displaced and dismembered relics as elements in a *genealogy* of and for the present. The function of this museological past sited within the space of the present is to signal alterity or otherness; to distinguish from the present an Other which can be reformatted so as to be legible in some plausible fashion as generating or *producing* the present.... This museological "past" is thus an *instrument* for the imaginative production and sustenance of the present; of modernity as such.' Donald Preziosi, 'The Art of Art History', in Donald Preziosi (ed.), *The Art of Art History: A Critical Anthology*, Oxford and New York, 1998, 511.

24 A recent study concentrates on the problem: L. Funda Şenol Cantek, *'Yaban'lar ve Yerliler: Başkent Olma Sürecinde Ankara* (The Newcomers and the Locals: Ankara in the Process of Becoming the Capital City), Ankara, 2003. For a discussion of the architectural context of this duality, see Zeynep Kezer, *The Making of a National Capital: Ideology, Modernity, and Socio-Spatial Practices in Early Republican Ankara*, unpublished PhD dissertation, University of California, Berkeley, CA, 1998.

25 Gönül Tankut, *Bir Başkentin İmarı* (The Construction of a Capital City), İstanbul, 1993, 79–80.
26 Quoted in Asuman Türkün Erendil and Zuhal Ulusoy, 'İronik Karşılaşmalar: Kale'nin Kentle ve Kentin Kale'yle İki Karşılaşması (Ironic Encounters: The Encounter between the Citadel and the City and between the City and the Citadel)', in *Şehrin Zulası, Ankara Kalesi* (The Ankara Citadel, the Cache of the City), İstanbul, 2004, 236.
27 http://travel.yahoo.com/p-travelguide-3680417-ankara_ankara-i;_ylt=Aku8SwIdwgrFd53GB.tdvFyKMmoL.
28 www.lonelyplanet.com/destinations/middle_east/turkey/attractions.htm.
29 Eric Fernie, 'Canon', in *Art History and Its Methods: A Critical Anthology*, Hong Kong, 1995, 329.
30 See Andrew Ballantyne's essay, 'Architecture as Evidence', in this volume.
31 See, for example, 'Atatürk', *Arkitekt*, 8, 1938, and 'Anıtkabir Proje Müsabakası (Competition for Atatürk's Mausoleum)', *Yapı*, 11, 1942, 15. The building is also found as 'architecturally' significant by architects, taking the third place in a list of twenty prominent buildings of the Republican period in Turkey that were chosen out of a questionnaire prepared by the Turkish Chamber of Architects. See Ali Cengizkan, 'Türkiye'de Çağdaş Mimarlığın Önde Gelen 20 Eseri (20 Prominent Works of Contemporary Architecture in Turkey)', *Mimarlık*, 311, 2003, 23–32.
32 *Ankara and the Central Anatolian Region*. Also quoted in www.allaboutturkey.com/ankara.htm.
33 Dana Arnold, 'The Illusion of Inclusion: The Guidebook and Historic Architecture', in *Reading Architectural History*, London and New York, 2002, 173.
34 http://travel.yahoo.com/p-travelguide-3680417-ankara_ankara-i;ylt=Aku8SwIdwgrFd53GB.tdvFyKMmoL (emphasis is mine). This is related to the fact that the writing of the history of early Republican architecture is also exclusionary in terms of building typology. Governmental or administrative buildings have mostly been accepted as significant buildings of the period, while contemporary private construction of housing or other characteristic buildings types such as industrial buildings have not yet been sufficiently studied and documented.
35 www.turkishodyssey.com/places/anatolia/ana3.htm.
36 'Çoktandır "hantal", "resmi" ve "bürokratik" bir Ankara'dan söz edilmektedir.' Derya Özkan, 'Dosya: İstanbul Ankara', *İstanbul*, 36, 2001, 48.
37 See Çağlar Keyder (ed.), *İstanbul: Küresel ve Yerel Arasında* (İstanbul: Between the Global and the Local), İstanbul, 2000.
38 '2000'ler kimi erken göstergelerine bakılırsa, Ankara'nın da piyasa ekonomisi gerçeklerine alıştığını düşündürmektedir. Bu kentte de mimari hedefini artık kamuya ucuz hizmet vermekle sınırlı görmeyen gerçek bir "serbest" mimari üretim sektörü doğmuştur. ... Ankara, ... devlet kaynaklarını kestirmeden kullanmakla tariflenmeyen "sivil" bir mimarlık üretmeye koyulmuştur belki de.' 'Ankara'da Mimarlığın Bir Yüzyılı (A Century of Architecture in Ankara)', in *Ankara 1910–2003*, İstanbul, 2003.
39 *Ankara and the Central Anatolian Region.*
40 Robert S. Nelson, 'Tourists, Terrorists, and Metaphysical Theater at Hagia Sophia', in Robert S. Nelson and Margaret Olin (eds), *Monuments and Memory, Made and Unmade*, Chicago, IL, and London, 2003, 59.
41 Feroz Ahmad, *The Making of Modern Turkey*, London and New York, 1993, 63; Eric J. Zürcher, *Turkey: A Modern History*, London and New York, 1993, 134.

42 As Bennett clarifies, museums 'stood as embodiments, both material and symbolic, of a power to "show and tell" which, in being deployed in a newly constituted open and public space, sought rhetorically to incorporate the people within the processes of the state.' Tony Bennett, *The Birth of the Museum*, London and New York, 1995, 87.

43 www.kultur.gov.tr/portal/default_EN.asp?BELGENO=1918; and also in *Ankara and the Central Anatolian Region*.

44 '[A] metaphor for Ankara, derived from the city's strategic importance during the nationalist war [before the foundation of the new state], was that of a benevolent mother who gave birth to the Turkish republic.' Sibel Bozdoğan, *Modernism and Nation Building: Turkish Architectural Culture in the Early Republic*, Seattle, WA, and London, 2001, 68.

45 The Ministry of Culture and Tourism complains that tourists prefer not to stay longer than an average of two days in Ankara although the city has a rich collection of historical buildings and museums. See: www.ankara.gov.tr/index.php?site=&module=cmsPage&page=page&cmsPage=61.

46 www.mytravelguide.com/attractions/ctattractions-17575602-Turkey_Ankara_attractions.html.

47 Uğur Tanyeli, *İstanbul 1900–2000: Konutu ve Modernleşmeyi Metropolden Okumak* (İstanbul 1900–2000: Reading the House and Modernization from the Metropolis), İstanbul, 2005, 28.

48 Kevin Walsh, *The Representation of the Past: Museums and Heritage in the Post-Modern World*, London and New York, 1992, 182.

49 Recent unification of the Ministry of Culture with the Ministry of Tourism in Turkey emphasizes how 'culture' is now defined within the limited and questionable boundaries of the idea of 'heritage tourism'.

50 Such a critique that also bases the canon formation in architectural historiography seems urgent in the case of Turkey because significant work to complete the inventories is yet to be undertaken in the archives to better develop the empirical information on the built environment in the country.

51 A recent study on Ankara similarly criticizes the dominating 'national–modern' and 'bureaucratic' images of the city and examines its history in detail in order to provide the necessary knowledge for overcoming such common understandings that identify Ankara as non-historical and non-spatial. See Suavi Aydın, Kudret Emiroğlu, Ömer Türkoğlu and Ergi D. Özsoy, 'Sonsöz: Ankaráyi Küçümseyerck Üretilen Yerli Oryantalizmin Sefaleti [Epilogue: The Poverty of the Native Orientalism that is Contemptuous in Ankara]', in *Küçük Asyánin Bin Yüzü: Ankara [A Thousand Faces of the Asia Minor: Ankara]*, Ankara, 2005, 612–14.

52 For a critique of the contemporary characteristics of the city, see Tanıl Bora, 'Küçük-Büyük Şehirle Mega-Taşra Arasında Ankara [Ankara between Small-Great City and Mega-Province]', in Tanıl Bora (ed.), *Taşraya Bakmak [Looking at the Province]*, İstanbul, 2005, 58–64.

53 The law (No. 2863) on the conservation of cultural and natural properties in Turkey defines that the 'immovable property' built prior to the end of the nineteenth century is to be conserved. See Emre Madran and Nimet Özgönül, *Kültürel ve Doğal Değerlerin Korunması* (The Conservation of Cultural and Natural Values), Ankara, 2005, 7. As such, a legal framework is not yet defined for the preservation and conservation of buildings and neighbourhoods of the twentieth century.

Part III
Reframings

12
Space, time, and architectural history

Nancy Stieber

Architectural history is not art history. Of course, the origins of architectural history as it is practised in the academy today lie both in art history and in the practice of architecture itself. Architectural history has long been suspended as a sort of stepchild between the two. On the one hand, it has had a shadowy presence in art history departments where it was subordinated to the history of painting. On the other hand, architectural history has often provided a service in architectural schools, a service sometimes not even seen as necessary, but in any case always viewed as secondary to the practical training in the studio. For that and other reasons, the discipline of architectural history has struggled to achieve autonomy.[1] The rise of the preservation and cultural heritage industry has introduced yet another pressure, or 'client'. But over the last few decades the discipline has been transforming itself into the cultural history of the built environment, embracing questions that arise from a curiosity about the relationships between culture, society, and design that have little or nothing to do with the standard art historical motivations for architectural history. The hagiographic monograph dedicated to the individual architect, the nationalistic defining of styles, the polemical justification of particular movements in architecture have long been staples of writing in architectural history and there are still forces at work to produce them. But the growth of the field as an autonomous area of inquiry has been, somewhat ironically, dependent on questions generated from outside the closed circle of the architects and patrons served by art historical approaches. The intellectual pursuits that make this an interesting topic have come to depend on methods and problems defined outside architecture.

A revolution in thinking about the relationship between objects and their makers has already taken place, as seen in the expansion of art history to include visual culture and the cultural history of the visible.[2] The move has been from construing the past as a series of stylistic waves, with the art historian's task that of taxonomer classifying visually, or of biographer explaining individual creativity, or of interpreter of monuments, to posing questions about the relations between objects, their makers, their users, and the relationship of all of those to social processes. Art history and perforce architectural history have for decades now been contending with that liminal, border location between the cultural and the social, that difficult to theorize location of making meaning that observes the human imagination caught in the web of conflicting social processes that constitute cultural change. As Fredric Jameson has put it: 'It is now the cultural production process (and its relation to our peculiar social formation) that is the object of study and no longer the individual masterpiece.'[3]

This is a transformation that has been evolving for the last thirty years as the humanities and social sciences have resituated themselves under the impact of such writers as Michel Foucault, Pierre Bourdieu, Raymond Williams, Clifford Geertz, Julia Kristeva, Edward Said, Hayden White, and others. While literary theory has consistently been the first field to respond to the methodological challenges of these authors, other fields such as anthropology and geography have also reconsidered their premises. Few fields have escaped from the self-examination and self-reflexivity this intellectual revolution has engendered. As I have argued elsewhere:

> The result has been a shattering of the project to construct large-scale explicative narratives of history and culture. Instead, the focus has come to be on the contingent, the temporary, and the dynamic, on processes rather than structures, on hybridity rather than consistency, on the quotidian as well as the extraordinary, on the periphery as well as the centre, on reception as well as production. Culture has come to be viewed as symbolic practice, productive of concrete expressions that can be mined to reveal their codes, making explicit both their agency and their contingency.[4]

Art history has moved away from its preoccupation with documentation, connoisseurship, and biography towards the history of the image construed broadly to encompass globalism, media, and popular culture. Architectural history has similarly shifted its sights from a focus on the individual architect and architectural monument to include vernacular architecture, the architecture of everyday life, and the ordinary landscape. The production of the built environment, and its imbrication with the social fabric, have replaced the more exclusive concerns with the heroic biography of the architect and the assumption of a historical perspective within the professional discourse of architecture. Instead, the life of the built environment, its reception, and its social functioning during and after construction have come under study, allowing investigations of such issues as gender, class, and colonialism. While aesthetic and formal issues have not been cast aside, they are viewed as socially contingent, the result of cultural dynamics that the historian aims to reveal in their complex interworkings.

An audience still exists for the monograph dedicated to the oeuvre of a particular architect, tracing the development of ideas and forms in the light of biography. However, the more interesting questions about architecture and its history are being posed by historians exploring problems and not styles: issues such as the nature of public space, the construction of nationalism and regional identity, changing conceptions of domesticity, the experiential history of architecture, and the broad problem of representation with all that it entails about understanding relationships between the viewer, the viewed, and the view-maker. The focus is on the work that architecture does within culture and society, rather than stylistic taxonomies and canonic developmental schemes. Architectural history has come to examine the historical circumstances that produce meaning and the social and cultural processes that continue to generate meaning in a site.[5]

The influences on architectural history from outside the field become evident if we examine space as an analytical term in architectural history. For much of the twentieth century, architectural history, and most particularly the history of modern architecture, was permeated with discussions of space. In 1957 Bruno Zevi wrote: 'space is the protagonist of architecture'.[6] The birth of architectural history as a field of inquiry occurred simultaneously with the discovery of space as an analytical term in the work of August Schmarzow and others.[7] This conception became central to the way modernists defined architecture and the way the historians of modernism defined architectural history. Siegfried Giedion, writing the polemical *Space, Time and Architecture* on the basis of his 1938–9 Charles Elliot Norton lectures, worked within this Swiss and German visual tradition to introduce modern architecture to several generations of scholars and architects.[8] While this was a book whose main purpose was to explain how the architecture of Walter Gropius, Le Corbusier, and Mies van der Rohe expressed the self-consciousness of the era through a new conception of space, in fact, Giedion articulates here and elsewhere the basis for an entire history of architecture grounded on the history of space.[9] Despite all the varying factors that influence architectural design, and he cites economic, political, social, and technological factors, Giedion argues that architecture is an organism unto itself with an autonomous line of development. He writes of 'architecture as an enterprise with a continuous and independent growth of its own, apart from questions of economics, class interests, race, or other issues.'[10] That line of development, he claims, can be understood as consisting of a series of space conceptions.

Giedion's bold attempt to create a grand narrative has a clear genealogy, which he in part makes explicit in the introduction to his book with its acknowledgement of Jakob Burckhardt and Heinrich Wölfflin. Of course, the scheme of identifying eras that express themselves consistently in all areas of human endeavour is a Hegelian conceit that was commonplace in the nineteenth century. What is interesting here is that Giedion places space at the centre of his history – an idea that has its roots in Gotthold Ephraim Lessing and Johann Gottfried Herder's attempts to identify the characteristic visual nature of each art form, but more relevantly is related to the nineteenth-century German project of understanding how the mind comprehends space – the psychological approach to the experience of vision that leads to August Schmarsow's theory of architecture as a spatial creation, the first full articulation of a theory identifying architecture as the shaping of space.[11]

Giedion's focus is the new space conception he identifies with modernism. Breaking with the space conception of Renaissance perspectival space, he claims, this occurs first in cubist painting, parallels the scientific insights into relativity, but finally gives rise to an architecture based on the interpenetration of hovering horizontal and vertical planes, the play of enormous forces held in equilibrium, the simultaneity of vision from above and below, inside and outside, introducing time, the fourth dimension into the perception of space, thus creating what Giedion identifies as space-time.

The formalism of this position was countered by Bruno Zevi, who, like Giedion, made space the centre of his call for a new architectural history, but who was also more interested in space 'as concretely experienced' rather than space 'as abstractly imagined'.[12] This experiential emphasis brings Zevi closer to Schmarzow who, as Mitchell Schwarzer has written, evinces 'a predilection for the vital space over the silent form, the space whose contours are shaped by the demands of human life'.[13] For Zevi, 'the specific property of architecture – the feature distinguishing it from all other forms of art – consists in its working with a three-dimensional vocabulary which includes man.... Architecture,' he writes, 'is like a great hollowed-out sculpture which man enters and apprehends by moving about within it'.[14] Space, internal and external, must be experienced through dynamic motion of the body; it can only be grasped through one's own movement through it.

Zevi complains:

> A satisfactory history of architecture has not yet been written because we are still not accustomed to thinking in terms of space and because historians of architecture have failed to apply a coherent method of studying buildings from a spatial point of view.[15]

But the kind of history he projects after all is based on a *Zeitgeist* scheme very similar to Giedion's: the aim of 'showing how the multiplicity of factors which make up history have acted in concert to give rise to various conceptions of space'.[16] Both Giedion and Zevi envisioned an architectural history that would place space at its centre, but neither was able to explain the motor of change from one space conception to the next and neither created a narrative model that acknowledged the 'factors' each recognized as intrinsic to architectural development: the economic conditions, patronage, life-styles, and class relations. Their basic model remained one of reflection and expression: architecture is the reflection of the age, the expression of the space conception. In this historiography space is passively shaped.

A more sophisticated view of architecture that places space at its centre can be found in William MacDonald's eloquent account of Roman imperial architecture, which brilliantly integrates the social, the technical, and the aesthetic. MacDonald demonstrates that 'What the Palaces, the Markets, and the Pantheon show above all else is the maturity of the concept of monumental interior space',[17] its 'transcendent characteristic' being 'its space-shaping, space-bordering quality'.[18] Here space becomes both a reflection of society and a tool of communication. The 'Roman stewardship of all antiquity and the imperial hope for one inclusive society,' MacDonald writes, '. . . were proclaimed by an architecture of splendid interior spaces'.[19] He meticulously defines for us the formula for Roman design: its axes, symmetries, and vaulted terminal volumes. He demonstrates how space was manipulated so that the observer was guided towards 'a large and well-lighted architectural volume from which the natural world was excluded, where enveloping and radially focused surfaces suggested permanence, stability, and security'.[20] He explains how the decoration, the linings of nonstructural materials, depreciated the mass and weight of the structural solids so the impression of a seamless envelope of space was increased while the play of light on the marble and other materials 'brought to life the purely spatial reality of the architecture'.[21] MacDonald describes the sensory implications of this design. He writes of a kinaesthetic sense alerted and instructed by the decoration as well as by the primary architectural forms. 'The vaulted style, with its relatively seamless continuity of surface, its tendency to rhetorical persuasion, and its capacity to call up a strong sensation of fixed and ordered place, reflected both the claims and the realities of imperial society', he writes.[22] It reflected those realities and the vaulted style became an imitation of the state, a tangible metaphor for its traditions and its claims to universal sovereignty.[23] We are taught, through this reading, to see the expressive nature of architectural space, its sources in tectonic structure, decorative form, axial planning, and billowing vaults, its coercive, controlling effect on the observer, and, above all, through all these, its role as marker of imperial ideology. Pure spatial reality is the reality of an architectural perception, akin to Giedion's premise of architecture as an enterprise with a continuous and independent growth of its own. The historian's role is then to read and interpret closely the message that spatial reality bears.

In recent years, however, that notion of space as passive and reflective has been radically challenged in sociocultural critiques launched outside architectural history. Sixty years after Giedion, the most provocative discussions of space, the space of the built environment, have not only come from outside architectural history, they have to a large extent ignored what the field has to offer. These discussions of space are taking place in geography, cultural studies, literary theory, gender studies, and postcolonial studies. There has been a vast outpouring of books dealing with the space of the built environment.

Not since around 1900, when, as Stephen Kern has described, space became a focus in sociology, philosophy, and science, as well as painting and architecture, has there been such rapt attention paid to the concept of space.[24] Most of these are studies that explore the spatial implications of French social theorists and philosophers, in particular Michel Foucault, Henri Lefebvre, Michel de Certeau, and Pierre Bourdieu.[25] The neo-Marxist geographers, David Harvey, Edward Soja, and Doreen Massey, have also made seminal contributions to the spatial turn.[26] As early as 1967 Foucault called for an alternative spatial history. He wrote: 'A whole history remains to be written of spaces – which would at the same time be the history of powers – from the great strategies of geo-politics to the little tactics of the habitat.'[27] An intellectual industry has now been put in place in answer to that challenge.[28]

Is the space that is presented in these texts recognizable? No single framework has emerged to unify their perspective and, indeed, given their postmodern methodological proclivities, none is sought. However, what stands out as a base assumption is the notion that space is socially constructed. This premise takes a number of forms, for instance David Harvey's statement that 'conceptions of time and space are necessarily created through material practices which serve to reproduce social life'.[29] Or Henri Lefebvre's thesis that 'The social practice of a society secretes that society's space'[30] and 'the social relations of production have a social existence to the extent that they have a spatial existence: they project themselves into space, becoming inscribed there, and in the process producing the space itself',[31] which is a version of his insight that space is socially produced but then becomes an agent itself in social relations, or, as Edward Soja puts it, social relations are both space-forming and space-contingent.[32] He writes: 'The production of spatiality in conjunction with the making of history can thus be described as both medium and the outcome, the presupposition and embodiment, of social action and relationship, of society itself.'[33] In other words, space is not simply the stage of social relations, it is operative in their formation.

The great advantage of such formulations is that they avoid the reductionist mapping of the material onto the social, the mere reflection or expression of the social in the material. Space comes to be seen as the result of process, produced by social processes, itself enabling social processes. The meaning of space is not something that is read into it, as if space were some empty extension that receives value passively or an inactive text requiring interpretation. Rather, space itself becomes active as a conduit for living social relations, not manifesting them as representation, but constituted through them and in turn shaping them.

The disadvantages of such formulations are twofold. First, their discussions remain at the level of theorizing, highly suggestive but empirically untested. When they do turn to history, they revert to the kind of untestable grand narrative tradition shared with a Siegfried Giedion, on the assumption that each society creates its own characteristic space, in Lefebvre and Harvey's case equating modes of production to spatial conceptions. Second, these accounts evince a consistent distrust of the visual. In the desire to demystify or demythologize the naturalization of space perceptions, the founding theories of space research have appropriately put into question the history of visuality, but with the unfortunate consequence that close visual analysis has itself become suspect.

In these schemes, as in Giedion's, the advent of perspective plays a pivotal role as the key to an age, as a scopic regime in Martin Jay's term,[34] or as a 'visual ideology' in Dennis Cosgrove's,[35] who defines perspective as a technology of power that turns the visual field or space into a commodity. In this view, perspective becomes the means to critique modern rationality. In Harvey's account, perspectivism conceives of space as abstract, homogeneous, and universal, useful for merchants and landowners, for the absolutist state, and for the bureaucratic state.[36] For others, it is Cartesian spatial ordering or Galilean extension of space that become the basis of a critique of modern or Enlightenment rationality. In these definitions, space is viewed as a tool of surveillance, control, segregation, and surveying in aid of ownership and oppression.

This distrust of perspectival and Cartesian space is further generalized as a distrust of the visual, the aesthetic, and of representation altogether. Martin Jay's account of the anti-ocular strain in French thought of the twentieth century explicates the various strains of this criticism of vision's complicity with political and social oppression through its application to spectacle and surveillance, its illusions that distract attention from social relations and control.[37] The representation of space is an illusion, in service to power and then with an eye to distracting from realities, covering up, misrepresenting, not simply in the propagandist sense, but thwarting recognition of the system at work, naturalizing what has been constructed to sustain oppression. The aesthetics of urban design and architecture are viewed primarily as part of an ideological armatorium that represents power while providing a veneer of beauty that conceals oppressive relations. Such beauty is suspect: illusory, seductive, false, and misleading, a bearer of ideology. 'We must be insistently aware of how space can be made to hide consequences from us,' Soja writes, 'how relations of power and discipline are inscribed into the apparently innocent spatiality of social life, how human geographies become filled with politics and ideology.'[38] Order and harmony are called into question as tools of oppression, whereas indeterminacy, flux, and hybridity become markers of liberation.

It follows then that the visual experience of the built environment, what the American historian William MacDonald called the 'spatial reality of architecture', is given scant attention. There is a virtual absence of reference to the formal qualities of architecture in the new literature on space. When Foucault, in a much-cited interview, refers to old age homes, prisons, and motels,[39] there is never a mention of the shaping of the space as designed, the impact of the forms as aesthetic, as built, or the lived experience of space that has been shaped. There is rarely a close-up view of the workings of an individual building. Indeed, like this essay, most of the recent writings on space are not illustrated. But, even when an author like David Harvey writes a well-illustrated account of the imbrication of nineteenth-century Paris's spatial and political history, he does so without reference to the main contributions of architectural historians to the understanding of how the buildings of Paris operated within the social fabric.[40]

At this point, it becomes evident that architectural historians have a lot to learn from the questions being posed in other fields, but, at the same time, they have much to offer in return. First, the lesson for architectural history is to ask the question: what is the cultural work that architecture does? The interpretive function of the historian who regards the built environment as a text or picture allows the symbolic and representational to be seen, but not processes. So what happens when the passivity of 'symbolize, represent, and reflect' is replaced with active verbs such as 'transform, perform, inform'? What happens when architectural history begins to look at those spaces that are indeterminate, rather than looking only at the places of order, or find the indeterminacy in places of order as they are used, distorted, reinvested with meaning? How can the often ambiguous but provocative theories be translated into case studies that allow the examination of how space is socially produced so that the dialectical relationship between the material and the social is the focus, not simply the relationship of the mental to the material? How can topics be defined that explore the experience of architectural space in life through history?[41] While studies inspired by spatial theory have privileged topics on gender, class, post-colonialism, and race, there are many social processes at work, often only visible in microhistory, in the specifics of the tensions that define a particular society, changing roles in family life, patterns of land ownership, methods of doing business, patterns of consumption, any of which can make concrete and evident some of the larger problems of state formation, capitalism, formation of class identity, and the commodification of space that are worked out through spatial design.

Eve Blau's study of housing in Red Vienna starts with a pertinent question inspired by Lefebvre and Soja: in what way can architecture (and by extension architectural space) be 'instrumental, operative, and strategic'?[42] This question leads her to analyse the experiential quality of space through which space itself became an active social and political agent, not simply the bearer of a particular political ideology. It leads to the investigation of how a specific set of architects developed spatial concepts and how these were then instrumentalized and then experienced. Such work can only be achieved by means of the most thorough empirical investigation. Suffice it to say that, through the specific analysis of architectural practice in Vienna, the spatial configuration of the city and its building typologies, this episode in architectural history, which was written out of Giedion's grand narrative of the modern space conception, clarifies with precision how space was invested with meaning. While informed by theory, the conclusions could only be reached by means of the most thorough empirical investigation, not by theory alone.

In the book *Dominion of the Eye*, Marvin Trachtenberg explicates the planned nature of trecento urbanism in Florence. By measuring piazze accurately, he is able to reveal a spatial order that he relates to intellectual and political practices, establishing not an explanation, but 'a historical ground of possibility'.[43] Trachtenberg, like Blau, rejects any model of architecture mirroring society, instead making use of the spatial implications of the sociocultural criticism of Foucault and Bourdieu to reveal urbanistic practices that work through power and knowledge, that is, through the processes that bring those into relation with each other. The theory prods him to investigate the imbricated relationships of politics, economics, visual theory, and spatial practice that give rise to the ordered planning of the Florentine piazza. The result is a minutely observed study of trecento urbanism whose methodologies owe little to traditional art historical approaches and in fact discard the staple presumption of Renaissance exceptionalism and the reductionism of stylistic labels.[44]

These two examples make evident what architectural history has to offer the contemporary discourse on space. Given the general absence of specific examples of building in spatial theory, given its avoidance of confronting specific instances of space in history, given the often ambiguous level of theory's abstraction, what architectural history can provide are concrete illustrations of what has been raised theoretically about space as both a social product and agent. There is still yet another history of space to be written, the one that emerges from testing theory empirically, that leads in turn to the revision of theory, and deepens the understanding of both theory and the built environment.

Equally important, architectural history can reinsert the formal analysis of the visual into the problematic of social space, whether the topic is Brazilian squatter settlements, Frank Gehry's Bilbao Museum, or ancient Chinese temples. There is an autonomous architectural knowledge of space and it plays a role in social construction. There are even signs that postmodernist anti-ocularism has turned and that beauty and wonder are being readmitted into intellectual discourse after decades in which they had been banished from the humanities. Beauty is identified as a source of justice rather than a tool of oppression in a recent book by Elaine Scarry, where she defends beauty as true and fair.[45] However, this argument should not be mistaken for a call to return to business as usual, a return to pure formalism. Rather, it is a call for theoretically informed, empirical research that recognizes the social agency of spatial form, the active social role of the purely spatial reality of architecture, a spatial reality that operates through its visuality.

Given the widespread interest in many fields about the very topic that is at the centre of architectural history, namely the shaping of space, the challenge to the field is one of demonstrating to others that the visual is not suspect, but rich with possibilities to reveal complex social and cultural relations, and that the visual needs not be subordinate to the textual. This is a position that can only be demonstrated through close visual analyses of case studies. Architectural historians should be engaged in a dialogue with cultural geographers, anthropologists, and literary theorists who have been writing about space, cities, and architecture, and should be contributing in essential ways to the transdisciplinary discourse of space. This will be easier to accomplish if the field sheds the narrow and parochial purviews of traditional art historical concerns, if its queries are defined in terms of the cultural and social work that architecture does, and if the centrality of the visual language of architecture is emphasized.

Notes

Previous versions of this essay were presented as the Plenary Talk, Annual Meeting of the Society of Architectural Historians, Toronto, April 2001, at the Eerste Architectuurhistorische Landdag, Nederlands Architectuurinstituut, January 2004, and at the symposium *Rethinking Architectural Historiography*, Middle East Technical University, Ankara, March 2004.

1 In the United States the Society of Architectural Historians was established in 1940 but did not separate from the annual meetings of the art historical disciplinary society, the College Art Association, until 1957. For an American perspective on the history of the discipline, see Elisabeth B. MacDougall (ed.), *The Architectural Historian in America: A Symposium in Celebration of the Fiftieth Anniversary of the Founding of the Society of Architectural Historians*, Washington DC, 1990.
2 On the relation of visual studies to art history, see W. J. T. Mitchell, 'Showing Seeing: A Critique of Visual Culture', in Nicolas Mirzoeff (ed.), *The Visual Culture Reader*, London, 1998, 86–101.
3 Fredric Jameson, 'Symptoms of Theory or Symptoms for Theory?', *Critical Theory*, 30: 2, Winter, 2003–4, www.uchicago.edu/research/jnl-crit-inq/issues/v30/30n2.Jameson.html.
4 Nancy Stieber, 'Architecture Between Disciplines', *Journal of the Society of Architectural Historians*, 62: 2, June 2003, 176.
5 Stieber, 'Architecture Between Disciplines', 176–7.
6 Bruno Zevi, *Architecture as Space*, New York, 1957, 22.
7 Harry Francis Mallgrave and Eleftherios Ikonomou, *Empathy, Form, and Space: Problems in German Aesthetics, 1873–1893*, Santa Monica, CA, 1994.
8 Siegfried Giedion, *Space, Time and Architecture; The Growth of a New Tradition*, Cambridge, MA, 1941.
9 Siegfried Giedion, *Architecture and the Phenomena of Transition: The Three Space Conceptions in Architecture*, Cambridge, MA, 1971.
10 Giedion, *Space, Time and Architecture*, 22.
11 Mitchell Schwarzer, 'The Emergence of Architectural Space: August Schmarsow's Theory of "Raumgestaltung"', *Assemblage*, 19, October 1991, 50.
12 Zevi, *Architecture as Space*, 23.
13 Schwarzer, 'The Emergence of Architectural Space', 55.
14 Zevi, *Architecture as Space*, 22.
15 Zevi, *Architecture as Space*, 22.
16 Zevi, *Architecture as Space*, 73.
17 William L. MacDonald, *The Architecture of the Roman Empire I: An Introductory Study*, rev. edn, New Haven, CT, 1982, 167.
18 MacDonald, *Architecture of the Roman Empire*, 167.
19 MacDonald, *Architecture of the Roman Empire*, 167.
20 MacDonald, *Architecture of the Roman Empire*, 171.

21 MacDonald, *Architecture of the Roman Empire*, 172.
22 MacDonald, *Architecture of the Roman Empire*, 179.
23 MacDonald, *Architecture of the Roman Empire*, 181.
24 Stephen Kern, *The Culture of Time and Space*, Cambridge, MA, 1983.
25 Michel Foucault, 'Space, Knowledge, and Power', *Skyline, The Architecture and Design Review*, March 1982, 16–20; Henri Lefebvre, *The Production of Space*, Oxford, 1991; Pierre Bourdieu, 'The Kabyle House, or The World Reversed', in *Algeria 1960*, Cambridge, 1990, 133–53; Pierre Bourdieu, *The Field of Cultural Production*, New York, 1993.
26 David Harvey, *The Condition of Postmodernity: An Inquiry into the Origins of Cultural Change*, Cambridge, 1989; Edward W. Soja, *Postmodern Geographies: The Reassertion of Space in Critical Social Theory*, New York, 1989; Edward J. Soja, *Thirdspace: Journeys to Los Angeles and Other Real-and-imagined Places*, Cambridge, MA, 1996; Doreen Massey, *Space, Place, and Gender*, Minneapolis, MN, 1994.
27 Michel Foucault, 'The Eye of Power', in C. Gordon (ed.), *Power/Knowledge: Selected Interviews and Other Writings, 1972–1977*, New York, 1980, 149. See also, Michel Foucault, 'Des Espaces Autres', *Architecture/Mouvement/Continuité*, October 1984 (English version: 'Of Other Spaces', *Diacritics*, 1986, 22–5); Interview with Michel Foucault, 'Space, Knowledge and Power', in Paul Rabinow (ed.), *The Foucault Reader*, New York, 1984, 239–56. On Foucault's project of a history of space, see Stuart Elden, *Foucault and the Project of a Spatial History*, London, 2001.
28 A number of sources discuss space from a variety of disciplinary perspectives: for urbanism, see Maria Balshaw and Liam Kennedy (eds), *Urban Space and Representation*, London, 2000; for geography, see Derek Gregory, *Geographical Imaginations*, Cambridge, MA, 1994, 364–411; for anthropology, see Denise L. Lawrence and Setha M. Low, 'The Built Environment and Spatial Form', *Annual Review of Anthropology*, 19, 1990, 453–505 and Setha M. Low and Denise Lawrence-Zúñiga (eds), *The Anthropology of Space and Place: Locating Culture*, Oxford, 2003; for social history, see George Benko and Ulf Strohmayer (eds), *Space and Social History: Interpreting Modernity and Postmodernity*, Oxford, 1997; for archaeology, see Michael Parker Pearson and Colin Richards, *Architecture and Order: Approaches to Social Space*, London, 1994; gendered space is discussed in Jane Rendell, Barbara Penner, and Iain Borden (eds), *Gender Space Architecture: An Interdisciplinary Introduction*, London, 2000; for social theory, Helen Liggett and David C. Perry, *Spatial Practices: Critical Explorations in Social/Spatial Theory*, Thousands Oaks, CA, 1995; for architectural practice, Kim Dovey, *Framing Places: Mediating Power in Built Form*, London, 1999; for film studies, Giuliana Bruno, *Atlas of Emotion: Journeys in Art, Architecture, and Film*, New York, 2002.
29 Harvey, *Condition of Postmodernity*, 204. For an extended discussion, see David Harvey, 'The Social Construction of Space and Time', in his *Justice, Nature, and the Geography of Difference*, Cambridge, MA, 1996, 210–47.
30 Lefebvre, *Production of Space*, 38.
31 Lefebvre, *Production of Space*, 129.
32 Soja, *Postmodern Geographies*, 126.
33 Soja, *Postmodern Geographies*, 127.
34 Martin Jay, 'Scopic Regimes of Modernity', in Hal Foster (ed.), *Vision and Visuality*, Seattle, WA, 1988, 3–28. Jay credits the term 'scopic regime' to the film critic Christian Metz.

35 Dennis Cosgrove, 'Prospect, Perspective and the Evolution of the Landscape Idea', *Transactions of the Institute of British Geographers*, 1, 1985, 46. For a useful summary of social interpretations of perspective, see Gregory, *Geographical Imaginations*, 389–92.

36 Harvey, *Condition of Postmodernity*, 254.

37 On ocularcentrism, see Foster (ed.), *Vision and Visuality*; David Michael Levin (ed.), *Modernity and the Hegemony of Vision*, Berkeley, CA, 1993; and Martin Jay, *Downcast Eyes: The Denigration of Vision in Twentieth-century French Thought*, Berkeley, CA, 1993. Arguing against the notion that vision is perforce hegemonic is Mitchell, 'Showing Seeing', 94–7, who considers this one of the fallacies of visual studies and argues that images have 'lives of their own'. Jay offered alternatives to Foucault's panopticism in 'In the Empire of the Gaze: Foucault and the Denigration of Vision in Twentieth-century French Thought', in David Couzens Hoy (ed.), *Foucault: A Critical Reader*, Oxford, 1986, 175–204. A second generation of authors working on visuality present more nuanced interpretations that eschew the notion of hegemonic scopic regimes without abandoning the precept that visuality is socially constructed. See, for instance, Teresa Brennan and Martin Jay (eds), *Vision in Context: Historical and Contemporary Perspectives on Sight*, London, 1996.

38 Soja, *Postmodern Geographies*, 6.

39 Foucault, 'Of Other Spaces'.

40 David Harvey, *Paris: Capital of Modernity*, New York, 2003. Missing from the bibliography of this book are works by such authors as David Van Zanten, Katherine Fischer Taylor, and Christopher Mead.

41 For examples of such work, see Steven Harris and Deborah Berke, *Architecture of the Everyday*, New York, 1997; Paul Groth and Todd W. Bressi (eds), *Understanding Ordinary Landscapes*, New Haven, CT, 1997.

42 Eve Blau, *The Architecture of Red Vienna 1919–1934*, Cambridge, MA, 1999, 12.

43 Marvin Trachtenberg, *Dominion of the Eye: Urbanism, Art, and Power in Early Modern Florence*, Cambridge, 1997, xvii.

44 I have argued in favour of theoretically driven microhistories of the built environment in Nancy Stieber, 'Microhistory of the Modern City: Urban Space, Its Use and Representation', *Journal of the Society of Architectural Historians*, 58: 3, December 1999, 382–9.

45 Elaine Scarry, *One Beauty and Being Just*, Princeton, NJ, 1999. See also, Philip Fisher, *Wonder, The Rainbow, And The Aesthetics Of Rare Experiences*, Cambridge, MA, 1998.

13
Visuality and architectural history

Belgin Turan Özkaya

Architecture is not only the built form; it encompasses diverse conceptual, representational, textual and spatial practices. In recent decades the 'linguistic' and 'pictorial turns' have made us all aware of that much larger and complex terrain that architecture covers. Alongside being the more readily visible act of making built environments to house human activity – in other words, a spatial practice – architecture is also a discursive and visual practice that embraces 'word' and 'image'.

One central, if intermittent, architectural 'practice' that is purely discursive is the architectural treatise, which was often produced with the sole intention of conveying architectural ideas, and which had become increasingly pictorial in time. In the case of buildings, on the other hand, their reception is often fashioned by accompanying texts and discourses generated concurrently or afterwards, mostly in the form of architectural criticism and history. The task of a critical architectural history is not to oppose such discourses and narratives to a pure physical/spatial immediacy, the possibility of which is suspect, but rather to reveal the mechanisms that engender them and privilege certain discourses and narratives over others, hence to make it possible to think differently; to develop other discourses, other narratives that defy the dominant ones. While being self-reflexive about its methodology, assumptions and biases and querying itself and its boundaries with interdisciplinary tools, critical architectural history, I argue, should also engage with conventional forms of architectural historiography. It is evident that new perspectives, theories and methodologies coming from different disciplines do transform architectural history by providing new theoretical and methodological tools and new objects of study. But the individual architect and architectural object, canonical or otherwise, hence architectural monograph, do not just disappear. The question is how to write 'non-operative', non-complacent histories that are not complicit with marketing strategies of architectural practice that favour certain architectures over others.[1]

The spread of architectural ideas, discourses and narratives that had accelerated after the invention of printing, as is very well known, gained huge momentum in the modern era with the developments in mass media. Today what gets disseminated by printed, and increasingly by digital media, is not only the word but also the image, both of which affect architecture. Recent scholarship on the modern era has disclosed the pivotal role the photographic record played in the reception of architecture. The easily reproducible and easily circulated photography, by making the image of buildings widely available, privileged the image of buildings over their experience. The study of buildings has come to depend on visual documentation of architecture as much as on-site studies. Accordingly, not only spatial and discursive qualities but also images of buildings have come to define architecture.

On the other hand, a certain critique about architecture's engagement with images has also emerged due to the presumed inaptitude of the two-dimensional image for conveying three-dimensional, spatial experience and its openness to manipulation and easy (commercial) consumption. One prominent example of the denigration of photographic image vis-à-vis architecture comes from the Marxist cultural critic Fredric Jameson. Jameson defines the photograph of the already existing building as 'bad reification' (as opposed to architectural drawing, which is 'good reification'), as the illicit substitution of one order of things for another. He writes: 'So it is that in our architectural histories and journals, we consume so many photographic images of the classical or modern buildings, coming at length to believe that these are somehow the things themselves.'[2] As an extension of this position, architecture that yields to being 'pictured' has come to be seen as an anathema to a genuine architectural practice. Jameson's argument on Frank Gehry's house in Santa Monica, if we keep the same example, revolves around what Jameson sees as a positive trait, i.e. the lack of ideal photographic points of view from which a unified image of the house can be construed, namely its resistance to being photographed.[3]

That is only one, and understandably not very welcome, consequence of the appealing and threatening potential visual technologies, first photography then film, provided for architecture. The enthusiasm of early modern architects about film, epitomized in the art historian Sigfried Giedion's words, 'only film can make the new architecture intelligible', and exemplified by the rapprochement between CIAM (Congrès International de l'Architecture Moderne) and the organization of avant-garde filmmakers such as Sergei Eisenstein and Hans Richter, the CICI (Congrès International du Cinéma Indépendant), both of which held their 1930 meeting in Brussels, is well known.[4]

Despite the growing literature on architecture and such visual technologies the further implications of architecture's potentially enriching dialogue with both 'the still image' and 'the moving image' needs to be further explored. In contradistinction to the earlier literature that is content with the more visible interaction between architecture and visual technologies, most notably how architecture is (mis-)represented in photography and portrayed/propagated in film, there are also publications that focus on the possibilities of a deeper, structural resemblance and interaction between these seemingly different media. One of the most prominent examples of these is, as will be seen later, the visual and environmental historian Giuliana Bruno's work, which is located at the spatiovisual interstices of art, architecture and film. Moreover, research into the impact of visual technologies and the changing points and modes of viewing on architecture, the city and spatial perception, from the seminal works of the French thinkers Paul Virilio and Michel de Certeau to some more recent publications, are growing. The latter include the architectural historian Mitchell Schwarzer's *Zoomscape*, the architectural and film historian Edward Dimendberg's *Film Noir and the Spaces of Modernity*, and *The Built Surface*, edited by the architectural historians Christy Anderson and Karen Koehler. While *Zoomscape* queries the ways within which the perception of architecture has been shaped by visual and transportation technologies and *Film Noir and the Spaces of Modernity* illuminates both early twentieth-century American urbanism and film noir, which are usually studied in isolation, by bringing them together, *The Built Surface* sheds light on the almost forgotten interaction between architecture and the pictorial arts (hence the still image) since antiquity.[5]

Along these lines, a complex conceptualization of architecture as a practice embracing 'word' and 'image' as well as built space points to a productive path for architectural history that is located at the intersection of architectural and visual cultures. Such a conceptualization disrupts the binary opposition, the visual (or the pictorial/representational) versus the spatial, or the image versus lived experience, or the image versus the discursive for that matter, that has long marked architectural historiography. We do not need to treat the visual/pictorial (or the image) as innately the site of objectification, reification or deception vis-à-vis an authentic spatial (i.e. bodily) experience. I am not arguing that these are not at stake at all and even that they are not pervasive ways within which images are consumed and that looking is never alienating or 'distancing', but, rather, that they are not essential, universal qualities of vision and visual technologies that cannot be done away with. Also, an original moment of architectural/spatial experience that is not visually and discursively mediated appears to be so elusive. Since the late 1990s a new group of work is developing that focus on different outlooks on vision, which had been 'denigrated' by an earlier body of literature.[6] The psychoanalytical theorist Kaja Silverman's work, as an excellent example, while revealing the undeniable and non-dismissible importance of vision in the formation of human subjectivity shows that, in the context of film, what is at stake is not simple ocular-centrism, and how the look fraught with the possibility of (visual) violence and objectification can be put to political use and made to see and identify with what is different from itself.[7] Likewise, Giuliana Bruno has forcefully argued that the visual experience, due to its possible emotive content, can be an 'embodied' haptic experience that falls outside mere opticality. Bruno, through a critique of some recent film theory that, she thinks, has failed to address the emotion of viewing and in line with cinema's etymological origin – to move, sees the spectator as a voyageur (rather than a voyeur) who has gone through a spatio-corporeal mobilization and 'who traverses a haptic, emotive terrain'. Bruno also detects continuity between architectural space and filmic space and makes us aware of how archetypal modern architectures such as arcades, railways, glass houses and exhibition halls – those sites of transit, in her words – by changing the relation between spatial experience and bodily motion, paved the way for the moving image – the quintessence of modernity.[8]

An outlook that combines such seemingly different media, the pictorial and visual spaces of image and film, with their emotive implications for the physical space of architecture is useful in shedding light on the work of the Italian architect Aldo Rossi, whose work defies such boundaries. Rossi who has come to be known for his architectural paintings and sketches as much as his built work, and whose diverse media of production have increasingly coalesced, has been both praised and reproached for this. They provided a pretext for dismissing him as not really an architect or for uncritically celebrating his work for its artistic 'touch'. The intricate actual ties between his diverse media of production have not been sufficiently probed. How do the suggestive, visionary 'spaces' of the painting and the photograph and his not well-known involvement with filmic 'space' illuminate the architecture of Rossi?

The affective 'space' of Aldo Rossi

The moving image

> I, however, am distorted by similarity to all that surrounds me here. Thus like a mollusk in its shell I had my abode in the nineteenth century, which now lies hollow before me like an empty shell. I hold it to my ear.[9]

The very little-known film, *Ornamento e Delitto* (Ornament and Crime), which Aldo Rossi made with the Italian architect Gianni Braghieri and designer Franco Raggi, with technical help from Luigi Durissi and Elver Degan Bianchet, for the 1973 Milan Triennial, begins and finishes with these enigmatic words of the German thinker Walter Benjamin from *Berlin Childhood Around 1900*.[10] In addition to the 'textual' start quite unusual for a sound film, the curious thing about the opening shot is that Benjamin's words are integrated within the film itself and not left to the para-filmic sites of titles or intertitles. Instead, the words are both aurally and visually animated – an anonymous male figure with his back turned to us and whose face cannot be seen writes them on a wall of what may well be one of those post-war low-cost tenement blocks that populate the *periferie* of Italian cities. And the voiceover reads it.

The 'graffito-zation', in other words, scratching in order to make public, can be seen as returning to streets the words of Benjamin, who had theorized about the life on streets, and taken the trivia of everyday and popular culture seriously as a basis for his philosophy. For us the more crucial question is: What is pictured between the first and second appearance of Benjamin's words in this seemingly repetitive 'un-progressing' film? Can those images and the words of Benjamin, who produced one of the most important critiques of (historical) progress as a linear continuum, illuminate the work of Rossi?

'Streets' and 'graffiti' certainly had a significance close to home in the context of 1970s Italy: it was the peak moment of the Student and Worker Movements – a time of demonstrations, marches and occupations, when political graffiti had become almost an art in itself. Ironically, in 1971, the Triennial had to cease because of the student occupation of Palazzo dell'Arte, where the exhibitions customarily take place and which was covered by graffiti back then. A couple of years later, Rossi and the others, by carrying the graffiti from the façade of Palazzo dell' Arte to the screen inside, were appropriating one of the daily practices of the students.

That is not the only thing that was borrowed in this idiosyncratic film. The title, *Ornamento e Delitto*, as is evident, comes from Adolf Loos' 1908 essay, which is one of the texts used in the film. Rossi writes: '*Ornamento e Delitto* remains an extremely beautiful title for an architectural essay because it alludes only indirectly to architecture.'[11] In the film, sequences of architecture and city views are juxtaposed with long fragments from Italian motion pictures by a curious *détournement*. There are scenes from Mauro Bolognini's 1962 film *Senilità*, Luchino Visconti's 1954 film *Il Senso*, and Federico Fellini's *Otto e Mezzo* of 1963 and *Roma* of 1972. The architectural and urban examples start with Stonehenge and include examples of Greek and Roman sites, Art Nouveau and Modern Movement, as well as the views of contemporary Milan that they shot at the outskirts of the city. Between the unseen but evoked turn of the century Berlin of Benjamin's childhood, recollected by him in exile, and Stonehenge, 'a great [architectural] beginning', in Rossi's words, the film cuts to the spring of 1866, and to the Venetian ghetto with Visconti's Countess Serpieri who is on her way to see her suitor Franz Mahler.[12] From the gracefully gliding Venetian *flâneuse* in the person of Livia Serpieri at the start of what will become a revengeful story of love and betrayal we are carried to Stonehenge. About the images of *Il Senso* and *Senilità* (specifically about the Venetian ghetto and the harbour of Trieste), Rossi writes that these are 'two of the most beautiful images of Italian cities [which are] consumed and disappeared behind a feverish love story which, whether it be forbidden or not, is always impossible'.[13]

Stonehenge is followed by examples of Greek architecture and the Athenian Acropolis flooded with tourists. Interestingly and uncharacteristically for an architecture film the long footage depicts rambling people, women, men, families, little children and babies more than the ruins, which become a backdrop also for the 'voice' of Karl Marx of *Grundrisse* on the 'Greek arts and the artistic pleasure that they still afford and how they constitute a norm and an unattainable model'. We travel from the Hadrian's Villa in Tivoli and other Roman ruins to the theatre of Epidarius and a performance of Sophocles' *Oedipus Rex* with Greek actors; and from paintings of industrial landscapes and city edges to the Austrian architect Adolf Loos' Steiner House and Villa Karma while 'hearing' Loos on the nature of dwelling, which is not as in the case of the artwork 'a private matter of the artist'. Loos' architecture also constitutes the background of the argument in defence of (uniformity and) tradition as opposed to 'aesthetic vanity'. We walk the harbour of Trieste with *Senilità*'s rejected and humiliated protagonist Emilio and his love interest Angiolina, overlaid with the Swiss architect Hans Schmidt's words from *Beiträge zur Architektur 1924–1964*, published in East Berlin, on monotony's being 'a social problem rather than an architectural and urban one'. In the film there is also footage from Lenin's funeral accompanied by a diatribe against the 'fatigued revolution'. Beyond the film's more apparent fragmented narrative it is possible to construe a sub-text that links one city to another, some of which have personal importance for Rossi; from the alluded Berlin of the turn of the century to nineteenth-century Venice to present-day Athens; from melancholy Trieste to *fin-de-siècle* Vienna to Lenin's Moscow; and from Fellini's Rome to 1970s Milanese *periferia*. Like Benjamin, if we hold the mollusc to our ears what do we hear?

The film was made for Triennial's international exhibition *Architettura-Città*, curated by Rossi with a group of younger colleagues, and was shown together with the German/American avant-garde artist and filmmaker Hans Richter's 1930 film *Die Neue Wohnung* (The New Dwelling), made for the Swiss Werkbund on the occasion of WOBA, the first Swiss housing exhibition in Basel. The Richter film celebrates the new life the then emerging modern architecture envisaged through a comparison of the conventional, turn of the century tenement house and the modern dwelling and its furniture. The Swiss Werkbund's choice of film, the script of which was partly written by Hans Schmidt, as their medium of expression originated from their faith in the effectiveness of film as advertising.[14] *Die Neue Wohnung* juxtaposes the good and the bad – the airy, sun-filled, unadorned architecture and 'efficient' built-in furniture with the dark, stuffy, kitschy conventional interiors – through a series of comical incidents showing the hazards of the latter.

If *Die Neue Wohnung* was about change and rupture, about changing lives and forms, the underlying theme of *Ornamento e Delitto* appears to be continuity. Continuity of not only architecture and spaces but also the lives that may take place in the settings architecture provides. It is about life and forms that do not change over centuries. By implication the early modern life depicted in *Il Senso* is still relevant for 1970s Italy. The views of Adolf Loos, who saw 'modernity as a specific continuation of tradition' and whose architecture and ideas appear prominently in the film are hence quite apposite.[15]

In his *A Scientific Autobiography*, Rossi writes:

> [I]t was a collage of architectural works and pieces of different films which tried to introduce the discourse of architecture into life and at the same

time view it as a background for human events. From cities and palaces we passed to excerpts from Visconti, Fellini, and other directors. Venice and the problem of the historical urban center, acquired further significance as a background to the impossible love described by Visconti in *Il Senso*. I recall a white, desperate Trieste, which only the story of Italo Svevo's *Senility* made clear, especially its architectural context. We later shot the final part of the film on the outskirts of Milan at dawn. I truly believe that I had gone beyond architecture, or at least explained it better. The problem of technique also vanished, and now I think that the realization of this film may be continuation of so many things I am seeking in architecture. . . . I consider any technique possible; I would go so far as to claim that a method or technique can be a style. To consider one technique superior to, or more appropriate than, another is a sign of the madness of contemporary architecture and of the Enlightenment mentality which the architectural schools have transmitted wholesale to the Modern Movement in architecture.[16]

What Rossi says about *Ornamento e Delitto* actually involves characteristics that traverse his entire work in different media – not only film but also architecture and painting. As I will try to show later, there is an emphatically visual logic that informs Rossi's what might be called trans-disciplinary production, which 'moves' from the flat surface of paintings and photographs to the 'spaces' of architecture and film. And his indifference to the type of 'technique' or in other words openness to any medium of expression is crucial in understanding his architecture, which is, for him, a 'technique' among others.

The governing principle of *Ornamento e Delitto* is the technique of collage, that is, putting together fragments coming from different contexts that do not necessarily end up in a unified whole; as Rossi states, this is also the idea behind his 1976 project of *La Città Analoga*. Of course an additive method or a logic of assemblage can be seen across Rossi's architectural oeuvre, where different architectural types and elements are brought together time and again in different compositions.

If we go back to the film, what is to be gained by putting *Senilità*'s melancholy views of the harbour of Trieste 'side by side' with Karl Ehn's residential complex, Karl Marx Hof of red Vienna? Or the architecture of Loos with turn of the century Italian writer Italo Svevo's immaturely aged protagonist Emilio's shadowy, overstuffed apartment, Emilio being tormented by his unrequited infatuation with Angiolina played by Claudia Cardinale? As we have seen, Rossi's aim is 'to introduce the discourse of architecture into life and at the same time to view architecture as a background for human events'.[17] That exchange between life and architecture is an underlying theme also in Rossi's architecture. And, I would argue, that theme has turned into a desire to capture something beyond the 'material' or 'physical' context of architecture, a desire to carry different lives, different 'worlds', what I call 'livedness' into architecture. In his *Quaderni Azzurri* Rossi writes: 'Throughout the film architecture is a tool, a background. It is shaped by sentiments.'[18] In other words, what Rossi wanted to create was an affective 'space'. It was an affective space that portrayed life as it may take place in the setting architecture creates, which is the continuation of already existing 'worlds' and lives rather than being new ones that architecture attempts to shape in the manner of modern architecture or as propagated in *Die Neue Wohnung*.

How is what I call 'livedness' captured in Rossi's work, how is life conveyed, how are different 'worlds' opened up? But first Rossi's other major interest should be mentioned – in the photograph historian Paolo Costantini's words, his 'concealed passion' for taking polaroids, his 'secret images'. As Costantini stated, 'the polaroid image is immersed in the language of existence'.[19] It is immersed in daily life. The polaroid captures instantaneous bits and pieces of life. Rossi collects such images but not only materially. He collects images mentally, too. And his creative process depends on this accumulation, which is later translated into his work. That is why he talks about his architecture as 'things, which have already been seen'.[20] Here the issue is not only repeating architectural types and elements but images as conveyors of (real) life moments. The images may come from his polaroids, from film or painting but they come with a 'content', with the implication of a world, of the real life beyond the material context of architecture. They bring associations of different lives, different worlds. Hence the palm tree that emerges here and there in his work can be the trace of a moment lived in Zurich or a moment from a trip or it may belong to past lives spent in the lake country of northern Italy. Or, for him, the *ballatoio* (gallery), the archetypal element of traditional Milanese tenements that he used in 1969–70 Monte Amiata Housing in Gallaretese, carries associations of 'a life style bathed in everyday occurrences, domestic intimacy and varied personal relationships'.[21]

One of the best illustrations of the 'conveyance' of a different world, of a different life, is the *Teatro Domestico* project, part of the *Progetto Domestico* exhibition curated by Georges Teyssot for the 1986 Milan Triennial (Figure 13.1). In one of the cells of the huge installation representing a three-storey dwelling in section that covered the whole landing of the main staircase in Palazzo dell'Arte, we are presented with an ordinary, a 'typical', even a poor interior. At the back, there is the Rossian trademark – that standard four-pane, square window. Furniture is sparse, only a table and two chairs; they are quite standard, too. As Rossi put it, they don't have any obvious style or distinguishing features, just like the lamp, which is a simple, run of the mill lamp with a visible light bulb. The most dominant element is the wallpaper, which has been deliberately aged, and which operates as a sign alluding to the 'real' life beyond architecture. It lends to the scene an air of what I call 'livedness'. What we see is not an immaculately finished, designed architectural interior. As a matter of fact, what we see is the ultimate eradication of architecture as intentional design. Here, architecture works under erasure. It undercuts itself while conveying us a 'world', a very ordinary world; that of the common people. That room might have belonged to the house of a

Figure 13.1 Aldo Rossi: detail from the *Teatro Domestico* for the exhibition *Il Progetto Domestico* at the Milan Triennial, 1986. (Photograph by Luigi Ghirri, negative exposed in 1986, Collection Centre Canadien d'Architecture/Canadian Centre for Architecture, Montréal © Archivo Ghirri.)

Lombard factory worker who lives in a tenement block at the periphery of Milan, or to any modest, poor household within the city. Or it can be a Ferrarese interior like the ones depicted in another Visconti film, *Ossessione* of 1942. Rossi writes:

> [I]n my early youth I was struck by the Ferrarese 'interiors' of the first film of Visconti, 'Ossessione'. Those 'interiors' . . . are full of, in a pictorial sense, black, shiny, silk petticoat of Clara Calamai, beautiful and covered by the sweat of the Ferrarese summer that made her even paler. There were also objects like lamps, coffeemakers, and food like those soups made with such ill will, and wine glasses. This whole interior was like an architecture of desire.[22]

Rossi's desire to 'carry' this world to his architecture is never more emphatic than when he pictures Clara Calamai in the corridors of his own projects. He adds, 'The love and crime of Clara Calamai in *Ossessione* could have easily unfolded in the passages and corridors of my projects.'[23]

The pictorial image

While Rossi could envisage the spaces of his architecture with figments of the moving image, the film he made presented a series of paintings as 'expressive' of modernity through their forms, lights and colours. Paintings of railways and industrial machines together with factory views precede views of Loos' Steiner House. Not only the drawings of the Russian avant-garde, such as Ivan Leonidov's project for the Commissariat of Heavy Industry in Moscow, but also the figurative art of the Italian metaphysical painter Mario Sironi; his alienating city edge paintings depicting vacant railway stations and skewed industrial landscapes with gasometers and warehouses are juxtaposed with the sequence of the arrival of a train to one of the 'gates' of Milan – the Vigentina station with passengers pouring out of it. For Rossi, whose interest in and inspiration from certain painters, most notably the Italian metaphysical painter Giorgio De Chirico, are well known, the attribution of such expressiveness to painting is not surprising.

In *I Quaderni Azzurri* he talks about De Chirico's depiction of the castle of Ferrara and Sironi's city edge paintings as being as informative as the city itself – that is, as informative as city plans and urban objects themselves that can teach us the ways within which city parts and urban objects are repeated and utilized to different effect.[24] These painters, Rossi argues, have understood the possibility of creating architecture with new signification out of existing urban and architectural forms. What can De Chiricoesque castles, *piazze* and arcades, together with Sironi's city edges, warehouses and gasometers, teach architects? (Figure 13.2). These remarks should be seen in relation to typological and morphological studies of the city that Rossi and the others were involved with in 1960s and 1970s Italy. In contradistinction to the functionalist city of modernist planning based on zoning and the Taylorist logic of production, Italian architects who were engaged in typological and morphological studies of the city were propagating a city of parts, urban artefacts and different typologies. Apparently, the sources for this, at least in the case of Rossi, were not only existing cities or urban plans and projects, but also paintings that 'clarified' different architectural and urban types and forms.

A product of such a line of thinking that has long been overlooked was on display in the *Architettura-Città* exhibition – the painting entitled *La Città Analoga* by the Italian architect and painter Arduino Cantafora. As the exhibition, whose catalogue was entitled *Architettura Razionale*, has come to be associated more than anything else with the international sanctioning of Neo-Rationalism and the Italian *Tendenza*, with Rossi as the most prominent advocate of both, and as Rossi's formulation of '*città analoga*' has come to be seen related to a later phase of his oeuvre because of his 1976 *La Città Analoga* project, Cantafora's painting, developed in collaboration with Rossi, has received scant attention by historians.[25] Rossi actually had come up with the idea of *città analoga* in 1969 in the catalogue of the exhibition *Illuminismo*

Figure 13.2 Mario Sironi: *Paesaggio urbano*, private collection, Venice. (Cameraphoto/Art Resource, NY.)

e Architettura del'700 Veneto, long before producing his own analogical city in 1976.[26] Based on the well-known painting, in its creator's words, on the *veduta ideata*, by the eighteenth-century Venetian painter Antonio Canaletto, which portrays, back then, several two-hundred-year-old projects in an imaginary Venetian setting, i.e. the sixteenth-century architect Andrea Palladio's unrealized design for the Rialto Bridge standing across the Grand Canal, with other Palladian buildings, Palazzo Chiericati and the Basilica of Vicenza on either *riva*, Rossi develops the idea of 'analogical city'.

He writes: 'The three palladian works one of which is an unrealized project constitute an analogical Venice formed by definite elements related to the history of architecture as well as to that of the city.' For him, by the geographical transposition of monuments a city is constituted that becomes a site of pure architectural values.[27] He adds:

> [W]e witness a logical-formal operation, a speculation on monuments and on the urban character which is unsettling for the history of art and thought.... *What is important in this painting is the construction of a theory, a hypothesis for a theory of architectural design where the signification that appears at the end of the operation is the authentic, unforeseen, original side of the research.* A rational theory of art does not claim to limit the

meaning of the work to be built; for if we know, and that is clear, what we wanted to say, we do not know if we said nothing but that.[28]

In other words, Canaletto's painting conveys an imaginary, non-existent urban totality made up of (experienced) architectural 'realities', and that unforeseen totality constitutes its original side. At this point, Rossi's interest in painting goes beyond simple inspiration. For him (architectural) paintings can be the location from which a logic of production that would be valid for different arenas of production, from painting to architecture to film, can be deduced. As mentioned before, exploiting the invisible potential of visible fragments coming from different contexts and playing with the elements of a well-defined vocabulary for creating a 'new' totality becomes a trans-disciplinary modus operandi for Rossi. Furthermore, for him Cantafora's painting, which brings together Adolf Loos' Michaelerplatz Building, Rossi's Monte Amiata Housing and Segrate Fountain, Etienne-Louis Boullée's truncated cone, and Ludwig Hilberseimer's seemingly endless urban blocks, among others, points to the constructed and cumulative nature of the city and the value of monuments as sites of collective memory.[29] In that sense analogical thinking is both a technique of design and a tool to understand the city, its singular constituents as well as different typologies. As it was observed in the pages of *Controspazio*, montage (seen here as the 'structuring principle' of Cantafora's painting) sheds light on the consistency of design principles related to the concept of 'type' and the aptness of instituting 'type' as the basis of architectural research.[30] Rossi's uncompleted book *La Città Analoga*, for which he signed a contract with Laterza publishers in September 1975, would also be based on 'analogy' as such a system of (architectural) composition.[31]

The parallel that Rossi establishes between two-dimensional pictorial representation and architectural production is evinced in his argument on architectural composition. In an entry in *I Quaderni Azzurri* he discusses the problem of 'architectural composition', starting from his *Città industriale con monumenti* and *Città con monumenti*, which are made up of elements coming from his architectural projects as well as existing urban types. He looks for ways to go beyond non-unified compositions and to achieve unity in architecture by drawing and redrawing the same architectural elements and types that he numbered in different compositions. The interesting thing about his argument is that what he calls 'architectural composition' is not confined to architecture but, as we have seen, can be located in pictorial practice as well.[32]

By moving smoothly among actual artefacts, his own built and un-built projects and pictorial figures Rossi defines for himself a trans-disciplinary, trans-media arena of production and his argument has implications for architecture itself as much as 'architectural paintings'. Hence, in addition to abstractions of De Chiricoesque arcades, of Mario Sironi's urban blocks, of beach cabins on the island of Elba, or of the lakeside statue of Carlo Borromeo, figures alluding to Lombard smokestacks, to the 'hut/tomb' of his Segrate monument, to the courtyard of De Amicis school, to the tower of Castello Sforzesco, or to New England lighthouses fill Rossi's paintings, drawings and architecture, which are brought together in different compositions (Figures 13.3 and 13.4).

Figure 13.3 Aldo Rossi: *Città con Architetture e Monumenti*, 1972. (Research Library, The Getty Research Institute, Los Angeles, 880319.)

Figure 13.4 Aldo Rossi: *Senza titolo su un'antica carta francese*, printed in 1989 (Collection Centre Canadien d'Architecture/Canadian Centre for Architecture, Montréal; Acquis grâce à l'apui de Gail Johnson à la memoire d'Edgar et Loretta Tolhurst/Acquired with the support of Gail Johnson in memory of Edgar and Loretta Tolhurst.)

The aim is to arrive at 'new' compositions by utilizing 'things, which have already been seen'. In this way, something unforeseen is hoped to be revealed at the end of a process, which may start from the singular and most often the personal and arrive at the 'universal' through abstraction and typification. As I have argued elsewhere, the strikingly trimmed-down forms, figures and images of Rossi with all the shades of their potential meanings are visually very evocative. Somehow, they seem to ring familiar with each and every addressee by provoking personal responses. In other words, originally they may be 'objects of affection' for Rossi but in the end they operate as 'universal' handles of memory, and trigger a process of remembering for us, of our own recollections.[33] In that sense the 'typical' is located at the affective interstices of the memories of the producer and those of the addressee.

Not surprisingly, then, the director of the other film screened at the exhibition, Hans Richter, was interested in the 'typical', too. Richter saw it as a means to intensify expression.[34] He wrote: 'We heighten the single event to the typical by suppression of the particular; we make "screaming people" excitement in itself out of the material.'[35] The aspiration to arrive at the general and the universal is also the idea behind *Ornamento e Delitto*, which brings together, among others, Fellini's Rome, Bolognini's Trieste, Visconti's Venice and Rossi's Milan, the last three of which evoke personal memories for Rossi. But, as in the well-known case of Fellini films, which start from the personal and eventually operate as larger cultural parables, *Ornamento e Delitto* tried to reveal the general, the universal, the unchanging both in architecture and in emotion. It is not a coincidence that the film finishes by repeating Benjamin's words from arguably one of the most autobiographical of his writings, whose project was to light up the history of an era through the narration of an individual past. As in Rossi's other work, from painting to architecture based on a singular visual logic, in *Ornamento e Delitto*, too, what is revealed to us is more about us than Rossi.

I, however, am distorted by similarity to all that surrounds me here. Thus like a mollusk in its shell I had my abode in the nineteenth century, which now lies hollow before me like an empty shell. I hold it to my ear.[36]

Notes

Different versions of this paper were presented at the conferences, *Realism(s) in European and American Architecture and Urban Design (1930–1960)* at Politecnico di Milano, 13–15 December 2001; *Rethinking Architectural Historiography*, at Middle East Technical University, 18–19 March 2004; and *Art and the Fragmentation of Urban Space: Global Links, Gated Communities, Non-Places* at the University of San Diego, 5–6 November 2004.

1 Here what I have in mind can be seen as an extension of the Italian architectural historian Manfredo Tafuri's concept of 'operative criticism'. Tafuri defines it as 'an analysis of architecture [or of the arts in general] that, instead of an abstract survey, has as its objective the planning of a precise poetical tendency, anticipated in its structures and derived from historical analyses programmatically distorted and finalised'. Manfredo Tafuri, *Theories and History of Architecture*, London, 1980, 141–70.
2 Fredric Jameson, *Postmodernism or the Cultural Logic of Late Capitalism*, Durham, 1994, 124–5.
3 Jameson, *Postmodernism*, 97–129.
4 Sigfried Giedion, *Bauen in Frankreich, Bauen in Eisen, Bauen in Eisenbeton*, Leipzig and Berlin, 1928, 92, cited in Andres Janser, '"Only Film Can Make the New Architecture Intelligible!": Hans Richter's *Die neue Wohnung* and the Early Documentary Film on Modern Architecture', in François Penz and Maureen Thomas (eds), *Cinema & Architecture: Méliès, Mallet-Stevens, Multimedia*, London, 1997, 34.
5 The full titles of the two volumes are: Christy Anderson (ed.), *The Built Surface Volume 1: Architecture and the Pictorial Arts from Antiquity to the Enlightenment*, Aldershot and Burlington, 2002, and Karen Koehler (ed.), *The Built Surface Volume 2: Architecture and the Pictorial Arts from Romanticism to the Twenty-first Century*, Aldershot and Burlington, 2002. See also, Edward Dimendberg, *Film Noir and the Spaces of Modernity*, Cambridge and London, 2004, and Mitchell Schwarzer, *Zoomscape: Architecture in Motion and Media*, New York, 2004.
6 By now the literature on vision and visuality is almost inexhaustible. For a seminal work that ambivalently surveys the 'anti-ocular' sentiment in twentieth-century French thought, see Martin Jay, *Downcast Eyes: The Denigration of Vision in Twentieth-century French Thought*, Berkeley, CA, and London, 1994.
7 Kaja Silverman, *The Threshold of the Visible World*, New York and London, 1996.
8 Giuliana Bruno, *The Atlas of Emotion: Journeys in Art, Architecture, and Film*, New York, 2002.
9 Walter Benjamin, 'Berlin Childhood Around 1900', in *Selected Writings Volume 3: 1935–1938*, Cambridge and London, 2002, 392. In the film the quotation appears as 'Io però sono deformato dai nessi con tutto ciò che qui mi circonda. Come un mollusco abita il suo guscio, così dimoravo nel dicannovesimo secolo il quale mi resta d'avanti come un guscio disabitato. Lo accosto all'orrecchio.' That is different

from the English translation in *Selected Writings*. In the essay I use the version in *Selected Writings*.

10 The film *Ornamento e Delitto* was on display between November 2003 and 2005 as part of the long-term exhibition 'Forms of Affinity' at the Bonnefanten Museum in Maastricht. I am grateful to Ton Quik, the curator of the exhibition, for generously sharing his knowledge of Aldo Rossi with me.

11 Aldo Rossi, *A Scientific Autobiography*, Cambridge and London, 1981, 74.

12 Francesco Dal Co (ed.), *Aldo Rossi: I Quaderni Azzurri*, no. 8, facsimile, Electa/The Getty Research Institute, Milan, 1999. *I Quaderni Azzurri* (Blue Notebooks) are diaries that Rossi kept between 1968 and 1992 and that are now at the Getty Research Institute in Los Angeles.

13 'due immagini tra le più belle delle città Italiane (il ghetto di Venezia e il porto di Trieste) si consumano e scompaiono dietro una storia d'amore febbrile, proibita o no, comunque impossibile'. *I Quaderni Azzurri*, no. 19.

14 Andres Janser, 'New Living: A Model Film? Hans Richter's Werkbund Film: Between Commissioned Work and Poetry on Film', in Andres Janser and Arthur Rüegg, *Hans Richter: New Living, Architecture. Film. Space*, Baden, 2001, 19.

15 For a short but lucid argument on Adolf Loos see, Hilde Heynen, 'Adolf Loos: The Broken Tradition', in *Architecture and Modernity: A Critique*, New York, 1999, 76–95.

16 Rossi, *A Scientific Autobiography*, 72–4.

17 Rossi, *A Scientific Autobiography*, 72.

18 'In tutto il film l'architettura è uno strumento, uno sfondo. Essa viene diritta dai sentimenti.' *I Quaderni Azzurri*, no. 19.

19 Paolo Costantini, *Luigi Ghirri–Aldo Rossi: Things Which Are Only Themselves*, Milan and Montréal, 1996, 13.

20 Aldo Rossi, 'The Meaning of Analogy in my Last Projects', trans. Nina Galetta, Typescript, Box 1, File 3, Getty Research Institute, Los Angeles, CA. Published in *Solitary Travelers*, New York, 1979.

21 Aldo Rossi', An Analogical Architecture', *A+U*, 65: 5, 1976, 74.

22 '[G]iovanissimo fui colpito dagli "interni" ferraresi del primo film di Visconti "Ossessione". Questi "interni", come gli amanti di cinema ben conoscono, sono pieni, in senso pittorico, della sottovèste di seta lucida e nera di Clara Calamai, bellisima e velata da un sudore da estate ferrarese che la rendeva ancora più pallida; vi erano poi oggetti come lampade e caffettiere e cibo come minestre fatte con malavoglia e bicchieri di vino. Tutto questo interno era come un'architettura del desiderio.' Aldo Rossi, *Architetture Padane*, Mantua, 1984, 11.

23 'L'amore e la colpa di Clara Calamai in "Ossessione" potevano percorrere in tranquillità gli anditi e i corridoi dei miei progetti.' Typescript, Box 1, File 17, Getty Research Institute, Los Angeles, CA.

24 *I Quaderni Azzurri*, no. 2.

25 *I Quaderni Azzurri*, no. 15. In the 24 July 1973 entry Rossi writes about their discussion about the painting with Arduino Cantafora.

26 Aldo Rossi, 'L'architettura della ragione come architettura di tendenza', in Manlio Brusatin (ed.), *Illuminismo e Architettura del'700 Veneto*, Castelfranco, 1969; reprinted in Aldo Rossi, *Scritti scelti sull'architettura e la città 1956–1972*, Milan, 1975, 370–9.

27 'I tre monumenti palladiani, di cui l'uno è un progetto, costituiscono così una Venezia analoga la cui formazione è compiuta con elementi certi e legati alla storia dell'architettura come della città. La trasposizione geografica dei monumenti attorno al progetto costi-

tuisce una città che conosciamo pur confermandosi come luogo di puri valori architettonici.' Rossi, *Scritti scelti*, 370.

28 '[A]ssistiamo a un'operazione logico-formale, a una speculazione sui monumenti e sul carattere urbano sconcertante nella storia dell'arte e nel pensiero.... Quello che più importa di questo quadro è quindi la costruzione teorica, l'ipotesi di una teoria della progettazione architettonica dove gli elementi sono prefissati, formalmente definiti, ma dove il significato che scaturisce al termine della operazione è il senso autentico, imprevisto, originale della ricerca. Una teoria razionale dell'arte non vuole infatti limitare il significato dell'opera da costruire; poichè se sappiamo, ed è chiaro, quello che volevamo dire, non sappiamo se dicevamo che quello.' Rossi, *Scritti scelti*, 371, my emphasis.

29 '15 Triennale 15', *Casabella*, 385, January 1974, 21.
30 'XV Triennale: Sezione Internazionale di Architettura', *Controspazio*, 5–6, December 1973, 62.
31 *Aldo Rossi Papers*, Box 12, Getty Research Institute, Los Angeles, CA.
32 *I Quaderni Azzurri*, no. 7.
33 Belgin Turan Özkaya, 'Memory and Loss in the Architecture of Aldo Rossi', talk given as part of the Visiting Scholars Seminar Series, December 2000, Canadian Centre for Architecture, Montréal.
34 Janser in Penz and Thomas, *Cinema & Architecture*, 42.
35 Hans Richter, 'Film von Morgen', *Das Werk*, 16–19 September 1929, 281; cited in Janser in Penz and Thomas, *Cinema & Architecture*, 42.
36 Benjamin, *Selected Writings*, 392.

14

The digital disciplinary divide
Reactions to historical virtual reality models

Diane Favro

In 1765 Giovanni Battista Piranesi published an engraving contrasting the myriad of sophisticated paraphernalia employed by an architect with the singular scrawny pen used by an author. The image was at once a vitriolic personal attack on a rival, and a hermeneutical assessment of instruments as shapers of disciplinary inquiry.[1] Every tool compels researchers to ask certain questions, and to frame their inquiries in specific ways. The advent of various digital technologies has facilitated extant modes of research, while also provoking different emphases and enquiries. Four-dimensional virtual reality models allow scholars to rebuild lost or fragmentary historical structures, to move through recreated environments in real time, to trace evolutionary phases, and to link the images with diverse supportive data.[2] A broad range of historical digital models has been created at the UCLA Cultural Virtual Reality Laboratory since 1997, including recreations of the Temple of Artemis at Sardis, sections of imperial Rome, Incan palaces, the church of Santiago de Compostela, and a modernist house by Richard Neutra.[3] Several thousand students, scholars, and lay people have flown through the CVRLab models. Their reception is revelatory. Most observers question specific issues relating to authenticity, presentation qualities, and applications. Few inquire about the impact of the tool itself on research methodology, knowledge production, or the scholarly positioning of archaeological recreation imagery in the twenty-first century. None questions how individual experiences differ across disciplines.

Within the last few decades history, art history, and archaeology have explored various (and often competing) approaches.[4] After years with very little self-reflection, architectural history has followed, producing vital publications exploring the history of the field, methods, and research trends.[5] Despite the overt promotion of inter- or trans-disciplinary approaches, the majority of these introspective publications address internal audiences within each field. Engagement with new technologies is provoking greater exchange.

The modelling of historic environments requires the same architectural expertise needed to erect physical structures, coupled with extensive historical, archaeological, topographical, and cultural knowledge of the specific site and period.[6] Viable virtual historic models result only when scholars from the humanities, social sciences, physical sciences, computing, arts, and architecture directly interact during all phases, from modelling to presentation. Such personalized contact reveals significant disciplinary divides in methodologies and significant discrepancies between levels of technological, visual, spatial, structural, and experiential literacy across fields.

New technologies spark strong responses, ranging from addiction to repulsion. These reactions, in turn, dramatically impact how scholars interact with virtual reality recreations of historic buildings. Not surprisingly, new technologies are more readily embraced by scholars in departments such as architecture, in which computing is an integral part of the curriculum. Archaeologists familiar with total stations, CAD, and various digital tools also accept the technology, though frequently expressing unease at the simulation properties. In contrast, art historians, classicists, and others from departments with limited technological support find the digital domain quite foreign, if not outright threatening. They have difficulty manipulating the models and interpreting the data, as well as determining how digital recreations impact traditional print publications and academic evaluations. Outside the university, lay audiences assume that anything shown on a computer is scientific, accurate, and thus beyond criticism.

Frequently, the distinction between technophobe and technophile is age-based. Younger scholars raised on computer games immediately engage with simulation technologies. As a result, their critiques of the CRVLab recreation models focus first on digital presentation quality, ease of mobility, complexity of the operating systems, and other technical aspects; only second do they turn to the historical content presented. These observers move seamlessly (and rapidly) between different types of information presentation such as the visual recreations and the supporting textual, photographic, and aural material archived in linked metadata. In contrast, more mature scholars have not developed digital skills. Unfamiliar with simulation capabilities they do not intuit the operation (or even the existence) of various tools such as the metadata links, pop-up windows, or various switches. In addition, they find themselves marginalized in group discussions with young technophiles who speak an acronym-filled technical jargon (vrml, 6dof) further complicated by obtuse theorization.[7]

More is at play here than either fear or love of something new, or mere familiarity with operations and vocabulary. Rather, these responses reveal distinctly different disciplinary emphases in how data is synthesized and organized. Scholars trained in connoisseurship and meticulous documentation are uncomfortable with the indeterminacy of virtual recreations. The CVRLab models are not hyper-realistic restorations of original environments; instead, they present the current state of knowledge about historical buildings, depicting only verified architectural information or hypothetical representations based on well-documented comparanda vetted by scientific committees. The images are knowledge representations, yet paradoxically they approximate reality in certain aspects.[8] Observers are expected to shift seamlessly between reading the digital images as buildings and as information. This challenge is in many ways antithetical to the rigorous training of archaeologists, classicists, and art historians. Similarly, the simultaneous presentation of the interactive models along with diverse hypermedia including textual, aural, and pictorial data causes a mental disconnect for scholars not trained in fuzzy logic.[9] As a result, group discussions frequently find participants talking at cross purposes, with some structuring their arguments around technologically inspired indeterminacies, and with others privileging isolated certainties. Of course, uniformity of thinking is not desirable; however, discussions about the architectural content represented in the virtual reality recreations would be enriched if all observers acknowledged not only that technology itself shapes evaluations, but that academic reception does as well.

Logically, the visual power of historical recreations focuses attention on the activity of the eye. People may look at the same object, but what they 'see' is shaped by both personal and culturally constituted practices. In the 1970s, art historian Norman Bryson coined the term 'visuality' to describe seeing mediated by culture.[10] While research has focused on how the 'period eye' impacts the perception of architecture in specific eras, little has been done to evaluate the 'disciplinary eye' of scholars in different fields. When interacting with the UCLA virtual reality architectural recreations, some researchers express discomfort with the dominant role relegated to the imagery. For example, classical archaeologists generally consider reconstruction images to be disseminators of information produced at the end of a research project, not as producers of knowledge integral to the research process.[11] The reactions of scholars to the models also affirm what Michael Baxandall identified as the 'class eye', that is, the eye shaped by social determinants.[12] Individuals in more academic, less visually based disciplines, argue that enticing visual presentations such as the digital models are useful for lower-level students or lay audiences, not scholars. Similarly, they find the kinetic aspects of viewing problematic in large part due to associations with adolescent gaming. In contrast, architects believe the three-dimensional representations are the research, preferring to close their eyes to the associated metadata as an encumbrance needed by academic scholars, but not by those who actually make architecture.

Optical engagement differs greatly across disciplines. Rudolf Arnheim, Erwin Panofsky, and other early pioneers of visual thinking confirmed that conceptual training is necessary to interpret any secondary representation of an object. Simply, one learns how to read an axonometric drawing of a building or any other architectural image. A similar education is needed for those entering four-dimensional digital realms.[13] Interactive virtual reality architectural environments are immersive and abstracted. They require viewers to suspend belief and draw on imagination to accept that surface textures wrapped around digitally constructed polygons depict thick stone course work or that a building shown on a flat computer screen or projected in a visualization portal simulates a real-world context (Figure 14.1). Architecture practitioners and scholars actively involved with design and computing readily project themselves into the recreated spaces; their visual training privileges the three-dimensional and contextual aspects of the digital models. Conversely, academics who work primarily with static images have difficulty crossing through the fourth-wall barrier of the computer screen. Unable to situate themselves in the recreated digital spaces, they see selectively and frequently fall back on familiar analytical strategies. Thus, art historians focus on the aesthetics of the architectural representations depicted in the models, rather than on the overall experience of the simulations. Archaeologists familiar with scientific line drawings criticize attempts at realism; they call for more abstracted representations that showcase the scientific content uncontaminated by artistic enhancements or kinetic distractions. In contrast, academics from film studies critique the models phenomenologically, basing their evaluations on holistic interpretations of the pictorial aspects in relation to the presentation narrative.[14] At issue are not just the differences between costly hyper-realism, verifiable minimalism, and immersive interactivity, but those

Figure 14.1 Recreated Arch of Septimius Severus; UCLA CVRLab, modelling by Dean Abernathy and Carmen Valenciano.

Figure 14.2 Colosseum with coded circulation paths; UCLA CVRLab, modelling by Dean Abernathy.

between different disciplinary views that shape thinking by foregrounding select features in the study of architecture.

Each field associated with architectural history has developed its own acceptable representational strategies. Realism dominates in some; abstraction in others. Reception of the virtual reality models reveals that these visual languages do not always translate easily. Each model created at the CVRLab addresses specific research goals, with images adjusted to suit the agenda and budget. In the Roman Forum digital model scholars wished to mark the location and approximate size of buildings known only from archaeological footprints. The modelling team represented the volumes by extruding transparent boxes from the ground plans. Some academic observers consider such architectural abbreviations appropriate; others maintain in a Vitruvian vein that transparent buildings do not exist and thus should not be included.[15] Notably, the combination of different representational typologies causes the greatest problems of legibility. In the digital model of the Colosseum the researchers distinguish between building levels and social groups by tracing paths with broad bands of transparent colour (Figure 14.2). The clash between the abstract depiction of the circulation routes and the realism of the Colosseum model creates a dissonance for scholars accustomed to reading visual representations as singular aesthetic pictorial images.

In addition to representational conventions, each discipline favours literal, as well as conceptual, views. Immersive digital environments allow researchers to analyse sightlines and view sheds from a simulated ground-level observation point, yet modern viewers do not always exploit this opportunity. Urban historians prefer the filmic trope of flying down into an environment. Such bird's eye overviews are obviously useful, but place the observer in a distanced, superior position unfamiliar to the original occupants of the depicted environment (Figure 14.3). Iconic images and presentation types in every field also subconsciously impact viewing. Scholars looking at the digital models invariably want to fly up and, elevated, see art works such as the reliefs on the Arch of Septimius Severus at a 90-degree angle, an undistorted (but unrealistic) angle of sight commonly shown in publications. Similarly, few academics

Figure 14.3 Sequential views flying down into Roman Forum Model; UCLA CVRLab, modelling by Dean Abernathy.

ever wish to move around to see the back of modelled buildings, preferring to look at the recreations from the same positions represented in iconic published images. The objectification of architecture has strengthened the scholarly preference for viewing from static, not moving, positions.[16]

Colour elicits conflicting reactions. Architectural paint and surface treatment change over time, complicating the accurate documentation of colour on historical buildings. This fact, along with the high cost of colour reproductions, for many decades promoted the teaching and publication of art and architecture in black and white. The dominance of architectural monochromaticism in academic circles tended to impart a scholarly, scientific value to black and white depictions. Including only verifiable data, the Roman Forum model currently shows colour when the specific material is known, but does not depict visually compromising factors such as aging and dirt. As a result, the architecture has a limited palette and the stones appear as if newly quarried. Some observers bemoan the inclusion of any architectural colour, arguing that the surface treatment, aging, irregularities, and related aspects cannot be verified. Archaeologists in particular find colour distracting or inexact, citing preference for less emotive, less culturally loaded, more 'pure' black and white line drawings. On the other hand, architects call for more colour, even if undocumented, to approximate realism. These opposing reactions to colour representation in the digital models affirm different valuation of architectural colour across disciplines.

The initial creation of visual simulation technologies resulted in a plethora of studies in computer sciences regarding the reading of digital environments.[17] In parallel, research on the visual culture of specific periods proliferated, investigating visuality in relation to both cities and individual buildings.[18] Interpretive viewing has also been considered within specific spheres of knowledge production. All this vital work has remained compartmentalized. The varying, and often contradictory, visual responses demonstrated by observers of the digital models affirm the need for trans-disciplinary historiographies of optical knowledge that explore the interstices of academic interaction. Such inquiries should expand the discourse and affirm the role of visual presentations as producers of knowledge at every step of research.

Like vision, space is culturally constituted. Traditionally, the study of 'spatiality' in historical (especially ancient) contexts has been compromised by the incompleteness of the physical remains. Research has centred on a few extant structures (Pantheon), or on plan analyses which naturally privilege space at ground level. New digital technologies should stimulate further explorations. By emphasizing holistic recreations and entire environments, such tools facilitate the study of voids as well as solids. Few have taken advantage of this capability. For example, scholarly observers of the Roman Forum model rarely raise space as a topic even though Roman architecture is relentlessly characterized as spatially oriented.[19] Not a single observer discussed the fascinating secondary or transitory spaces evident between structures in the Forum model. Significantly, an underdeveloped spatial literacy seemed common to scholars and practitioners in all disciplines. In this instance, the viewing of the virtual models reveals not only the need for disciplinary comparison of spatial literacies, but for the trans-disciplinary promotion of the subject as essential to the understanding of architecture.

A building cannot stand without a solid foundation and structure. During the process of creating the models scholarly deficiencies in structural understanding became apparent. Traditionally, scholars generate selective two-dimensional drawings of reconstructed buildings; only rarely do they fashion more costly, but structurally precise, small-scale physical models. In general, axonometric and elevation drawings are preferred since they minimize distortion and allow for true measurements. At the same time, these drawn representations promote the conceptualization of buildings as composed of individual planes. Difficulties become apparent when such images are used to create three-dimensional digital models. The archaeologist Heinrich Bauer presented his exhaustive research on the Basilica Aemilia in a set of plans, sections, and elevations. Modellers using these to build the digital version of the Basilica soon discovered some anomalies. The stairs that appeared to be logically positioned in the plan and section did not fit in the allotted space and an entire portion of the upper gallery had no access.[20] In effect, the two-dimensional renderings minimized the conceptualization of the building as a three-dimensional structure.

Vitruvius noted that an architect is distinguished by the ability to put all the pieces together in his mind, that is, to conceptualize the entire finished building.[21] However, certain disciplines focus on the documentation of architectural fragments. For instance, archaeological training emphasizes the parts over the whole. As a result archaeologists do not readily develop recombinant skills. Historians and other scholars who work with textual materials and secondary two-dimensional representations of historical buildings likewise do not have the opportunity to develop expertise in structural complexities. Gone are the days when some architectural history curricula required students to have hands-on training in design and structures. Focused and intense disciplinary criteria leave little room for art or architectural historians, archaeologists, historians, or classicists to learn in depth about structures. As a result, they are compelled to develop proficiency in three-dimensional, tectonic thinking ad hoc. No wonder the observers of the digital models are largely uninterested in the three-dimensional structural knowledge represented. Furthermore, the multimedia display invokes a sensory overload. In particular, the kinetic interaction with historic recreations shifts attention from individual buildings to the overall experience. To pause and closely examine the structure of one building seems counter to the dominant kinetic and immersive character of the presentation.

The simulation of real-time movement through recreated historical environments is enticing and controversial. From an academic viewpoint, such animation has negative associations with popular entertainments, including cinema and gaming. Beyond academic snobbery, the subject is also devalued as being unquantifiable, undocumentable, and too subjective. On the whole, architectural researchers have few mechanisms for evaluating movement historically. Kinetic research in architecture has centred on first-hand observation of contemporary, not past, users. Methodologies for assessing the impact of movement on the perception and cognition of architecture in distant historical periods have yet to be developed fully. Simply, the prior lack of study on this topic has minimized scholarly interest.

Architecture, as Le Corbusier noted, requires 'the foot that walks, the head that turns, the eye that sees'.[22] The virtual reality models refocus attention on kinetic factors in relation to historical architecture. The topic is important. Speed of movement impacts visibility; buildings erected by pedestrian cultures tend to have more detailing than those for automobile cultures. By modulating the pace, presenters of recreated digital models can approximate real-time movement for different eras. Such simulations allow observers to evaluate how architectural design responded to the 'period foot'. In particular, recreations of era-specific movement draw attention to sequencing as an important design consideration. For example, simulated movement through the digital models at ground level emphasizes the visual interplay and impact of structures experienced sequentially. However, observers who follow the triumphal route through the modelled recreation of the Roman Forum discuss individual buildings and the route, not the kinetic, experiential interrelationships of elements along the path. This response mimics contemporary scholarship, especially semiotic readings, which likewise privilege the route and specific structures over the continuous experience.[23] The animated interaction with the procession seems dangerously close to subjective (and juvenile) role playing.

Time is a factor in movement and in the overall experience of architectural environments. Virtual reality technology allows for a greater exploration of the fourth dimension in historical architecture, from the time taken to traverse a space to urban evolution. In several CVRLab models, observers can trace evolutionary developments by switching between models of different periods. Representatives of all disciplines respond favourably to this feature, since it reinforces standard commodification of time into distinctly characterized eras.[24] Time, however, is not a series of select moments, but, as Borges wrote, a river.[25] Architects favoured the visualization of time made possible by such tools as a time-slider and urban evolution simulator.[26] Academic observers were less appreciative, minutely questioning the complex data sources to such a degree that they lost track of the overall emphasis on evolutionary fluidity.

Overall, many temporal issues relating to architectural history remain largely unexplored. Environments, like people, age; few historical studies explore this topic in depth. Steward Brand in *How Buildings Learn: What Happens After They're Built*, calls for architects and scholars to consider how structures change over time.[27] Formal variability, however, is not valued in academia, which still privileges the moment of conception as the most pure expression of architecture. When viewing the Forum digital model, several observers commented on the cleanliness of the rendered environment, but not on the 'new' appearance of all the buildings as a temporal anomaly. This omission in part responds to the state-of-knowledge premise underlying the models, but it also reflects a common scholarly reverence of original form and concept at the expense of other aspects, including subsequent alterations of form and use. Such thinking highlights the tendency in academia to compartmentalize time in relation to objects as well as to styles and theoretical developments.

Solar orientation and available lighting greatly impacted building design in pre-industrial societies. Some of the CVRLab models use meticulously calibrated data on the sun's path in specific years to evaluate architectural alignments.[28] In other cases, the models depict natural and artificial lighting at different times of day and year to facilitate assessment of use patterns and other considerations (Figure 14.4). Response to the simulated historical lighting was mixed. Academic observers across disciplines laud the incorporation of scientific solar ephemera data; in contrast, they devalue more emotive renderings of lighting in recreated environments as being hard to verify and too emotive. Obviously a clear distinction is made between rationalized observation and the embodied experience of observers projecting themselves into a recreated space.

Passively situated outside the digital environments all observers had trouble placing themselves within the models. Initial hypotheses posited that scholars

Figure 14.4 Lightscape analysis of Curia (Senate House) model, Rome; UCLA CVRLab, modelling by Dean Abernathy.

unfamiliar with technology would require some perceptual training in moving through the digital spaces, yet this would be offset by familiarity with the sites; techno-savvy people unfamiliar with the historic location would compensate with skill at navigation learned from gaming. Both premises were incorrect. Almost all observers had difficulty situating themselves in the recreated historical environments. The disorienting diminution of peripheral vision in digital models partially explains the positional difficulties, yet other factors are also at play. Obviously, maps, drawings, and other familiar presentations have historically been static and two-dimensional; people locate themselves as a point on a horizontal plane. In gaming, the narrative propels movement, making the player's specific location less relevant. The CVRLab addressed the observers' spatial disorientation by creating a pop-up map showing their position while moving through the model. However, the need for such a locational device underscores an academic predilection to think two-dimensionally even when dealing with three-dimensional subject matter, and to favour interacting with architecture from fixed points. Both factors minimize experiential assessment of architecture.

Though viewed from a stationary, external point, virtual reality historical environments are sensorially rich. They portray not only visual complexity and movement, but also sound, interactive human figures, and other features to simulate historical experiences. The CVRLab model of Santiago de Compostela includes period-specific music localized at various points within the Romanesque pilgrimage church. Usually, observers respond positively to this enhancement, acknowledging sound as an important means to improve understanding of the space and cultural context depicted. Such interpretations are useful, but superficial. Scant research has been conducted on how sound interacts and impacts architecture and urban spaces in history.[29] The same holds true for other experiential characteristics, including haptic responses to surface textures, temperatures, and the most intangible aspect of all, mood.[30] Scholars shy away from perceptual archaeology as unverifiable, and inherently subjective. Most contend that the experiential enhancements are simply too distractingly seductive; to rephrase Fredric Jameson, 'the experiential is essentially pornographic'.[31]

While Michael Shanks and Christopher Tilley have called for the reintegration of subjectivity into archaeology, scholars in that and other fields have not immediately responded.[32] Current research on architectural experience has been largely subsumed under more intellectualized considerations of collective memory and identity.[33] However, studies of contemporary environments affirm that visitors to physical sites recall not only the monuments seen, but, with equal force, the weather, crowding, mood, sounds, and other sensorial responses. These vibrant aspects of the human–architecture connection need to be evaluated for historical environments. While the argument can be made that modern researchers rooted in contemporary worlds and values can never fully comprehend (or even simulate) historical experiences, this is true as well for all historical reconstructions and historical studies in general.

The digital historical recreations are not time machines to the past, but visualizations of current knowledge. Both this concept and the technology itself promote alterity. The CVRLab models include alternative reconstructions and diverse assessments of intangible sensorial data. Many of the academic observers' overall criticisms are mitigated by presenting the virtual reality historical environments as laboratories where experimentation occurs, rather than as imagined snapshots of the past.

The reactions to the UCLA historic virtual reality models discussed here admittedly are anecdotal, representing a sampling of about 5,000 observers who in most cases interacted with the models as groups. The interpretation of the responses naturally reveals the disciplinary eye of the author, an architectural historian trained and working in professional architecture programs. Yet it also highlights the existence of significant differences in visual, spatial, structural, and experiential literacy across academic fields. Virtual reality models of historical environments, like all implements, shape and reflect current thinking. By nature inclusive, four-dimensional, and kinetic, as well as costly and collaborative, new technologies compel scholars to re-evaluate research paradigms for how they approach architectural history, what they study, and with whom. Historical digital recreations encourage scholars to consider past environments holistically, integrating a mesh of aesthetic, structural, theoretical, visual, and experiential factors. Equally important, this tool provides academics with real and simulated realms in which to contemplate their disciplinary differences.

The utilization of digital reconstruction technologies has already begun to shape architectural historiography. Significantly, digital modelling tools are promoting profound scholarly exchange. Interdisciplinarity has been a scholarly buzz word for years, yet true collaboration and the integration of methodologies have been limited. Too often borrowings have been one-sided or superficial, emphasizing what has been critically labelled as 'disciplinary poaching'. The creation of effective and accurate digital models of historic environments requires a sustained and close collaboration between individuals from different disciplines. Equally important, the cooperation is broadly based, involving not just scholars in academic fields such as the humanities and social sciences, but also those in the sciences and practising architects. Interdisciplinary exchange offers numerous benefits, but care should be taken to ensure the integrity (and methods) of individual disciplines.

Significantly, the digital modelling of historic environments is gradually redefining scholarly evaluation in the field. Within the American academic system, promotions in the humanities have traditionally been based on singular products (articles, books) by an individual author (or at most two authors) working within a well-defined field. Being the product of many minds, digital reconstruction models have multiple 'authors'; undergoing continued modification they do not result in finished, 'published' products. Academic promotion reviewers are beginning to acknowledge these differences, drawing on evaluative paradigms from the sciences where multiple authorship and non-print products are common. Collectively, architectural historians need to establish evaluative criteria for research utilizing new technologies; such guidelines will also benefit other scholarly undertakings, including diverse collaborative studies, oral histories, software design, and built projects, thus expanding and enriching the field.

Interactive digital models of past architecture refocus attention on the experiential, constructional, and temporal aspects of historical architecture. Visually appealing digital models give primacy to the activity of the eye. The power (and cost) of sensorially rich digital images imparts a sense of veracity further strengthened by the inbuilt association of computer-based creations with scientific accuracy. Inherent in such emphases is the potential minimization of other significant factors, such as the social and political aspects of architectural design. The variability and mutability of digital depictions are shifting thinking about architectural reconstructions in general. Increasingly they are considered not only as the end visualization of completed research, but also as environments where experimentation can be conducted. In effect, digital environments provide architectural historians with laboratories parallel to those used in the sciences. Once that notion gains acceptance, experimentation should increase in number and complexity. New technologies allow contemporary architectural historians to manipulate far more intricate, extensive, and diverse data than previous generations. A single model can present not only multisensorial information, but it can also be linked to innumerable archives of support materials. The threat of informational overload looms. The field will be challenged to develop new strategies to handle the collation, presentation, and useful integration of metadata. Above all, architectural historians must always keep in mind that they, not the technologies, should drive the research.

Notes

1 Giovanni Battista Piranesi, *Observations on the Letter of Monsieur Mariette*, introduction by John Wilton-Ely, trans. Caroline Beamish and David Britt, Los Angeles, CA, 2002, 33–40.

2 Mark Gillings, 'Engaging Place: A Framework for the Integration and Realisation of Virtual-Reality Approaches in Archaeology', *Archaeology in the Age of the Internet*, BAR International Series 750, 1999, 247–54.

3 www.cvrlab.org; Bernard Frischer, Dean Abernathy, Diane Favro, Paolo Liverani, and Sible De Blaauw, 'Virtual Reality and Ancient Rome: The UCLA Cultural VR Lab's Santa Maria Maggiore Project', *Virtual Reality in Archaeology*, BAR International Series S 843, Juan Barceló, Maurizio Forte, and Donald H. Saunders (eds), London, 2000, 155–62. At UCLA, the CVRLab models are now overseen by the Experiential Technologies Center; www.etc.ucla.edu.

4 Vernon Hyde Minor, *Art History's History*, Englewood Cliffs, NJ, 1994; Donald Preziosi, *The Art of Art History: A Critical Anthology*, Oxford, 1998; Ian Hodder, *Archaeological Theory Today*, Cambridge, 2001; Dana Arnold, *Art History: A Very Short Introduction*, Oxford, 2004.

5 Gwendolyn Wright and Janet Parks (eds), *The History of History in American Schools of Architecture 1865–1975*, New York, 1990; Hazel Conway and Rowan Roenisch, *Understanding Architecture: An Introduction to Architecture and Architectural History*, London, 1994; Panayotis Tournikiotis, *The Historiography of Modern Architecture*, Cambridge, MA, 1999; Dana Arnold, *Reading Architectural History*, London and New York, 2002; Linda Groat and David Wang, *Architectural Research Methods*, New York, 2001; Andrew Ballantyne, *Architectures*, Oxford, 2002.

6 The majority of CVRLab modellers are architects.

7 Barceló *et al.*, *Virtual Reality*, 260–3; Gregory L. Ulmer, *Heuretics: The Logic of Invention*, Baltimore, MD, 1994, 17.

8 Randall Davis, Howard Shrobe, and Peter Szolovits, 'What Is a Knowledge Representation?', *AI Magazine*, 14: 1, 1993, 17–33.

9 BAR on augmented reality; Eviatar Zerubavel, *The Fine Line: Making Distinctions in Everyday Life*, Chicago, IL, 1991, 5–20; J. F. Baldwin (ed.), *Fuzzy Logic*, New York, 1996.

10 Norman Bryson, 'The Gaze in the Expanded Field', in Hal Foster (ed.), *Vision & Visuality*, Seattle, WA, 1988, 91–2.

11 Mark Sorrell (ed.), *Reconstructing the Past*, London, 1981, 26.

12 Michael Baxandall, *Painting and Experience in Fifteenth-century Italy*, Oxford, 1986, 29–39.

13 Rudolf Arnheim, *Visual Thinking*, Berkeley, CA, 1974; Erwin Panofsky, *Perspective as Symbolic Form*, trans. Christopher S. Wood, New York, 1991; Richard L. Gregory, *Eye and Brain: The Psychology of Seeing*, New York, 1966; Stephanie Moser, 'Archaeological Representation: The Visual Conventions for Constructing Knowledge about the Past', in Hodder, *Archaeological Theory*, 264; Kevin Robins, *Into the Image: Culture and Politics in the Field of Vision*, London, 1996, 129–46; Brian Molyneaux, 'From Virtuality to Actuality: The Archaeological Site Simulation Environment', in Paul Reilly and Sebastian Rahtz (eds), *Archaeology and the Information Age*, London, 1992, 312–22.

14 Vivian Sobchack, 'Towards a Phenomenology of Cinematic and Electronic Presence: The Scene of the Screen', *Post Script*, 10, Fall, 1990, 54–5.

15 Vitruvius, *De architectura*, 7.5.3.

16 Beatriz Colomina, *Sexuality and Space*, New York, 1992.

17 Jay D. Bolter and Richard Grusin, *Remediation: Understanding New Media*, Cambridge, MA, 1999; Ron Burnett, *How Images Think*, Cambridge, MA, 2004.

18 See for example, Marvin Trachtenberg, *Dominion of the Eye: Urbanism, Art, and Power in Early Modern Florence*, Cambridge, 1997.

19 Sigfried Giedion, *Space, Time and Architecture: The Growth of a New Tradition*, Cambridge, MA, 1962.

20 For another example, see James E. Packer, *The Forum of Trajan in Rome: A Study of the Monuments in Brief*, Berkeley, CA, 2001, 192–217.

21 Vitruvius, *De architectura*, 6.8.10.

22 Spiro Kostof, *A History of Architecture: Settings and Rituals*, New York, 1993, 11.

23 Diane Favro, 'Reading the Augustan City', in Peter Holliday (ed.), *Narrative and Event in Ancient Art*, Cambridge, 1993, 230–57.

24 Michael Shanks and Christopher Tilley, *Re-Constructing Archaeology: Theory and Practice*, Cambridge and New York, 1987, 9–11.

25 Jorges Luis Borges, *Conversations*, ed. Richard Burgin, Jackson, MI, 1998, 206.

26 Abdul Ballam, *An Advanced Digital*

Solution for Representing Continuity in Urban Architectural Change: A Virtual Urban Architectural Evolution, PhD thesis, UCLA, 2004.
27 Stewart Brand, *How Buildings Learn: What Happens After They're Built*, New York, 1994.
28 Charles Stanish, 'Island of the Sun', www.cvrlab.org.
29 Dell Upton, 'Sounds Stranger and More Complicated Than Any I Ever Imagined: The Racial Soundscape of Antebellum New Orleans', lecture, Constructing Race Conference, University of Illinois, 5 March 2004.
30 Giuliana Bruno, *Atlas of Emotion*, New York, 2002, 15–72.
31 The original quote was: 'The visual is essentially pornographic'; Fredric Jameson, *Signatures of the Visible*, London, 1990, 1.
32 Shanks and Tilley, *Re-Constructing Archaeology*, 1–28; Michael Shanks, *Experiencing the Past: On the Character of Archaeology*, London 1999, 130–43.
33 M. Christine Boyer, *City of Collective Memory: Its Historical Imagery and Architectural Entertainments*, Cambridge, MA, 1994.

15
The afterlife of buildings
Architecture and Walter Benjamin's theory of history

Patricia A. Morton

> For the materialist historian, every epoch with which he occupies himself is only a fore-history of that which really concerns him.[1]

This essay looks at writing architectural history at the edges of historiography. It considers the ways Walter Benjamin used architecture as an essential example of capitalism's workings over time and speculates on a Benjaminian theory of architectural history that focuses on marginal and neglected things. Benjamin's materialist theory of history and his complex understanding of the conditions in which works of art are produced and interpreted have enormous resonance for architectural histories and theories. His non-progressive notion of history and his concept of the 'afterlife' of an artwork pose a challenge to architectural historiography, one that sets different subjects for historical inquiry, shifts interest away from the products of genius, and reconstructs the role of the critical historian. This essay serves as a retrospective manifesto for my own work, deeply informed by my reading of Benjamin.

In an early note for the *Arcades Project*, Benjamin gave architecture a central place in his theory of history, calling it 'the most important witness of the latent "mythology". And the most important architecture of the nineteenth century is the arcade'.[2] The 'mythology' to which Benjamin referred is the positivist ideology of automatic historical progress. The materiality of architecture made it one of Benjamin's most important 'witnesses' because it can physically demonstrate the operation of reification and commodity fetishism. Architecture makes visible the transience of the 'new' and the lie of the promise of progress in commodity culture by physically embodying outmoded styles and functions beyond their moment of fashion. Precisely because of the delay between the generation of new modes of consumption and the production of architectural forms, architecture served him as a gauge for the 'progress' of fashion under capitalism. The intractable nature of architecture's gross physicality was the measure of its value to Benjamin's struggle against the myth of progress. Architectural artifacts, rather than the intentions of architects or architectural theory, are his 'witnesses'. The *Arcades Project* itself was Benjamin's attempt to write a collective history of nineteenth-century Paris, not as it was recorded in history, but as it had been forgotten.

The arcades were Benjamin's primary example of such concrete manifestations of the archaic, along with the interior of the bourgeois home, the ruin, and Paris as transformed by Haussmann, which served as metaphors for and images of the operation of history. Benjamin's method of historical analysis was influenced by imagistic conceptions of knowledge in Aragon, Breton, and Freud, and reflected in the theoretical method of the *Arcades Project*, which Susan Buck-Morss has described as a 'dialectics of seeing'.[3] This method was a means for finding philosophical insight in the debris of mass culture, the 'ruins of the bourgeoisie': gambling, mirrors, street signs, souvenirs, hashish, wax figures, panoramas, boredom, kitsch, prostitution, streets, metros, and architecture.

For Benjamin, art provided the most visible example of those things left out of history's dynamic; for him, the artwork marks and represents historical experience. The durability of the artwork (i.e. its fame or lack of fame over time) is important to the process by which the critic reveals its 'truth content'. Benjamin's theory of history was concerned to decipher those 'waste products' that persisted beyond fame, but were neglected by conventional history. He saw certain epochs as incapable of creating stable traditions and 'great' works of art, and believed this incapacity made them the most important eras for history because of the anachronistic or extreme character of the art they produced. He wrote his doctoral thesis (*Habilitationsschrift*) on the much-reviled German Baroque drama (*Trauerspiel*). At times of uncertainty like the German Baroque, he asserted, the art produced reflects a lack of coherence in the world at large. In these times, a 'vigorous style of art' is required to 'seem equal to the violence of world events'.[4] These eras cannot produce well-wrought works, according to Benjamin, so the artists of the time become obsessed with extravagant form and technique. The *Trauerspiel* study was the first instance of Benjamin's search for those crucial, neglected works that destroy the seeming continuity and coherence of history itself.

Theodor Adorno summarized the dynamic Benjamin established between history of dominant culture and history of the repressed:

> If Benjamin said that history had hitherto been written from the standpoint of the victor, and needed to be written from that of the vanquished, we might add that knowledge must indeed present the fatally rectilinear succession of victory and defeat, but should also address itself to those things which were not embraced by this dynamic, which fell by the wayside – what might be called the waste products and blind spots that have escaped the dialectic. . . . Theory must needs deal with cross-grained,

opaque, unassimilated material, which as such admittedly has from the start an anachronistic quality, but is not wholly obsolete since it has outwitted the historical dynamic. This can most readily be seen in art.[5]

While Adorno and Benjamin famously differed over the relation between aesthetics and politics, they were united in a search for those things that outwitted the dynamic of history and their critical placement outside canonical histories. Benjamin privileged criticism for its power to reveal the truth content of a work and for exposing the contradictions and myths of modern life, a task he formulated in an essay on Goethe's *Elective Affinities*: 'Criticism seeks the truth content of a work of art, commentary its material content.'[6] In his study of German *Trauerspiel*, he elaborated on the process by which historical content is transformed into philosophical truth:

> This transformation of material content into truth content makes the decrease in effectiveness, whereby the attraction of earlier charms diminishes decade by decade, into the basis for a rebirth, in which all ephemeral beauty is completely stripped off, and the work stands as a ruin.[7]

The material content of a work of art consists of its historically determined structure and detail. The truth is obscured by the material content of the work as in a palimpsest in which a faded text is covered by a more graphic script. The script must first be deciphered before the underlying text can be read. In the same manner, the critic must start with commentary before criticism can begin because the material content has to be examined in order for the truth content to become manifest.

The critic performs a transformation on the work, a destructive act, in revealing the truth content of a work, much as alchemy changes base matter into precious metal: 'If, to use a metaphor, one views the growing work as a flaming funeral pyre, then the commentator stands before it like the chemist, the critic like the alchemist.'[8] The truth lives in the ruins of the past, in history, and in the experience of what is past. Time operates on the work of art and separates the truth content from the material content; the commentator analyzes the residual content; and the critic completes the process of destroying everything extraneous to the truth. 'Criticism means the mortification of the works.'[9]

History and criticism work in tandem to expose the underlying truth in the work and are, therefore, inextricably linked. As Benjamin made clear in his book on German *Trauerspiel*, while the substance of the work must be destroyed in order to reveal the truth content, the material content requires analysis because of its historical character. Benjamin's emphasis here on the decline of the superficial appeal of the artwork is imperative to his valorization of works in decay, such as the Parisian arcades. The truth of their fetishization comes to the fore as their popularity disappears. And the hidden truth content of the work 'is only to be grasped through immersion in the most minute details of material content'.[10] This program for submersion in the minutia of material content became the directive for the *Arcades Project* (*Das Passagen-Werk*), Benjamin's unfinished study of the nineteenth century.

As is well known since its publication in German, French, and English, the *Arcades Project* is a vast set of notes that Benjamin collected on aspects of Paris and the nineteenth century, organized into lettered folders (convolutes) with titles such as 'A: Arcades, *Magasins de Nouveautés*, Sales Clerks', 'I: The Interior, the Trace', and 'P: The Streets of Paris'.[11] Quotations and fragments of commentary were the blocks out of which Benjamin built his works, believing that criticism 'looks for that which is exemplary, even if this exemplary character can be admitted only in respect of the merest fragment'.[12] He used these fragments to assemble wholes that, like mosaics, 'preserve their majesty despite their fragmentation into capricious particles'.[13] The parts making up the mosaic of the *Arcades Project* were the quotations, with which he wrote his history of the nineteenth century. 'To write history therefore means to *quote* history. But the concept of quotation implies that any given historical object must be ripped out of its context.'[14]

Benjamin's method consisted of 'ripping' these fragments out of their historical context, providing commentary on them and putting them together using what he termed the 'montage principle'. Not only is this ripping activity the process by which history is written, it has a critical charge as well. Criticism completes the revelatory operation begun by time and makes explicit what is discovered. The critical historian can, therefore, penetrate the superficial aspect of works, understand their pre- and post-histories and gain a demystified picture of the 'design of history'.

As Adorno stated, art provided Benjamin with the most visible example of those things evading history's dynamic. The work's usefulness to the critic arises out of two different periods of its life: the 'prehistory' of a work of art in other works and historical phenomena and its 'afterlife'. Benjamin developed the notion of an artwork's 'afterlife' in 'The Task of the Translator', an introduction to his translation of Charles Baudelaire's *Tableaux Parisiens*. In this essay, he described how translations create the afterlife of a literary work:

> A translation issues from the original – not so much from its life as from its afterlife. For a translation comes later than the original, and since the important works of world literature never find their chosen translators at the time of their origin, their translation marks their stage of continued life.[15]

The translation is not a literal likeness of the original, however, but performs a transformation on it. This transformation is, in part, the product of historical processes that change languages and their usage. The translation should never attempt to imitate the original because it would then efface the alteration the original undergoes in its afterlife. Like the translation, the afterhistory of an artwork is grounded in the manner in which it reaches us through

Figure 15.1 Galerie Vivienne, Paris, 1823, interior view (photograph by the author).

history. In Benjamin's model of history, the artwork ceases to be located in the empty, homogeneous time of historicism.

In his essay on collector Eduard Fuchs, Benjamin amplified the concept of the 'afterlife' in terms of his theory of historical materialism:

> For a dialectical historian, these works incorporate both their pre-history and their after-history – an after-history in virtue of which their pre-history, too, can be seen to undergo constant change. They teach him how their function can outlast their creator, can leave his intentions behind.[16]

Later in the same essay, he contrasted Fuchs' 'contemplation of unknown craftsmen and the work of their hands' with the 'cult of the leader' prevalent in art history and gaining ascendancy in politics under fascism.[17] For architectural history, the concept of the afterlife shifts critical attention away from the 'context' and intention of the architect and the moment of creation and toward the translations of use and interpretation that occur over time. It deflects focus from the heroic figure of the artist or architect to the status of the work over time. The history of a work's 'afterlife' is not, however, an account of reception, as understood in reception theory, or a simple historic record.[18] Architectural works such as the arcades accrue meanings, functions, and associations that cannot have been anticipated in their original conception; rather than a fixed meaning established by the creator, they are transformed by time, leaving material content for the critic's alchemical analysis.

Benjamin's afterlife concept is not equivalent to the teleological scheme of history posited by Sigfried Giedion, for example, but involves a complex interaction between past and present:

> 'Apart from a certain *haut-goût* charm, the artistic trappings of the last century have gone musty', says Giedion. (Giedion, *Bauen in Frankreich*, Lpz Berlin, 1928, p. 3) By contrast, we believe that the charm they exert on us reveals that they still contain materials of vital importance to us – not, of course, for our architecture, the way the iron truss-work anticipates our design; but they are vital for our perception. . . . In other words: just as Giedion teaches us we can read the basic features of today's architecture out of buildings around 1850, so would we read today's life, today's forms out of the life and the apparently secondary forgotten forms of that era.[19]

Whereas Giedion saw nineteenth-century iron and glass constructions as precursors to twentieth-century steel and concrete buildings, they had no current importance for him except as precedents to modernism. The teleology of historical progress left them 'musty' and irrelevant. Benjamin, by contrast, repudiated this instrumental Hegelianism and recuperated the arcades, among other phenomena, as kernels of overlooked historic truth content. Their very

Figure 15.2 Passage de Choiseul, Paris, 1824, exterior view
(photograph by the author).

mustiness provided Benjamin with the opportunity to construct an alternative historical narrative of technology and economy, anticipating aspects of contemporary revisionist histories of 'heroic' modernism.[20]

Architecture's importance to Benjamin lies in the fact that it is both a product of culture and implicated with economic structures of development. One of architecture's most important attributes is its physicality, its material content, in Benjamin's terms. It is vital as a material 'witness' because it resists easy erasure and remains within the city as a reminder of the lack of progress and the transience of the 'new' in modern life. The 'afterlife' of buildings is critical evidence of the origins of the present in the 'trash of history'. The arcades illustrate how Benjamin used architecture to produce dialectical images in opposition to the phantasmagoric illusions of capitalism. The arcade was one of Benjamin's '*Urphänomene*', physical forms in which objective laws are made visible, a concept he borrowed from Goethe's writings on biology. The Ur-phenomenon, in Goethe's theory, is a primal, natural form that makes instantaneously visible fundamental principles more generally applicable to a species of phenomena. The general is contained in the particular. Further, the Ur-phenomenon contains within it the future development of that class of things. In the *Arcades Project*, Benjamin transferred Goethe's notion 'from the realm of nature to that of history':

> I pursue the origins of the forms and the mutations of the Paris arcades from their beginning to their decline, and I locate this origin in the economic facts. Seen from the standpoint of causality, however (and that means considered as causes), these facts would not be primal phenomena; they become such only insofar as in their own individual development – unfolding: might be the better term – they give rise to the whole series of the arcade's concrete historical forms, just as the leaf unfolds from itself all the riches of the empirical world of plants.[21]

Economic facts do not exclusively determine the life history of the arcades, as in the traditional Marxist matrix of base and superstructure.[22] Rather, Benjamin posits a more complex relationship between economy and the history of Ur-phenomena, in which their forms develop out of changes to their economic foundation:

> The economic conditions under which a society exists are expressed in the superstructure – precisely as, with the sleeper, an overfull stomach finds not its reflection, but its expression in the contents of dreams which, from a causal point of view, it may be said to 'condition'. The collective, from the first, expresses the conditions of its life. These find their expression in the dream and their interpretation in the awakening.[23]

The upheavals of the market economy allowed Benjamin to characterize the Ur-phenomena, the monuments of the bourgeoisie, as ruins 'even before they have crumbled'. By means of his critical method, he read the history of social, technological, and economic change in the afterlife of the arcades, as the expression of a dynamic relation to the superstructure.

While such revelations can be glimpsed in the Ur-phenomena, they require another critical transformation to make their meaning clear: the creation of what Benjamin called the 'dialectical image'. The dialectical image is formed by a momentary conjunction of elements of the past and the present and is built through 'ripping' i.e. removing historical entities from history's continuity. 'The dialectical image is . . . the very object constructed in the materialist presentation of history. It is identical with the historical object; it justifies its being blasted out of the continuum of the historical process.'[24] It is not arbitrarily developed, but has a particular utility with regard to the dialectical problem of the present. Images come to 'legibility' at a specific time with regard to the needs of that moment:

> It isn't that the past casts its light on the present or the present casts its light on the past: rather, an image is that in which the past and the present flash into a constellation. In other words: image is dialectic at a standstill.[25]

The historian reassembles fragments of the past that have been left by time's destructive power and the critic's alchemical 'ripping' operation into dialectical images that give a truer picture of the present than the phantasmagorias of modern life. At the moment when they become recognizable, they initiate a wakening from the myth of capitalist progress; they are the interpretation that expresses the collective's awakening.

Buildings themselves are not 'fleeting images' in the literal sense of Benjamin's dialectical images. As they are experienced, however, they can flash into unintentional constellations with other phenomena. As Benjamin pointed out in his 'Work of Art' essay, architecture is perceived through use and habit rather than contemplation.[26] The 'distracted state' with which architecture is understood is analogous to the cognitive mode of hashish trances or dreams. In Benjamin's early work on the *Arcades Project*, dreams reveal historical knowledge that has been repressed. Whereas the dream in Surrealist theory is privileged as an end in itself, Benjamin viewed it as a means for gaining insight into historical phenomena that must then be brought to consciousness.[27] Habit is one of his foremost devices for eliminating the distancing of 'aura' and demystifying reality, a compelling feature of the perception of built form:

> What makes the very first glimpse of a village, a town, in the landscape so incomparable and irretrievable is the rigorous connection between foreground and distance. Habit has not yet done its work. As soon as we find our bearings, the landscape vanishes at a stroke like the facade of a house as we enter it. . . . Once we begin to find our way about, that earliest picture can never be restored.[28]

The initial image, born of a distanced view, is lost and replaced by a habitual and haptic comprehension not based on the optic. Once the process of awakening from the phantasmagoria of capitalism has begun, the earlier picture, or dream state, cannot be restored.

In this way, the arcade as an Ur-phenomenon makes visible the general laws of capitalism. Like other Ur-phenomena, they consisted of a range of activities and economic processes as well as the material object itself. Benjamin built up a myriad of images out of the life in and around the arcades: the *flâneur* and *flânerie*, gambling, prostitution, consumerism, glass architecture, and advertising. The general principle they illustrate is that of commodity fetishization. The arcade is itself fetishized, contains fetishes, and furthers the process of fetishizing objects into commodities. It obscures the concrete social relations housed within it with the image of a 'fairyland' of pleasure. Buying and selling are not the exhibited activities of the arcade; the phantasmagoric pleasures of display substitute for the economic transactions concealed behind the arcade shop fronts.

The redemptive aspect of the arcades lies in their 'afterlife' in the city as outdated forms of commodity culture. While, at a certain moment in their history, they represent capitalism in its most virulent incarnation, after they have been left behind by fashion, they embody the demystifying potential of the survival of neglected things. According to Benjamin, the Surrealists were the first to

> perceive the revolutionary energies that appear in the 'outmoded,' in the first iron constructions, the first factory buildings, the earliest photographs, the objects that have begun to be extinct, grand pianos, the dresses of five years ago, fashionable restaurants when the vogue has begun to ebb from them.[29]

As with all of Benjamin's examples, the arcades are both fallen in their collusion with capitalism and redeemed by the fragments of historical truth they retain. This truth is found in the incongruous images that flash up among the objects and activities housed in the arcade and the incongruity of the arcades themselves within the city.

Studies of glass architecture, world's fairs, *flânerie*, Parisian urbanism, and Surrealism have been inspired by the *Arcades Project*, yet many appropriations of Benjamin's theory ignore one of its central tenets: that it examine neglected and outdated things. His edicts to blast the past, disrupt history's comfortable continuum, and look at what does not fit into dominant ideologies are often ignored in favor of an instrumentalized Benjamin. Equally, the lack of a critical approach to his theory glosses over the lacunae within the *Arcades Project* and his other works. His inattention to imperialism and racism, for example, is remarkable given their centrality to capitalist political economy in the nineteenth and twentieth centuries. Although feminists have used

Benjamin extensively, they have done so 'against the grain' of the masculinist underpinnings of his writings.[30] While it would be anachronistic to make Benjamin into a proto-feminist, his method intersects with the feminist endeavor to dissect the teleological, logocentric foundation of historical knowledge, to recuperate creators and artworks neglected by canonical history, and to probe the edges of dominant discourse for moments of aberrant resistance. The aporia in Benjamin's work, from the perspective of contemporary feminist discourse, lies in his blindness to phallocentrism and its implication with capitalist political economy. The family was essential to bourgeois social and economic systems, and was dependent on woman's unpaid work and confined her to the margins of productive labor, but these conditions are unrecognized within Benjamin's work. In fact, the *Arcades Project* relegates women to the conventional realms of prostitution or the wifely domestic domain. As Janet Wolff, Sally Munt, Elizabeth Wilson, and others have observed, there is no *flâneuse* in Baudelaire or Benjamin, but she can be constructed.[31]

So it is not a matter of getting Benjamin 'right'. Benjamin's use of architecture provides a model for examining architectural artifacts in terms of their life histories without placing them in a normalizing 'context' that denatures them of political content. As he put it in his Fuchs essay:

> [The materialist historian] breaks the epoch away from its reified *historical continuity*, and the life from the epoch and the work from the life's work. But the result of this construction is that *in* the work the life's work, *in* the life's work the epoch, and *in* the epoch the course of history are suspended and preserved.[32]

The critical historian assembles this architectural history, based on this constructive principle, with concern for the specificity of a time and a place, including the present. This is not the Annales School's *longue durée*, although it has resonance with the School's critique of political history and genius. It is the inverse, a dialectical moment when the trash of history flashes up into a dialectical image. The imagistic nature of these flashes of truth runs deeply counter to the seeming continuity and flows of narrative history and contradicts the notion that we can see a building 'in its context' and 'as it was', except in momentary images.

Benjamin's theory prompts us to look more closely at those moments when history seems *not* to suit our purposes as historians. Manfredo Tafuri, by contrast, argues for examining 'felicitous moments' when 'architecture, techniques, institutions, urban administration, ideologies and utopias converge in a work or formal system'.[33] While these instances are important to architectural history, moments of *divergence* are more revealing of the aporias in history. 'Progress lodges, not in the continuity of the course of time, but rather in its moments of interference . . . .'[34] A Benjaminian construction of architectural history looks to the marginal and outmoded for escape values from the totality of instrumental reason and its cultural hegemony. This task is grounded in the recognition of the material conditions of a time and a place, including the 'trash' as well as the 'culture'. Further, the emphasis Benjamin placed on the 'afterlife' of works transfers the critical historian's attention from the intentions of the architect at the moment of conception to an unpredictable social and political history of works. Built works can be examined as provisional witnesses without the fixed value tied to the intent of their ostensible author. Benjamin overturned the 'cult of the leader' and history's hierarchies of 'genius', 'masterpiece', and 'precedent' by his insistence on the importance of non-heroic creations and the detritus left by history's dynamic.

Benjamin's devaluation of the author has enormous resonance with the contemporary feminist criticism centered on what Donna Haraway calls 'situated knowledge', as opposed to the distanced, universalist model of historical scholarship based on 'a conquering gaze from nowhere'.[35] His model challenges traditional history that reads works either as transcendent or as a mirror reflecting the world. He proposes, instead, a constellation of contingent, local knowledge that flashes up into dialectical images constructed out of history's detritus. His valorization of Fuchs and ordinary objects of study was an implicit critique of history's universalizing conception of the historian and (his) location in a detached, abstract space of criticism, and this critique has served as a starting point for extended critiques of ways of looking, spectatorship, and the articulation of difference in visual culture. Benjamin undermines the presumption that a stable location – within disciplinary, national, racial, geographic, or psychic boundaries – determines the historian's access to truth and the meaning of the work. The architectural historian, then, is just one of many potential readers, not the privileged holder of the discerning eye.

Following Benjamin's lead, the historian recontextualizes and reinterprets masculinist discourse and assumes the role of *a* reader of works rather than *the* authoritative/authoritarian historian. The intersections of ethnicity, race, gender, and sexuality are not disentangled and rationalized in this work, but made explicit and central. Rather than create another universalizing narrative of art and history, this history situates knowledge and meaning in local, discursive, and/or subject positions. This is not a revisionist project – the simple addition of token people of color and women to the canon – but a reconceptualization of architectural history's means and methods that foreground questions of power, difference, and sexuality.

To approach 'what has been' means to treat it not historiographically, as heretofore, but politically, in political categories.[36] The politics of this exercise lies in making history 'actual', in Benjamin's sense, by reference to what Tafuri calls the 'historic space':

> Historical space does not establish improbable links between diverse languages, between techniques that are distant from each other. Rather, it explores what such distance expresses: it probes what appears to be a *void*, trying to make the absence that seems to dwell in that void speak.[37]

If history, for Benjamin, is that construction that 'leads the past to place the present in a critical condition',[38] the void between languages is the space that allows the divergences of history to speak about the discontinuities within architecture culture's apparent monolithic uniformity.

Notes

1 Walter Benjamin, 'N [Theoretics of Knowledge; Theory of Progress]' (from *Das Passagen-Werk*), trans. Leigh Hafrey and Richard Sieburth, *The Philosophical Forum*, XV: 1–2, Fall–Winter, 1983–4, N9a, 8.

2 Walter Benjamin, *Das Passagen-Werk*, Frankfurt am Main, 1982, 1002 (Do, 7). Benjamin used the term '*Passagenarbeit*' (Arcades Work) or '*Passagen*' in reference to his notes on Paris in the nineteenth century. The editors of his *Collected Works*, Rolf Tiedemann and Hermann Schweppenhäuser, gave the manuscript the title *Passagen-Werk*. It has been published in English as Walter Benjamin, *The Arcades Project*, trans. Howard Eiland and Kevin McLaughlin, Rolf Tiedemann (ed.), Cambridge, MA, 1999. On the reception of Benjamin's work, see Terry Eagleton, *Walter Benjamin; or, Towards a Revolutionary Criticism*, London, 1981; Michael Jennings, *Dialectical Images: Walter Benjamin's Theory of Literary Criticism*, Ithaca, NY, 1987; Gary Smith (ed.), *On Benjamin: Critical Essays and Recollections*, Cambridge, MA, 1988; Bernd Witte, *Walter Benjamin: An Intellectual Biography*, Detroit, MI, 1991; Richard Wolin, *Walter Benjamin: An Aesthetic of Redemption*, Berkeley, CA, 1994.

3 Susan Buck-Morss, *The Dialectics of Seeing: Walter Benjamin and the Arcades Project*, Cambridge, MA, and London, 1989.

4 Walter Benjamin, *The Origin of German Tragic Drama* (*Ursprung des deutsches Trauerspiels*), trans. John Osborne, London, 1977, 55.

5 Theodor Adorno, *Minima Moralia: Reflections from Damaged Life*, trans. E. F. N. Jephcott, London, 1974, 151.

6 Walter Benjamin, 'Goethes Wahlverwandtschaften', in *Gesammelte Schriften*, Frankfurt am Main, 1974, I, 125. Benjamin restated this equation in 'Central Park', a series of notes for his book on Baudelaire: 'The duration of the literary work's influence stands in reverse relation to the conspicuousness of its material content.' 'Central Park', trans. Lloyd Spenser, *New German Critique*, 34, Winter, 1985, 54; translation altered.

7 Benjamin, *The Origin of German Tragic Drama*, 182.

8 Benjamin, 'Goethes Wahlverwandtschaften', 126.

9 Benjamin, *The Origin of German Tragic Drama*, 182.

10 Benjamin, *The Origin of German Tragic Drama*, 29; translation altered. See also Benjamin, 'Rigorous Study of Art' (Strenge Kustwissenschaft), trans. Thomas Y. Levin, *October*, 47, Winter, 1988, 88.

11 Benjamin, *The Arcades Project*, 29.

12 Benjamin, *The Origin of German Tragic Drama*, 44.

13 Benjamin, *The Origin of German Tragic Drama*, 28.

14 Benjamin, 'N [Theoretics of Knowledge; Theory of Progress]', N11, 3.

15 Walter Benjamin, 'The Task of the Translator', in *Illuminations*, trans. Harry Zohn, New York, 1969, 71.

16 Walter Benjamin, 'Eduard Fuchs, Collector and Historian', in *One Way Street and Other Writings*, trans.

Edmund Jephcott and Kingsley Shorter, London, 1979, 351.
17 Benjamin, 'Eduard Fuchs', 386.
18 See Hans Robert Jauss, *Toward an Aesthetic of Reception*, trans. Timothy Bahti, Minneapolis, MN, 1982.
19 Benjamin, 'N [Theoretics of Knowledge; Theory of Progress]', N1, 11.
20 See, for example, Beatriz Colomina, *Privacy and Publicity: Modern Architecture as Mass Media*, Cambridge, MA, 1994; Mark Wigley, *White Walls, Designer Dresses: The Fashioning of Modern Architecture*, Cambridge, MA, 1995; Reinhold Martin, *The Organizational Complex: Architecture, Media, and Corporate Space*, Cambridge, MA, 2003.
21 Benjamin, *The Arcades Project* (N2a, 4), 462.
22 For speculations on Benjamin's relation to Marxism and the Frankfurt School, in light of the publication of *The Arcades Project*, see T. J. Clark, 'Should Benjamin Have Read Marx?', in Kevin McLaughlin and Philip Rosen (eds), *Benjamin Now: Critical Encounters with The Arcades Project*, Special issue of *Boundary 2*, 30: 1, Spring 2003, 31–50.
23 Benjamin, *The Arcades Project* (K2, 5), 392.
24 Benjamin, *The Arcades Project* (N10a), 3.
25 Benjamin, *The Arcades Project* (N3), 1.
26 Walter Benjamin, 'The Work of Art in the Age of Mechanical Reproduction', in *Illuminations*, trans. Harry Zohn, New York, 1969.
27 This emphasis on the dream and the 'dreaming collective' in Benjamin's *Exposé* of 1935 is the source of his famous dispute with Theodor Adorno. Adorno asserted that Benjamin's characterization of the commodity as a dream subjectivized the commodity into a mythical category akin to Jung's 'collective unconscious': 'The fetish character of the commodity is not a fact of consciousness; rather, it is dialectical, in the eminent sense that it produces consciousness.' Theodor Adorno to Walter Benjamin in *Aesthetics and Politics*, London, 1977, 111.
28 Walter Benjamin, 'One Way Street', in *One Way Street and Other Writings*, 78.
29 Walter Benjamin, 'Surrealism', in *Reflections*, trans. Edmund Jephcott, New York, 1978, 181. On Surrealist depictions of Parisian arcades, see Robin Walz, *Pulp Surrealism: Insolent Popular Culture in Early Twentieth-Century France*, Berkeley, CA, 2000.
30 See Janet Wolff, 'Memoires and Micrologies: Walter Benjamin, Feminism and Cultural Analysis', in *Resident Alien: Feminist Cultural Criticism*, New Haven, CT, and London, 1995, 41–58.
31 Wolff, 'Memoires and Micrologies'; Sally Munt, 'The Lesbian Flâneur', in Iain Borden, Jane Rendell, and Joe Kerr, with Alicia Pivaro, *The Unknown City: Contesting Architecture and Social Space*, Cambridge, MA, 2001, 246–61; Elizabeth Wilson, *The Sphinx in the City: Urban Life, the Control of Disorder, and Women*, Berkeley, CA, 1991.
32 Benjamin, 'Eduard Fuchs', 352.
33 Manfredo Tafuri, *The Sphere and the Labyrinth*, trans. Pelegrino d'Acierno and Robert Connolly, Cambridge, MA, 1987, 13.
34 Benjamin, 'N [Theoretics of Knowledge; Theory of Progress]', N9a, 7.
35 Donna Haraway, 'Situated Knowledges: The Science Question in Feminism and the Privilege of Partial Perspective', in *Simians, Cyborgs, and Women*, New York, 1991, 188.
36 Benjamin, *The Arcades Project* (K2, 3), 392.
37 Benjamin, *The Arcades Project* (K2, 3), 13.
38 Benjamin, 'N [Theoretics of Knowledge; Theory of Progress]', N7a, 4.

16
Beyond a boundary
Towards an architectural history of the non-east

Dana Arnold

Architecture remains one of the most potent symbols of western civilization and culture. In terms of architectural history this has led to the establishing of canonical histories and narratives that privilege western traditions of thinking. There is no doubt, however, that over recent years architectural history and its historiography have been transformed as fields of academic enquiry. The frameworks, subjects and objects, themes and methods of the discipline have expanded beyond its traditional boundaries. This dynamic interaction with other disciplines continues to produce fresh perspectives and conceptual groundings for how we think about architecture and formulate its histories. My aim here is not to chart the expansion of the field of architectural history; rather, I want to concentrate on the intellectual boundaries of the subject as evident in its canonical and non-canonical narratives. In addition, I consider how the expanding geographical boundaries of architectural history also influence our conceptualization of the discipline.[1] And, as a kind of concluding dialogue with many of the essays in this volume, I offer alternative readings of the questions of globalization and Marxist theory, specifically here with reference to the post-colonial world.

Much is made of the concept of globalization in all aspects of the academy, as well as social, cultural and political life. But what impact do these ever-expanding geographical boundaries have on the intellectual parameters of architectural history? This is especially the case for a discipline such as architectural history, where ideas of migration and diaspora remain somewhat alien. Moreover, global architectural histories, or world histories of architecture, bring with them colonial baggage that post-colonial theory does not always unpack. The master narratives of architectural histories formulated within the western canon are mapped on to the analysis of the built environment of the 'non-west'. As a consequence, issues of style and authorship, together with the notion of historical progress, all of which are recognizably western preoccupations, become the narrative structures of histories of architectural production that may have very different sets of values. These master narratives of architectural production in the west have remained largely undisturbed by historians and operate as discrete entities. For instance, classicism and the classical style produces a stream of history that flows from antiquity to the present day untouched by and largely independent of other narrative structures. Similarly, the reliance on the named author genius, as manifested for example in the persona of the architect, establishes a genealogy of architectural production where the importance of the building is determined by its designer, rather than by its own intrinsic qualities. It is my contention that these narrative structures endorse the white western male subject as the predicate of architectural historical discourse. This not only impacts on our reading of architectural histories of the west, but also on how we view architecture in a global context. Clearly, the act of reading is culturally determined and how the 'west' reads architecture is different from how it might be read by the 'east'. Moreover, cross-culturalism also requires the crossing of paradigms – we need to think differently about otherness by avoiding the western preoccupations with the search for patterns and coherence in history, and the desire for closure.[2] Post-colonial theorists have indeed articulated the need for western historians to refocus and accept contradictions, ambiguities and discontinuities.[3] But these cries are not unique to post-colonialism as they form a central plank of post-structuralist theory. Nor are they necessarily heeded, as post-colonial discourses frequently confirm the white western narrative as the primary, if not the only narrative, as seen, for instance, in the evocative phrase 'non-western'. It is, however, not my intention to single out individual studies or authors for analysis and critique. If anything, I would prefer to work towards the proposition of constructing an architectural history of the 'non-east' as an antidote to the colonizing proclivities of western narratives. In this way it may be possible to offer a reflexive view of histories and the historiography of the west.

It is here that my choice of title 'Beyond a boundary' comes to the fore.[4] It is borrowed from the writer and political commentator C. L. R. James, who wrote from both within and without the colonial frame. As a black man from the West Indies he was part of the African diaspora – the colonized – but equally he was middle-class, educated and an important Marxist historian and activist, attributes perhaps more readily, though not accurately, associated with the colonizer. James's book entitled *Beyond a Boundary* is *inter alia* a quasi-autobiographical text about James's own intellectual and political development together with the history and aesthetics of cricket and an account of the anti-colonial struggle in the British Caribbean. The potential for tensions and interactions between these various narrative threads is clearly manifest, but my point here is to show that the study of a racial boundary can also provide other histories, which may at first appear to be in opposition. And, I contest that this kind of diversified intellectual frame can be used in the analysis of architectural history.

What I am getting at here is the subject–object relationship – James remains both subject and object showing that there is no single history, just a series of culturally determined narratives. And this is an important starting point for our rethinking of architectural historiography. In the Marxist spirit of James's own thinking, Fredric Jameson summed up this relationship and its importance to history in the opening pages of *The Political Unconscious*. 'Always historicize,' Jameson states, going on to note that 'the historicizing operation can follow two distinct paths, which only ultimately meet in the same place: the path of the object and the path of the subject.'[5] This certainly sounds an apposite note for my essay, and I want to extend the binary notion of subject–object relationships with Jameson's notion of dialectical thinking, as this idea elucidates the complexities about thinking and rethinking architectural history.[6] Moreover, this concept reveals the fluidity and changeability of architectural history and its historiography as the acts of reading and writing histories are always culturally determined.

A brief return to C. L. R. James adds another dimension to my discussion. The choice of a biographical subject as a starting point for this essay is not haphazard. It is already evident how the specificities of James can illuminate the way in which I can interrogate architectural history. But, in order to move away from our established sense of biography and autobiography, or the 'great man' theory of history, we have to go right to the heart of the predicate of the master narratives of architectural history: the white western male subject, whose persona is inscribed in the discourses of the discipline. And it is here that the paths of the subject and the object collide.

My first task, then, is to point out instances in architectural history where the discourses underpin the hegemony of the white western male subject as a mode of viewing and interpreting subjects. Perhaps one of the most obvious examples where the white male subject is inscribed in the narratives of architectural history is in the discourses of authorship, where architect or patron reigns supreme.[7] By contrast, the move in Marxist historical writing towards an everyday or bourgeois subject can promote the notion of inclusivity through tropes such as the social history of architecture, the analysis of space and the question of agency. And there is no doubt that these are important shifts in the way in which we think about architecture and structure historical narratives about it. Here, I intend to dig a little deeper into the scholarly predicates and different formulations of architectural history to see what lies beneath and beyond these seemingly more egalitarian constructs. It may be possible to remove the mask of Marxist respectability from certain narrative tropes of architectural history, as it serves only to hide the all-pervading nature of the colonizing white male subject. My discussion might then both prompt ways in which we can rethink architectural historiography and remove the status of its narrative structures from the realms of absolute truth. Indeed, questioning the relationship between truth and narrative helps us to see how the white male subject is the predicate of the linguistic constructions and the aesthetics of these histories. Post-colonial theory might at first appear to offer a possible alternative to the Eurocentric formulae of white, masculinist narratives, whether Marxist or not. Any theory should increase our capacity to think and by doing so resist the forces of intellectual domination. My juxtaposition of post-colonial theory and Marxist analysis, as manifest in social histories of architecture, is intended to prompt an inquiry into how the white western male subject pervades architectural history. This subject activates a kind of internal and external colonialism, which operates as a dominating force driving the discourses of west and east, canon and other.

I want to look at three discrete areas of architectural history; each is a distinct territory with its own set of boundaries, but together they present a series of position statements about how we might begin to rethink architectural historiography. First, the classical style, a mainstay of canonical histories, prompts us to think about the notion of the aesthetic and the divisions this sets up within the discipline, for instance between polite and vernacular architecture. Second, I want to look at the notion of place, here specifically the idea of 'home', which may seem to stand beyond the canonical boundaries of the discipline. This allows me to think about gender and how this plays out in the formulation of the established perimeters of the subject. Finally, I want to think about the colonial/post-colonial world and how the expansion of the physical geographical boundaries inflects on architectural history and its subjects and objects.

The aesthetics of domination

Style is the product of the formal analysis or a description of the ornamentation of a building. It may represent a specific set of ideals from the moment of the building's production. We, the viewer, will see this within the context of our own culture; in this way the understanding of the formal qualities of a building are the product of the convergence of past and present. Perhaps more than any other order of narrative, style reinforces the notion of progress in architecture, as well as dialectical modes of historical analysis. Attention is focused on the chronological development of ornament – the most obvious manifestation of style. We can only perceive this advancement through the backwards glance of the historian that does not transform the object, only its histories.[8] This is not to devalue the importance of style or the aesthetics of architecture. These qualities enable the recognition of a work of art, and indeed in our case architecture, as an object in its own right and as intelligible and valuable as such. Histories of architecture exist where buildings are no more than the stylistic analysis of their facades – their aesthetic is their history. The aesthetic is only one element in a complex set of interactions between past and present and, although it might offer a framing device for viewing architecture, it is not the only explanation. Style is a means of identifying, codifying and interrogating the aesthetic, breaking it up into its constituent parts. I want here to use it as a way of exploring the taxonomies of architecture and the impact this has on how we construct the boundaries of its narratives and its histories.

The classical style is a hermetically sealed formulation and it is a dominant narrative in the discourses of the architectural aesthetic. It is important to explore how our knowledge of the classical architecture of the past promotes and maintains the sovereign white male subject and how these preferences continue to the present day. This is especially significant for architectural history as both its tropes of language and its visual discourses conform to 'linguistic' principles. And it is these principles that guide our understanding of the architecture of the past and have informed the hierarchies of quality that can still dominate our judgement of classical design, and more generally the aesthetics of architectural production. I am not claiming here to give an analysis of the complex manifestations of the classical style. Instead, I wish to discuss specific exemplars that highlight some of the issues raised in this essay.

The impact of verbal discourses on our perception of subjects is evident in, for instance, the predisposition to accept whatever *is* as natural, whether in regard to academic enquiry or our social systems.[9] This impacts on architectural history as well as other modes of cultural production where the white western male viewpoint is unconsciously and unquestioningly accepted as *the* viewpoint of the historian.[10] I want to show here that this is inherent in the discourses of the architecture of classical antiquity and its derivatives, but that it is also only a construct. There are other ways of *engaging with* the past based on different predicates.

This analysis of the gendered construction of the languages of classical architecture might at first appear to jar against the comfortable image of genteel, gentlemanly custom of engaging with classical culture. And this is precisely one of the problems within architectural historiography that needs to be addressed. The classical architecture of the past is coloured by the world of antiquarianism and the polite activities involved with the rediscovering of the antique, such as the grand tour in eighteenth-century Europe. These present an image of well-established cultural practices. But these practices are also processes of exclusion as they become *the history* of classical architecture, rather than one aspect of a multifaceted cultural phenomenon. It is exactly this cosy image of our knowledge of classical architecture or, if you will, the boundaries that both exclude and include subjects from the discourse, that needs to be disrupted and unsettled. The rational enlightenment project was not objective; its subjectivity continues to impinge on our understanding and qualitative evaluation of antique architecture as well as the construction of its histories. And this takes us right to the heart of the Cartesian rationalist system of imposing pre-formulated ideas of order on the known world. This issue relates more generally to the way culture is constructed and evaluated – culture can be viewed as masculine and nature, just as that which is unruly and irrational, or not subject to rational laws, is feminine. But there must be a moment before the male subject began to dominate our linguistic and knowledge systems and create the boundaries that govern the narratives of architectural history. Here I want to raise questions about the discourses of classically inspired architecture and retrace their evolution back to a moment before the linguistic constraints of the rational male subject were imposed. In other words, instead of accepting the discourses around classical architecture, I want to see this cultural phenomenon as a site of struggle. Classical architecture becomes a problem, a product of historical discourse – an effect rather than a cause.[11] In this way classical architecture is, then, indexical of the predominant notion that the white male subject/object is what the past is all about. This essay seeks to disturb such a view.

It is important to think about how the verbal and visual languages of architectural history both inform and maintain western preoccupations with patterns and continuities. Here our knowledge systems of the architecture of antiquity come into play, as does their role in the promotion of the classical style. Indeed, it may at first appear that the male human subject does not take centre-stage in these contexts, but the actuality is otherwise. The enduring western predilection for the classical can be traced back to the architectural criticism of antiquity and is very much part of the way in which our knowledge of the past is constructed. The knowledge systems used to explore and present the past found expression in the architectural treatise, a collection of which formed a core part of any learned gentleman's library. One of the most influential texts in this regard is Vitruvius' treatise *De architectura* (*The Ten Books on Architecture*), written in the first century BCE, it is a survey of classical (principally Greek) architecture by a Roman author. The book provided a comprehensive survey of the classical style of building and supplied a ready-made taxonomic apparatus with which to discuss architectural design.[12] Vitruvius codified the classical orders of architecture and instilled into them a language and grammar, which made them intelligible, and this technique of representation was well in advance of methods of recording and representing architecture visually. Vitruvius also maps out the anthropocentric proportions and associations of the different orders; for instance, Doric being based on the masculine body and Ionic the feminine body. This strengthens the relationship of classical architecture to a human-based appreciation of style. This perhaps finds its apogee in the idea of the Vitruvian man, where the perfect forms of the circle and the square are shown as directly related to masculine proportions. The reinforcing of classical architecture with these associated values enabled the construction of an enduring canonical style or ideology imbued with a set of social and cultural beliefs expressed through a system of proportions based on the male body. In this system otherness is *mastered* and subdued in the process of representing the architecture of the past.[13]

There is no doubt about the importance of Vitruvius for the development of the abstract ideas around classical architecture and the value system it promoted and represented. The confluence of the verbal and the visual produced potent manifestos for classical architecture as seen in Andrea Palladio's *I Quattro Libri dell'Architettura* (*The Four Books of Architecture*) (1570), which discussed the architecture of antiquity as well as Palladio's own buildings, and which was translated into several languages. The veneration of classical architecture was also promoted through the Academies of Art and Design, which flourished throughout Europe, where architectural design was taught through rules and formulae.[14] Academic architecture relied heavily on these textual (i.e. linguistic) sources for the formulation of its classical style; moreover, many architects and cognoscenti also used them as guides to the buildings of antiquity and renaissance Italy. But I want here to present the emphasis placed on the cultural practices concerned with classical architecture as evidence of the western preoccupation with patterns and norms, and that these are part of an exclusionary process. This is apparent, for instance, in the notions of stylistic progress, genealogy and precedence in historical narratives, together with a disregard for the architectural production that stands outside the pattern of normative classical architecture. My purpose here is not to try to give a comprehensive account of the classical style, rather it is to suggest that in the specific domain of the narratives of the classical style there is a predilection for methods and techniques of representation that codify architecture through a set of linguistic principles. The rationalizing system of representing and interpreting architecture was part of a reductive process based on logos – the philosophical method for revealing the truth through linguistic means. These principles work to confirm the white male subject as the predicate of classical architecture and exclude others and otherness from the discourse. Moreover the aesthetic and the rules of classical architecture are both important parts of our cultural reading of the built environment, either by our acceptance or rejection of them. In turn, they can influence the way in which other forms of cultural production, including the architecture of the east, are viewed.

Hegemonies

There remains a reluctance in architectural history to take account the implicit value system, where we find an overlap between subject and object of historical investigation. Our brief survey of the notion of 'classical' is indicative of the continuing domination of white male subjectivity in the assumptions and writing of histories. I am proposing that the subjects or holders of the hegemonic discourses of architectural history should work towards de-hegemonizing their position.[15] This can be achieved in part by learning how to occupy the subject position of the other, and in part by an increased awareness of the presuppositions inherent in the languages and structures of scholarship. And one of the aims of this essay, together with many of the chapters in this volume, is to signal a series of intellectual distortions that must be corrected in order to achieve a more adequate and accurate view of historical situations.

My second area of consideration is the idea of 'home', which may appear to have feminine associations through notions of domesticity and so move away from the white male subject. Indeed, in the last twenty years the domestic environment has become a subject of academic study – albeit largely by feminist historians.[16] For instance, in the United States the domestic environment has come under close scrutiny from its beginnings in colonial architecture, such as the Puritan townscape, through to present-day towns and planned communities. But the emphasis here is on these homes as being part of the post-revolutionary American dream, albeit that they are riddled with contradictory messages.[17] The aesthetic also emerges as a means of expressing democratic freedom, refined taste and a good-quality American national style of building.[18] Gwendolyn Wright's *Moralism and the Model Home*, which specifically addresses the relationship between architects and builders, argues that a popular press to promote democratic equality, as expressed through the right of the ordinary citizen to a well-designed home, was created by builders. These texts gave practical advice on construction, together with examples of model houses, but they also encouraged individual expression in architecture. This free play of forms as encouraged by these builders' publications was criticized by architects as being 'democratic excess'. Instead, an appropriate national style should be developed where builders follow the example of trained architects, who would promote the kind of refined taste that could elevate the quality of American housing and produce an appropriate aesthetic for this emerging national identity. The dialogue between architect and patron is undoubtedly an essential part of the design process, but here again women can be excluded from the discourse. Alice T. Friedman demonstrates that an unexpectedly large number of the most significant and original houses built in Europe and America in the twentieth century were commissioned by female clients.[19] Friedman shows that these houses represent not only the epitome of Modern Design but also innovative approaches to domestic space, but this was the result of the joint efforts of client–architect pairs, such as Sarah Stein and Le Corbusier and Edith Farnsworth and Mies van der Rohe. The notion of home sets up important tensions and interactions between vernacular and academic architecture, as well as ways in which patriarchal hierarchies of style and modes of living, imposed through design, pervade the production of the built environment. And these are issues to which I shall return.

Any investigation of the architectural historiography of feminine spaces that 'home' may prompt leads us once more to the problem of projecting our own culturally determined views back onto the past, specifically here my view as a woman. Once again the subject–object relationship is germane to this question and surely a feminist historian is committed to challenging oppression, which the historical subject may fail to identify. Indeed, history can be seen as evidence that things can and do change.[20] But does the concept of 'women' in fact become a kind of *conceptual persona* that enables the historian to enact his/her own interpretation of another's life? And if this is the case is this not just another hallmark of masculinist methodology. Obviously, women who are no longer living cannot be asked about what they thought. Diaries and other kinds of evidence offer only limited insights into the historical condition of women and their thinking about themselves. Moreover, this kind of evidence is, of course, coloured by the way it is read by the historian. The relationship between the female subject/object and her historical counterpart can, then, remain opaque. But what of those who write about the recent past whose 'women' may still be living? Perhaps here history should learn from the present rather than vice versa. Mary McLeod recently wrote of her research into Charlotte Perriand, who worked with Le Corbusier and Pierre Jeanneret, and who is often presented as one of the unsung 'heroes' or 'heroines' of the European Modern Movement.[21] Like many women practitioners and writers, such as Ray Eames, Alison Smithson and Jaqueline Tyrwhitt, Perriand's work was collaborative and has been overshadowed by her male partners. But the presentation of Perriand as a victim is a construct of twentieth-century feminist historians. When interviewed by McLeod in 1997, Perriand expressed some irritation at this interpretation and expressed a far more positive view of her own professional career.

Any revision of the narratives of history to include women presents us with further dilemmas. Assumptions that the category of 'women' can represent all women from the past and present regardless of their age, ethnicity, sexual orientation and so on merely replaces one hegemony with another.[22] Moreover, feminist architectural historians have sought to reposition women in the grand narratives of the discipline by focusing on women's spaces, women architects, and women as part of the social web woven through the built environment.[23] The danger here is that women can just become a subcategory of the master narrative. Whilst women may make an appearance in histories of architecture, they can remain marginalized – a topic for women and about women – and a mere ripple on the pond of smooth masculinist narratives. And it is fair to say that, perhaps partly due to the limitations of its own success, the feminist project has slowed. This aspect of feminist scholarship has been remarked upon and prompted a re-evaluation of the female subject, but I contest that architecture presents a more urgent problem.[24] It is not simply a case of finding women who practised architecture or examining the spaces women occupied, although these are undoubtedly important topics. Women, and, indeed, all categories of 'other' including children, the infirm and non-western subjects, used and experienced architecture and urban environments in their entirety. Their exclusion from the primary narratives is blatantly obvious, and yet paradoxically remains acceptable. Moreover, it is important to remember that male-dominated power structures marginalize and subordinate not only women, but also people who would like to choose a same-sex relationship. Discrimination against gays and lesbians is a way of enforcing the familiar hierarchically ordered gender roles. These discourses of difference replicate themselves across the generations and the ubiquity of these mechanisms of replication enables us to understand how what is artificial can nonetheless be nearly ubiquitous. In this way they become an ideology – one function of which is an idealizing appeal to the values of an outdated system to endorse the present system.[25] The family is used as a means of promoting this male hegemony and its architectural expression in the family 'home' is a good example. For instance, the phrase 'a man's home is his castle'[26] harks back to the mastery of feudal times, evoking an image of an inherited home and birthright into the idea of present-day mortgaged property. Subversion of this male 'domain' through alternative sexuality or the privileging of female sex would undermine this ideology. Furthermore, phrases such as 'housewife' and its more evocative French equivalent 'la femme au foyer', literally translated as 'the woman in the hearth', put women firmly in their place in both the language and architectural/cultural geography of 'home'.

Subversion of a dominant ideology is also a hallmark of Marxist critique, which works in tandem with feminist theories and theories of other in this regard. Sexism and patriarchy can be seen as the survival of forms of alienation relating to one of the oldest modes of production in human history – the division of labour between men and women, young and old. An analysis of the narrative structures of architectural history can reveal the persistence of such structures of alienation, so a reworking of the narratives of gender also requires a radical restructuring of the archaic methods of production of architectural history. The 'history-effect' of these narrative texts – the reorganization of inert historical linear, chronological data or empirical information, as what happened had to happen the way it did – is one of the principal methodological problems that spring from the dominant masculinist ideology of architectural history. There appears to be no other logical course of history other than the one presented in these alienating narrative structures. In this way history can be seen as just an interpretative code – replacing it by language here I mean the concept of inter-subjectivity or a symbolic system of signs, as another interpretative code gets me no further forward. As Donna Haraway has remarked:

> Feminisms and Marxisms have run aground on Western epistemological imperatives to construct a revolutionary subject from the perspective of a hierarchy of oppressions and/or a latent position of moral superiority, innocence, and greater closeness to nature. With no available original dream of a common language or original symbiosis promising protection from hostile 'masculine' separation.[27]

This gets right to the heart of the problem of the investigative priorities inherent in my project. Causality, albeit a mainstay of Marxist historical investigation, becomes then just one trope of the restructuring of history. My search becomes, then, for those methods that will allow me to re-textualize history, while not proposing a new vision or replacing one hegemony with another.

The aesthetics of complicity and resistance

I want now to combine the aesthetic, the notion of home and the idea of national style and patriarchal identities in order to push out the geographical and intellectual boundaries by looking at how architecture is interpreted as a colonial presence. My example is the relationship between eighteenth-century classical British and the domestic architecture of the American colonies. Houses across Anglo-America show an increasing formality in design as the eighteenth century progressed, and were bilaterally symmetrical, both in facade and floor plan. Such broad similarity, with its origin among the urban elite, is one more hallmark of the re-Anglicized popular culture of America on the eve of the Revolution. This raises an interesting question about the distinction between vernacular and academic building traditions, since each is usually seen as reflecting different aspects of the culture that created the buildings. Vernacular building is usually seen as folk building, without formal plans and built by the occupant or, if not, by someone within the occupant's immediate community. In other words, it is architecture without architects. The change in Anglo-American building from the early seventeenth century to the end of the eighteenth century is essentially a picture of the slow development of vernacular forms under an increasing influence of the academic styles that were their contemporaries.

James Deetz has suggested that style, here he means academic architecture, makes distant the social and cultural conditions of production and importantly diminishes the role of human agency. Stepping back from this we can see how perceived stylistic uniformity and readily identifiable, classifiable elements and/or architects enable historians to construct macro histories where human agency, as expressed in this case in vernacular traditions, is subjugated to larger forces.[28] Indeed, the emphasis on the uniformity of town house and urban planning in the long eighteenth century as a stripped-down form of the classical ideal means that individuality in design is subsumed into a meta-narrative that privileges academic architecture. And we have already seen how the white male subject underpins this form of discourse. The divide suggested by Deetz between vernacular and academic architecture can be explored further if we ignore style, or the aesthetic, and formulate alternative classificatory schemes. We are as a result able to consider patrons, architects, viewers and architecture as equally important agents and establish dynamic relationships between these groups, and we benefit from the seemingly democratizing forces of social history. But this approach is not unique to vernacular architecture and attention remains focused on the masculinist predicates of historical discourse. Rather like the history-effect of the discourses of gender discussed above, the deck chairs of history are only re-arranged and not replaced. Marxism, or an approach to history derived from it, merely masks the fact that we do not ask fundamentally different questions. Moreover, why is the more widespread adoption of Anglicized classical architecture on the eve of the American Revolution seen as an appropriate expression of the growing objection to British rule? Vernacular architecture is still presented as being influenced (and therefore improved or progressed) through its contact with a purer classical style. Perhaps there is another way of thinking about this.

C. L. R. James can help us here. First, we can consider the broader implications of his choice of cricket as both an object of study and a metaphor for the colonial condition. The opposition of batsman and bowler serves as a metonym for the broader antagonism between not only colonizer and colonized, but between leader and led, between nation and individual, and between competing class and race factions in James's own Trinidadian home. Cricket is distinct in so far as its origins are primarily rural, pre-industrial, and particular to the landed elite who in turn spread it across the British Empire.[29] Moreover, James argues that cricket is a form of art worthy of the 'classical' (in the evaluative sense) status given opera, theatre or painting. Importantly, however, cricket's aesthetics enact a stylization of social resistance against British colonialism. As James remarks:

> I haven't the slightest doubt that the clash of race, caste and class did not retard but stimulated West Indian cricket. I am equally certain that in those years social and political passions, denied normal outlets, expressed themselves so fiercely in cricket (and other games) precisely because they were games.... The British tradition soaked deep into me was that when you entered the sporting arena you left behind you the sordid compromises of everyday existence. Yet for us to do that we would have had to divest ourselves of our skins. From the moment I had to decide which club I would join the contrast between the ideal and the real fascinated me and tore at my insides.... The class and racial rivalries were too intense. They could be fought out without violence or much lost except pride and honour. Thus the cricket field was a stage on which selected individuals played representative roles which were charged with social significance.[30]

Here we begin to understand the nuanced aesthetics of cricket whereby the batsman's posture and stroke become a mode of social representation. James's observations about British tradition betray his view of cricket as a British art form that must be both adopted and adapted in order to be a meaningful instrument of anti-colonial resistance. Indeed, James's intricate balancing of complicity and resistance is at stake here. In order to turn a residual colonial practice into a subversive anti-colonial one, the cultural practice must first be learned and assimilated according to the terms of the dominant colonial order.

Cricket as a mode of resistance against oppression or as a means of expressing identity is not the sole preserve of James. Indeed, the aesthetic of cricket translates well in to filmic representations of struggle, which inevitably connect to British colonial and post-colonial identities and cultural practices. Unusually for Bollywood, Ashutosh Gowariker's *Lagaan* (2001) is set during the Raj in 1893 and it is the story of a village's resistance to colonial oppression. The town of Champaner is hit by drought, and the villagers ask the British authorities for a halt to their taxes or 'Lagaan'. However, the authorities decide to raise the taxes unless the villagers can win a game of cricket against the local army platoon. Despite having no one who can play cricket when the challenge is made, the villagers go on to beat the British at their 'own game'. The all-important match is the main substance of the narrative and the viewing and the aesthetics of play comprise more than half of the film, which runs for over three hours in total.

In Avi Nesher's *Turn Left At The End Of The World* (Sof Ha'Olam Smola) (2004) cricket moves out of the expected arena of Anglo-Indian relations within a colonial frame. The story is set in 1969 in an isolated Israeli village on the edge of the Negev desert just after the Six-Day War and amid the turbulent climate of social change and post-colonialism. Two Jewish immigrant families, both of non-western descent, one from Morocco and the other from India, become unlikely neighbours who have nothing in common but the dream of a new life. However, the bottle factory in this run-down, remote village is the only work permitted to them, and the conditions are harsh and the pay abysmally low. At first both sides view each other with suspicion, both seeing the other as 'primitive'. The Moroccans look down upon the Indians for their darker skin, and are put off by their reserve, while the Indians consider the Moroccans to be boisterous. Even their common exploitation does little to bring them together as the Indians regard themselves as British, the Moroccans as French, and both as superior to the other. Each family tries to assert its particular cultural identity, the Indian family by putting together a cricket team, while the Moroccans play football and watch the cricketers mocking the moves and strokes – in James's terms, the aesthetics of the game. Despite the initial scepticism about playing in the desert, cricket catches on, and the British take notice and send their team out for a friendly match. The Moroccans are gradually drawn into the game and join the 'home' team. Throughout the match the British team remains anonymous, representing perhaps a state that promised a better life to both sets of immigrants. The emphasis is instead on the use of cricket as a means of unifying disparate strands of an exploited community through their complicity in a colonial game. The aesthetics of the posture and movement of the players, together with the oppositional forces of batsman and bowler, enable a form of resistance against oppression.[31]

Clearly, this line of argument maps on to the field of architectural production and the writing of its histories. It is not the idea of the game but James's notion of the aesthetic that is important here.[32] If the white male narrative is the dominant colonial order, then we can appreciate that complicity and resistance are effective techniques for an historian to use. Moreover, the emphasis on the aesthetic as a mode of opposition, as a way of articulating difference and resistance rather than compliance and assimilation, means that alternative narratives can be inscribed in the architecture itself, rather than relying on the social history to bring forth the authentic voices of different subjects. Can we then really only see complicity on the part of colonized builders in the workings of colonial oppression, since they like James have a colonial cultural practice as their only mode of resistance, or are we (and James) conceding too much by privileging academic architecture (or cricket) over indigenous cultural practices? Perhaps instead this mode of analysis offers another way of looking at colonial architecture, and indeed the vernacular tradition of building as variations of the dominant style, which become manifestations of resistance.

Are then complicity and resistance useful modes of analysis for the historian? In order to answer this I return to the idea of trying to occupy the subject position of other in order to rethink architectural history and its historiography. Here again post-colonial writing can help, but we need to look through the 'other' end of the telescope to view ourselves from without rather than within. Stuart Hall, commenting on the black experience, remarked how the dominant white western discourses had 'the power to make us see and experience *ourselves* as "Other"'.[33] And there is no doubt that this is common for those on the receiving end of oppression. However, those who most often find themselves on the other side of oppression have few skills for seeing themselves 'otherwise'. In order to think differently about architecture we need to develop analytical tools to enable historians, and especially here I mean those in dominant positions in society who have never been forced to do so, to see themselves as others. Without this empathy, attempts at inter/cultural analysis or revisionist histories will result in superficial 'understanding' without any move towards real change. As a result the colonized subject will simply be re-inscribed within the boundaries of colonial discourse. Once again this helps us to think about how the post-colonial view can assist us to understand the problematics of the master narratives of architectural history and how we can begin to rethink them. In a broader context, and to return to my opening remark about globalized societies, the issues raised here show us that we should begin to view the world differently if we are to respond effectively to the increasingly urgent demands of multiculturalism.

This essay is not intended to be a negative one that picks holes in the primary narratives of architectural history without offering alternatives. The intention is more to raise questions and prompt awareness of our narrative practices as well as their potential consequences. This is why architectural history from all periods needs rethinking, not just contemporary architecture, which has received most attention in this regard. There is no doubt that post-colonial theory helps us move on and away from white male narratives, albeit with certain caveats, and to this end it helps to unblock the log jam of the feminist project. Moreover, any call for change cannot, in the space of the few thousand words in this essay or indeed in an exploratory and provocative volume such as this, hope to reconfigure centuries of historical writing that has mapped out the terrain of the discipline. This canonical body of work is, in any event, an intrinsic part of the discipline and its historiography. All that said, an awareness of the implications of the master narratives of the discipline is essential and enables us to begin to rethink architectural historiography, as well as how we formulate new histories and begin to move away from the need for progression and closure. The 'non-west' is not a monolith, and we must not colonize this new territory by mapping it using only our shop-worn western narrative structures. Instead, we must appreciate its complexity and diversity, as well as the different sets of values that operate within its various cultural frames. An exploration of these 'non-western' values is, then, my next project – and perhaps they will help me to see western architecture from beyond a boundary as the 'non-east' and so offer me the possibility of understanding it afresh.

Notes

My thanks to Catherine M. Soussloff for her insightful comments. Any errors and omissions remain my own.

1 This essay draws on keynote addresses given at Tweede Architectuurhistorische Landdag: De Grenzen van de Architectuurgeschiedenis, Leiden, 28–29 January 2005, and *Rethinking Architectural Historiography*, Middle East Technical University, 18–19 March 2004.
2 On this point see, for instance, Trinh T. Minh-ha, *Woman Native Other*, Indianapolis, IN, 1989.
3 See for instance, H. K. Bhabha, 'Of Mimicry and Man: The Ambivalence of Colonial Discourse', *October*, 28, 1983, 18–36, and 'Signs Taken for Wonders: Questions of Ambivalence and Authority Under a Tree Outside DeIhi, May 1817', *Critical Inquiry*, 12, 1985, 144–65; S. Hall, 'Cultural Identity and Diaspora', in P. Williams and L. Chrisman (eds), *Colonial Discourse and Postcolonial Theory*, 1994, 392–403; and G. Spivak, *In Other Worlds: Essays in Cultural Politics*, New York, 1988.
4 C. L. R. James, *Beyond a Boundary* (1963), reprint edn, Durham, 1993.
5 Fredric Jameson, *The Political Unconscious: Narrative as a Socially Symbolic Act*, Ithaca, NY, 1981, 9.
6 This concept can be described as 'a thought thinking about itself in which the mind must deal with its own thought processes as much as the material it works on – the content and style of thinking are held in the mind at the same time.' See Fredric Jameson, *Marxism and Form: Twentieth-century Dialectical Theories of Literature*, Princeton, NJ, 1971, 45.
7 I have explored this question in my book, *Reading Architectural History*, London and New York, 2002. See especially ch. 2, 35–50.
8 I have explored this question in my book, *Reading Architectural History*. See especially ch. 3, 83–108.
9 This is aided, for instance, by our linguistic acknowledgement of woman as 'different'. For example, we use 'she' instead of the presumably neutral 'one' – in reality the white-male-position-accepted-as-natural, or the hidden 'he' as the subject of all scholarly predicates. For a further discussion of these issues see Kathleen Canning, 'Feminist History After the Linguistic Turn: Historicising Discourse and Experience', *Signs*, 19, 1994, 368–404.
10 My discussion centres on the white male subject both as the predicate of ways of thinking about the past as well as in the historiographic sense of this bias being perpetuated in architectural histories that do not re-examine these approaches to antiquity.
11 On this point see G. Spivak, *The Postcolonial Critic: Interviews, Strategies, Dialogues*, New York, 1990, 123.
12 On the point of language and criticism see the full discussion in Michael Baxandall, *Giotto and the Orators*, Oxford, 1971.
13 I have discussed these issues more fully

in my essay, 'Unlearning the Images of Archaeology', in S. Smiles and S. Moser (eds), *Envisioning the Past*, Oxford, 2004, 92–114.
14 For example the Royal Academy in London was founded in 1768.
15 On this point see, for instance, Spivak, *The Post-colonial Critic*, 121.
16 See, for instance, Alice Friedman, 'Domestic Differences: Edith Farnsworth, Mies van der Rohe, and the Gendered Body', in Christopher Reed (ed.), *Not At Home: The Suppression of Domesticity in Modern Architecture*, London, 1996 and *House and Household in Elizabethan England*, Chicago, 1989; Dolores Hayden, *The Grand Domestic Revolution: A History of Feminist Designs for American Homes, Neighborhoods, and Cities*, Cambridge, MA, 1981; and Gwendolyn Wright, *Building the Dream: A Social History of Housing in America*, Cambridge, MA, 1983, and *Moralism and the Model Home: Domestic Architecture and Cultural Conflict in Chicago, 1873–1913*, Chicago, IL, 1980.
17 Wright, *Building the Dream*.
18 Wright, *Moralism and the Model Home*.
19 Alice T. Friedman, *Women and the Making of the Modern House*, New York, 1998.
20 On this point see Glenn Jordan and Chris Weedon, *Cultural Politics: Class, Gender, Race in the Postmodern World*, Oxford, 1995.
21 Mary McLeod (ed.), *Charlotte Perriand: An Art of Living*, New York, 2003; and Mary McLeod, 'Reflections of Feminism and Modern Architecture', *Harvard Design Magazine*, 20, Spring/Summer, 2004. Also *ex info* Mary McLeod.
22 It has been argued that the white western female also imposes an all-encompassing notion of 'woman' on the past that merely replaces the hegemony of the white western male subject. Gender becomes then a signifier of power through its discourses. See Judith M. Bennett, 'Feminism and History', *Gender and History*, 1, 1989, 251–72.
23 See, for instance, the early 1990s: Beatriz Colomina (ed.), *Sexuality and Space*, New York, 1992.
24 The female subject has been diversified in feminist writings. See, for instance, bell hooks, *Feminist Theory: From Margin to Centre*, Boston, MA, 1984; Catherine Hall, *White Male and Middle Class: Explorations in Feminism and History*, Cambridge, 1992; and Vron Ware, *Beyond the Pale: White Women, Racism and History*, London, 1992.
25 See Juliet Mitchell, *A Woman's Estate*, Harmondsworth, 1971, where she discusses this aspect of Marx's *The German Ideology*.
26 See Eve Sedgwick, *Between Men: English Literature and Homosocial Desire*, New York, 1985, especially 1–15. In her book *Yearning: Race, Gender and Cultural Politics*, London, 1991, bell hooks suggests, however, that certain 'homeplaces' constructed by women can function as refuges or havens from white, male oppression. But she admits women can be forced into these spaces by these forces before making them their own.
27 Donna Haraway, 'A Cyborg Manifesto: Science, Technology and Socialist Feminism in the Late Twentieth Century', in *Simians, Cyborgs and Women: The Reinvention of Nature*, New York, 1991, 176.
28 James Deetz: of his many writings see, for instance, *In Small Things Forgotten: An Archaeology of Early American Life*, New York, 1996 and 'Cultural Dimensions of Ethnicity in the Archaeological Record', Keynote address, 28th annual meeting of the Society for Historical Archaeology, Washington, DC, 1995.
29 On this point see Neil Lazarus, *Nationalism and Cultural Practice in the*

Postcolonial World, Cambridge, 1999, esp. chapter 3, 'Cricket, Modernism, National Culture: The Case of C. L. R. James', 144–95.

30 James, *Beyond a Boundary*, 66.
31 My thanks to Dr Alona Nitzan-Shiftan for bringing this film to my attention.
32 The implications of the game in the work of James has been discussed elsewhere. See, for instance, Douglas Hartmann, 'What Can We Learn From Sport if We Take Sport Seriously as a Racial Force? Lessons from C. L. R. James's *Beyond a Boundary*', *Ethnic and Racial Studies*, 26, 3, May 2003, 451–83.
33 S. Hall, 'Cultural Identity and Diaspora', 394.

Index

Aalto, Alvar 66–7
abstract expressionism 117
Academies of Art and Design 235
Ackerman, James 50
Adams, Nicholas 3
Adorno, Theodor 216–17
aesthetics 5, 9, 40, 47–8, 177, 204, 211, 230, 232–3, 239, 241
Africa 3, 22, 47, 146, 230
Alexander the Great 62
alienation 238
American dream, the 236
Anatolia 89, 92, 94, 97, 100–2
Anderson, Christy 185
Ankara xviii, xx, xix, 9, 151–64
Annales School 225
anthropology xvi, 10, 22, 56, 180
antiquarianism 25, 233
Antiquaries Journal 25
Arabia 91, 93, 96–8
Archaeologica 25
Archaeological Journal 25
archaeology xvi, xvii, xx, 4–6, 20–1, 24–33, 36, 41, 48, 158, 200–3, 206–7, 210
architectural canon xvi, 75, 86, 151, 159–60, 173, 183, 225–6, 229, 232, 242
Arel, Ayda 88–90
Arnheim, Rudolf 202
Arnold, Dana 3–5, 10, 77; *Reading Architectural History* 3, 4
art criticism 135
art history 3–5, 17–18, 20–2, 39, 55, 63–4, 76, 88, 95, 99, 171–2, 179, 200, 202–3, 217, 235
Asia Minor 88–9

Association of Collegiate Schools of Architecture (USA) 54
Aston, Mick 26
Athens 41–2, 187–8
authenticity xvii, 20, 200
author, concept of xvi, xvii, 20, 62, 135, 211, 226, 229–30, 234
autobiographical writing 142–3, 231

Baghdad 98
Balkans 100–1
Bal, Mieke 138, 142
Barragan, Luis 67
Baroque 39, 53, 216
Barthes, Roland 121, 123
Bataille, Georges 37–9, 46
Baudelaire, Charles 218, 225
Bauer, Heinrich 207
Bawa, Geoffrey 67, 70
Baxandall, Michael 202
Belgium 184
Benjamin, Walter 9, 10, 54, 186–8, 196–7; *Arcades Project* 215–27
Berlin 8, 110–18, 186–8
Berlin Wall 112–13, 118
Bhabha, Homi 136
biography, of the architect xv, 171–3, 183, 231
Birmingham University 24
Black Sea Region xviii
Blair MacDougall, Elisabeth 3
Blau, Eve 3, 7, 178–9
Boer, Inge E. 138
Bold, John 24
Bollywood 240–1
Bolton Castle 25
Bonnell, Victoria E. 55–6

Borden, Iain 3, 136
Borges, Jorge Luis 208
Bourdieu, Pierre 54, 172, 176, 179
bourgeoisie 38, 216, 222, 231
Boyle, Jeremy 117
Bradford 44
Braidotti, Rosi 140
Brand, Stewart 208
Bristol, 28, 31, 33; University of 28
British Academy Black Sea Initiative xx
British Caribbean 31–2, 230, 240
British Institute of Archaeology, Ankara xx
Bronze Age 158
Bruno, Giuliana 185
Bryson, Norman 202
Buck-Morss, Susan 216
built environment 36, 48, 60, 74, 110, 229, 236–7
Burckhardt, Jakob 173
Byatt, A. S. 143
Bynum, Caroline 55
Byzantium xviii, 42, 158

Calamai, Clara 192
Calvino, Italo 67, 143
Canadian Centre for Architecture 114
Canaletto, Antonio 194
Cantafora, Arduino 193–4
capitalism 47–8, 139, 215, 222, 224–5
Cartesian: rationalism 233; space 177
cartography 1, 17–18
Çelik, Zeynep 3, 79
Centre for Research in Arts, Social Sciences and Humanities (University of Cambridge) xx, 17
de Certeau, Michel 185
Charles II (England) 40
Charlottenburg Palace (Berlin) 112–13
Chartier, Roger 122
Chicago 111–12, 114
China 155, 179
Cihanoğulları 88–9
cinema 184–97, 240–1
City of London 42
civic architecture 31, 33, 38–47, 110–18, 151, 161–3, 173
Civil War (English) 28
classicism 19, 86, 102, 111, 187, 230, 232–3, 235
class relations 36, 48, 125–7, 139, 172, 174, 178, 232, 240

client: architect versus 39–48; within architectural history 38, 53; see also patronage
collective memory 194, 210
College Art Association (USA) 4, 54
colonialism xviii, 172, 229–32, 235, 238–42
Colonial Williamsburg Foundation 28
Colosseum (Rome) 204
commercial buildings xvii, 44, 154, 164
commodity fetishism 139, 215–17, 224
connoisseurship 22
Constantinople 19, 92; see also İstanbul
Cornell University 6, 50–2, 54–5
Cosgrove, Dennis 177
Costantini, Paolo 190
Covent Garden (London) 28
craft, tradition of xvii, 26
critical theory 136–48
cross-culturalism 230, 241

De Chirico, Giorgio 192
Deetz, James 239
Deleuze, Gilles 40, 137–8
Denmark 67, 70
Derrida, Jacques 63–5, 137
design: academies of 235; architectural 52, 135, 177, 194; computer aided 201, 212; domestic 90–1, 236, 238–9; history 218; interior 190; political context of 18, 50, 212; pre-industrial 209; principles of 60; Roman 175, 234; social context of 50–1, 125, 171, 173–4, 209, 236; tradition of xvii, 26
Dimendberg, Edward 185
disciplinary boundaries xix, 2, 10, 20, 76, 135–6, 143, 148, 200–2, 204, 206, 208–9, 211, 226, 229, 242; see also interdisciplinarity; multi-disciplinarity; trans-disciplinarity
Duettman, Werner 112

Eames, Ray 237
eastern perspective xix, 74, 155, 159, 229–30, 232, 242
Edinburgh 37, 42, 44
Egan, Pierce 139
Egypt 67, 86, 91, 98
Eisenman, Peter 43–4
English Heritage 25, 33
Enlightenment 177, 189
Enzenberger, Hans Magnus 143

ethnicity 54, 61, 93, 97, 114, 226, 230, 232–5, 238, 240–1
Eurocentric approach xviii, 155–6, 231

Far East 74
Farnsworth, Edith 236
Fellini, Federico 187–9, 196
feminist theory 54, 99, 135, 138–40, 224–6, 230, 233, 235–7, 242
Fernie, Eric 3, 4–6
Ferris, Ian 24
Filarete 122–9
Fischer Taylor, Katherine 5, 9
flâneur/flâneuse 187, 224–5
Flax, Jane 140
Foster, Sir Norman 21, 116; *see also* Swiss Ré
Foucault, Michel 40, 138, 172, 176, 179
Fountains Abbey (North Yorkshire) 46
Frampton, Kenneth 66
France xviii, 1, 18–20, 25, 38, 145, 155, 177–8, 215–27, 238
Frankfurt School 137
Frei, Otto 116
Freud, Sigmund 147, 216
Friedman, Alice T. 236
Friedrich, Caspar David 80
Frome (Somerset) 26–8
Fuchs, Eduard 220, 225–6
functionalism 193
Furness Abbey 25

Gaddis, John Lewis 80
Geertz, Clifford 56, 172
de Gaulle, Charles 20
Gehry, Frank 184
gender studies 7, 54, 96, 99, 114, 138, 172, 175, 178, 226, 231
genealogy 235
genius, architect as xv, xvi, 39, 85, 215–16, 225–6, 230–1
genius loci 65–6
geography: architectural context of 3, 121, 136, 175–6, 229; cultural 238; impact of xix, 17, 18, 89–92, 180, 226
Georgian villa 28, 91
Germany 18–20, 25, 39–41, 110–18, 155, 173–4, 186–8, 216
Ghirardo, Diane 40
Gibb, E. J. W. 94
Giedion, Sigfried 4, 173–8, 184, 220

globalization 7, 45, 67, 70, 80, 161, 163–4, 172, 229–30
Goethe, Johann Wolfgang von 217, 222
Gothic 88
Great Britain xviii
Greece 41–2, 67, 86, 88, 90, 101, 187
Gropius, Walter 55, 173
Guattari, Félix 40, 137
guides to historic buildings xv, 151

Hadrian's Villa (Tivoli) 187
Hall, Stuart 95, 242
Haraway, Donna 140, 226, 238
Harries, Karsten 66–7
Harrison, Wallace 118
Harvey, David 176–7
Haussmann, Baron Georges-Eugène 216
Hegel, George Wilhelm Friedrich 137
Hegelian: dialects 137; essence of history 118; formulations 7
Hegelianism 220
Heidegger, Martin 64–5
Henry III (France) 1
Henry VIII (England) 46
Herder, Johann Gottfried 173
hero 61, 222, 226; architect as xv, 39, 172, 220, 231
Hill, Jonathan 141
Hitler, Adolf 40
Hobsbawm, Eric 157
Hunt, Lynn 55–6

imperialism xviii, 85–6, 93, 99, 103, 240
India 240–1
Institut national d'histoire de l'art (Paris) xx
Institute of Field Archaeologists 25
interdisciplinarity 2, 3, 25, 135–7, 200, 211
Ireland 46
Irigaray, Luce 139–40
İstanbul 96–7, 99, 154, 161
Italy 19, 122–9, 155, 179, 186–94, 196, 235

Jacobs, Stephen W. 50–1, 54–5
James, C. L. R. 230–1, 239–40
Jameson, Fredric 172, 184, 210, 231
Jamestown (Virginia) 28, 31
Jansen, Hermann 154, 156, 158
Jarzombek, Mark 76
Jay, Martin 177
Jeanneret, Pierre 237
Johnson, Philip 39

Journal of Architectural Education 3
Journal of the Society of Architectural Historians 3, 7, 79

Kahn, Louis 65, 67
Kern, Stephen 175
Klingensmith, Samuel John 53
Koehler, Karen 185
Kostof, Spiro 51, 77
Kristeva, Julia 135–6, 172
Kulturforum 116–18

LaCapra, Dominick 64, 122, 129
Lancaster University 25
language *see* translation
Latin America 3, 179
Lavin, Irving 54
Le Corbusier 38, 173, 208, 236–7
Leeds International Medieval Congress 17
Lefebvre, Henri 176, 178
Lenin, V. I. 188
Leppert, Richard 76
Lessing, Gotthold Ephraim 173
Levi, Primo 143
Lincoln Cathedral 61
linguistic structures 10, 61, 93, 183, 233, 235
literary theory 10, 180
London 20–1, 39–42, 138–42, 144, 147
Loos, Adolf 186–9, 192, 194
Louis XIV (France) 19
Louvre, the 38

MacDonald, William L. 77, 175, 177
McLeer, Brigid 142
McLeod, Mary 237
Mahler, Franz 187
Manchester 40, 44
Marxism 61, 70, 176, 184, 222, 229, 231–2, 238–9
Marx, Karl 137–9, 187, 189
masculinity 230–1, 233–8, 241
Massey, Doreen 176
Medici, Piero di Cosimo de' 122–9
Mehmed II (Ottoman Empire) 97–8
Merlin 46
Mesopotamia 91
Middle East Technical University (Ankara) xviii, xx
military power xviii, 42–3
Millar, Deborah 142
Miralles, Eric 37

modern architecture 67–70, 155–9, 161, 163–4, 184, 187–9, 192, 200
modernism 70, 111, 118, 186, 193, 220, 222, 236–7
Molyneux, Nicholas 25
monuments 38, 47, 88, 98, 111–18, 151–2, 163, 194, 200, 204–6, 208–10
Morriss, Richard 25, 33
Moxey, Keith 63
Mugerauer, Robert 65
multidisciplinarity 2, 6, 60, 135–6
Mumford, Lewis 77–8
Munt, Sally 225
museums 38, 123, 158, 163
Mussolini, Benito 76

Napoleon 20
nationalism 40–4, 85–95, 100–2, 112–13, 154–7, 159–60, 163–4, 171, 173, 236
National Socialist Party 112–13; *see also* socialism
Neo-Rationalism 193
Netherlands 18
Neumann, Ignaz Michael 20, 22
Neutra, Richard 200
Nevis Heritage Project 31
New National Gallery (Berlin) 8, 110–18
New York 112, 114, 118
Norbert-Schultz, Christian 65

Orient, the xviii
Osborne, Robin 5
Ottoman Empire 7, 42, 79, 85–103, 153, 158, 163
Ovalle, Iñigo Manglano 8, 110–18

Palladianism 194
Palladio, Andrea 234
Palestrina 74
Panofsky, Erwin 202
panoramas 216
Paris 38, 178, 215–21, 224
patronage 61, 85, 88, 101, 125–8, 174, 239
Payne, Alina 4, 5
Peloponnesian War 41
Perec, George 143
Perriand, Charlotte 237
Persia 96, 98
Persian poetry 93–4
Pevsner, Nikolaus 21, 61

phenomenology 65, 203, 220, 222–4
Piano, Renzo 67
Picasso, Pablo 20
Piranesi, Giovanni Battista 200
Pollak, Martha 3
Pope Gregory VII 19
popular culture 45, 151, 172, 184, 187, 207, 216, 239
post-colonialism 7, 61, 96, 175, 178, 229–32, 240, 242
post-modernism 66
post-structuralism 7, 135, 140, 230
Probyn, Elsbeth 140
Puritan townscape 236
Prussian Cultural Heritage Foundation 112–13

queer studies 54, 93, 237; *see also* sexuality; sub-cultures

radicalism 43
Ramelli, Agostino 1
reader, concept of xvii, 48, 56, 62, 110, 121–3, 128–9, 143–8
regionalism 65–7, 173
Renaissance 39, 174, 179, 235
Rhine, the 18–19, 21
Richter, Hans 184, 188, 196
Robia, Luca della 123
Rococo 53
Rodwell, Warwick 25
Rohe, Mies van der 41, 110–18, 173, 236
Roman Forum 203–6, 208–9
Roman Republic 74, 79, 92, 158, 175, 187, 234
Rome xviii, 18, 19, 39, 42, 46, 61, 126, 188, 196, 200, 204, 207, 210
Rossi, Aldo 185–97
Rowe, Colin 51–5
Royal Academy (London) 21
Royal Commission on the Historical Monuments of England 24–6, 33
Russia 94, 155, 188, 192

Said, Edward 172
St Bartholomew's Fair (London) 28–30
St Michael's Hill (Bristol) 28–31, 33
St Paul's Cathedral 40
St Peter (Rome) 19
Salvation Army 38
Sartre, Jean-Paul 65
Scarpa, Carlo 66–7

Scarry, Elaine 179
Scharoun, Hans 113, 116
Schinkel, Karl Friedrich 111–12, 114
Schmarsow, August 174
Schmidt, Hans 188
Schofield, John 28
Schwarzer, Mitchell 174, 185
Schweder, Rolf 112
Scotland 37
Scottish Assembly building 37, 44
Seagram Building (New York) 112, 114
semiotics 63–5
Sewell Jr, William 55–6
sexuality 7, 54, 226, 234, 238
Sforza, Francesco (Duke of Milan) 124–5, 127–8
Shanks, Michael 210
Silverman, Kaja 185
Sironi, Mario 192–3, 195
skyscrapers 118
Smithson, Alison 236
socialism 187
social ritual xvi, 5
Society of Architectural Historians (USA) xx, 4, 54–5
Soja, Edward 176–8
Southampton, University of xx, 31
Spain xviii
Spartans 41–3
spatial boundaries xix
Speer, Albert 40, 113
Speyer Cathedral 18–22
Stein, Sarah 236
Stieber, Nancy 3, 9–10
Stirling, James 113
Stonehenge 46, 187
stylistic categories xv, xvi, 21–2, 53, 88–91, 110–11, 140, 171, 174; challenging existing 50, 159–60, 173, 215–16, 229–30, 232–3, 239, 242
sub-cultures 95–6, 216, 242
Süleyman I (Ottoman Empire) 85, 96
Surrealist theory 223–4
Svevo, Italo 189
Swiss Ré, St Mary Axe 21, 42
Switzerland 188

Tafuri, Manfredo 7, 225–6
Tati, Jacques 116
technological developments, impact of 61, 110, 118, 173, 200–12, 222–3
Third Reich 111, 113

Tilley, Christopher 210
Tocqueville, Alexis de 47
Topkapı Palace 99
tourism 151–2, 156–8, 159–61, 163
Trachtenberg, Marvin 2, 3, 21, 77–8, 178–9
trans-disciplinarity 180, 189, 195, 200, 206–7
translation 218, 226–7, 233–4, 238
Tunisia 91
Turkey 86, 98, 101–2, 151–64
Turkish Academy of Sciences xx
Turkish Republic 79, 90, 153–4, 156–9, 161, 163–4
Turkish Scientific and Technological Research Council (Ankara) xx
Tyrwhitt, Jaqueline 237
Tzonis, Alexis 66–7

Ungers, Oswald Matthias 116–17
United States of America xviii, 20, 41, 43–4, 46, 55, 63, 111–12, 114, 184, 188, 195, 200, 235–6, 239
University College Los Angeles 200, 202–3, 208–11
urbanism 50–1, 55, 77, 139–40, 161, 204, 208, 224
urban planning 140, 187, 193, 195, 204, 225, 239
utilitarianism 5, 9

value, systems of 36–8, 40, 44–8, 176, 230, 235
Varnelis, Kazys 3
Venice 194
Vernacular Architecture Group 24
Victoria and Albert Museum (London) 123
Vikings 47

Virilio, Paul 185
virtual reality 200–12
Visconti, Luchino 187, 189, 192, 196
visual culture 9, 76, 180, 184–97, 201, 239
Vitruvius 60–2, 78–9, 126, 204, 207, 234

Wales 26
Watkin, David 2; *The Rise of Architectural History* 2, 3
Weber, Max 56
Weimar Republic 110
western perspective xviii, xix, 1, 155, 159, 229, 231–2, 237–8, 242
Westheim, Paul 112
West Indies 230, 240
Westminster Abbey 19
White, Hayden 172
Wilford, Michael 113
Williams, Raymond 172
Wilson, Elizabeth 225
Winckelmann, Johann Joachim 21
Wittkower, Rudolf 53
Wolff, Janet 225
Wölfflin, Heinrich 21, 173; *Principles of Art History* 39
Wood, John 31, 33
World War I, impact of 110, 157
World War II, impact of 20, 33, 40, 53, 67, 70, 74, 111–12
Wren, Sir Christopher 20, 39
Wright, Frank Lloyd 20
Wright, Gwendolyn 3, 236

Zeitgeist 118, 174
Zevi, Bruno 173–4
zoning 193
Zurich 190

eBooks – at www.eBookstore.tandf.co.uk

A library at your fingertips!

eBooks are electronic versions of printed books. You can store them on your PC/laptop or browse them online.

They have advantages for anyone needing rapid access to a wide variety of published, copyright information.

eBooks can help your research by enabling you to bookmark chapters, annotate text and use instant searches to find specific words or phrases. Several eBook files would fit on even a small laptop or PDA.

NEW: Save money by eSubscribing: cheap, online access to any eBook for as long as you need it.

Annual subscription packages

We now offer special low-cost bulk subscriptions to packages of eBooks in certain subject areas. These are available to libraries or to individuals.

For more information please contact webmaster.ebooks@tandf.co.uk

We're continually developing the eBook concept, so keep up to date by visiting the website.

www.eBookstore.tandf.co.uk